Negotiating Place and Space Through Digital Literacies

Research and Practice

A Volume in Digital Media and Learning

Series Editors

Danielle Herro
Clemson University
Remi Kalir
University of Colorado, Denver

Digital Media and Learning

Danielle Herro and Remi Kalir, Editors

Negotiating Place and Space Through Digital Literacies: Research and Practice (2019)
edited by Damiana G. Pyles, Ryan M. Rish, and Julie Warner

Mobile Learning: Perspectives on Practice and Policy (2018)
edited by Danielle Herro, Sousan Arafeh, Richard Ling, and Chris Holden

Negotiating Place and Space Through Digital Literacies

Research and Practice

edited by

Damiana G. Pyles
Appalachian State University

Ryan M. Rish
University at Buffalo (SUNY)

Julie Warner
Independent Researcher

INFORMATION AGE PUBLISHING, INC.
Charlotte, NC • www.infoagepub.com

Library of Congress Cataloging-in-Publication Data

CIP record for this book is available from the Library of Congress
http://www.loc.gov

ISBNs: 978-1-64113-483-5 (Paperback)

978-1-64113-484-2 (Hardcover)

978-1-64113-485-9 (ebook)

Printed in the United States of America

CONTENTS

PART II: DIGITAL LITERACIES FROM WITHIN

PART III: TRACING LITERACIES ACROSS TIME AND SPACE

FOREWORD

THE SPATIAL TURN IN LITERACY THEORY

Kathy A. Mills

A spatial turn has sparked a revolution in approaches to educational research since the early 21st century. This follows the rise of notable spatial thinkers across a wide range of disciplines, such as cultural and physical geography, economics, anthropology, media and communication studies, international relations, and many others, throughout the late 20th century (Soja, 2004). Spatial research does not simply invoke the use of à la mode terms and spatial metaphors, such as those that circulate on Twitter and in academic discourse—of networks, rhizomes, maps, and transcultural borders. Rather, the spatial turn is a groundswell of research that begins with the fundamental realization that all space is socially produced—in other words, it arises from purposeful social practices (Lefebvre, 1991; Mills, 2010; Mills & Comber, 2015; Soja, 1980). Therefore, it could be reasoned that space is not merely a reflection of society—it is society (Castells, 1983). The meanings and organization of space are outcomes of social experience, and the social relations of production are both space contingent and space forming, as a dialectic or recursive relationship (Mills, 2010; Soja, 1989). Framed within such a perspective, this highly original collection theorizes the ways in which space is conceptualized and operationalized in digital research to see literacy and space differently.

Negotiating Place and Space Through Digital Literacies: Research and Practice, pp. ix–xiii

Each chapter in the book contributes to an emergent, vibrant, and transformative rethinking of digital literacy practices and research, and toward radically different forms of thinking about social space. As Soja (2004, p. x) argues, "something remarkable happens when literacies and spatialities are conjoined in a process of mutual construction, a dialectic if you will. For literacy scholars and educators, the traditional confines of the classroom explode with new possibilities of interpretation." Some of these include expanded worlds of cultural hybridities, identity formations, new formations of critical consciousness, political positionings, and layers of geographical scale, from the local to global, and back again. Amidst the rapid transformation of networked digital media environments, the information explosion, and the digital data deluge (Mills, 2017), the spatializing of literacy research is a field replete with new opportunities to incorporate the study of virtual spaces, online communities, different mobilities, and cyborg bodies, of complex geospatial and agentive spaces of contemporary literacy practices. The authors of *Negotiating Place and Space Through Digital Literacies* have recognized these transformative potentials in bringing original research together in a unique and future-orientated monograph.

A consistent and powerful theme undergirding the studies is a distinctive critical and "spatial justice" (Soja, 2010) stance on digital literacies that seeks to reveal, rather than render obsolete, the inequitable geospatial distribution of digital literacy practices, such as for those in rural and remote regions of the world, or those with nondominant identities. These are still the blackspots of both physical and social geographies, and the blackspots in current thinking about literacy research. This critical stance is tied to a knowledge of the politics and power relations of social space and digital literacies, whether economic, political, social, cultural, geographical. or gendered, that are caught up in its stratification (Mills & Comber, 2015). It is a necessary basis for interpreting the sometimes in/visible and complex geopolitics and contestation of the private and public spaces of digital communication, and geographies of digital marginalization and exclusion.

The authors explode our understandings of the ways in the which digital media is caught up in the imagined or real social identities that traverse urban, rural, suburban and exurban spaces, and online and offline worlds, presenting agentive research of digital literacies from multiple of identities or subjectivities to disrupt notions of "metronormativity" (Herring, 2010). This work cuts across the politics of difference, including intersections of race, class, gender, sexuality, ability, and language, geography, and nation-state, and the entwining of cultural practices with digital media across time and space.

An outstanding feature of many chapters in the collection is a willingness to challenge existing notions of digital literacies and their associated spatial assumptions, such as disrupting in-school and out-of-school spatial binaries (see Bruce, Sullivan, Barrett, & Gonzalez, this volume), urban-centrism in digital literacy research, and overly celebratory views of digital literacies. For example, one study demonstrates how clusters of literacy practices that were initially performed face-to-face by the authors in tangible work carrels, and later when they worked in geographically diverse, online "virtual carrels," were often very analogous (Buchholz et al., this volume). A central realization is that virtual and physical spaces constitute interrelated social practices that are connected via multiple channels, involving relationality, multiplicities, and the movement of people, artefacts, ideas, and emotions within a community.

The book provides accounts of digital practices that rupture the English centrism of online spaces, such as the chapter by Song and Cho, who found that teens used the resources of Korean and English for different purposes depending on cultural and linguistic features in the online spaces. The volume challenges deficit views of social loafing in online spaces—the tendency to reduce individual effort in a group (see Neal & Vicars, this volume). It offsets deficit views of rurality and digital practices (see Connors & Daugherty, this volume; and Bruce et al., this volume), and theorizes both the new mobilities and "im/mobilities"—the emotionally paralysing or uncomfortable effects of literacy practices—without valorizing digital technologies (see Rust, this volume).

The book follows a spatial turn in digital literacies research, offering a contemporary and edgy reterritorializing of digital practices that obliterates homogenization. It achieves this by repositioning accounts that are typically marginalized, while acknowledging that places are shaped by oppressive institutional and social forces. Edward Soja, the noted American urban geographer and social theorist, would approve, because *Negotiating Place and Space Through Digital Literacies* speaks to his central proposition that critical social theory needs to take space seriously if it is to make sense of society (Soja, 1996). Each account in the book contributes to a digital literacies landscape that connects practices and places as lived, multiple, intersecting, fluid, and contested; interlinked yet interdependent; social and political, and located in power geometries (Hubbard & Kitchin, 2011).

The book makes a compelling case for the profound importance of spatiality in research of digital practices and intersecting relations of spatial power. A vivid example of this is an account of Indigenous activism of the Kiowa people near Carnegie, Oklahoma (see Woodward, this volume). The Kiowa established a social activist Facebook site to save Longhorn Mountain (SLM)—a place of cultural, historical and spiritual significance—from destruction by a mining company. Here, we see evidence of the contestation and power geometries that arise through shifts in the spatial organization of capitalist relations. The SLM Facebook page became an online space for Kiowas, residents, and supports of the SLM movement to build alliances across space-time. In this way, globalized forms of digital practices through social media spaces performed an integral role in the fight to preserve the sacred spatial organization of place and relations, and to resist capitalistic claims to spatial power (Massey, 1991).

The intersecting relations of power in digital literacy spaces are recurring in other chapters of the book. For example, Saunders and Salazar narrate the messy politics of adolescents' social media uses that entangle students, schools, and the public in the wilderness of online spaces, breaking down the spatial boundaries between school and public arenas. Similarly, highlighting the contested nature of digital practices and power, Thomas-Reid posits a "queering" of trolling texts online. This unique work highlights the pedagogical potentials of queering the offensive comments that are socially and spatially "in the margins" of online texts to reconfigure spaces, while pointing to evidence that humans are in fact, different people in online spaces than when interacting face-to-face. Jurich's chapter could be read as a response to both online studies (i.e., Sauders & Salazar, this volume; Thomas-Reid, this volume), sharing an original model for mediating dialogue in online affinity spaces, where even participants with a shared passion in an online community frequently encounter contested and "off-topic" viewpoints. Each of these studies illustrates the interstitial spaces of online interaction that can function as symbolic meeting places of both homogeneity and difference, conflict and mediation, identity politics and authentic community. Power geometries are also creatively uncovered in Sikkema and colleagues' research of art-based curricula that involved creating and wearing headdresses, literal masks, and digital posters to aesthetically negotiate and challenge identity politics and cultural representation as change agents.

Space and literacy practices are consistently seen to be enmeshed and mutually constitutive. For example, Abas traced signs and objects, such as portraiture and art installations in public places, and then followed the online reposting of photographs of those portraits, mapping the interactional spaces and audiences entangled with their tangible and digital circulation. Narrating a journey of a digital street performance from a taxi, Jackson's innovative research foregrounds the remaking of the urban working-class city of Hull, a place which was socially and theatrically produced, negotiated, lived, remembered, and enacted. In Opmeer and colleagues' research of digital heritage practices using 3D geospatial modelling in an ecomusuem, identities, places, and practices are seen as inextricably linked. Abram and Rowsell trace tacit modalities—the meanings that are felt or implied without being stated, including sentimentality and emotions that one connects to artefacts, whether a tangible object or a memory. Such explorations push back against the fixity of space, while pointing to the ever-evolving nature of meanings as they are perceived, experienced, remembered, and reexperienced tacitly across time and space.

In sum, the vibrant contributions to this new work forges new ground in current conceptions of digital literacy practices. Together, these studies are united by three central propositions in Massey's (2005) volume, "For Space," in which space is seen as constituted in interactions and interrelations, as spheres of coexisting heterogeneity and plurality, and perhaps most outstandingly in this volume, as always being remade.

REFERENCES

Castells, M. (1983). The city and the grassroots: A cross-cultural theory of urban social movements. Berkeley, CA: University of California Press.

Herring, S. (2010). *Another country: Queer anti-urbanism*. New York, NY: New University Press.

Hubbard, P., & Kitchin, R. (2011). *Key thinkers on space and place* (2nd ed.). London, England: SAGE.

Lefebvre, H. (1991). *The production of space* (D. Nicholson-Smith, Trans.). London, England: Blackwell.

Massey, D. (1991). A global sense of place. *Marxism Today, June*, 24–29.

Massey, D. B. (2005). *For space*. London, England: SAGE.

Mills, K. A. (2010). Filming in progress: New spaces for multimodal designing. *Linguistics and Education, 21*(1), 14–28.

Mills, K. A. (2017). What are the threats and potentials of big data for qualitative research? *Qualitative Research, Online first*, 1–13. doi:10.1177/1468794117743465

Mills, K. A., & Comber, B. (2015). Socio-spatial approaches to literacy studies: Rethinking the social constitution and politics of space. In K. Pahl & J. Rowsell (Eds.), *Handbook of literacy studies* (pp. 91–103). London, England: Routledge.

Soja, E. (1996). *Thirdspace: Journeys to los angeles and other real-and-imagined places*. Oxford, England: Basil Blackwell.

Soja, E. W. (1980). The socio-spatial dialectic. *Annals of the Association of America Geographers, 70*(2), 207–225.

Soja, E. W. (1989). *Postmodern geographies: The reassertion of space in critical social theory*. Oxford, England: Verso.

Soja, E. W. (2004). Preface. In K. M. Leander & M. Sheehey (Eds.), *Spatialising literacy research and practice* (pp. ix–xv). New York, NY: Peter Lang.

Soja, E. W. (2010). *Seeking spatial justice*. Minneapolis, MN: University of Minnesota Press.

PREFACE

Damiana Pyles, Ryan Rish, and Julie Warner

Imagine the folded, paper map you might pick up at the entrance to a large amusement park, or the giant store directory map mounted behind glass on one side of those large standalone three-sided advertising structures in the middle of a mall. Those maps probably include arrows or stars or dots with large text declaring, “You are here.” But if you look away from those maps, you may not be able to figure out where you are at all. Wherever the map says “here” often does not represent your position in the world. And even when the mapped representation accurately identifies where you are, it hardly accounts for the smell of the food vendor a few feet away, or the sound of children playing close by, or the piece of gum you just stepped in, or your feelings of anxiety or joy or relaxation. Even though the map presumptuously proclaims, “You are here,” the way you experience your “hereness” may not on the map at all—or barely there. Your hereness is likely complex, nuanced, multidimensional, historical, and fluid. How are you regarded in this place? When were you last here? What’s different around you? What do you see around you that is not represented on the map at all? Did you once kiss a teenage crush in a spot a few feet away? Are you frustrated that you can’t find, on the map, the one store you came to shop at? Who was “here” before there was a mall? The map has something to say about your hereness in the world and the things around you, but you quickly realize so much is missing from the map’s representation.

Negotiating Place and Space Through Digital Literacies: Research and Practice, pp. xv–xxxii

As early-career researchers who have worked in southern regions and/or rural communities in the United States we initially came together years ago as a research and writing group in reaction to what we recognized as a lack of representation of southern and rural places in digital literacies research, which started with a single tweet and moved forward from there (see Figure 1).

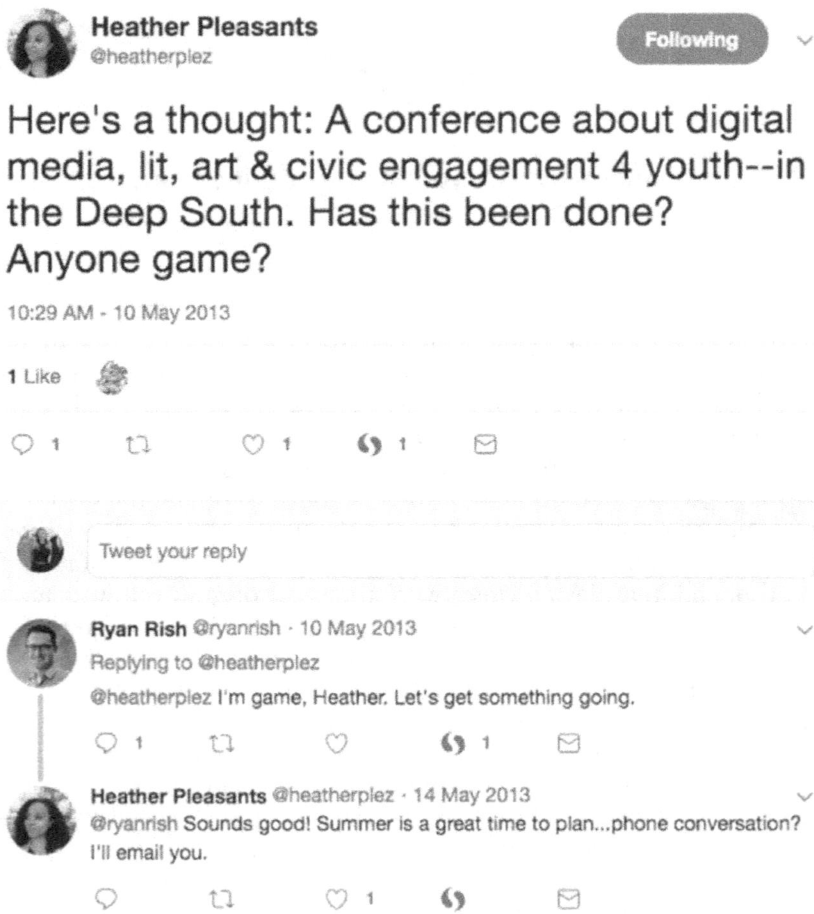

Figure 1. The Tweet that Sparked Southern Places Digital Spaces.

Along with a handful of other scholars,[1] we formed the Southern Places Digital Spaces collaborative and met over the course of a few years each month both online and offline, and we shared what with learned with others, often in online spaces. Although we came together initially because of our shared experience of doing digital literacies research in the U.S. South, our collective critical engagement with place-based and spatial theories in education research has broadened our focus. Rather than examining representation of the U.S. South exclusively, we came to consider the issue of representation of places and spaces more expansively (Literacy Research Association, 2014) (see Figure 2).

Figure 2. Southern Places Digital Spaces on LRA Research to Practice.

Through discussions rooted in readings on place-based and spatial theories, we sought to critically consider what kind of social spaces and which geographic places were and were not represented in the literacies research and what shaped those convergences and gaps.

What our explorations taught us were that digital literacies research has, for the most part, centered on urban places, spaces, and voices. In addition, we noted that in social and spatial imaginaries (Appadurai, 1996) we encountered in conversations and in the articles and books in our field, the U.S. South was often constructed as a monolith; yet, in actuality, notions of what the U.S. South is/is not, was/will be are continually contested, negotiated, reified, and renegotiated across large landscapes (Lewis Ellison, Noguerón-Liu, & Solomon, 2016). By considering the heterogeneity of the U.S. South across intersections of differences, including but not limited to race, class, gender, sexuality, ability, and language, we were beginning to see through our reading and discussions that studies of digital literacies had great potential for informing how the investigations of other regions within and outside of the U.S. could be conducted with regard to social, spatial, and historical considerations. And, as our own mobilities for work and life changes took us to different regions, we came to recognize a need to understand the intersections between geographic places, social spaces, and the ways that people navigate their relationship to those places through their use of digital technologies and locative media. In doing so, we sought to follow the lead of researchers in literacy studies who have considered how space is produced and experienced (mediated by analog and digital means) as people engage in literacies practices (Green & Corbett, 2013; Leander & Sheehy, 2004; Leander, Phillips, & Taylor, 2010; Mills & Comber, 2013).

With this volume, we widen our scope and bring together the work of global colleagues who conduct research into how people take up digital technologies as they teach, learn, and move across diverse physical and digital landscapes. This book represents an exploration with national and international scholars about how the field of literacy research could (re) conceptualize both geographic places and digital spaces, and the extent to which particular spaces and places are represented and considered integral to the way humans live, work, and play within an increasingly digitally-mediated world.

Digital Literacies, Place, and Space

Digital literacy practices have often been celebrated as means of transcending the constraints of the physical world through the production of new social spaces (Avila & Zacher Pandya, 2013; Pleasants & Salter, 2014). Indeed, in our own work, we have seen youth use digital tools and practices to create new spaces that went beyond the immediate boundaries of the physical spaces of their lives to explore their identities and connect with others (Gibbons, 2010, 2014; Rish & Cun, 2018; Rish, Cun, Gloss, & Pamuk, 2018; Warner, 2016, 2017). Gibbons (Pyles) (2010, 2012, 2014), in a study of youth filmmakers in rural and urban nonprofits, she worked to conceptualize rural media literacy and considered youth media production as a way of representing self, place, and social space in ways that respected their communities and fostered new senses of identities. She found that youth explored the potential of digital literacy practices and available tools to share their stories across time and space with different iterations of their own work refined and shared with others in their community and online in social spaces. Rish and his colleagues (2018) have examined how student inquiry can be supported by the use of mobile devices and the collection of locative data and media. Warner (2016, 2017) described the practices of youth composing with mobile phones and found that they moved not only with but also through new media. She looked at the ways identity markers, ideas, and relationships created new spaces as youth traveled with/through their mobile phones across physical or geographical boundaries.

However, we, like many other digital literacies researchers, have been wary in our work of taking on an overly-propitious view of technology as a panacea that can or will deliver resources to under-resourced places and marginalized peoples or render physical and material realities irrelevant (e.g., Warschauer, 2006; Wilder & Dressman, 2006). We have seen first-hand the way that, for example, challenges associated with geography, such as how rugged terrain or dense forested land can constitute infrastructural constraints to bringing broadband Internet to some schools and towns. To deny the importance of the material world to digital inequities would be disingenuous at best and, at worst, perpetuate disparities between resourced and under-resourced places by obscuring or ignoring those disparities (Watkins, 2018). To us, providing equitable access to resources for digital literacies and learning and working within spatial and historical complexities are issues of spatial justice (Soja, 2010).

In this volume we take a deep dive into investigations into the social, cultural, historical, and political aspects of literacies. We consider how the sociohistorical, sociocultural, and sociopolitical are enacted in/through landscapes that traverse urban, rural, and suburban/exurban, with emphasis placed on the ways digital technologies participate in the creation of identities and do work within social, digital, and material worlds. In particular, as we conceptualized this volume, we sought chapters that explored agentive work in digital literacies from a variety of perspectives that disrupted "metronormativity" (Herring, 2010) or urban centrism. We wanted to focus on how learning and teaching is fostered in often under-explored spaces where people worked for authentic engagement with their communities and with surrounding communities. Looking across/through intersections of difference (including, but not limited to race, class, gender, sexuality, ability, and language) and places, these studies of digital literacies have potential for informing how investigations of place, space, and mobilities within and across national and transnational contexts can be conducted in regard to the throwntogetherness of people, spaces/places, and texts (Massey, 2005). That is to say, these studies investigate various dimensions of the challenges, possibilities, inequities, and relationships inherent to negotiating space and place vis-à-vis digital literacies.

Part I: Reconsidering Digital Literacies From the Edges

Part I of this volume, Reconsidering Digital Literacies From the Edges, includes chapters with perspectives on how digital literacies intersect with learning and meaning making within and across various spaces with a special emphasis on the interactions between people, often familiar from school settings or from engagement in social spaces, and between people and digital texts. Some of these chapters focus on how people's interactions with one another and with texts foster learning, or in some case, include enough space for what appears to be a distancing from the learning interactions. Others focus on how people's interactions with texts are impacted by their own social and/or linguistic positionality, and the inherent complexities those bring. And, some chapters in this section explore what happens when people interact with one another in online spaces in ways that are both contradictory and uplifting. All of these chapters attempt to engage in the question of digital literacy from the edges as each chapter in Part I builds on and challenges current theoretical constructs around digital literacies, such as affinity space, social presence, multimodality, and monolingualism, by shedding light on the ways that people come to literacies from a new angle or from a different identity marker to help us understand the need to continually adjust the ways we consider and make meaning within and across spaces.

The social sciences over the past 50 years have seen several "turns" or foci in new directions that highlight different dimensions of literacy practices. While literacies researchers have, in part, adopted a spatial lens as a means of addressing the inequitable distribution of material resources, connections, and other capital (Mills & Comber, 2013), the "spatial turn" was a reaction to the digital turn's focus on the ways digital media challenged dominant conceptions of space as a container (Mills, 2010). Before the digital turn and spatial turns, literacy practices were often dichotomized into "in school" and "out-of-school" literacies, thus foregrounding physical space; this bifurcation of literacies as, in the case of "out of school" literacies, at-home, unsanctioned, nonacademic, and informal was contrasted with at-school literacies that are sanctioned, academic, and formal literacy practices. This spatial bifurcation was problematic because the divided conception of how literacy practices are framed, by definition, causes us to see them as fragmented; whereas, in reality, they are more fluid, with continuity (and surprising discontinuities) between what occurs across spaces. A bifurcated view results in a kind of a myopia where observers fail to acknowledge school-like practices at home or home-like practices at school (Hull & Schultz, 2001, 2002) amid the flows of modern life (Appadurai, 1996). The spatial turn engendered a more panoramic view of digital literacy practice.

Within this more panoramic view of literacies, some of the chapters in this section highlight how youth resist and respond to constraints imposed by particular spaces. In "Translanguage as a (Meta)cognitive Tool for Navigating and Learning in the Online Environment," Song and Cho challenge the common perception of English language centrism in online spaces of learning as they reveal the complex ways two Korean teens in the U.S. engaged in translanguaging. They found that the teens used the resources of both of their languages for different purposes depending on the cultural and linguistic features in the online spaces where they interacted. This finding is in keeping with other studies that show how people are blending online spaces to better navigate and express transnational identities (Christiansen, 2017). In much the same way, some digital literacies research has focused on how youth construct multimodal texts as a way to connect with other people and things, such as music, media, and so forth, in their places (Burn & Parker [Needs reference], 2003; Domingo, 2011). Sikkema and his coauthors' chapter, "Digital Media Explorations: How Space and Identity Become Sources of Learning" situates this conversation of resistance and response within an urban context as the chapter explores how teachers set up inclusive learning environments using digital tools and material products to help teens explore their own identities and positionalities in their Chicago neighborhoods.

Other chapters delve into the power dynamics at play in how people (re)use, communicate with, and/or foster identities with and through media in online spaces (Christiansen, 2017; Leander, Phillips, & Taylor, 2010). In "Social Loafing and Participatory Learning in a Networked Space," Neals and Vicar widen the scope of what is considered social interaction in online learning as they put a posthuman lens on digital participatory learning. Rather than viewing social loafing (the idea that people do less work when they are working in groups than alone) as a detriment to online learning, Neals and Vicar found that social loafing actually offered a new way to learn online and enrich students' experiences and connections to one another. Jurich's "Mediating Dialogue in Public Affinity Spaces," also challenges previously held notions of social interactions and meaning making within affinity spaces as primarily driven by a shared passion by demonstrating how disagreements and conflicts are negotiated in online affinity spaces for bass guitar players. In "Queering Text: Literacies Surrounding Cyber Trolling," Thomas-Reid considers the significance of what he calls "trolling artifacts" in online spaces designed for social justice teaching. Through the lens of queer theory, he suggests that these artifacts can be used for interrogation and enriching collective understandings of people's responses to social justice dialogue. In "trolling for truth" in negotiated, and often troubled, online spaces, Thomas-Reid's piece asserts a new kind of queered pedagogy that creates hope for more inclusive and truthful learning.

In this section, we hope to shed light on how "social space is not a static background against which activity develops, but rather space is both produced and productive" (de Haan & Leander, 2011, p. 320). These chapters call into question how different relationships in different spaces complicate ideas around agency and identity in both school and nonschool settings bringing the edges of space more to the center.

Part II: Digital Literacies From Within

Part II, Digital Literacies from Within, explicitly asks how digital literacies are fostered or contested in particular places given the spatial turn. We have come to understand space and place as relational constructs. Our considerations of social space that is constructed among people who are copresent and/or virtually remote include the significance of the materiality of a place and its history for what actions were taken therein and by whom. The people constructing the social space matter in relationship to each other, but they also matter in relationship to that particular place. For example, Finney (2014) documents how the legacies of Jim Crow, slavery, and racial violence have shaped cultural understandings of natural places and who should have access to them. People of color creating the social space of a conversation in a U.S. national park are doing so in relationship to a place in which they were historically excluded in a shared understanding of who should visit national parks. Likewise, places as built environments are designed for particular purposes with particular people and social relationships in mind. These purposes often do not only come from individuals or groups with special interests, but they may also come as part of larger government-sponsored agendas to separate people in systemic ways that are written into policies and laws and reinforced through the practices of people. Historically in the United States, this has taken the shape of state-sponsored segregation (Rothstein, 2017), which has created a legacy and entrenched practices of designing places based on preferences for particular classes and races of people. For example, in cities and suburbs across the U.S. basketball hoop removal from parks has been used to prevent the gathering of young men of color (Armborst, D'Oca, & Theodore, 2017). This is a very intentional reshaping of the material conditions of the place to thwart particular people from creating a particular social space (e.g., pickup basketball game). These two parks use examples that demonstrate the relationships between space and place. With national parks example, the access to the natural place has been defined in part by the aggregate of social spaces shared there by particular people over time. With city and suburban parks example, the places have been intentionally re-designed to discourage the sharing of particular social spaces by particular types of people.

However, we do not consider these constructs of space and place to be deterministic of the actions and meaning that is taken therein. We understand space as a "practiced place" (de Certeau, 1984), but not irrespective of the history and ideologies that gave shape to that particular place. Conversely, we understand place not only as "an order of distributed relationships, location, and fixity" (Talburt, 2000, p. 19), but also as sites where the social imaginary and acts of resistance can reinvent and transform through the social spaces that are shared there (Kinloch, 2010). Pressed further for a more precise definition of space and place, we respond by holding the two constructs in tension with one another in considerations of how the history and materiality of a place is significant when determining the "so what" of work involving digital media and literacies. We attempt in this volume to bring to the fore examples of how examining the relationships between space and place help us to understand digital literacies and their significance to the people involved. In these chapters, place is foregrounded or central to the argument. The chapters in this section interrogate the relationship between place and digital literacies across less studied settings.

Some of these chapters widen the lens on digital literacies in place(s) by exploring rurality, which has been a blind spot in the research on digital literacies. While literacy researchers have carried out robust research in the area of digital literacy practice over the past two decades, most of this research has focused on the engagement of people in urban contexts (e.g., Black, 2009; Chandler-Olcott & Mahar, 2003; Davis, 2010; Guzzetti & Gamboa, 2005; Hull & Nelson, 2005; Mackey & McClay, 2008). While this scholarship on urban areas doesn't discount rurality per se, a fuller understanding of "rural literacies" (Donehower, Hogg, & Schnell, 2007, 2011), in comparison, there is still much to be known about how rurality intersects with and/or constrains/fosters literacies in ways that are different than in other types of places (Green & Corbett, 2013), especially in terms of digital literacies (Pyles, 2016). In "Full of Sound and Fury," in their study of a professional development institute called Writing with Video, Bruce and his coauthors demonstrate the relationship between student digital composing processes and issues of identity within space by showing how both real and imagined aspects of space(s) are leveraged by participants. The work in this chapter illustrates the ways in which issues of space and place complicate the notion of "the field" and situatedness (Baron, 2008; Buckingham, 2008; Ito Okabe, & Matsuda, 2005; Ling, 2004; Livingstone, 2008; Mazzarella, 2005; Stornaiuolo, Smith, & Phillips, 2009) while avoiding a deficit perspective of rurality. Instead, the authors show the ways that the students used the "available resources of their ruralities" as they created video projects. In "Leveraging Digital Literacies to Critique Narratives about Southern Spaces and Places," Connors and Daugherty examine how digital media can be used to present opportunities for producing and disseminating counterstories (Delgado, 1989) about people and places in the southern United States. The digital videos the preservice teachers were asked to produce brought together the oral histories and the emerging teachers' own analytical perspectives on the people, places, and literacies of the Arkansas Ozark region. These chapters offer a rich picture of digital media and people from rural communities. These chapters further our argument that the digital divide binary, often applied to discussion of education in rural places, is, in essence, a deficit approach, but by refusing a deficit perspective, such studies offer insight into rich and meaningful uses of technologies by people in particular places.

Researchers have also attended to the conceived nature of space (Lefebvre, 1991; Soja, 1989), and technology integration has been explored as a means of addressing the educational needs of particular places. When it comes to rural places, in particular, researchers have approached technological tools and digital texts as a means of countering the lack of literacy resources and geographic isolation of some rural places (e.g., Howley, Wood, & Hough, 2011; Larson & Murray, 2008; Mitra, Dangwal, & Thadani, 2008). This research also foregrounds agency for the people living in those places. Woodward's "Indigenous Activism in the Digital Sphere: A Transrhetorical Analysis of the 'Save the Longhorn Mountain,' " applies a view of a social media site as a transrhetorical means toward preserving a geo-sacred site from mining. Woodward's study of Indigenous activism in the digital sphere demonstrates a digital literacy of social action dependent upon alliance building and reveals the need to further explore the ways in which digital literacies are influenced and created through social action. Woodward challenges us to consider how digital platforms contribute to change in the physical realm.

Other chapters explore how place as the central focus can lead to newer ways of utilizing digital media to re-see and re-conceptualize the place and/or its people. In "Innovative Technologies in Support of Local Heritage Management," Opmeer and his coauthors examine how GIS and 3D modeling facilitate people in a local community to create and share not only the history of the region in an ecomuseum but also their own relationships to the history and that area through the mapping and mobile apps that they created together in workshops. In this way, the local residents are marking their place in history as well as in their actual geographic area in ways that transcend both. Jackson's "From the Screen to the Streets: A Digital Performance Project to Remember and Reimagine Hull's Sense of Place," too, highlights the ways in which literacies travel across places and spaces. Through a series of interactive performance journeys traveling through a city entitled *Now|Then* (as one reviewer noted, a literal trip down memory lane) that evoked and explored relationships to the city of Hull in the United Kingdom over time. Translating digital media into performance becomes for Jackson a means for "establish[ing] heritage from below, and transcend[ing] grand narratives, so that individual stories and narratives can become contributors to a city's sense of place." Jackson maps the ways place is constructed centrifugally through human lives and memory, speaking back to hegemonic stories of place imposed from without through centripetal force.

The chapters in this section explore agency and space in new ways. The contributors demonstrate that people use literacy practices to reconfigure and conceptualize space in ways that are both concrete as well as conceived. These pieces call into question notions of agency defined simply as *the power to act* by highlighting the real ways that spaces both digital and conceived catalyze impacts in the physical world.

Part III: Tracing Digital Literacies Across Time and Space

In this last section, Part III, Tracing Digital Literacies Across Time and Space, the chapters offer some models for the use of digital literacies within lived experiences to promote social good within the "throwntogetherness" (Massey, 2005) of communities. In some ways, with the inclusion of these chapters, we are asserting a new digital politics that harkens back to Massey's recognition that we need a way of being together as people (and things) that:

> pays attention to the fact that entities and identities (be they places, or political constituencies, or mountains) are collectively produced through practices which form relations; and it is on those practices and relations that politics must be focused.... [W]hat this means in turn is that the politics itself might require a different geography: one which reflects the geography of those relations. (p. 148)

This call by critical geographers, such as Massey, has been taken up in these chapters by attempting to de-center digital literacies in pedagogy, collaboration, language, and community in different ways. By exploring how a variety of groups have used digital practices within their work for social change, we encourage others to imagine possibilities for engaged digital literacies within their own spaces and places. Despite a rich body of scholarship on space and digital literacies, questions about the role of the material world when one takes on a spatial perspective persist.

To grapple with the role of the physical world from a spatial orientation, many researchers have acknowledged the material as just one part of the "field of relations" or nexus of practice (Olwig & Hastrup,1997). In this view, space is not thought of as a container or "simply a static background 'upon' which human activity is played out" (Leander & McKim, 2003, p. 212); instead, one may think of space as an intersection, a never-ending expanse of connections, which includes (but is not limited to) the material/physical aspects of space. Yet, spatially-focused research has also acknowledged that space is, in part, conceived or imagined (Lefebvre, 1991; Soja, 1989). For instance, we know people use literacy practices, digital or analog, to "be part of the story," to claim a space, construct an identity, or take a social position (Moje, 2000). In this way, some literacy researchers have theorized space as similar to agency, as in the space people create for themselves to participate (De Hann & Leander, 2011; Moje, 2000; O'Brien, 1998, 2003; O'Brien, Springs, & Stith, 2001).

Mobile digital literacy practices in particular inspire a need to reconsider how we conceptualize space and agency. Mobile interfaces, and in particular GPS-enabled, locative media, affect how people think about and experience space (Farman, 2011). Taking this idea further, Farman (2011) posits that space is always "constructed simultaneously with our sense of embodiment" (p. 18). In much the same way, Wargo (2015) examined how one youth participant used digital mobile applications to mediate affective experience, and in doing so presents a laminated view of the material and digital as embodied experience, challenging us to reconsider the role of the material in relation to the digital with regard to mobile technologies. Mobile technologies allow us to bring the digital into the everyday spaces of our lives and thus reconfigure space.

The authors in this section also present challenges to long-standing theoretical constructs through their critique of static notions of multimodality by asking how time and space play a role in understanding subjective, sensory-based meaning making. In their chapter, "Immateriality Redux: Tacit Modalities and Personal Meaning Across Timescales," Abrams and Rowsell consider the tacit nature of modalities beyond typical considerations of affordances and constraints to consider how meaning making with artifacts changes over time and across space, foregrounding the significance of affect in meaning making. Artifactual meaning making is presented as ever evolving. Abas, in her chapter, "Repatriating Desaparacidos Across Time and Space," examined the ways that signs created by an artist-activist traveled from their physical origin, an art installation, to many nodes on a network through their posting to digital media. By focusing on place as linguistic landscape (centering upon linguistic texts, often markers and signs, in public spaces) they saw the way that language and space are enmeshed. In this way, the many spaces touched by the signs were shown to be inextricable and fluid. Abas shows us that flow can be a characteristic of space that can be leveraged for teaching and learning. In "Virtual Carrels," Buchholz and her co-authors shift from communicating in face-to-face carrels in their graduate studies to a range of online and offline spaces, such as Google Hangouts, Google Drive, and SMS/texts, in their first academic jobs. They find that the way they communicate creates a range of opportunities for personal and professional development as they navigate tricky political situations in their new jobs. These chapters represent an intriguing addition to the research on literacy and globalization, diasporas, and transnational communication (Brouwer, 2006; Lam, 2000, 2004, 2006, 2009; Skop & Adams, 2009), illuminating the ways people engage across a multitude of boundaries and borders. Such views of space are salient now, as the online adds a new layer to (or new nodes within) social space for literacy researchers to consider.

In this section, the chapters also work through some of the contestations that happen when people, places, and things are "thrown-together." By including these chapters, we are attempting to move away from prior assumptions that digital literacies will level the educational playing ground for students in underresourced places and spaces toward a more nuanced understanding that digital literacies are operating within existing power structures in communities but when one can see the "diffractions" (Barad, 2007) of the literacies, new understandings can emerge. For instance, in this last section, in particular, we are interested in exploring transliteracies, specifically how "..materials, persons, practices, and texts are dynamically configured across varied temporalities and spaces (Stornaiuolo, Smith, & Phillips, 2017, p. 70), including how people interact with *things* with similar complexities in power relationships. For instance, Rust's chapter, (Im)mobilizing Literacies," explicitly uses Storniaiuolo, Smith, and Phillips (2017) concept of immobilities to discuss how young people in different schools created digital media that was shared with other students both digitally and in a face-to-face workshop. Through examining the phases of the project, Rust found that some children experienced insecurity due to age and race when creating and responding to the youth media created, and those immobilities were present in different ways even when they were in a face-to-face workshop. The focus on immobilities provides a counter-narrative to an idea that media production helps all children equally, suggested by the proliferation of 1–1 tablet programs, connectivity, or coding initiatives in the early 2000s.

Living, Being, Learning Together Through Digital Literacies

Although these views of space predate "networked society" (Castells, 1996), digital literacies research has necessitated a re-theorization of space. The purpose of this volume is to consider through a variety of scholarly inquiries from global contexts how researchers and practitioners conceptualize and operationalize space and place in digital literacy research specifically. In our own respective inquiries into matters of space and place in digital literacy and in reading across the works submitted for inclusion in this volume, what we have recognized is that places are made up of elements that Massey (2005) calls *throwntogetherness* [author's italics] in which "places pose in particular form the question of our living together" (p. 151), and we would contend, of our learning together as well. "Place, in other words, does—as many argue—change us, not through some visceral belonging (some barely changing rootedness, as so many would have it) but through the practising of place, the negotiation of intersecting trajectories; place as an arena where negotiation is forced upon us" (Massey, 2005, p. 154). Therefore, in this volume, we consider how space/place, identities, and the role of digital literacies create opportunities for individuals and communities to negotiate living, being, and learning together in ways that have been unexplored or underexplored.

Conducting research on digital literacies practices always entails the risk of focusing too much on the tools that mediate literacy practices—at looking at the world from the angle of the tool at the expense of the world and its people around it. We have found that a focus on place and space is one means toward avoiding such reductionist views of digital literacy practices. Looking across the contributions in these pages one thing is clear: understanding the world around us and our place in it is a shared human endeavor. We view the chapters in this collection as significant contributions to our emergent understandings.

NOTE

1. Heather Pleasants, Lindy Johnson, Sean Connors, Darren Crovitz

REFERENCES

Armborst, T., D'Oca, D., & Theodore, G. (2017). *The arsenal of exclusion and inclusion.* Bacelona, Spain: Actar.

Appadurai, A. (1996). *Modernity at large: Cultural dimensions of globalization.* Minneapolis, MN: University of Minnesota Press.

Avila, J., & Zacher Pandya, J. (Eds.). (2012). *Critical digital literacies as social praxis: Intersections and challenges*. New York, NY: Peter Lang.

Barad, K. (2007). *Meeting the universe halfway: Quantum physics and the entanglement of matter and meaning*. Durham, NC & London, England: Duke University Press.

Baron, N. (2008). *Always on: Language in an online and mobile world.* New York, NY: Oxford University Press.

Black, R. W. (2009). Online fan fiction, global identities, and imagination. *Research in the Teaching of English, 43,* 397–425.

Buckingham, D. (Ed.). (2008). *Youth, identity, and digital media.* Cambridge, MA: MIT Press.

Brouwer, L. (2006). Giving voice to Dutch Moroccan girls on the Internet. *Global Media Journal*, 5(9). Retrieved from http://dare.ubvu.vu.nl/bitstream/handle/1871/25786/194682.pdf

Castells, M. (1996). *The rise of the network society: The information age: Economy, society, and culture* (Vol. I). Oxford, England: Blackwell.

Chandler-Olcott, K., & Mahar, D. (2003). "Tech-savviness" meets multiliteracies: Exploring adolescent girls' technology-mediated literacy practices. *Reading Research Quarterly, 38,* 356–385.

Christiansen, M .S. (2017). Creating a unique transnational place: Deterritorialized discourse and the blending of time and space in online social media. *Written Communication, 34*(2), 135–164.

Davis, K. (2010). Coming of age online: The developmental underpinnings of girls' blogs. *Journal of Adolescent Research, 25,* 145–171.

de Certeau, M. (1984). *The practice of everyday life.* Berkeley, CA: University of California Press.

De Hann, M., & Leander, K. (2011). The construction of ethnic boundaries in classroom interaction through social space. *Culture & Psychology, 17*(3), 319–338.

Delgado, R. (1989). Storytelling for oppositionists and others: A plea for narrative. *Michigan Law Review, 87*(8), 2411–2441.

Domingo, M. (2011). Analyzing layering in textual design: a multimodal approach for examining cultural, linguistic, and social migrations in digital video. *International Journal of Social Research Methodology, 14*(3), 219–230. doi:10.1080/13645579.2011.563619

Donehower, K., Hogg, C., & Schell, E.E. (2012). *Reclaiming the rural: Essays on literacy, rhetoric, and pedagogy.* Carbondale, IL: Southern Illinois University Press.

Donehower, K., Hogg, C., & Schell, E. E. (2007). *Rural literacies.* Carbondale, IL: Southern Illinois University Press.

Farman, J. (2011). *Mobile interface theory: Embodied space and locative media.* New York, NY: Routledge.

Finney, C. (2014). *Black faces, white spaces: Reimagining the relationship of African Americans to the great outdoors.* Chapel Hill, NC: University of North Carolina Press.

Gibbons, D. (2010). Tracing the paths of moving artifacts in youth media production. *English Teaching: Practice and Critique, 9*(1), 8–21.

Gibbons, D. (2012). Developing an ethics of youth media production using media literacy, identity, & modality. *Journal of Media Literacy Education, 4*(3), 256–265.

Gibbons, D. (2014). Rural places meet media literacy: Representing truth and self in rural social space. *Journal on Images and Culture, 6.*

Green, B., & Corbett, J. (2013). *Rethinking rural literacies: Transnational perspectives.* New York, NY: Palgrave MacMillan.

Guzzetti, B., & Gamboa, M. (2005). Online journaling: The informal writings of two adolescent girls. *Research in the Teaching of English, 40,* 168–206.

Herring, S. (2010). *Another country: Queer Anti-Urbanism.* New York, NY: New York University.

Howley, A., Wood, L., & Hough, B. (2011). Rural elementary school teachers' technology integration. *Journal of Research in Rural Education, 26*(9), 1–13.

Hull, G., & Nelson, M. (2005). Locating the semiotic power of multimodality. *Written Communication, 22,* 224–261.

Hull, G., & Schultz, K. (2001). Literacy and learning out of school: A review of theory and research. *Review of Educational Research, 71,* 575–611.

Hull, G., & Schultz, K. (Eds.). (2002). *School's out! Bridging out-of-school literacies with classroom practice.* New York, NY: Teachers College Press.

Ito, M., Okabe, D., & Matsuda, M. (Eds.). (2005). *Personal, portable, pedestrian: Mobile phones in Japanese life*. Cambridge, MA: MIT Press.

Kinloch, V. (2010). *Harlem on our minds: Place, race, and the literacies of urban youth*. New York, NY: Teachers College Press.

Lam, W. S. E. (2000). Second language literacy and the design of the self: A case study of a teenager writing on the Internet. *TESOL Quarterly, 34,* 457–482.

Lam, W. S. E. (2004). Second language socialization in a bilingual chat room: Global and local considerations. *Language, Learning and Technology, 8*(3), 44–65.

Lam, W. S. E. (2006). Culture and learning in the context of globalization: Research directions. *Review of Research in Education, 30,* 213–237.

Lam, W. S. E. (2009). Multiliteracies on instant messaging in negotiating local, translocal, and transnational affiliations: A case of an adolescent immigrant. *Reading Research Quarterly, 44,* 377–397.

Larson, R. C., & Murray, E. (2008). Open educational resources for blended learning in high schools: Overcoming impediments in developing countries. *Journal of Asynchronous Learning Networks, 12*(1), 85–103.

Leander, K., & McKim, K. K. (2003). Tracing the everyday "sitings" of adolescents on the Internet: A strategic adaptation of ethnography across online and offline spaces. *Education, Communication & Information, 3,* 211–240.

Leander, K., & Sheehy, M. (Eds.). (2004). *Spatializing literacy research and practice*. New York, NY: Peter Lang.

Leander, K. M., Phillips, N. C., & Taylor, K. H. (2010). The changing social spaces of learning: Mapping new mobilities. *Review of Research in Education, 34*(1), 329–394.

Lefebvre, H. (1991). *Critique of everyday life* (Vol. 2). New York, NY: Verso.

Lewis Ellison, T., Nogueŕon-Liu, S., & Solomon, M. (2016). Co-constructing place, space, and race: African American and Latinx participants and researchers' representations of digital literacy research in the South. *Journal of Literacy and Technology, 17*(3), 62–99.

Ling, R. (2004). *The mobile connection: The cell phone's impact on society*. San Francisco, CA: Morgan Kaufman.

Literacy Research Association. (2014, Nov. 12). LRA Research to Practice—Episode 13. Retrieved from https://youtu.be/lr5ykG3AnPE

Livingstone, S. (2008). Taking risky opportunities in youthful content creation: Teenagers' use of social networking sites for intimacy, privacy and self-expression. *New Media & Society, 10,* 393–411.

Mackey, M., & McClay, J. K. (2008). Pirates and poachers: Fan fiction and the conventions of reading and writing. *English in Education, 42*(2), 131–147.

Massey, D. (2005). *For space*. London, England: SAGE.

Mazzarella, S. (2005). *Girl wide web: Girls, the internet, and the negotiation of identity*. New York, NY: Peter Lang.

Mills, K. A. (2010). A review of the "digital turn" in the new literacy studies. *Review of Educational Research, 80*(2), 246–271.

Mills, K. A. (2015). *Literacy theories for the digital age: Social, critical, multimodal, spatial, material and sensory lenses*. Bristol, England: Multilingual Matters.

Mills, K. A., & Comber, B. (2013). Space, place and power: The spatial turn in literacy research. In K. Hall, T. Cremin, B. Comber, & L. Moll (Eds.),

International Handbook of Research in Children's Literacy, Learning and Culture (pp. 1–26). London, England: Wiley-Blackwell.

Mitra, S., Dangwal, R., & Thadani, L. (2008). Effects of remoteness on the quality of education: A case study from north Indian schools. *Australasian Journal of Educational Technology*, *24*(2), 168–180.

Moje, E. (2000). To be part of the story: The literacy practices of gangsta adolescents. *Teachers College Record*, 102, 652–690.

Moje, E. (2004). Powerful spaces: Tracing the out-of-school literacy spaces of Latino/a youth. In K. Leander & M. Sheehy (Eds.), *Spatializing literacy research and practice*. New York, NY: Peter Lang.

O'Brien, D. G. (1998). Multiple literacies in a high school program for "at-risk" adolescents. In D. E. Alvermann, K. A. Hinchman, D. W. Moore, S. F. Phelps, & D. R. Waff (Eds.), *Reconceptualizing the literacies in adolescents' lives* (pp. 27–49). Mahwah, NJ: Erlbaum.

O'Brien, D. G. (2003). Juxtaposing traditional and intermedial literacies to redefine the competence of struggling adolescents. *Reading Online*, *6*(7). Retrieved from http://www.readingonline.org/newliteracies/lit_index.asp?HREF=obrien2/

O'Brien, D., Springs, R., & Stith, D. (2001). Engaging at-risk high school students: Literacy learning in a high school literacy lab. *Constructions of literacy: Studies of Teaching and Learning in and Out of Secondary Schools*, 97–116.

Olwig, K. F., & Hastrup, K. (Eds.). (1997). *Siting culture: The shifting anthropological object*. London, England: Psychology Press.

Pleasants, H. M., & Salter, D. E. (Eds.). (2014). *Community-based multiliteracies and digital media projects: Questioning assumptions and exploring realities*. New York, NY: Peter Lang.

Pyles, D. G. (2016). Rural media literacy: Youth documentary videomaking as a rural literacy practice. *Journal of Research in Rural Education, 31*(7), 1–15.

Rish, R.M., & Cun, A. (2018). Co-navigating mobilized student inquiry across multiple contexts. *Proceedings of the International Conference on the Learning Sciences*. London, England.

Rish, R. M., Cun, A., Gloss, A., & Pamuk, M. (2018). Mobile asset mapping as community inquiry. In S. Arafeh, D. Herro, R. Ling, & C. Holden (Eds.), *Mobile learning: Perspectives on practice and policy* (pp. 119–141). Charlotte, NC: Information Age Publishing.

San Pedro, T. J. (2015). Silence as Shields: Agency and Resistances among Native American Students in the Urban Southwest. *Research in the Teaching of English, 50*(2), 132–153.

Rothstein, R. (2017). *The color of law: A forgotten history of how our government segregated America*. New York, NY: Liverlight.

Siegel, M., & Panofsky, C. P. (2009). Designs for multimodality in literacy studies: Explorations in analysis. In K. M. Leander, D. W. Rowe, D. K. Dickinson, M. K. Hundley, R. T. Jimenez, & V. J. Risko (Eds.), *58th Yearbook of the National Reading Conference* 5 (pp. 99–111). Oak Creek, WI: NRC.

Skop, E., & Adams, P. C. (2009). Creating and inhabiting virtual places: Indian immigrants in cyberspace. *National Identities, 11,* 127–147.

Soja, E. W. (1989). Postmodern geographies: The reassertion of space in critical social theory. New York, NY: Verso.

Soja, E. W. (2010). *Seeking spatial justice*. Minneapolis, MN: University of Minnesota Press.

Stornaiuolo, A., Smith, A., & Phillips, N. C. (2017). Developing a transliteracies framework for a connected world. *Journal of Literacy Research, 49*(1), 68–91.

Talburt, S. (2000). *Subject to identity: Knowledge, sexuality, and academic practices in higher education*. Albany, NY: State University of New York Press.

Wargo, J. (2015). Spatial stories with nomadic narrators: Affect, Snapchat, and feeling embodiment in youth mobile composing. *Journal of Language and Literacy Education, 11*(1), 47–64.

Warner, J. (2016). Adolescents' dialogic composing with mobile phones. *Journal of Literacy Research, 48*(2), 164–191.

Warner, J. (2017). *Adolescents' new literacies with and through mobile phones*. New York, NY: Peter Lang.

Warschauer, M. (2006). *Laptops and literacy: Learning in the wireless classroom*. New York, NY: Teachers College Press.

Watkins, S. G. (2018). *The digital edge: How Black and Latino youth navigate digital inequality*. New York, NY: New York University Press.

Wilder, P., & Dressman, M. (2006). New literacies, enduring challenges? The influence of capital on adolescent readers' Internet practices. *Reconceptualizing the Literacies In Adolescents' Lives, 2,* 205–229.

PART I

RECONSIDERING DIGITAL LITERACIES FROM THE EDGES

CHAPTER 1

DIGITAL MEDIA EXPLORATIONS

How Space and Identity Become Sources of Learning

Scott Sikkema
Chicago Arts Partnerships in Education

Louanne Smolin
LIS Curriculum Research

Joseph Spilberg and Mark Diaz
Chicago Arts Partnerships in Education

Erin A. Preston
External Research Consultant, Chicago Arts Partnerships in Education

Classrooms are contested spaces. Compliance measures, educator professional development focused on alignment with mandates, punitive oversight systems, and notions of universal curriculum potentially threaten to remove the individuality and identity of classrooms (Darling-Hammond,

Negotiating Place and Space Through Digital Literacies: Research and Practice, pp. 3–20

2013; Kohn, 2011; Ravitch, 2010). Digital literacies offer a process for teachers and students to unpack this context, to reshape it, and in the process, redefine their identities as learners. Digital literacies move beyond adding technology into the mix of learning activities. Rather, they offer a collaborative process for learners to investigate and redefine their worlds both in and outside of the classroom. Our work is drawn from digital media arts partnerships between Chicago Arts Partnerships in Education (CAPE) and urban, public school classroom teachers in both professional development and classroom settings. The potential to shift perceptions of school space led CAPE collaborators to pedagogies that examined space, including alternate community spaces, and identity as site for art making.

The purpose of this chapter is to examine the digital literacy practices within our arts integrated school curriculum, affording opportunities for arts teachers and students to transform their learning spaces and reconceptualize their identities as learners. Specifically, we ask: How can the possibilities of digital media accelerate or deepen student and teacher exploration and production of space and identity? How can digital media, expressed through artmaking, be used as material to reproduce or perform space and identity through the act of making?

This chapter includes three sections. We begin by discussing the digital literacy foundations that ground our arts integration partnerships. We, then, explore digital media as artistic material. Finally, through curricular cases, we examine how arts teachers and students investigated space and identity through arts integrated curriculum.

THEORETICAL FOUNDATIONS OF DIGITAL LITERACY PRACTICE

As teachers and students engage in digital literacies, they activate processes that necessitate their engagement in multiple modalities where "the textual is also related to the visual, the audio, the spatial, the behavioral, and so on" (The New London Group, 1996, p. 64). The New London Group (1996) redefined literacy, shifting the field from a focus on text based literacy to multiple "literacies" that recognize there are "multiple ways of communicating and making meaning" (Leander & Boldt, 2012, p. 23). These multiliteracies are "complemented by, or replaced by, other ways of crossing time and distance, such as recordings and transmissions of oral, visual, audio, gestural and other patterns of meaning" (Kalantzis & Cope, 2012, p. 2). This redefinition raises two important implications for learning: (1) meaning is shaped by multiple modes of representation and (2) the contextual boundaries in which we experience these modes become expanded as well. In other words, students encounter multiple forms of literacies in multiple contexts.

Although these ideas have shaped the field of new literacies, over the years, critique has been voiced. For example, Leander and Boldt (2012) raised concerns about how the work of the New London Group (1996) has been taken up in research and practice. In particular, they see as problematic the notion of "youth literacy practices as purposeful rational design" which involves a "domestication that subtracts movement, indeterminacy, and emergent potential from the picture" (p. 24). Their critique sought to reconceptualize learners' literacy engagement as "the moment-by-moment unfolding or emergence" of experience (p. 25). CAPE's arts integration methodologies are, in fact, more reflective of emergent practices rather than structured design, and have shaped the ways in which digital media has been explored in our partner classrooms.

Additionally, we have often found in the urban educational settings in which we work, classrooms are becoming "non-places" disconnected from anything relational or historical, and so also unconcerned with any sense of individual or collective identity (Augé, 1995). In this context space is not used and individuality is not valued. Therefore, identity is not considered to be material or product with which to work. However, in our work we seek to reclaim these spaces through an expansion of classroom literacies, including digital literacies.

Digital literacies inclusive of space and identity bring multiple variables into play. First, *students' experiences* contribute to multiliteracies. This has instructional implications because "in bringing space and place into the frame of literacy studies we see a subtle shift—a rebalancing of the semiotic with the materiality of lived, embodied, and situated experience" (Mills & Comber, 2013, p. 412). Therefore, students' experiences become a part of the curriculum. Sheehy (as cited in Mills & Comber, 2013) discusses this dimension of curriculum as a permeable territory, defining it as "in between spaces." These in between spaces consist of: The difficult interactional negotiations that can occur when teachers attempt to shift from reproducing literacies that are disembodied from the materiality of students' lives—worksheets, tests, and typical school knowledge—to focus on the meaningful events, objects, literacy practices, and knowledge inherent in students' own lives (Mills & Comber, 2013, p. 414). As students' lifeworlds, including the spaces surrounding students' interactions in their classrooms, homes, peer relationships, and digital explorations, are factored into the literacy curriculum, their voice and generative creativity become valuable resources for learning, expanding curricular options and, therefore, their potential for meaning making.

Second, within a digital literacy framework, *space is situated within a social context*. Multimodal interactions are embedded in social spaces, and, therefore, the space becomes defined through relationships. As Massey (2005) describes, space is built through the

> [p]ractices of engagement and the power-geometries of relations, of the structuring of space (both through enclosure and through flow) through such relations, and through an understanding of those relations as differentially (and unequally) empowering in their effects. Such practices do not so much measure space as create it, the "distances" they engender may be ones of physical force, of political (dis)alignment, of imagination. (p. 100)

In CAPE's digital media partnerships, teachers and students create space by examining the relations of power between and among them and by exploring how those relations move within defined spaces, such as the classroom. This relational conception of space can transform teaching and learning. As Leander and Boldt (2012) described, "when social space is reimagined as activity or process rather than as dimension … freedom, dislocation, and surprise characterize our sense of the social" (p. 39). Using digital literacy practices and the multimodalities they encompass, classrooms can develop into participatory learning cultures. In this process, space and relationships are created anew. The normative power relationships between teachers and students becomes disrupted. The learning environment becomes inclusive of "a more heteroglossic authentic interaction—a new area of negotiation and representation, where official and unofficial, formal and informal spaces become permeable and create potential for new kinds of learning" (Mills & Comber, 2013, p. 413). This counters oppressive classroom structures and situates learning in a context where students have voice, expertise, and agentive power (Mills & Comber, 2013).

Finally, digital literacies encompassing of space foster possibilities for *identities to become dynamic and fluid*. As teachers and students form new space and relationships, they develop new understandings of their identities. Massey's (2005) view of space as relational leads to the continual negotiation of relations and differences, a process never totally settled. Identities shift between individual and collaborator as teachers and students explore digital media, and these negotiations are "productive of political, and personal, identity" (p. 182). This description is counter to the normative classroom culture that typically contains formal roles, limited opportunities for collaboration, and a narrow to nonexistent audience. A classroom that embraces participatory culture can be transformed by its liberatory qualities, including dialogic practices and a flattening of authority and expertise (Mills & Comber, 2013).

Digital Media as Artistic Material

The framework described above contextualizes digital literacies in social spaces and created by each individual's experiences, dynamic identities, and relationships (Leander & Boldt, 2012). This has implications for digital arts practices. Massey (2005) described space as being composed of the interrelations of our practices, and, as such, space is never finished being constructed by those of us interacting within the space. Thus, to examine, deconstruct, and reconstruct space is to do the same via ourselves and our identities. When students experiment with technology as material, then digital space affords them an environment where "forms of expression and bodies (content) are more or less in constant movement between stasis and change" (Leander & Boldt, 2012, p. 39). In manipulating digital material, students and teachers directly experience simultaneity and disconnections from the new, and they are always in the flux of determining new relations (Massey, 2005). As a result, students can use digital media as artistic material to examine and construct space and identity.

Moreover, when students use digital media as material, what they construct embodies their thinking which can then be used to experiment with evolving understandings of space (Papert, 1990). In this way, digital media gives materiality and physicality to one's mental model (Papert, 1990). Students can use digital media to better understand technology by "seeing the process" in material and "also see representation of the process as it plays out" (Resnick & Rosenbaum, 2013, p. 174). For example, when editing digital video footage, students can immediately see the effects of editing decisions on their film in playback. When combined with a participatory culture where students learn with and through technology, they are afforded the opportunity to see the relational processes of creating space. When creating digital products, such as digital videos, students can take on various roles with each other including screenwriter, director, actor, and editor. Students can examine and (re)create the structures of relations or power in their classroom, their school, their neighborhood, or their community. Creating digital space is a way for students to disrupt normative power structures and restore emergent potential for relations. In this process, a student's relationship to both technology and space can transform into one more individualized and transparent (Turkle & Papert, 1990). Technology and space can become material to think with in order to gain command of expression and communication (Massey 2005; Turkle & Papert, 1990).

Digital space impacts how students develop identity. Boyd (2008) described digital environments as spaces where students experiment with and perform their identity, taking on identities, such as community members, tinkerers, and experts (Ito et al., 2009). When students make choices about how to perform identity and create forms of expression in digital spaces, it is a nonlinear practice emerging from interrelations and multiliteracies (Leander & Boldt, 2012). The interplay between the virtual and physical impacts a student's sense of body and identity due to "a constant 'reproduction' of the self without the body" (Paul, 2015, p. 165).

This fluctuation of presence and identity across digital spaces prompts students and teachers to rethink the precepts of identity, body, and space, and enables the potential to form new statements of identity in spaces, whether digital, physical, or a combination (boyd, 2008; Ito et al., 2009; Palfrey & Gasser, 2008; Wilson, 2017). By embracing the ways digital space has changed how and where students develop their identities and engage in literacy practices, teachers can activate the liminal qualities between a classroom and digital spaces where norms, roles, and identities can be renegotiated.

If transforming spaces can play a role in transforming identities, and if digital media can become artistic material rather than merely a tool, how can the possibilities of digital media accelerate or deepen student and teacher exploration and production of space and identity? How can digital media, expressed through artmaking, be used as material to reproduce or perform space and identity through the act of making? The cases below provide examples in which we explore how CAPE's arts teachers and students transformed their learning spaces and how this transformation helped them reconceptualize their identities as learners.

CURRICULAR CASES

CAPE's partnerships utilize a conceptual approach to art and art making, generating opportunities for exploring site or location, as a way into space and identity (Kwon, 1997). In this conceptual approach CAPE's teacher artists, student artists and viewers utilize technology as artistic material, collaboratively constructing cultural and sociopolitical inquiries in multiple spaces within and surrounding schools and enabling these spaces to transform the identities of all the collaborators. In the curricular examples that follow, we examine this digital literacy framework, describing how space and identity are transformed when digital media is conceived of as material through which students and teachers learn.

Connectivity and Collaboration: Curricular Example 1

In CAPE's professional development for teachers, we reconceive how technology is used and understood. To achieve this, we engage teachers in experiences that help them see and use digital technology as a material in-and-of-itself rather than using it simply as a tool to create known end products, such as self-portraits or movies. During the *connectivity and collaboration* workshop, teachers explored the physicality of digital devices versus learning basic operations, enabling them to find new ways to manipulate digital media. Teachers were shown examples by contemporary artists where digital devices not only captured something about a space, they were set up in the space itself to redefine the experiencing of that space. This way of thinking about devices as a literal, physical part of the art was a new way of thinking for our teacher participants. They were tasked to utilize digital devices in small groups to create a new understanding of their identity as a group in relation to the space they were in. They investigated group dynamics, stories, and the workshop space itself. They performed for video or captured sounds or images of the space and shared with each other the array of media they created. They then examined each media file to identify patterns and ideas that emerged from the footage. After settling on a connective theme, they reworked or created new media files to execute the final project.

One group realized a common current running through their thoughts and feelings were reactions to the 2016 election. They created individual voice recordings of their reactions and set these recordings on each of their devices to an appropriated video of a campfire. They arranged their devices with the voice recorded campfire videos around the workshop space for their colleagues to encounter.

Figure 1.1. Campfire.

This group's creation, installation, and encounter reflects Massey's (2005) notion that space is a "sphere of dynamic simultaneity, constantly disconnected by new arrivals, constantly waiting to be determined (and therefore always undetermined) by the construction of new relations" (p. 107). As one teacher stated:

> I learned a lot about the value of collaboration as well because I never would have thought about that alone. Although I had parts in coming up with that idea. We do a giant fireplace on the stage during our winter dance, and I was like, "Oh, yeah. So everyone brings something to the table." And so we got thrown into it over and over again. (CAPE, 2018a)

The teachers created this new, "campfire" space through extended negotiations with each other as to their differences and relations, a negotiating process that was as much digital as it was verbal. This process created new spaces, generating a "political, and personal, identity" (Massey, 2005, p. 182). As the above teacher stated:

> Just the idea that we were using technology in a way I had never thought of using it before.... And everyone that day, everyone did really interesting pieces of, iPads inside of iPads.... [The facilitator] also just left that really open for us. You're pulling from every experience of your life.... Everyone used it in such different ways. (CAPE, 2018a)

This teacher aptly describes how exposure to her peers' ideas not only opened her up to new ways of thinking, but also helped her to dig deeper to mine her own experiences. In this professional development example, and all of those above, teachers were given permission to build on their basic understanding of technology by directly connecting with aesthetic concerns in the arts integrated lessons they teach, strengthening their knowledge of both aesthetic and technological realms. For example, they created both sculpture and aural composition through installation of iPads as artistic material and digital recording processes. As Qvortrup (2003) described, "the artwork object to be observed by the audience is not just the resulting image or projection" but a "complex system of material interferences and of textual interreferences" (p. 251). In Figure 1.1, iPads were used as sculptural material and communication medium, going beyond their normative use as personal information device. Together teachers created an intertextual experience for their audiences, an experience that invited them to make meaning of the multiple modes of expression present in the installation. In this way, the creators of the art and the audience could acknowledge and process their thinking and emotions about the election.

Other groups investigated interferences and interreferences. For example, one such group experimented with the space around them, as depicted in Figure 1.2 and explained below.

Figure 1.2. Space reproduced.

Figure 1.2 displays still shots from this group's video. The video is composed of multiple iPad devices simultaneously playing back slow tracking shots from multiple perspectives of the expanse of the space. As digital artists, this group of teachers moved away from creating a discrete art object. Rather, the "digital technologies offer multiple possibilities for an enhanced cinematic representation in installations, a continuation of the spatialization of the images in a physical environment" (Paul, 2015, p. 96). Their installation created a hybrid form that disrupted a linear narrative in which participants are presented with a single projection on a wall with the support of a picture plane. Participants reconceptualized the narrative flow by moving through the space to view the multiple channels. In creating this installation, the teacher-artists chose to *emphasize experience* by assembling multiple objects and digitized spaces. This led them to raise different questions than they might have considered if emphasizing art as object. Can the digital technology transform how an audience might interact and participate with the art? How might the audience see and experience the space they are in when they are immersed in every angle of it at once? Using questions such as these to guide their installation, teachers created an experience for participants to examine their relationship with space.

In the *connectivity and collaboration* case, teachers developed an understanding of how devices themselves occupy space, how they can be arranged to activate a location, and how they then can enhance the meaning of an artistic experience. Their experiments in technological approaches forefronted communication, collaboration, and the materiality of the technology itself. In contrast to artworks as objects, these examples of digital art challenged viewers to see digital media as material. In the process, teachers re-imagined their space of learning as well as creating a space for exploring their relationships as co-creators of conceptual art.

Me Behind the Mask: Curricular Example 2

This curriculum was implemented in an alternative urban high school that provides students with academic, behavioral, and truancy challenges a second chance to complete a high school diploma. World Literature and Journalism teacher Avery G. partnered with teaching artist Charles J., an interdisciplinary digital/visual artist. Avery and Charles wanted students to consider what characterized a social problem while also working through design and engineering problem solving methods. Students studied world cultures through an inquiry: What are ethnocentric views, and what is the appropriate way to learn respectfully about another culture? The learners were also interested in analyzing through a study of media, identity politics, and cultural reproduction, how identities, including their own, are visualized and performed. Considering their own alternative high school as a culture and identity as well as a particular and unique space, they analyzed how their own culture and identities are stereotyped and what they themselves want to project about their culture and identity.

The medium for this examination became masks. Students researched how cultures around the world created masks and headgear that had social value and represented aspects of their culture. They created their own headdresses and wrote text or messages that carried a personal meaning for them. The messages they incorporated functioned as life mottos or rules to live by. For example, one student wrote: “Being humble is not being weak.” Upon close inspection, the shapes of the headpieces made of crisscrossed rods are visually connected to the text. A young woman wears a shoe shape construction which bears the phrase “Take a walk in my shoes.” In the below image, a young man is adorned by something that appears to cage his head and holds up a sign stating “Mind your own business” (see Figure 1.3). Figure 1.3 is provocative in its portrayal of a body encaged. It sparks our engagement, prompting us to learn more by participating in a thoughtful dialogue with the artist. We might think about cages and where we actually see them. Perhaps we think about where they

Figure 1.3. Mind your own business.

exist but are unseen? How does our knowledge that this image appears in a school impact the meaning we might make? Is this student-artist making a statement about classrooms as cages? Is he communicating with and admonishing those who have opinions about classrooms and students? In this example the student is not only thinking about how material can convey ideas, but also how it can provoke questions.

In the final iteration of this project, students photographed each other adorned with their structural headdress and holding up their bold text and created digitized posters. They discussed where their posters might go up in the school, wanting to create "democratic public spaces … operating with a sense of spatiality which keeps always under scrutiny the play of social relations which construct them" (Massey, 2005, p. 153). This was realized as the students debated who they wanted to encounter the posters, and thus what kinds of dialogue and ideas they hoped the posters would prompt. This debate was particularly appropriate to the space of this alternative school, which occupies a floor within a much larger, multistory building. There is little outside this building to identify it as a school or educational setting. Additionally, the school itself has a number of spaces typically closed off from any general public. Considering all these factors, it was critically important to the students to choose places where the posters could spark debate from their peers and raise consciousness with school visitors. As such, social space, digital media and shared dialogue came together, creating a participatory culture that altered "the focus of literacy from individual expression to community involvement" (Jenkins, Clinton, Ravi, Robinson, & Weigel, 2009, p. 6). As the social space of the school was made a site for inquiry, the nature of the dialogue became transformed. The ratio of teacher and student talk was rebalanced, student voice became amplified, and their engagement with their original inquiry intensified.

The network of who the students communicated with and learned from went beyond the classroom teacher. Through this engagement of others, students confronted "what is typically unmentionable in an institutional setting" (Mills & Comber, 2013, p. 414), such as who they are as students, how stereotyped expectations of students of color exist in school settings, and what the potential is for nontraditional students to achieve. As the classroom teacher stated: "The projects were received very well and the posters created quite a buzz around school, which was a special experience for the student artists" (CAPE, 2018b). These transformations enabled the students to re-form their identities as actors within their schools, becoming agents of change, creating spaces for their reflection and generating new potential for their learning.

In the *Me Behind the Mask* curriculum, technology afforded students the ability to produce physical products and redefine school spaces, crafting opportunities for naming and challenging the hegemony of school spaces. Their use of mediated imagery went beyond their own individual identities to a broader sociocultural context, challenging the culture of school space. Their process highlighted how technology informs understandings of identity, and specifically, how identities become stereotyped, enculturated, and reproduced. They effectively pulled back the curtain that renders unseen the normative learning practices dominating classrooms.

Anger Pets: Curricular Example 3

Teacher Kindra H. is an art teacher at an urban elementary school. She, teaching artist Adrianne S, and a seventh grade class of students examined the use of social media in history and its role in personal contexts for a curriculum project, called *Anger Pets*. Students began their inquiry by analyzing how print media depicted people's struggles and mass protests during the Civil Rights Movement. They then investigated the present-day manifestation of civil rights within the Black Lives Matter movements, examining how young activists used social media to express their concerns about racial issues in the United States. These engagements deepened students' knowledge of how technology shapes information.

Using "anger" as a big idea, students investigated expressions of anger through this historical lens and made connections to their personal experiences with anger. Identity thus became a part of the curriculum, as students examined their own identities through the anchor of anger. They fabricated "anger pets"—sculptural embodiments of anger—out of various materials, including clay and fabric. Students then created videos and animations incorporating these figures. They thought about the causes, effects, and consequences of anger as they grappled with how to create sculptures that could "perform" their chosen emotional attributes. Students' conceptions of anger became expanded in the process.

As the unit progressed, opportunities to utilize the videos presented themselves, and the use of digital technology became materials that students shaped in order to communicate their messages. These technologies included cell phone videos, stop motion animation, and audio recordings. Students used this digital media to further explore how anger is depicted and shared in digital spaces, both personally and in a sociocultural context. The use of phones for video recording was convenient, but it is also the same technology used to document police brutality as a criminal justice tool as part of the Black Lives Matter movement. This connection was an important learning tool; it enabled students to interrogate the sociocultural implications of how anger, violence, and activism are depicted in digital spaces.

Kindra remarked on the relationship between technology and identity. As Kindra stated, digital media explorations enabled her students to "personify their anger, look at it objectively, and appraise how it impacts them" (CAPE, 2018c). As such, they had an opportunity to examine an aspect of their identity typically not addressed within academic curriculum. To concretize anger, students experimented with ways to make the attributes of their anger pets visible through technology explorations, and, as Kindra stated, making "choices in camera angles and movement, sound and some special effects that they invented" (CAPE, 2018c). She maintained that "using the technology allowed students to separate themselves from their own anger (something very personal), and view it objectively" (CAPE, 2018c). As such, "self-reflection and analysis were both possible because of the use of technology" (CAPE, 2018c). Further, digital media enabled the students to see from themselves to the other in their classroom. They gained new understandings of the commonality of anger, forging what Massey (2005) calls a "grounded connectedness" (p. 188). In Figure 1.4, an anger pet is surrounded by student reflections of different attributes of anger characteristics such as "anger is a lonely place." With this installation, they remade their classroom space by establishing a new collective identity, or connectedness, within it using media itself to express identities, emotions, and connectedness.

Kindra expanded curriculum to encompass the potential of their digital literacies for learning. For example, the particular uses of media in this

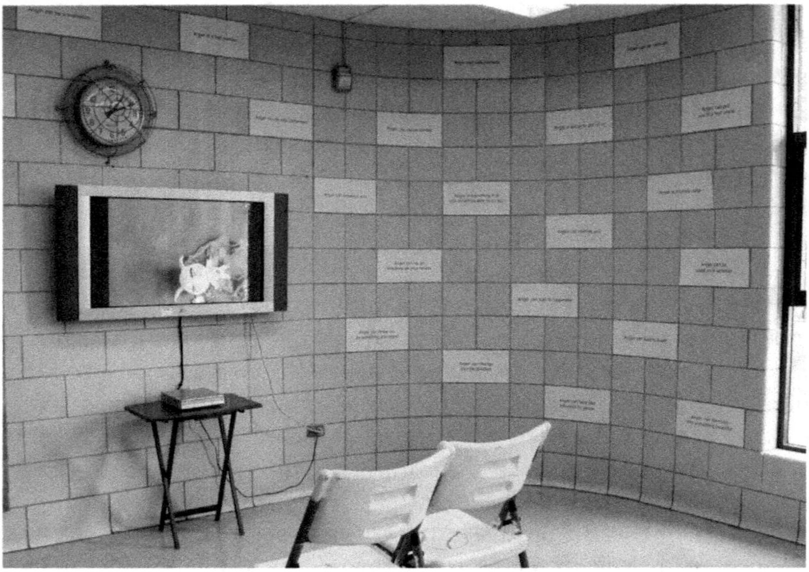

Figure 1.4. Anger pets installation.

unit connected students' life experiences and digital communication with historical research. As Kindra stated:

> The concept of anger with middle schoolers is strongly expressed on social media today. Cell phones play an important role in their lives. Using the cell phone's video camera was the natural choice. We took the same tool that is often used as their "weapon of destruction" and used it as a tool of expression. Students walked in with a great deal of prior knowledge in terms of the subject as well as the vehicle. This allowed them to concentrate on how they would express their ideas rather than learning the nuts-and-bolts of a new art medium. (CAPE, 2018c)

Counter to Leander and Boldt's (2012) contention that "design leaves out movement and surprise" (p. 43), Kindra's curriculum design enabled students to investigate and experiment with anger in multiple modalities. In this process, students were able to play with their expression, understanding, and representation of anger which resulted in "emergent combinations that [took] flight into something anew" (p. 43). Students had authorial control to visualize and give voice to their anger based on their individual conceptualizations and technological choices. By extending students' exploration of anger through digital media, representations became visceral and, when combined with the sculptural forms, called into question whose anger is valued and what anger must look like in order to be valued. Connecting this back to the sociocultural context, digital media allowed students to materialize something ephemeral, like an emotion, into an artifact which could then be examined to better understand identity.

Digital media flattened the normative hierarchy between students and teachers, adults and schoolchildren. As Kindra stated: "Because of the technology aspect, my students and I did quite a bit of role reversal, making them the teacher and me the student" (CAPE, 2018c). This enabled students to have a greater voice throughout the entire process, and because of that Kindra's students learned that "taking the lead is a responsibility and that there is a seriousness that has to be maintained in order to take the reins and direct what your artwork will say and how it will speak" (CAPE, 2018c). Her students rose to the occasion. This project expanded Kindra's instructional repertoire and her identity as a teacher, artist, and learner. She stated in her written reflections that she became "more flexible and willing to change, and release control" (CAPE, 2018c).

CONCLUSIONS

The above curricular cases examined how CAPE's arts teachers and students investigated space and identity through media arts integrated curriculum. We began by asking the following two questions: How can the possibilities of digital media accelerate or deepen student and teacher exploration and production of space and identity? How can digital media, expressed through artmaking, be used as material to reproduce or perform space and identity through the act of making? CAPE's teachers and students cocreated curriculum that diverged from the linearity of instruction, conceiving of digital technology as material to produce space and identity and creating opportunities for all to better understand the world and themselves. Through their agentive work, they conceived of space as dynamic, social, and permeable. In the *connectivity and collaboration* professional development workshop, teachers used technology to redefine the experiencing of space and incorporating the personal and political into their identities as co-creators. In *Me Behind the Mask*, students challenged the status quo concerning what constitutes a school space by elevating their voices within that space and becoming agents of change. In the *Anger Pets* curriculum, students' digital media use enabled them to examine anger personally and in a wider sociocultural and historical context.

An aesthetic pedagogy changed the emphasis of the type of materials and practices used for instruction including how to rethink the use of digital media. Rather than acquiring content knowledge through traditional literacies, such as written texts, students engaged with academic content using digital media as material. For example, in the *Me Behind the Mask* unit students examined world cultures through paper tubing, digitized posters, and the participation of their school community. As middle school students created *Anger Pets* and discussed their interpretations on films they made, they learned about the impact of media in historic and contemporary contexts. In both projects, technology was intrinsic to the artistic practice of production, and it enabled a process for students to delve into the complexity of academic concepts, such as understanding civil rights, posing problems, and to conveying their ideas.

Key to understanding technology as a material is the emphasis on manipulating and reassembling existing information or forms to achieve hybrid forms. iPads moved beyond a simple tool to become installations that enabled audiences to rethink the space around them. Digital images build upon what spaces, such as lunchrooms and hallways, are typically used for, redefining them so that they become sites of dialogic inquiry. In the curricular examples described above, a disruption in thinking and doing occurred around digital media that immersed teachers and students in remaking space, producing and reproducing identities. Students engaged with big ideas, such as conceptualizing how space creates norms of behavior and how they can disrupt such norms, thinking in new ways about who they are in school, and in turn, understanding how school has shaped their identities as learners. Through this process, their identities as agents of change, generative learners and active communicators grew.

As learners experimented with technology as material, their relationship with technology became a personal one shaped by their individuality, including their interests, aesthetics, and approaches to knowledge construction (Papert, 1990). Using digital media as material, multiple and personal approaches to meaning making were made possible, and thus the learners described above had the potential to create an "epistemological pluralism" (Turkle & Papert, 1990) in their learning spaces. As a result, normative classroom strategies for thinking and learning were expanded from one of "logic and planning" (Resnick & Rosenbaum, 2013, p. 167) to include personal and exploratory approaches to knowledge construction.

Learning spaces were rethought. The novel spaces exemplified in this chapter probed new understandings of individual, collective, and social identities through investigations and enactment of the materiality of digital media and space. Hallways, cafeterias, streets and community centers became materials to disrupt and reshape. CAPE students, teachers, and artists experienced and articulated their interrelatedness in working with digital material, and such interrelatedness was inherently spatial, reflecting the concept that sociability implies and requires spatiality (Massey, 2005). In experiencing and creating with the digital as material, learners saw and forged new identities, thus making new spaces for identities to interrelate.

Student voice was elevated and they became active agents of sociocultural debate. They took up the responsibility of making their own decisions while creating their own artistic products. They mined their own experiences, thoughts, and perspectives to drive their creations.

Through their participation in CAPE's arts integration professional development programs, teachers explored theoretical ideas about literacy and digital media, making these ideas more accessible within the realities of their instructional contexts. For these teachers and their students, digital media became an effective part of space reproduction, transformation, and identity formation because of its use as a material. This provided a context in which teachers and students could interrogate and push beyond the constraints of school spaces, countering hegemonic school based practices. This disturbance of the normative curriculum engendered by digital media encouraged teachers to diverge from the linearity of instruction and enabled students to experiment, shape, and convey their deeper understandings of the world. As such, they both teachers and students stepped out of their respective normative roles, collaboratively questioning and reimagining learning in classrooms, contesting and reclaiming their shared spaces.

REFERENCES

Augé, M. (1995). *Non-places: An introduction to supermodernity*. (J. Howe, Trans.). New York, NY: Verso.

boyd, d. (2008). Why youth (heart) social network sites: The role of networked publics in teenage social life. In D. Buckingham (Ed.), *Youth, identity, and digital media* (pp. 119–142). The John D. and Catherine T. MacArthur Foundation Reports on Digital Media and Learning. Cambridge, MA: The MIT Press.

Chicago Arts Partnerships in Education (CAPE). (2018a). *Project ATLAS (year 3 teacher interview)* [transcription data file]. Chicago, IL: Author.

Chicago Arts Partnerships in Education (CAPE). (2018b). *Artist/researcher partnerships* [digital portfolio documentation]. Retrieved from http://at.bulb.re/pYu

Chicago Arts Partnerships in Education (CAPE). (2018c). *Project ATLAS (year 2 performance measure)* [digital portfolio documentation]. Retrieved from http://at.bulb.re/pYt

Darling-Hammond, L. (2013). *Getting teacher evaluation right: What really matters for effectiveness and improvement*. New York, NY: Teachers College Press.

Ito, M., Horst, H., Bittanti, M., boyd, d., Herr-Stephenson, B., Lange, P. G., ... Robinson, L. (2009). Living and learning with new media: Summary of findings from the digital youth project. *The John D. and Catherine T. MacArthur Foundation Reports on Digital Media and Learning*. Cambridge, MA: The MIT Press.

Jenkins, H. (with Purushotma, R., Weigel, M., Clinton, K., & Robison, A. J.). (2009). Confronting the challenges of participatory culture: Media education for the 21st century. *The John D. and Catherine T. MacArthur Foundation Reports on Digital Media and Learning*. Cambridge, MA: MIT Press.

Kalantzis, M., & Cope, B. (2012). *Literacies*. New York, NY: Cambridge University Press.

Kohn, A. (2011). *Feel-bad education: And other contrarian essays on children and schooling*. Boston, MA: Beacon Press.

Kwon, M. (1997, October). One place after another: Notes on site specificity., *80*(Spring), 85–110.

Leander, K., & Boldt, G. (2012). Rereading "a pedagogy of multiliteracies": Bodies, texts, and emergence. *Journal of Literacy Research*, *45*(1), 22–46.

Massey, D. (2005). *For Space*. London, England: SAGE.

Mills, K. A., & Comber, B. (2013). Space, place and power: The spatial turn in literacy research. In K. Hall, T. Cremin, B. Comber, & L. Moll (Eds.), *International handbook of research in children's literacy, learning and culture* (pp. 412–423). London, England: Wiley Blackwell. Retrieved from https://doi.org/10.1002/9781118323342.ch30

New London Group. (1996). A pedagogy of multiliteracies: Designing social futures. *Harvard Educational Review*, *66*(1), 60–93.

Palfrey, J., & Gasser, U. (2008). *Born digital*. New York, NY: Basic Books.

Papert, S. (1990). A *critique of technocentrism in thinking about the school of the future* (circulated title: *M.I.T. Media Lab Epistemology and Learning Memo No. 2*). Media Lab, School of Architecture + Planning, Massachusetts Institute of Technology, Cambridge, Massachusetts. Retrieved from http://papert.org/articles/ACritiqueofTechnocentrism.html

Paul, C. (2015). *Digital art* (3rd ed.). New York, NY: Thames and Hudson.

Qvortrup, L. (2003). Digital poetics: The poetical potentials of projection and interaction. In G. Liestol, A. Morrison, & T. Rasmussen (Eds.), *Digital Media revisited: Theoretical and conceptual innovations in digital domains* (pp. 240–261). Cambridge, MA: MIT Press.

Ravitch, D. (2010). *The death and life of the great American school system: How testing and choice are undermining education*. New York, NY: Basic Books.

Resnick, M., & Rosenbaum, E. (2013). Designing for Tinkerability. In M. Honey & D. Kanter (Eds.), *Design, make, play: Growing the next generation of STEM Innovators* (pp. 163–181). New York, NY: Routledge.

Turkle, S., & Papert, S. (1990). Epistemological Pluralism and the Revaluation of the Concrete. *SIGNS: Journal of Women in Culture and Society*, *16*(1), 128–157.

Wilson, N. (2017). Sociotechnical and pedagogical barriers to technology integration. In M. Grassetti & S. Brookby (Eds.), *Advancing next generation teacher education through digital tools and applications* (pp. 19–36). Hershey, PA: IGI Global.

CHAPTER 2

MEDIATING DIALOGUE IN PUBLIC ONLINE AFFINITY SPACES

Chuck Jurich
University of North Carolina, Wilmington

Outside of our safe and comfortable Web 3.0 ideological bubbles, contemporary online discourse is increasingly marked by anti-social and uncivil commenting practices (Cheng, Bernstein, Danescu-Niculescu-Mizil, & Leskovec, 2017; Coe, Kenski, & Rains, 2014). Reagle (2015) describes "comment" as a kind of genre marked by short, asynchronous, and reactive communication, and while online comments can function to inform and improve, they are regularly used to manipulate, alienate, and shape readers and participants. Online discussion forums are open venues for "trolls," "haters," and "cyberbullies" who provoke, flame, intimidate, and victimize fellow commenters, often to regulate spaces (Phillips, 2015). From subtle jabs to the abhorrent invasion of privacy of "doxing" (or publicly documenting someone's contact, financial, and/or health information), online spaces can feel unwelcoming and unsafe.

Readers with any passing experiences with online commentary can attest to comments' general lack of intelligence, contention, and cruelty. The idea of authentic and sincere interaction amongst strangers online, in the year

Negotiating Place and Space Through Digital Literacies: Research and Practice, pp. 21–40

2018, may seem laughably naive, yet, these spaces exist. One such space is Talkbass (http://talkbass.com), a heavily trafficked public online discussion forum and virtual affinity space for people who play, or have an interest in, the bass guitar or upright bass musical instruments. Despite the massive size, heavy participation, and long history of the space (270,000 registered members and over one million discussion threads), the negative practices mentioned above are virtually nonexistent on Talkbass and helpfulness and civility are normalized behaviors.

This chapter investigates how people from diverse and distant locations, with wide ranging backgrounds, experiences, and world-views, engage with and learn from one another within online interactions in a coconstructed online affinity space. The purpose of this study is to examine and describe how discussion and interaction on Talkbass works with the belief that these insights can be used to improve dialogue and discussion in other contexts. I consider online discussion forums as virtual shared spaces for the potential negotiation, development, and mediation of human interactions through asynchronous dialogue.

Talkbass as an Affinity Space

Affinity spaces are physical, virtual, or hybrid spaces of shared passion, organized around a common interest or activity where the user generated content and interactional organizations reflexively shape each other (Gee, 2004). Affinity spaces offer multiple paths of participation, opportunities to engage with and learn with others, and a complex web of interest-driven interaction (Lammers, Curwood, & Magnifico, 2012). Affinity spaces are accessed via a "portal" such as the Talkbass website but also through common search engines which attract and invite new participants. Focusing on the space itself (content, signs, organization, portals) versus the community and "belongingness" of its individual members, Gee (2004) describes affinity spaces as having 11 specific characteristics but cautions that an affinity space is not an all-or-nothing concept, rather, the more the space has these characteristics, the closer it is to being a "paradigmatic affinity space" (p. 77). Using these criteria, Talkbass is a well-defined affinity space (see Table 2.1) with a clear common endeavor, multiple routes to participate and garner status, and the acceptance of a variety and range of knowledge.

The Off Topic Subforum of Talkbass and Authentic Dialogue

In an online affinity space, Gee (2004) argues that variables such as race, class, gender, sexuality, ability, and education level, while not eliminated, are backgrounded to a common or shared interest. Online affinity spaces

Table 2.1.
Characteristics of Affinity Spaces (Gee, 2004) and Talkbass.com as an Affinity Space

#	Characteristics of Affinity Spaces (Gee, 2004)	Talkbass as an Affinity Space
1	Common endeavor is primary, not race, class, gender, or disability	The "bass" is the common endeavor and all other member demographics are secondary to the shared interest.
2	Newbies, masters, and everyone else share common space	Experience, skill, real world fame (some members are notable musicians) are not requirements to participate.
3	Some portals are strong generators	On the web, top searches on information concerning the bass frequently lead to Talkbass.com.
4	Content organization is transformed by interactional organization	Members give feedback to and request features from gear manufacturers, particularly "boutique" builders who cater to players "geeking out" (Ito et al., 2010).
5	Both intensive and extensive knowledge are encouraged	Members help each other design and buy their bass "rigs" and encourage the modification of instruments, amplifiers, speaker cabinets, and more.
6	Both individual and distributed knowledge are encouraged	Members teach and learn how to be better bass players via discussion on technique, equipment, professionalism, band management, and more.
7	Dispersed knowledge is encouraged	Members discuss and link to topics that are outside the scope of the bass, particularly true for the Off Topic sub-forum addressed in this study.
8	Tacit knowledge is encouraged and honored	The most common inquiries in the space are questions based on tacit knowledge and real world experience: "Has anyone tried ____?"
9	There are many different forms and routes to participation	Participation takes place in a variety of ways including reading (views are counted), "liking" posts, starting a thread, contributing a post, and moderating a subforum.
10	There are lots of different routes to status	Status comes in many forms including being a moderator, "Supporting Member," or super-user, starting a popular thread, accumulating "likes" and "points," contributing highly specialized knowledge, and more.
11	Leadership is porous and leaders are resources	Overt leaders include paid staff and moderators. Some superusers have earned leadership roles and can influence member behaviors and interactions. All members can report posts for moderation.

are unique in that they provide opportunity for individuals who may not share the connections typically associated with one another to gather and share common ground (Black, 2007). While the bass is the endeavor that initially brings participants together on Talkbass, there is also an active "Off Topic" subforum where the same members congregate to discuss anything and everything *except* playing the bass. After receiving good advice on what bass or amplifier to buy, appreciative participants return to the site inquiring about nonbass related subjects such as their career, relationships, health concerns, or how to deal with road rage, deadbeat landlords, grief/death, and countless other personal topics. Much like an "edge city" (Garreau, 1991), a growing satellite city that would not exist without the larger and more established central city, the Off Topic subforum has become its own destination for many members. Off Topic is a unique space to study in that the one interest that brought participants together is relegated but the social connections from the larger affinity space still links members. As a result, Off Topic discussions are diverse and unpredictable, like putting all motorcycle enthusiasts together to discuss their relationships with their parents, and this diversity provides opportunities for rich dialogue.

The term *dialogue* is used to describe an act of creation by people who authentically want to understand one another and solve problems (Freire, 1970). The Freirian concept of *authentic dialogue* is about unveiling the limit-situations and the obstacles that come with revealing the truth itself. When discussing topics and problems, what are the obstacles (limits) that create these problems and what are the actions (limit-acts) that might help solve them? I approach the study from a critical perspective of new literacies where online affinity spaces such as Talkbass have the potential to foster authentic dialogue between participants who have conflicting and contrasting value systems and world views. In many ways, online affinity spaces behave as "culture circles" where posters ask questions and generate themes of inquiry and the resulting discussions are attempts of the participants to make sense of their lives and the world by "reading the word" and "naming the world" in their posts and comments (Freire, 1970). Applying this framework to Talkbass, authentic dialogue may or may not occur in the discussions; however, disagreements and differing viewpoints are excellent starting points for potential dialogue.

The research question guiding the study was: what are the characteristics of dialogue in online affinity spaces when the discussion and subjects move away from the focal shared interest and what does this dialogue tell us about the spaces in which it occurs? Through studying the language of the comments, I looked to describe and map out threads and posts to better understand how discussions develop and how disagreements and conflict is negotiated. In this chapter, I first describe the research site and share the methods used in the study. Next, I outline the structure and attributes of Talkbass discussions using examples from recent threads. I conclude by detailing the characteristics of this affinity space that make it different from other online forums and identify five specific actions participants in any forum can do to help mediate and move discussions towards authentic dialogue.

METHODS

Site and Participants

Celebrating its 20th year in January of 2018, Talkbass (http://talkbass.com) has over 20 million public posts logged. There are over 80 subforums available for members that target various aspects of bass playing such as "Technique," "Strings," "Effects," and many more. The site of the research is the Off Topic subforum which is the third most popular subforum (2.4 million posts) behind "Basses" (5.1 million) and "Amps and Cabs" (2.8 million). All discussion threads are public and open for anyone in the world to read. (Note: Readers can view all the threads mentioned in this chapter and follow along with the data presented.) Membership is required in order to post however anyone can browse, read, and search the forums. There are vast numbers of "lurkers," members and nonmembers, who only read threads as well as highly visible "super-users" with thousands of authored posts. Any member can be reprimanded and/or banned from making posts for breaking forum rules. Membership is free but "Supporting Members" and "Gold Supporting Members" pay an annual membership fee and have additional benefits, most notably the ability to buy and sell musical equipment/gear on the site and an advertisement-free spatial environment.

Data Collection

Data for the study comes from the publicly available Off Topic discussion subforum (found at http://www.talkbass.com/forums/off-topic-bg.34/). Over a 4-month period, I read and sorted the most recent Off Topic threads (n = 680) searching for "data-rich" discussions for close post-by-post analysis. Specifically, I looked for threads that had: (1) an original post with an identifiable question or generative theme posed, (2) a focus on social or political issues where participants had differing perspectives, experiences, and/or opinions, (3) at least 40 posts in the thread at the time of analysis (evidence of engagement), and (4) evidence of multiple voices and many participants within a thread (not just 3–4 people contributing all the posts in a thread). At the time of this writing 22 of the 680 threads met this criteria; within these 22 threads, approximately 1,800 posts were collected for analysis.

Data Analysis

Data was analyzed using the method of *categorical aggregation*, or the sorting and rendering of information into large clusters of ideas and providing details that supported the themes (Creswell, 2007). Specific strategies used were reading posts and assigning codes to them, reducing related codes to themes and categories, writing analytical memos, relating categories to one another, and relating categories to the theoretical framework. I used a *process coding* scheme, focusing on the actions and interactions of participants in response to situations or problems (Saldaña, 2009). I chose this scheme because interactions between posters were often done with an objective or goal in mind (e.g. "complimenting," "clarifying," or "telling their story") or dealing with a problem or issue (e.g. "disagreeing"). For example, in the thread "How do you deal with road rage?" (MJ5150, 2017), the member Funkhead posted a comment and mentions another member, @OP>>. (Note: all "screen names" mentioned in this chapter are real however they are likely pseudonyms.)

> **Funkhead:** I am a trucker and I have to constantly remind myself of all that is at stake. I don't want to ruin my career or risk hurting someone. @ OP>> Thanks for posting this. I really needed a reminder after this week. (MJ5150, 2017, post 32)

Funkhead's post was coded as "agreeing" (with the preceding comment) and "appreciating" for thanking the member @OP>>. Process codes exclusively take on the form of gerunds (verbs used as nouns) and can suggest or capture the processes taking place in the data.

THE STRUCTURE OF ONLINE DISCUSSION SPACES

Threads and posts on Talkbass have consistent and identifiable structures and characteristics. Threads begin with an original post where the "Original Poster" (OP) poses a question or a generative theme for discussion. For example, Ironbar started the Off Topic thread: "Advice needed: Seriously considering divorce." In the first lines of the initial or "original post" he writes:

> **IronBar:** I ask this question here because with the exception of BassCliff, I've never met any of you in person, and this forum provides a modicum of anonymity. For reasons I won't dwell on, I'm seriously considering divorce from my spouse. (Ironbar, 2017, post 1)

The theme of divorce is introduced and the question of what the poster should do is presented. Sometimes the question/theme is in the thread title itself such as in the thread "Anyone here have any stories/advice about immigration abroad?" (anavar, 2017).

After the start of the thread, there are three main categories of posts that follow: (1) *My Two Cents*, brief monologues where posters share their thoughts and ideas, (2) *Contention to Moderation,* posts which center on winning the debate and being "right," and (3) *Community to Mediation,* posts which focus on social relationships and discovering the object of knowledge of the topic. Figure 2.1 outlines the structure of online discussion spaces on Talkbass and shows the relationships between the original post and the three main categories of posts in a thread. After the original post, early comments that follow are typically *My Two Cents* posts but as participants start to respond to each other and not just the OP, discussions fracture and grow in many dialectic directions at once. Threads simultaneously turn to contentious disagreements that can lead to interventions by the Talkbass staff moderators (described in the *Contention to Moderation* section*) and* evolve into community building spaces leading to mediated dialogue (described in the *Community to Mediation* section). While the model appears linear, the actual processes and interactions in a discussion thread are dynamic and multiple.

My Two Cents Posts

In *My Two Cents* posts, participants share their stance, thoughts, and opinions on the question or generative theme introduced in the Original Post. The name originates from the casual, opinionated, and often flippant feel to the posts. They are ubiquitous, easily representing over half of all posts studied. While they can appear at any time, *My Two Cents* posts are particularly prevalent early in threads. A typical *My Two Cents* post is *Think/Splaining* which has the general structure of "I think (blank) because (blank)." In response to the OP, geegeedemocracy, in the thread "Going to lunch with my ex," Chicory Blue, *Think/Splained*:

> **Chicory Blue:** Trying to hold together a relationship that's in the process of falling apart is just delaying the inevitable and hurting yourself more in the process.... If there's any hope for you at all, it isn't here and now, not

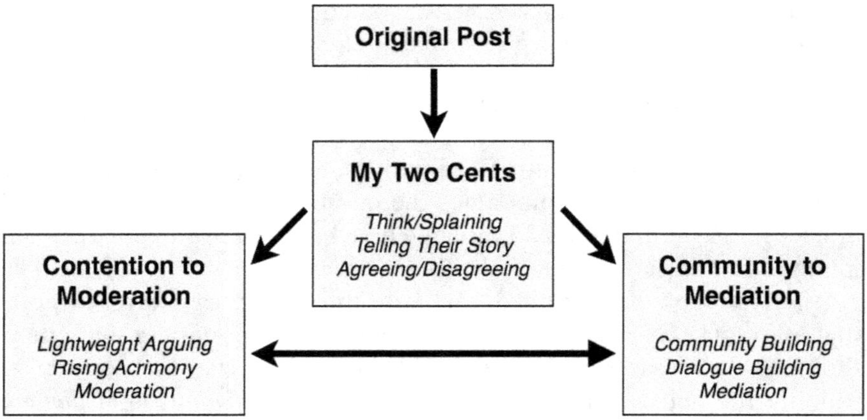

Figure 2.1. The structure and relationships between post categories on Talkbass.

> while everything is still in flux and volatile. Be brave, let it go, and find your peace elsewhere. (geegeedemocracy, 2017, post 9)

Chicory Blue states what he/she thinks, "let it go" for now, but also explains why, (because) "everything is still in flux and volatile." The post is thoughtful and his/her explanation is evident however many posters emphasize the "I think" portion but are light on the "because." For example, Joedog responded to the OP: "Go into it w/an open mind, but don't expect much. Best of luck!" (geegeedemocracy, 2017, post 21). The post is casual and supportive but does not explain why the OP should not expect much from the lunch meeting.

Some posters use narrative structure to express their stance or opinion. *Telling Their Story* posts highlight a similarity or connection between the OP's situation with their own. Stories are engaging, personal, and compelling but they also function as a rhetorical device to organize an argument. For example, member Funky Ghost shared his story about trying to get back together with his ex:

> **Funky Ghost:** I am currently dating my ex wife.... We have talked about all the reasons why we came to an end and were completely honest about it all. We accepted our parts in it (an important step to have a real shot at a reboot imo) and we have cautiously been working our way back to a full relationship. I made it clear, yesterday in fact, of my intention to win her heart back. It was received well Take it slow, talk and be honest with yourself and her about your reasons for being there. (geegeedemocracy, 2017, post 23)

Through his story, Funky Ghost shared his stance on the topic and his explanation is embedded in the narrative itself suggesting that if he and his ex can make it work, maybe it can also work for the OP. He advises, "take it slow, talk and be honest with yourself and her."

Another common variety of *My Two Cents* category is *Agreeing/Disagreeing* posts. Here, participants post in an affirmative or negative response to the question or generative theme of the OP or posts that come before them. The posts tend to be accompanied by a quote or reference to what they are agreeing/disagreeing with. In the thread "Man, are we really this sensitive? Do we need to be offended THIS badly?" the OP, two fingers, does not so much ask a question as much as *Think/Splains* on a topic and then asks who agrees with him. The subject of the thread is a Dove soap TV commercial where a Black woman takes off her shirt to reveal a Caucasian woman underneath. The OP became aware of the commercial when he saw many posts on Facebook that were critical of the ad, commenting on its racist undertones because it visually suggests that soap cleans the Black woman and transforms her into a Caucasian. After viewing the commercial, two fingers vehemently *Think/Splained* in a lengthy initial post that he did not think it was racist at all and inquired who agreed or disagreed. Mayatch disagreed:

> **Mayatch:** It's an ad for soap; it shows a black woman turning into a white woman. I don't think it should require huge logical leaps to see how that could offend someone. Did you see the pictures in the linked article of old soap ads literally showing scrubbing the black off people? (two fingers, 2017, post 56)

The tone of posts matters. In general, "agreeing" feels affirming and "disagreeing" feels more like a slight; however, variations of *Agreeing/Disagreeing* can often flip the tone of the post. Further, "agreeing *but*" may be perceived as picky and argumentative and "disagreeing *but*" can feel open-minded and compromising. For example, bholder who was the first to reply in the thread, agreed with the OP two fingers but in a variation ("agreeing but") commenting: "I'm not terribly offended, personally, but I think it was an incredibly stupid move and understand those who are offended." (two fingers, 2017, post 2).

Alone, *My Two Cents* posts read like a series of monologues, and considered alone are not dialogic in the sense that the comments are only in relation to the Original Post. However, *My Two Cents* posts serve as important raw discussion materials needed when moving towards potential dialogue later in the thread. While expressed opinions and lived experiences are important to the ones sharing, Freire and Macedo (1995) argue that stories are only useful to authentic dialogues if they can be connected to the larger issues that they frame. Lived experiences are good points of departure but participants have to universalize them. The exchanging of stories turn dialogue into conversation overly focused on the individual and removed from the "object of knowledge" while universalized posts are arguably the most convincing.

Contention to Moderation Posts

After sharing their initial "two cents" comments, participants in *Contention to Moderation* posts start to respond to each other's comments and not just the OP. These posts focus on the debate between thread posters, from "contention" (when two posters express that they disagree with one another) to "moderation" (when the rules of the virtual affinity space are enforced or threatened to be enforced). Talkbass has 10 rules that guide member interaction including "respect your fellow members" and strict moderation of culturally insensitive remarks and trolling (Talkbass, 2018). The Off Topic subforum has additional rules with a heavy emphasis on the restriction of discussions concerning religion and politics:

> Religious/political discussions are challenging enough to moderate when people are face-to-face.... In an impersonal, anonymous medium such as this, such threads tend to require constant moderation, create enemies out of prior friends, and generate more hate and anger than anything else.... If you want to discuss religion on TalkBass, the limited-access Lounge Lobby forum is available for such discussion (Supporting Membership required). (john turner, 2007, post 6).

The moderators recognize the limitations of the medium and the potential for contention with these topics. Off Topic moderators often remind participants of forum rules and adapt rules to current events. For example, gun advocacy/gun control is now a banned topic. The moderator Robert R. Tyler explained: "Much like politics, these threads tend to only breed contention amongst the membership even if the initial intention of a thread was good" (Brian R. Tyler, 2016, post 1). Violators of any forum rules face warnings, suspensions, and possible banishment.

Even with nonforbidden topics, contention and disagreement still occurs. I describe contentious posts as *Lightweight Arguing*. Here participants keep to the topic but dig in their heels and try to convince the other side that their proof is suspect, thinking is flawed, or experiences are irrelevant. The primary goal is to win the argument. The thread "Is Billy Joel disgusting for having a kid at age 68?" is an insightful example of how *Lightweight Arguing* can develop. After a series of *My Two Cents* posts, two camps formed. Arguing against Billy Joel having kids at age 68, blue4 wrote: "There's enough data out there to suggest that very old parents have a higher risk of having autistic children so myself I would never do it, regardless of the womans age. !" (GK Growl, 2017, post 46). Jazz Ad rebutted:

> **Jazz Ad:** First it's only the mother's age. Then it increases for younger moms too. Finally, the risk goes from .5 to 2%. Which basically means you have no control over it. It isn't a sound enough reason to orient a personal choice. (Gk Growl, 2017, post 63)

Typically, debate would continue however blue4 did something unusual in *Lightweight Arguing* and acknowledged the point. Referencing Jazz Ad, blue4 wrote: "There's enough for me. That's sound enough. I didn't criticize him in my post, just stating I wouldn't do it myself." (GK Growl, 2017, post 73). The comment from blue4 that the evidence was "sound enough," was a courteous concession, though blue4 did reiterate in the end "I wouldn't do it myself." However, this exchange represents only one small strand in a complex rope of interactions from multiple members on the topic. Jumping in and agreeing with Jazz Ad's earlier post, Buldog-5151bass sarcastically added "How DARE you start arguing facts here. : D" (GK Growl, 2017, post 75). This comment provoked blue4 to rebut and reiterate: "A quick Google search shows that the 'facts' are far from settled. As I stated before, there's enough there regarding not just autism but other mental health issues to give me pause." (GK Growl, 2017, post 76). This exchange shows how, even if two participants can come to an understanding on an issue, the dynamic and multiple nature of online forums keeps the interaction on edge. There is a bit of uneasiness involved in *Lightweight Arguing* and while it typically ends in a "tie," where both sides make their point but no one changes their mind, there is always the threat that it may escalate. While tolerated, *Lightweight Arguing* does not help build positive relationships leading to community.

Escalating beyond *Lightweight Arguing* are posts that dispense with the care of civil debating and moves towards antisocial and negative behaviors. I call these posts *Rising Acrimony* in order to highlight the "bitterness" that is central to the comments and they include posting practices such as dismissing, judging, jabbing, sarcasming, name calling, and more. In the thread concerning the Dove soap advertisement, Pbassmanca viewed the commercial and agreed with the OP: "Whats the problem? To me this is just smug idiots looking under every rock to find something racist" (two fingers, 2017, post 148). Here, he/she calls anyone who disagrees with them a "smug idiot" and dismisses the issue/topic outright. Sarcasm in particular is used to silence, dismiss, belittle, or negate another posters response. In response to the Billy Joel question, Gravedigger Dav wrote

"Trouble finding something that offends you this morning?" (GK Growl, 2017, post 39), effectively dismissing the OP. Practiced under the guise of humor, sarcasm divides and polarizes. As I will elaborate in the next section, humor is essential to developing positive social relationships in Talkbass, but sarcasm creates two groups: those who agree with the quip and those who are stung by it. *Rising Acrimony* such as name calling and sarcasming is regularly reported and watched closely by moderators because it leads to division, something Talkbass moderators take great measures to avoid.

Moderation

Off Topic has four moderators who participate in discussions and enforce the general rules of Talkbass as well as the specific rules of the Off Topic subforum. The two biggest areas of concern on Off Topic are politics and "divisiveness." When the threads dip into forbidden topics (e.g., guns and gun control, politicians) or specific posts are deemed in violation of rules, moderators privately contact the poster and issue warnings and consequences using a point system similar to the one used for driver's licenses (soulgeezer, 2007). While moderation takes place mainly in the background and is rarely addressed openly, the status of suspended or banned members shows up in all of their prior posts which remain even if they are banned. Anyone can report a post for being in violation of forum rules as all posts have a "Report" button at the bottom of the post. Although there are only four moderators in Off-Topic, every member is essentially an apparatus of the site's moderation team (Althusser, 1971).

Nearly all references to moderation that I observed in the threads studied were self-imposed. For example, in the thread "Anyone here have any stories/advice about immigration abroad?" the poster MJ5150 hinted that the United States was not necessarily the ideal country it is typically depicted. When asked by another member to elaborate with some details (*Lightweight Arguing*), MJ5150 responded by naming four or five issues but stopped him/herself short saying "There are others, but it will quickly become argumentative and divisive it I were to go into details." (anavar, 2017, post 37). Later on, in the same thread, member Oddly agreed and added to MJ5150's sentiment but limited his/her comments writing: "And that's all I'm gonna say because expanding on that will get this thread closed and me banned" (anavar, 2017, post 39). Self-silencing is common and highlight how hegemony (Gramsci, 1971) works in Talkbass; the four moderators do not control the behaviors of the posters as much as the members controlling themselves via self-censorship and reporting. The situation is dialectic; a top-down *and* grassroots power dynamic. When challenging topics are introduced, such as the Dove soap advertisement, both self-moderation and site-moderation come into play. Commenting on the tenuous civility, the OP, two fingers, wrote: "Hey we are almost 8 pages into a civil conversation about this! Yay us! (:hyper:)" (two fingers, 2017, post 139). Ultimately, the moderators decided to shut down the thread as it was deemed "divisive" and "too political" to continue. Moderator Chris Fitzgerald explained:

> **Chris Fitzgerald:** Interesting discussion. Unfortunately, the issues of race relations, racial sensitivity, race baiting, and racial "dog whistles" have become embedded in the national consciousness as a political football at this time.... After some mod discussion, the consensus seems to be that the subject of "is this racist or are people too sensitive to racial issues these days" is inherently political in today's current divisive climate; to imply that something appears racist is easily construed as taking a side, as is denying that something is racially charged. Personally, I find this sad, but have to admit that these are the times we live in. For this reason, this topic is considered too political for TB because it is too likely to divide. (two fingers, 2017, post 177)

The Talkbass users' fear of divisiveness prevent discussions to linger too long in contention because the well-being of the affinity space is more important that the individual members' right to debate. While the moderators' decision can be viewed as silencing perspectives and voices, the moderators argue it is to protect the community as a whole. The strategy of the moderators is to restrict certain subjects, but perhaps it is not topics that are divisive but how participants discuss with one another that divides.

Community to Mediation Posts

Community to Mediation posts build positive, playful, and meaningful interactions between posters and lead towards the mediation of dialogue. Community building in Talkbass is accomplished through persistent attention to the spatial mood as well as the contributions and well-being of other members. In the thread "How we react to death," the OP, OldDog52 (2017), shared a story about how he did not cry when his parents died, nor when 58 people were killed in the Las Vegas shootings, but he did cry when the musician Tom Petty passed away recently. He felt guilty about it. After 20 posts of sincere and personal discussion, the OP wrote "Thanks everyone for the thoughtful comments." *Community Building* posts show appreciation, sympathy, empathy, support, and more. Joking in particular was one of the most common types of *Community Building*. No matter how dire the topic, participants joked frequently, and members showed appreciation for the humor.

In the thread "Advice needed: Seriously considering divorce," member Catcauphonic joked that the OP should consider the timing when scheduling the sit-down talk with his wife: "I'd move that ultimatum date up till the week before Christmas ... gives you enough time to get her some gifts if she accepts. Otherwise, you get yourself something nice ;). I kid, I kid." (Ironbar, 2017, post 35). Even the serious acts of rule enforcement come with humor and positivity: "Transgressions will result in a thwack from the Modstick. You don't want that, do you?" (john turner, 2007, post 5). Joking was done to lighten the mood, to provide a break from intensity, but also to keep participants engaged and reading. Unlike sarcasming, which functions to divide, joking is for everyone and thus helps build community.

Dialogue Building posts address and focus on the object of knowledge in the question or generative theme. These posts involve making connections, speculating, observing, contextualizing, and universalizing ideas from specific stories to larger themes. Before the Dove soap ad thread was shut down by the moderators, member mellowinman focused on the complexities of the object of knowledge in his story:

> **mellowinman:** Let me offer some attempted wisdom. I have been dating interracially for quite some time now, and one thing I've learned is that I'm about 1/2 as smart as I always thought I was. So when people of other ethnicities talk to me, I really try to listen and understand, and let go of my preconceived notions. I was raised in the 60s white suburbs, and I harbor all kinds of dumb stereotypes, and false assumptions. I caution the women I date that I may be an absolute idiot at times, and ask that they be understanding, and help me to learn.... Before we make an assumption about anything, it's a good idea to try and look at it from the other person's point of view. I would rather be a bit silly, and oversensitive towards others than just blatantly disregard anyone's feelings. (two fingers, 2017, post 51)

mellowinman's post starts by *Telling Their Story* ("I have been dating interracially ...") and then later *Think/Splains* his stance on the topic when he writes (I think that) "before we make an assumption about anything, it's a good idea to try and look at it from the other person's point of view." What makes this post different than a *My Two Cents* post is how he helps build dialogue by positioning himself as someone who, though he doesn't intend to, has made and will continue to make "dumb stereotypes" and "false assumptions" concerning race. He has learned that he is "half as smart as I always thought I was" and if you listen to his "wisdom," you'll be smarter than him. It highlights the object of knowledge of the thread and suggests that understanding race is complicated so we should "really try to listen and understand." The post helps pose new questions: Can I be a good person and also say and do things that are perceived as racist?

Mediation posts were the most rare of all the subcategories of posts however they are some of the most important kinds of posts on the site. *Mediation* posts attempt to identify the "limit-situation" of the object of knowledge. Freire (1970) describes limit-situations as obstacles to ones' liberation with dialogue as the primary tool to reveal and overcome these limits. Limit-situations are not closed borders where possibilities end, but instead, exposed borders where possibilities begin. For example, in the thread "How do you deal with road rage?" (MJ5150, 2017) posters responded with their tactics but ultimately the topic developed into a debate between two world views, "the world is full of idiots who happen to be driving" versus "the world is full of good people who happen to make errors while driving" but this observation was never shared overtly in the thread. It takes an unusual participant to read all the posts, synthesize what has been written, identify the themes in the thread, and then summarize the findings for all the other participants. It is rare but exactly what is needed to push a typical *My Two Cents* discussion into mediated dialogue. Participants did come close. After many anecdotes of road rage committed and averted, ToneMonkey commented: "I'm starting to appreciate that certain threads here at TB are excellent training for the discipline of just walking away, ignoring the people, and breathing deeply." (MJ5150, 2017, post 73). ToneMonkey shows appreciation (*Community Building*) but also makes a key act in mediation which is to summarize contributions to the thread. Responding to a poster complaining about bicyclists on roadways, member slobake refocused the thread to the object of knowledge and began to connect this post with the larger limit-situation.

> **slobake:** Anyone can see insane/jerky people using all sorts of transportation. If there is an us vs them it is regular folks who are just trying to get to work and or home and morons who think the roads were built for them alone. What form of transportation they are using is not the problem but attitude is. (MJ5150, 2017, post 91)

The post draws attention to the idea that it is not cars or bicycles that are the problem (limit) but the attitude of drivers who believe the road space is theirs alone. Finding the limit-situation is a challenging act requiring effort, attention, and mediation. While rare, it is certainly doable, especially when posters know that it is even a possibility.

WHY IS TALKBASS SO ... NICE?

While I was able to describe posts and see definite patterns and characteristics within threads, I began to wonder why discussion on Talkbass stay civil and do not devolve in ways I have observed in other forums and comments sections of websites. There are similarities between the members (English speaking, mainly Western, generally males) but differences that matter (region, age, socioeconomic status, political leanings, and affiliations) are regularly revealed in discussions, yet, there is consistent civility. I posed the question "Why is Talkbass so nice?" to members and many responses pointed towards the role of enforced moderation on the site but a second factor that emerged was the focus on positivity and community in the affinity space. hrodbert696 wrote:

> **hrodbert696:** I think the thing about stricter moderation is that it not only cuts back the weeds but also helps make more room for positive growth to flourish. The mods can't make the positivity happen, that's to the credit of a lot of great TBers who share their experiences and insights generously here.... So for a healthy community you need both - people willing to contribute as positive members of the community, and some enforcers to allow the positive stuff room to breathe so it doesn't get choked out. (SLIV, 2018, post 31)

The poster asserts that the "mods can't make the positivity happen." So while moderation is really important, it only "makes room" for members to do the work of contributing community building, and dialoging. He/she credits the Talkbass community's positivity and generosity. Highlighting the sharing culture of Talkbass, PWRL wrote:

> **PWRL:** I think it's partly the rules, but I think there's more to it. For one thing, this site is a tremendous knowledge base for all things bass-related. If you treat others well, people will be more likely to share knowledge with you, but if you're a jerk and you turn everybody off, you're likely to get ignored (SLIV, 2018, post 8)

The Off Topic subforum is an active space of the larger affinity space of Talkbass as a whole. This "tremendous knowledge base" is a highly desirable resource for everyone with an interest in the bass. Members give and receive and if you're a "jerk" you will not receive any help which is the central reason for participants to join the space in the first place. For many members sharing and giving through pleasant interactions are a satisfaction in itself. As member D M C wrote, "TalkBass, come for the bass info, stay for the joy of the membership" (SLIV, 2018, post 53).

Thus, on Talkbass, two conditions are present that help members learn and grow together: (1) active moderation and (2) supportive, positive interactions. Still, a strong "police" presence and "nice neighbors" do not inherently make a community and neither moderation nor courteousness can create dialogue where diverse people can learn from one another. Dialogue requires the skills and motivation to listen, appreciate, synthesize, connect, and mediate. I observed that threads with strong dialogue all had one or more key posts with certain characteristics. These are specific actions that posters can do to help move discussions towards mediated dialogue. The first two actions help build community, the second two help build dialogue, and the last one, mediating dialogue, is the most challenging but the ultimate goal.

- ***Demonstrating listening.*** Participating in threads is important but responding to specific posters builds community. Referencing, quoting, and acknowledging other posters demonstrates listening. Even a simple "I agree" with some elaboration (or clicking the "Like" button) makes posters feel like their contributions matter.
- ***Showing appreciation.*** One of the most simple ways to build community is to show appreciation for those who took the time to post thoughtful and reflective comments. "Thank you" or "I appreciate" go a long way towards supporting participants who oftentimes make themselves vulnerable in posts.
- ***Synthesizing.*** Synthesizing, summarizing, and looking for patterns in threads is a way of moving from personal opinions to identifying the object of knowledge.
- ***Making connections.*** Making connections and adding new contexts helps move individual stories to universalized themes. While anecdotes can be powerful, taking people's personal stories and generalizing them gives new life and potency to these anecdotes.
- ***Mediating dialogue.*** Through mediated dialogue, thread participants learn to identify and name the limit-situations, or the obstacles/limits that create the problems in their lives that they wish to solve. Once uncovered, the "limit-acts" of the generative theme can be addressed, explored, and acted upon to overcome the limit-situation.

CREATING CONDITIONS AND SPACES FOR DIALOGUE

I believe the data presented here shows that affinity spaces like Talkbass have the structure, stability, affordances, and diverse leadership to help participants mediate human interactions and better understand one another. I do not want to overstate the volume and magnitude of *authentic dialogue* (Freire, 1970) that occurs in discussions on Talkbass but the conditions for potential dialogue are well developed in the space. At its dialogic best, the Talkbass Off Topic subforum functions as a "third space" community (Gutierrez, Rymes, & Larson, 1995) that sits between the first "official script" of bass knowledge distribution and the second "counterscript" of trolling and flaming (which is actively squashed by moderation.) In these third space discussions, many participants experience meaningful moments, when they entered looking for specific information or casual company but instead found themselves learning something new about the human condition or perhaps themselves. The affinity space brings people from far-away places together, positive interactions gives them important and meaningful experiences, but it is perhaps the community that develops, via third space discussion, that keeps them coming back.

As Gee (2004) defines them, most online discussion boards and comment sections lack a clearly articulated shared interest and are not well-defined affinity spaces. Without this "official script" of the space, counterscripts such as flaming and trolling can run rampant. In order to reign these practices in, the trend of popular news websites such as USAtoday.com and chicagotribune.com is to remove anonymous commenting with the hope that "real world" identities and the lack of anonymity would discourage transgressive practices and create greater accountability and more civil discourse (Shanahan, 2013). Despite these changes, *Lightweight Arguing* and *Rising Acrimony* are still normative behaviors on these sites. ESPN.com converted to Facebook-linked commenting in 2013 but quietly removed *all* comments from their site in July of 2018, even choosing not to archive comments from past content. ESPN isn't the first major site to eliminate comments altogether. *Popular Science* shut down its comments section in 2013 after expressing concern that comments could not only trigger flame wars, but change people's interpretation of the articles themselves (LaBarre, 2013). On these sites, the counterscript has overwhelmed the official script of the actual articles and content. The two factors that appear to matter the most in creating dialogic conditions in the Talkbass affinity space, moderation and community building, are rarely if ever present.

Writing in the late 1960s, and predating electronic communications as we know them, Freire's ideas on dialogue are very much applicable to contemporary online discourse and particularly to affinity spaces such as Talkbass. Freire (1970) argues that dialogue is not achieved when one person, expressing their opinion "deposits" ideas into another. It is not a simple exchange of ideas to be "consumed" by the posters as they read each other's anecdotes and stories. Dialogue is about discovering and acting upon the obstacles that come when new truths are revealed. For authentic dialogue to grow, participants must join willingly, participate if it matters to them, generate their own topics, and contribute what they are comfortable in contributing. Affinity spaces like Talkbass bring diverse people together to discuss their shared endeavor, but in the act of learning together via dialog, a shared social space is cultivated. This is evident in the popular Off Topic subforum where online identities develop, evolve, and change alongside parallel real world identities. For many members, this is a comfortable, engaging, and safe *place*, and places change us, even if they are digital.

REFERENCES

Althusser, L. (Ed.). (1971). Ideology and ideological state apparatuses. In *Lenin and philosophy and other essays*. New York, NY: Monthly Review Press.

Anavar. (2017, November 21). Anyone here have any stories/advice about immigration abroad? [Electronic message board]. Retrieved from https://www.talkbass.com/threads/anyone-here-have-any-stories-advice-about-immigration-abroad.1314086/.

Black, R. (2007). Digital design: English language learners and reader reviews in online fiction. In M. Knobel & C. Lankshear (Eds.), *A new literacies sampler* (pp. 115–136). New York, NY: Peter Lang.

Cheng, J., Bernstein, M., Danescu-Niculescu-Mizil, C., & Leskovec, J. (2017). Anyone can become a troll: Causes of trolling behavior in online discussions. *CSCW : Proceedings of the Conference on Computer-Supported Cooperative Work. Conference on Computer-Supported Cooperative Work, 2017*, 1217–1230.

Coe, K., Kenski, K., & Rains, S. A. (2014). Online and uncivil? Patterns and determinants of incivility in newspaper website comments. *Journal of Communication, 64*(4), 658–679.

Creswell, J. W. (2007). *Qualitative inquiry and research design: Choosing among five approaches* (2nd ed.). Thousand Oaks, CA: SAGE.

Freire, P. (1970). *Pedagogy of the oppressed*. New York, NY: Heinemann.

Freire, P., & Macedo, D. (1995). A dialogue: Culture, language, and race. *Harvard Educational Review, 63*(3), 377–402.

Garreau, J. (1991). *Edge city: Life on the new frontier*. New York, NY: Anchor Books.

Gee, J. P. (2004). *Situated language and learning: A critique of traditional schooling*. New York, NY: Routledge.

Geegeedemocracy. (2017, August 30). Going to lunch with my ex. [Electronic message board]. Retrieved from https://www.talkbass.com/threads/going-to-lunch-with-my-ex.1301411/

GK Growl. (2017, October 24). Is Billy Joel becoming a father again at 68 disgusting? [Electronic message board]. Retrieved from https://www.talkbass.com/threads/is-billy-joel-becoming-a-father-again-at-68-disgusting.1309478/

Gramsci, A. (1971). *Selections from the prison notebooks*. New York, NY: International Publishers.

Gutierrez, K., Rymes, B., & Larson, J. (1995). Script, counterscript, and underlife in the classroom: James Brown versus *Brown v. Board of Education*. *Harvard Educational Review, 65*(3), 445–471.

Ironbar (2017, November 26). Advice needed: Seriously considering divorce [Electronic message board]. Retrieved from https://www.talkbass.com/threads/advice-needed-seriously-considering-divorce.1314777/

Ito, M., Baumer, S., Bittanti, M., boyd, d., Cody, R., Herr-Stephenson, B., … Tripp, L. (2010). *Hanging out, messing around, and geeking out: Kids living and learning with new media*. Cambridge, MA: MIT Press.

john turner. (2007, April 20). Off topic forum rules: Read before you post. [Electronic message board]. Retrieved from https://www.talkbass.com/threads/off-topic-forum-rules-read-before-you-post.952126/

LaBarre, S. (2013, September 24). Why we're shutting off our comments. *Popular Science*. Retrieved from https://www.popsci.com/science/article/2013-09/why-were-shutting-our-comments

Lammers, J. C., Curwood, J. S., & Magnifico, A. M. (2012). Towards an affinity space methodology: Considerations for literacy research. *English Teaching: Practice and Critique, 11*(2), 44–58.

MJ5150 (2017, November 18). How do you deal with road rage? [Electronic message board]. Retrieved from https://www.talkbass.com/threads/how-do-you-deal-with-road-rage.1313514/

OldDog52 (2017, October 3). How we react to death [Electronic message board]. Retrieved from https://www.talkbass.com/threads/how-we-react-to-death.1306342/

Phillips, W. (2015). *This is why we can't have nice things*. Cambridge, MA: MIT Press.

Reagle, J. (2015). *Reading the comments: Likers, haters, and manipulators at the bottom of the web*. Boston, MA: MIT Press.

Saldaña, J. (2009). *The coding manual for qualitative researchers*. Thousand Oakes, CA: SAGE.

Shanahan, M. (2013, July 16). More news organizations try civilizing online comments with the help of social media. *Poynter*. Retrieved from https://www.poynter.org/news/more-news-organizations-try-civilizing-online-comments-help-social-media/

Soulgeezer. (2007, February 13). Can someone explain "infractions" and "points"? [Electronic message board]. Retrieved from https://www.talkbass.com/threads/can-someone-explain-infractions-and-points.309494/

SLIV. (2018, January 6). Why is Talkbass so… nice? [Electronic message board]. Retrieved from https://www.talkbass.com/threads/why-is-talkbass-so-nice.1321436/

Talkbass. (2018). Terms of service and rules. [Electronic message board]. Retrieved from https://www.talkbass.com/help/terms

two fingers. (2017, October 9). Man, are we really this sensitive? Do we need to be offended THIS badly? [Electronic message board]. Retrieved from https://www.talkbass.com/threads/man-are-we-really-this-sensitive-do-we-need-to-be-offended-this-badly.1307120/

Tyler, B. R. (2016, August 15). Gun and gun control threads are no longer permitted here. [Electronic message board]. Retrieved from https://www.talkbass.com/threads/gun-and-gun-control-threads-are-no-longer-permitted-here.1238665/

CHAPTER 3

QUEERING TEXT

Literacies Surrounding Cyber Trolling

Matthew Thomas-Reid
Appalachian State University

If at its basic level literacy is concerned with the ability to read and write *text*, our present digitized reality requires us to stretch our collective imaginations to understand the word *text* in this new virtual context. What constitutes text, and who makes these decisions? When teachers using digitized versions of 30-year-old textbooks are still warning students to stay away from Wikipedia, it seems clear that the same antiquated processes by which we have vetted text to be suitable for educational purposes are often being employed in digital contexts, and that these processes could do with a good queering. In general terms, I mean to suggest here that a queer methodology can potentially reorient perspectives to destabilize tacit assumptions about a given topic. A queer methodology allows a consumer of contemporary digital texts in a higher education context the opportunity to construct a more robust set of meanings by considering

---

This chapter is based in part on a paper presented by the author at the Philosophy Education Society (PES) 2017 conference entitled "Trolling Toward the Human, Cyber Artifacts, Social Justice, and Queering of intercorporeality."

Negotiating Place and Space Through Digital Literacies: Research and Practice, pp. 41–57

not only the body of an online text, but perhaps also the comments that troll underneath. Rhetorically, both "queer" and "troll" take on multiple meanings, and I to some extent 'play' with these meanings throughout this chapter. Methodologically, I begin with a theoretical framework for reconsidering how trolling comments might be understood as the articulation of oppressive opinions that are denied within normative public discourse. I then conclude by grounding the theory in a more concrete scenario of a discussion board about privilege used on a college campus. This chapter ought not be thought of as a set of instructional methods, rather an exploration of how, as university educators, we might reorient our relationship with particular types of online texts.

Beyond the slur that you might have heard during your school playground days, the word queer in an academic context has a more nuanced meaning, though it does manage to retain its irreverent disruptive quality, even as it is reclaimed and appropriated by the academy. Adam Greteman (2014) parses out the term succinctly through its versatility as multiple parts of speech:

> queer we realize here at the outset is a slippery term operating as a noun used to define people's identity (e.g., LGBT) and an adjective to modify theory. It might even come to operate as a verb that "makes strange" or queers something. (p. 420)

It is really in action, in this verb form, that queer has power, both as the action of queering text and also as the verb of doing queer work, the praxis and pedagogy of teaching queerly. Deborah Britzman (1995) points this out by suggesting that while many might "think the term queer as a noun or an identity, ... the queer and the theory in queer theory signify actions, not actors. It can be thought of as a verb, or as a citational relation that signifies more than the signifier" (p. 153).

In this way, when I talk about queering *text*, it does not necessarily imply gender or sexuality related textual content in the text; rather I use a queer methodology to disrupt the very idea of what text is and can be. Text might, in a postmodern sense, have a wide possible range of meanings, from Mark Lamont Hill's (2009) use of hip hop music as text to Kate Kedley's (2004) suggestion that teachers' bodies themselves might be read as text. Queer theory is well positioned as a lens through which to disrupt understandings of text in a digital era as queer because queer theory cannot be constrained into a single fixed definition and explication of method. Queer theory requires an understanding that normative, or dominant, culture is not fixed, and therefore the approaches to challenging these dominant structures also cannot remain fixed. Deborah Britzman (1995), "refuses to secure queer theory to a fixed content, to a set of guidelines" (p. 155).

Instead Britzman is attempting to "articulate a thought of a method rather than a pronouncement of content," to bring to pedagogical spaces consideration of what Edelman terms "unstable differential relations" (p. 155).

When reading an article online how often do you to scroll to the bottom and read the comments? As a consumer of these texts, it is almost a compulsion for me at this point to scroll down and see the trolls at work; somehow reading the candid, often angry comments contextualizes something for me, allowing a glimpse into a world outside of my sphere of influence. If we accept, as Nicola McClung (2017) writes, that "all texts are ideological, and all readers (and writers) are complicit in upholding or confronting the injustices reinforced in print," then why should we ignore the confrontations that play out in the spaces right below the text (p. 403)? There is something queer about these texts, these cyber artifacts that lurk just below the surface:

> I may provisionally call queer a text ... that not only works against narrativity, the generic pressure of all narrative toward closure and the fulfillment of meaning, but also pointedly disrupts the referentiality of language and the referentiality of images, what Pier Paolo Pasolini, speaking of cinema, called "the language of reality." (de Lauretis, 2011, p. 244)

Academic discourse has rules, and when you read the comments section under online articles there is a subversion of the rules, or what de Lauretis (2011) called the language of reality. There is something else queer in the comments of online trolls, and this is their ability to break the rules in reference to the taboo language of sex, although generally in oppressive and offensive ways. There is something queer in this action: "an antisocial politics of queer theory" (p. 254). de Lauretis goes on to suggest that the antisocial aspect in queer theory is beyond "political contestation, opposition, or antagonism," it is the inclusion of the overtly gendered and sexual. You do not have to go far in any comments section to see this highly sexualized language, often designed to emasculate their political enemies, as in the example of calling liberals "butthurt" or "Progressive Snowflake effeminate male cucks" (Neff, 2016, comments). Butthurt, a clear allusion to anal sex, and cuck, a term used to describe a man who lets other men have sex with his wife, are commonly used antiliberal epithet in online comments. Imagine a space where a person would hurl that type of insult at another—it certainly does not resemble the discourse in the academy or the digital spaces that the academy attempts to create. Returning to de Lauretis (2011), we might think of these comment sections as queer because they are "the space of a transit, a displacement, a passage and transformation, not a referential but a figural space (p. 246). I envision cyber trolling as a powerful contextual reference point for academic ideas;

in this space below the official text, one can examine often complex and important social responses to academic ideas. In short, the educator can see the often ugly truths about how ideas are being received by particular cross sections of the public.

Can the university educator ignore these spaces or texts held in them? Might anything be gleaned from these texts beyond the understanding that some people are just mean? What might it mean to teach with these digital artifacts created by cyber trolls? Employing another queer methodological technique, I come from a place of personal queer identity and draw on queer traditional practices like trolling to make sense of this online trolling phenomenon. Rich lessons can be gleaned from queer histories. Online spaces have proven replete with opportunities both for queers to troll their marginalized desires as well as queer consumers of cyberspace to witness hateful trolling by those who feel empowered in anonymous spaces (Adkins, 1998, p. 446) (Herring, Job-Sluder, Scheckler, & Barab, 2002, p. 371). How might texts gleaned from these spaces, which we might think of as *trolling artifacts,* be viewed as texts to be critically analyzed and from which new literacies might be developed? This critical analysis relates to Friesen's (2008) words that "when compared to their counterparts in the 'real' world, virtual artifacts manifest a pliability, brilliance, discontinuity, and disposability that can have educational value" (p. 111). Might we develop a literacy utilizing trolling artifacts to enrich learning experiences, and what lessons might pedagogues take from the phenomenon of cyber trolling in both of these contexts?

Using a phenomenological methodology and queer theoretical framework I seek to posit a queer approach to cyber trolling with a view to realizing its pedagogical potential in higher education classrooms. To clarify this purpose, suggesting value or potential in the examining of cyber artifacts does need to be approached with caution. Racism, sexism, homophobia, and transphobia abound in the realm of these comments, and any attempt to validate a perspective of hate is always problematic. The value of these trolls, as I suggest throughout this chapter, is often in their ability to elucidate the tacit beliefs that some consumers of texts might have and to more fully interrogate these trolls as a straw person as opposed to direct confrontation with students, and to address potentially problematic reception of the official text.

I juxtapose two specific usages of the word troll, contrasting the queer usage "wander[ing] around looking for sex" (Atkins, 1998, p. 446) with the online parlance of flaming and harassing hate speech (Herring et al., 2002). Trolling then becomes a linguistic bridge linking the queer experience of trolling for sex with the contemporary usage of troll, where online users fill discussion boards and chat rooms with offensive content that would likely not be used in civil face to face discourse (Herring et al., 2002,

p. 372). If we think of trolling in its simplest form as *to bring to the surface that which is hidden,* we might posit a shift from online technologies being used solely for students to demonstrate understanding toward trolling that which students might keep hidden both about themselves and others. In other words, to peek into the often dark and problematic ways that our students at the collegiate level interpret texts but may never share in class.

First, I explore how the phenomenon of trolling developed from queer nonnormative experiences intent on connection and how this notion of trolling evolved into modern day Internet parlance intent on disconnection. Next, I consider how we troll past normative spaces into hidden worlds created in response to the normative confines of dialogue in social justice classroom spaces. Finally, I suggest that these trolling responses to social justice topics might actually be used as "cyber artifacts," or texts (in a post-modern sense) to be critically interrogated within university classrooms, enriching collective understanding of human responses to social justice dialogue. Ultimately, I believe that using queer traditions, we might refigure trolling responses to social justice topics to push at the hidden desires for connection, however contentious, embedded in their meanderings. In short, how might the queer experience of trolling inform pedagogies?

A Queer Journey: An Alternate History of the Troll

My first lesson about flirting came with a warning: "stop looking at me like that faggot, or you will get a fist to the face." I suppose I must have stared a little too long at my middle school crush, and I learned a valuable lesson from the experience: I must keep this side of myself hidden from view. This was the mid-90s, and for the most part queer adolescence was about keeping a low profile. The year I went off to college, Matthew Shepard was beaten and left for dead on a Wyoming fencepost; that year I learned that the cost of inciting "gay panic" in straight guys could be death. I learned to be subtle in my advances; I learned to observe others and see their interest, while at the same time learning how to convey mine without drawing too much attention to myself. In short, I learned how to troll, in a very different sense of the word than we often consider today. No, this is not a memoir of a gay man cruising for sex, rather an exploration of a queer subjectivity, a history of how a community learned to keep certain "fragments of human capacities," hidden from view (Williams, 1995, p. 84). What lessons, if any, might the teacher take from the tradition of queer trolling? Considering this alternative meaning of trolling, I agree with Ernesto Martinez's suggestion that the educator might "think from … an understanding of identity and experience as useful resources for the acquisition of better, more accurate knowledge" (Martinez, 2012, p. 6).

When facilitating discussion in my classrooms I have, recently, began to think of myself as trolling my students. Lest you all begin harboring thoughts of calling my dean to warn her of a predator on campus, let me be clear about what I mean here: Fearing that students will simply parrot that which they see as "politically correct," I long to troll their thoughts, their feelings, their visceral understandings of the kinds of issues that arise from dialogue surrounding social justice in the classroom. Thinking from personal queer identity and experience is salient to my concern about dialogue in social justice classroom spaces insofar as there might be a limitation to what we can learn about each other, as "I will never know how you see red and you will never know how I see it. But this separation of consciousness is recognized only after a failure of communication" (Merleau-Ponty, 1964, p. 17). Because, you see, I consume the texts available in social media, I visit blog sites, I read the kinds of comments that students make about "liberal indoctrinating professors," and I look out over my classes and wonder, "just what are they thinking?"

With a queer mindset, I accept this limitation and seek acquisition of knowledge differently: *trolling* for these human fragments. I argue these trolling artifacts might actually be able to inform instruction. As an example, after reading numerous trolling artifacts that used 'human nature' as an argument against social justice education, I now actually teach a lesson interrogating the very notion of human nature. Drawing on both the phenomenological language of above referenced Maurice Merleau-Ponty (1964) and the queer methodological approaches of Britzman, Ahmed, and Butler, we can enrich classroom conversations around social justice by legitimizing the use of what I will refer to as cyber-trolling artifacts as a *straw person* entry point for interrogating social justice ideas in academic discourse. As a follow-up, we can develop means by which we might manage to troll student understanding much as the youthful version of me trolled to find out if that cute guy in the corner liked me.

Queer history is steeped in a tradition of both hiding fragments of human identity and developing techniques for trolling these fragments, therefore becoming a framework with which to uncover deeper human understanding. While a more detailed exploration of my multiple usages of queer and troll will unfold later in the chapter it is useful to understand that the term "trolling" has deeply queer roots, and can be traced to the ostensibly dead gay language known as *British Polari*, meaning to "wander around looking for sex" (Atkins, 1998, p. 446). As an artifact of gay history, trolling manifests itself beyond gay language codes into the gay hanky codes of the United States in the 20th century and even into hookup applications used commonly today.

Imagine in a cafe there is a businessman in an expensive suit at another table. Perhaps you are able to read his performance in terms of race, class, gender, mannerisms, and so forth. Imagine further that you have an application on your smartphone called Grindr, which allows users in close proximity to see their hidden queer desires. Imagine the surprise when the man pops up on your Grindr app with a profile that reads: *leather daddy ISO hookup*. Outside queer culture, this description seems baffling: you would need to know that *ISO* means in search of, and that *leather daddy* means an older dominant man. Consider the implications of trolling for fragments of humanity in this queered illustration: we are limited in our understanding of another's *meaning making* because we keep fragments of our identity in other worlds, often in cyber space, hidden from view. We phenomenologically structure our own realities in this way, as Norm Friesen (2008) writes, "the life world that the computer presents has its own, manifold, experiential times and spaces" (p. 111).

A queer perspective illustrates how virtual spaces harbor particular manifestations of identity that do not fit in normative discursive spaces. It should be made clear at this point that while historically marginalized communities have trolled to express aspects of self, modern cyber trolls are often manifestations of normative perspectives lashing out against a perceived loss of power. With this said, I invite you to join me in *trolling* these hidden worlds in order to enrich our encounters with others in the public world. If something of our identity and understanding is hidden in private spaces, then it is worthwhile to examine evidences of these private spaces that we might enrich our public dialogue around social justice.

Queers, Trolls, and the Intercorporeal

I use trolling as a linguistic bridge linking the queer experience of trolling for sex with the contemporary usage of the word where online users troll discussion boards and chat rooms with offensive content that would likely not be used in civil face to face discourse (Herring et al., 2002, 372). Imagine a person alone in their self-structured surrounding where a screen allows them perceived freedom to express themselves without regard for conventions of normative, or indeed even civil, discourse. Lacking in this scenario is a connection with others, which I identity as intercorporeality. Marjorie O'loughlin defines intercorporeality in *Embodiment and Education* as a "carnal bond between human subjects, indicating that embodied subjects are connected in their belonging to a common world" (Friesen, 2008, p. 94). Rather than suggesting a common bond is present in online spaces, I argue the lack of intercorporeality in the act of Internet trolling is what makes these thoughts salient—they are the result of private thought devoid of an encounter with the corporeal *other*.

Maurice Merleau-Ponty (1968) suggests in *The Visible and the Invisible* that intercorporeality outlines two connected spheres, the sphere of physical living and the sphere of empathy (Friesen, 2008, p. 94). Withdrawing from empathy of others in order to express often malicious and normatively inappropriate comments mirrors the tradition of trolling for queer sexual encounters insofar as they are both, at least in perception, rejected by a normative society that does not want to deal with the fact of their existence. My approach of connecting these ideas is queer because queer theory often utilizes "techniques to make sense of and remark upon what it dismisses or cannot bear to know" (Britzman, 1995, p. 154). When one reads a particularly inflammatory trolling comment online, a sort of queer moment occurs, "when the world no longer seems the right way up … [and] the effect is "wonky" (Ahmed, 2006, pp. 561–562).

Perhaps you have read a comment in a discussion forum and thought to yourself "who could possibly write such a thing, let alone actually believe it?" Indeed, in an online post about a "privilege board" installed on my university campus, a commenter suggested that "The white male students need to start wearing masks and doing a little push back" (Hutchison, 2016, comments section). Rather than dismissing this type of comment as disingenuous or sociopathic, refer back to the example of the businessman on Grindr and consider that both of these examples illustrate a very real piece of human identity that is not apparent in public spaces governed by normative rules of discourse.

With this juxtaposition of public and private identity in mind I posit a novel approach: this kind of discourse might provide a glimpse into the private self-structured surroundings that exist just below the surface of normative discourse. These online artifacts might serve as fragments of how some tacitly react to issues of social justice. There might be, to use the words of Marc Lamont Hill (2009), a "realness" in these fragments, if so there might also be pedagogical application. Realness does not imply that these ideas are legitimate, but might allow the teacher an inroad into interrogating problematic perspectives. Well-chosen comments, therefore, might be usable texts within class discussions of social justice themes, and further these artifacts of online trolling might be used to troll classroom spaces to probe more deeply into what our students might really be thinking about critical perspectives in race, class, gender and sexuality. Ultimately, pedagogical use of trolling comments might actually serve to create learning experiences that disrupt students' current understandings of social justice.

These fragments, or trolling artifacts are important precisely because although intercorporeality in a classroom allows for empathy, there is the potential that face to face dialogue can be disingenuous. It is this classic "I will say one thing and think another" which makes trolling artifacts potentially useful. Outside of the empathetic intercorporeal sphere, individuals will more often share what they really think, particularly when these thoughts are toxic and hurtful. Specifically, some students might simply decline to speak about topics of race or gender in front of the perceived other. From an exploration of the interconnectedness of queering and trolling, I hope to glean from the carnage of online trolling that cyber artifacts can become queer incursions that provide powerful pedagogical interruptions in intercorporeal classroom spaces.

Obvious Troll Is Obvious: Queer Trolls to Cyber Trolls

In 1950s England, one might well stroll through a park and hear a man say to another: "charper that butch omme ajax; if we flutter our ogle riahs he might just troll over;" the Polari-English translation being: check out that the straight acting "man nearby; and if we fluttered our eyelashes, he might just wander over" (McCullagh, 2011). If nobody understands the exchange, the two men can continue to speak openly about their queerness without fear of recourse from authorities. Sarah Ahmed (2006) suggests the need to develop a private space for queer dialogue is because "the queer subject within straight culture hence deviates and is made socially present as a deviant" (p. 554). In this way queer spaces develop under the radar of intercorporeality because our physical actions and words can belie actual thoughts in public encounters (Merleau-Ponty, 1964, p. 114).

Two salient features emerge: first, we cannot know what another is thinking, and second, because we cannot know this, we use information from the body to fill in the narrative about the interaction (Merleau-Ponty, 1964, p. 114). Referring back to the Polari encounter above we see a clear limitation: the gestures and words used are coded in precisely such a way as to obfuscate understanding. We would have to familiarize ourselves with the language of trolling in order to enrich our meaning making of the encounter. Trolling for sex in queer communities, then, often relied on false intercorporeal impressions to hide their intentions from a disapproving world. Referring back to the fictional example of the business man and Grindr, in his dress and bearing he uses signifiers of heteronormativity to hide his actions, while trolling in a distinct world just under the surface of the normative world. It is as if a queer discursive space develops in the cracks of a constructed world that denies this voice, and the apparent shared corporeal reality is in juxtaposition with a new shared reality of the psyche manifesting itself in spaces of coded language, behaviors, and of course, online spaces. To develop meaning as an outside observer would require exploration in order to crack this code.

Recontextualizing this concept in the normative space of contemporary discourse, in a society claiming to embrace norms of respectful dialogue, queer thoughts and actions might be framed differently. Imagine when a student is confronted with what they perceive as *politically correct* culture in the public sphere and thus retreats to the cyber world to express their thinking. Bracketing out for a moment the overtones of *politically correct*, at play here is a new normativity that regulates public discourse to the point that individuals who dissent feel uncomfortable sharing their thoughts and feelings publically. This phenomenon leads to the development of discursive spaces that mirror that of the queer experience, but in this instance, the trolling is not for sex, rather for the articulation of an oppressive opinion that is denied to them within normative public discourse. In this sense, we can easily see how

> online discussion forums provide a new arena for the enactment of power inequities such as those motivated by sexism, racism, and heterosexism. The relative anonymity of the Internet releases some of the inhibitions of a civil society, resulting in flaming, harassment, and hate speech online. (Herring et al., 2002, p. 371)

Now, contextualize online spaces as queer or perhaps as producing queer incursions into straight spaces, much in the same way historical queer trolling has done for decades. Though clearly the queer community is responding to oppressive heteronormativity and the online trolling community is responding to a *perceived* suppression of their privileged hate speech, the end result is the same— a retreat into online spaces to articulate their position. Precisely for this reason both examples might be thought of as "queer." The double meaning of queer here might seem at first confusing until queer is understood as both a noun or state of being in terms of identity, as well as an adjective describing phenomenon of making blurry that which was once clear. As Deborah Britzman (1995) points out,

> Queer Theory does not depend on the identity of the theorist … rather … Queer Theory anticipates the precariousness of the signified: the limits within its conventions and rules, and the ways in which these various conventions and rules incite subversive performances, citations, and inconveniences. (p. 153)

Returning to our cyberspace troll, we note that their performance in public [read normative] spaces might have a particular signification, but the signification might not provide a full picture of what the individual really thinks.

Returning to intercorporeality with these above examples in mind, a queer disconnect forms. Merleau-Ponty (1964) suggests that consciousness is observable through our comportment in the world, and it is in "the manner in which the other deals with the world, that I will be able to discover [their] consciousness" (p. 117). Merleau-Ponty is suggesting that an intercorporeal encounter with the other is predicated on my ability to empathize with the body of the other-to see a smile and understand it because I smile when I am happy (p. 117). The potential fallacy here is that I can discover consciousness through conduct; if the history of gay trolling tells us anything, aspects of consciousness are often obfuscated from view in normative spaces where these aspects are deemed inappropriate or unappreciated. So, to posit, in the words of Susan Herring (2002), "internet trolling as a manifestation of a much broader phenomenon whereby individuals take pleasure in disrupting the social order out of anger, perversity or contempt" might not necessarily always be true (p. 382).

Internet trolling might then be a phenomenon of hiding aspects of consciousness because these aspects are not acceptable in public spaces, with very good reason, of course. Confronted with an intercorporeal encounter with the other, I might not give voice to what I am truly thinking, and this manifests itself in the only outlet that I have available for my aggression: online spaces. Herring (2002) goes on to suggest an important idea that will drive my further inquiry: "It would be interesting to compare online disruption with disruptive behavior in face-to-face groups in playgrounds, classes, meetings, support groups, and social events" (p. 371). Now rather than a correlation there is in fact a disconnect between online activity and face to face encounters in public spaces, or in Merleau-Ponty's (1964) language, a disconnect between the "perceptual fields that can be given in his experience ... and his relations with his human and social surroundings" (p. 108). Applying this disconnect to pedagogy, I now turn to specific examples of trolling on my own university campus to more clearly illustrate the disconnect between personal perception and social relationships.

Troll in Campus: The Political Becomes Personal

Conversations about power and privilege are common at mine and many other institutions of higher education across the country in recent years. While occasionally in my classes I encounter what Merleau-Ponty (1964) calls "psychological rigidity," or the inability to see beyond a clearly delineated sense of black and white truth, generally there is a sense of mutual respect or at least civility (p. 101). The reason for general civility in face to face interactions might connect to intercorporeality, or transferring the intimate experience of one's own body to that of an "other" (p. 115). I can see a flushed face, hear shaking in a voice, and generally sense angry muscles tensing in someone that I am talking to; in this sensory experience, I connect these significations to my own body, and therefore develop a sense of empathy— if not empathy to ideas, then at least empathy to individuals manifesting in surface politeness.

And yet when attending to cyberspace there are at least some students (maybe even my own, though it is precisely my lack of knowing that becomes problematic) who have rather angry and dissenting opinions that they are willing to articulate in very aggressive ways. After a group of student leaders put up a *privilege board* in a residence hall the campus of the university where I teach, the event was reported to the conservative website www.campusreform.com, and an article was written berating the board. The article points out significant social media reaction to this privilege board, citing comments from students such as "if you can express your political opinions without being called racist, sexist, bigot, etc. you have liberal privilege" (Hutchison, 2016, comments). Further, the comments under the article teemed with angry posts, some claiming to be authored by university students, and some not. One comment declares "white Christian males ... founded and made this country great," while another commenter suggests that it is their "privilege to work 40 hours a week to pay for [the university's] girly men" (Hutchison, 2016, comments). Note again the queer connection to gender and implicit sexuality in the last comment.

Why does the vitriol of anonymous Internet trolls matter? Queer phenomenologist Sarah Ahmed (2006) provides language to put these comments into context by suggesting that we consider our orientation to phenomena (p. 545). In an academic context, if I want to consider how students are engaging with issues of social justice I likely draw on a rather narrow set of evidences, including classroom dialogue and student assessment and reflection. Because of the limitations of these evidences, I really cannot know if these very students are retreating into the cyber world and articulating very different points of view. Reorienting our thinking, imagine taking seriously online comments as "moments of disorientation, which involve not only 'the intellectual' experience of disorder, but the vital experience of giddiness and nausea, which is the awareness of our own contingency and the horror with which it fills us" (Ahmed, 2006, p. 544).

Perhaps we are so quick to dismiss online trolling because it does horrify, and with good reason. With comments calling universities a "four-year rape apology seminar" and professors "lesbianic femenists" (sic), it is easy to first react with anger and then almost instant dismissal, and yet what happens when the trolling hits closer to home, and makes the transition from cyberspace space to physical space (Neff, 2016, comments)? Shortly after the privilege board scenario, a group of students literally trolled the streets, using chalk to post messages over the walls and walkways of the campus with slogans like "white privilege is a lie" (Cole, 2016, comments). When a group of students reacted against the "chalkings," wiping them away, people once again took to social media to troll the situation with comments like "I'm actually concerned with how butthurt (sic) these students are getting" (Cole, 2016, comments). Specifically I am referencing comments made on the forum itself, but similar comments were peppered throughout facebook and other social media with hashtags including #liberalprivilege, and those on the other side of the issue including #racismatappalachian.

In civil public discourse we do not refer to people being genuinely offended as *butthurt*, but this speaks to the sense that online spaces provide the opportunity to say cruel things without having to see the faces of the targets of the cruelty. When uttering a cruel remark to the face of another person I can see signifiers including flushed faces, teary eyes, physical recoiling, and aggressive posturing begin to arise. These signifiers become together a totality of expressions presented to me, and as I decode them "I witness, I project, so to speak, what I myself feel of my own body … I transfer to the other the intimate experience I have of my own body (Merleau-Ponty, 1964, p. 115). While certainly not everyone will decode and project in the same ways, these projections of bodily understanding can prevent us from saying the hurtful things that we might feel in face to face public encounters, and instead retreat to the anonymity of the Internet perhaps not so that the "other" does not see them, but that they do not have to see the "other."

Troll as the Straw Person: Implications for Classroom Spaces

Consider the normative space the exists in a university classroom: there are norms of civil discourse, and particularly when faced with critical conversations of social justice centering on race, class, gender, and sexuality, "artful facilitation is imperative in order to effectively manage the content, conflict, and emotions that invariably arise in any meaningful classroom engagements" (Bettez, 2008, p. 280). This facilitation of dialogue allows for interruptions and encounters with difference, but as noted, there might be a limitation to what we can genuinely learn about each other in face to face discourse. Cyber-trolling artifacts might serve to provide an important secondary facet to the understanding of a person's consciousness: the part kept hidden in normative spaces. If, as some of the trolling comments are to be believed, students might feel "intimidated by liberal professors," the cyber world might provide examples of how some students' consciousness's respond to divisive issues of social justice without students having to disclose in discussion (Hutchison, 2016, comments). Given the intercorporeal space of the physical classroom, imagine being able to critically interrogate a controversial or dissenting opinion without a student having to risk a sense of safety by voicing this opinion; further consider the opportunity for self-reflection and interrupted thinking without the student fearing judgement (Friesen, 2008, p. 95). One fascinating product of this queering of the conversation is that the trolling artifact begins to mediate the conversation in such a way that students who might actually agree with the troll are able to witness, and even participate in, a relatively safe critical engagement with the idea. I have had multiple students reflect after classes that they secretly agreed with the troll at first, but through the process were actually able to see the alternative in a more positive light, and in some cases these student experienced a complete reversal of their previous opinions, all happening completely out of view of their fellow classmates. The troll becomes the "straw person" here because the class can interrogate this unembodied artifact as opposed to interrogating each other.

Returning now to the lens of intercorporeality, we can more clearly see a radical disconnect between what a student says in class versus their articulation of thought in cyber spaces. Through the lens of intercorporeality it becomes clear that we are bound by space and place in terms of both meaning making and expression of thought: "the specificities of place and all environments have body-subjects who are at different times, in differing cultures, related to them" (O'Loughlin, 1997, p. 27). As the body subject relates to space and place differently as these variables move, we might begin to think for the constitution of consciousness variable based on space and place, or that in fact we ARE different people in front of a screen than face to face: Judith Butler (1990) writes "the body is not a 'being,' but a variable boundary, a surface whose permeability is politically regulated" (p. 239). Further, Butler notes "there is no 'I' who stands behind discourse and executes its volition or will through discourse," meaning in this context that in a social justice classroom conversation, the intercorporeal moment might constitute a consciousness different from that of the same person sitting in front of a screen with only their thoughts and the surroundings of their room to constitute their consciousness (p. 18).

Might there be value to interacting with the kinds of ideas that students would not utter in class? At this point it should be made clear that I am not suggesting a professor stalk the Facebook feeds of their students, quite the contrary. An anonymous representation of tacit student thinking can be presented through simply setting up trolling comments as a "straw person" for continued interrogation, and in Norm Friesen's (2008) words, "when compared to their counterparts in the 'real' world, virtual artifacts manifest a pliability, brilliance, discontinuity, and disposability that can have educational value" (p. 111). It is this disposability that makes a trolling comment useful —students are not required to interrogate personalized values, rather ideas that some might have encountered. In reading student reflections after such lessons, I have observed on multiple occasions students admit to having shared perspectives with the cyber trolls, and that the lesson and subsequent discussion allowed them to reconsider these perspectives. Whether ideas confronting ideas like "I don't see color" or "women are just naturally different," reading cyber artifacts can be useful in bringing these ideas to the surface to critically interrogate.

Rich understanding might be attained by challenging the hateful online trolling as text to be critically considered, extending "beyond its physical limitations through its engagement with other figurative bodies, such as the 'body' of the text ... an 'enlarged' view of all human being" (Friesen, 2008, p. 95). Here we might think about the background of online spaces, or what students think when they are not paying attention to the public or foreground: inhabiting the familiar makes things into backgrounds for action ... the background is a "dimly apprehended depth or fringe of indeterminate reality" (Ahmed, 2006, p. 549).

I have also taken to actively trolling my students through using anonymous tools to collect responses. I literally call these sessions "trolling for the truth." The danger here, of course, is to allow the voices of oppression a platform to further marginalize vulnerable groups. Here is where the before mentioned artful facilitation of dialogue becomes important: unpacking student comments together with both empathy and judgement is the responsibility of the artful facilitator of discussion. The addition of judgement here is critical, as the educator must be able to critically trouble the waters of student opinion, and interrogating anonymous comments together can develop real movement toward critical social consciousness. This is difficult work, as trolling in order to open up dialogical spaces can be volatile, and can easily lead to destabilization of traditional structures of power in the classroom. It is for this reason that the goal of this chapter, as stated earlier, is not to provide a systematic guide for the pedagogical use of cyber artifacts, rather to reorient the dialogue around what types of text might be considered usable within the context of classroom spaces. Deeper considerations of pedagogical practice is absolutely necessary and will inform further inquiry on this topic. But approaching this topic queerly also means having the courage to leave application more open ended.

I would like to believe optimistically that the phenomenon of intercorporeality creates spaces of empathy, and that the social justice pedagogue might embrace queer cyber artifacts, not as pieces of truth, rather as texts that might be seen as authentic fragments of humanity to be used to move toward developing greater empathy in social justice classroom spaces. However, the sea change in victim politics in this country has left social justice discourse in this country in a queerer state than it has been in recent years, a state that I cannot gloss over with a happy ending— the stakes are just too high. With the dominant culture pushing back at the suppression of their oppressive speech, sanitizing classroom discourse ironically plays right into the narrative that is being created.

The dominant culture in this country has embraced what Lauren Berlant (2006) might refer to as a *cruel optimism* (p. 20). In this cruel optimism, those with power have repositioned themselves as the powerless, and have, however erroneously, taken on the mantle of the oppressed. With this in mind, those with historical privilege have developed a strange kinship with the historically marginalized queer; they have embraced the identity of Troll as a false sense of voice, a simpatico that allows them to project themselves into cyberspace with a sense of liberation, a cruel optimism that they are fighting against forces of oppression.

This "condition of projected possibility" in fact "creates a fake moment of intersubjectivity" (Berlant, 2006, p. 22). In Berlant's (2006) words, those historically with power have developed a "rhetorical animation that permits subjects to suspend themselves in the optimism of a potential occupation of the same psychic space of others" (p. 22). With this in mind, the project seems now to require the pedagogue to find new kinds of texts in order to "troll," that we might displace this cruel optimism, to reclaim queer for the marginal, for the wonky, for the skewed, for the misfits ... in short, those who claim to be opposed to the queer ought to be confronted with the cyber evidences of their own misguided attempt at queering.

The power in this confrontation is that trolls like staying in the shadows. There is an interesting occurrence when you take a thing like a troll out of its habitat. Like a fish out of water, it does not survive very well. The sort of visceral vitriol that happens in online spaces tends to cool a great deal when faced with real people in real world spaces. For this reason the use of the troll to mediate conversation does not become an extension of cyberspace; it does become tempered with intercorporeality, and this seems to be where there is real value behind this approach: by bringing the troll into the intercorporeal light of day, they will turn to stone.

REFERENCES

Atkins, D. (1998). Skinny, 'White' chicks and hung, buff boys: Queer sex spaces and their disconnects. In D. Atkins (Ed.), *Looking queer: Body image and identity in lesbian, bisexual, gay, and transgender communities* (pp. 439–454). Binghamton, NY: Haworth Press.

Ahmed, S. (2006). Orientations: Toward a queer phenomenology. *GLQ: A Journal of Lesbian and Gay Studies, 12*(4), 543–574.

Berlant, L. (2006) Cruel optimism. *Differences, 17*(3), 20–36.

Bettez, S. (2008) Social justice activist teaching in the university classroom. In J. Diem (Ed.), *Unsettling beliefs: Teaching theory to teachers* (pp. 297–300). Charlotte, NC: Information Age.

Britzman, D. (1995). Is there a queer pedagogy? Or, stop reading straight. *Educational Theory, 45*(2), 151–165.

Butler, J. (1990). *Gender trouble: Feminism and the subversion of identity*. New York, NY: Routledge.

Cole, M. R. (2016). Appalachian state students of color become target of harassment after racist chalkings on campus. *Fresh U*. Retrieved from https://www.freshu.io/mia-renee- cole/appalachian-state-students-of-color-target-of-harassment-after-chalkings

de Lauretis, T. (2011). Queer texts, bad habits, and the issue of a future. *GLQ: A Journal of Lesbian & Gay Studies, 17*(2–3), 243–263.

Friesen, N. (2008). *The place of the classroom and the space of the screen: Relational pedagogy and Internet technology*. New York, NY: Peter Lang.

Greteman, A. J., & Wojcikiewicz, S. K. (2014). The problems with the future: Educational futurism and the figural child. *Journal of Philosophy of Education, 48*(4), 559–573.

Herring, S., Job-Sluder, K., Scheckler, R., & Barab, S. (2002). Searching for safety online: Managing "trolling" in a feminist forum. *The Information Society, 18*, 371–384.

Hill, M. L. (2009). *Beats, rhymes, and classroom life: Hip-hop pedagogy and the politics of identity*. New York, NY: Teacher College Press.

Hutchison, S. (2016). 'Priveldge board' gets prominent placement at App State. *Campus Reform*. Retrieved from https://www.campusreform.org/?ID=8022

Kedley, K. (2015). Queering the teacher as a text in the English language arts classroom: Beyond books, identity work and teacher preparation. *Sex Education, 15*(4), 364–377.

Martínez, E. (2012). *On making sense: Queer race narratives of intelligibility*. Stanford, CA: Stanford University Press.

McClung, N. (2017). Learning to queer text: Epiphanies from a family critical literacy practice. *The Reading Teacher, 71*(4), 401–410.

McCullagh, J. (2011). Polari, a secret gay language born of homophobia. *PositiveLite*. Retrieved from http://www.positivelite.com/component/zoo/item/polari-a-secret-gay-language-born-of-homophobia

Merleau-Ponty, M. (1964). *The primacy of perception and other essays on phenomenological psychology, the philosophy of art, history and politics*. Evanston, IL: Northwestern University Press.

Merleau-Ponty, M. (1968). *The visible and the invisible* (Alphonso Lingis, Trans.), Evanston, IL: Northwestern University Press.

Neff, B. (2016). Video: Students erase pro-trump chalk, threaten to run creators off campus, *The Daily Caller News Foundation*. Retrieved from http://dailycaller.com/2016/09/15/video-students-erase-pro-trump-chalk-threaten-to-run-creators-off-campus/

O'Loughlin, M. (1997). Corporeal subjectivities: Merleau-Ponty, education and the postmodern subject. *Educational Philosophy and Theory, 29*(1), 20–30.

Williams, B. (1995). *Making sense of humanity: And other philosophical papers 1982–1993*. New York, NY: Cambridge University Press.

CHAPTER 4

LIFTING THE VEIL

Social Loafing and Participatory Learning in a Networked Space

Greg Neal and Mark Vicars
Victoria University

INTRODUCTION

Participation in digital networks is an ever-expanding social phenomenon that has brought together a constellation of previously unimagined communicative practices. Social network sites such as LinkedIn, My Space, Facebook, Twitter, and Snapchat are all high traffic social sites worldwide in which many young people "socially loaf" or "hang out" on-line. "Social loafing," defined as "the tendency to reduce one's efforts when working collectively" (Karau & Williams, 1993, p. 683) is associated with individual production where responsibility within a group, is diffused. However, narratives from students who participated in a global collaboration project have suggested how asynchronous opportunities allowed participants to peruse content at their leisure, read widely in a nonlinear style, access information in their own place and space and determine when/if they wanted to contribute online.

Negotiating Place and Space Through Digital Literacies: Research and Practice, pp. 59–76

Bijker and Law (1992) have noted how "Technologies … are subject to contingencies" (p. 8) and Hutchby (2001) suggests "When people interact through, around or with technologies, it is necessary for them to find ways of managing the constraints on their possibilities for action that emerge from those artefacts' affordances" (p. 450).

"Hanging-out" online as Gee (2008) has identified, invariably involves the "other stuff" of language, namely: "social relations, cultural models, power and politics, perspectives on experience, values and attitudes, as well as things and places in the world" (p. 1) that encapsulate the "new ethos" (Lankshear & Knobel, 2006) of new literacies. If, as we are suggesting in this chapter, social loafing draws on the "other stuff" in maintaining an online identity then it could be argued how "Being [online] in every sense is entangled, connected, indefinite, impersonal, shifting into different multiplicities and assemblages" (St Pierre, 2013, p. 653). Paradoxically not being visibly present formed constructive learning opportunities for students who had not worked in this kind of distributed online environment before. While social loafing might not fit within constructing conventional understandings of deep learning, it does in the context of the project provide an understanding for how content information, despite periodic lack of connection, was exchanged and interrogated across spatial and temporal divides.

Davies (2012) has noted the need to be aware of how contemporary literacy behaviors involve "all kinds of social 'stuff'" (p. 20) that surrounds texts, and she argues for an acknowledgment of how these have generated multiple textual affordances (Gibson, 1979) that "do not exist apart from the social practices in which they are embedded and in which they are acquired" (Lankshear & Knobel, 2006, p. 13). As digital technologies increasingly transform and multiply opportunities for literacy practices, both within and beyond educational domains, the epistemological and ontological 'new' situates literacy is an ever-emerging assemblage of meanings, practices, technologies and contexts. Luke (2003) has noted how "texts of the new technologies have mutated into complex hybrid systems that have made new demands on reading and writing, viewing, social exchange, and communication" (p. 401). As an articulation of the "new," social loafing is an under documented phenomenon that we suggest is an effect of digital, distributed, asynchronous online communication.

The production and consumption of texts online is increasingly becoming an open-ended joint construction: a "we" space. A space in which learning involves intra-action of social environment and identities across time, place and multimodal affordances (Keene & Zimmerman, 1997). Becoming ontologically and epistemologically re/attuned to the principle of the "We-hermeneutic" is one that Sepie (2017) suggests draws on an understanding of self that is derived from "our awareness of the fundamental human relationships that we have within the broader ecologies within which we are embedded" (p. 2).

While there continues the "race to the top" for students to achieve social and academic objectives, there are fewer opportunities for students to linger in their learning and occupy a different kind of literacy practice. The social and cultural expectations of literacy in a schooling context demand a prescribed compliance: literate behaviors look and sound in a very particular way (Gee & Gee, 1990). However, as readers and writers are enacting identities in textual practice(s) and relationships, the learning of and about literacy is always in constant evolution: "new literacies have emerged ... embodied in new social practices—[in] new ways of participating as a citizen in public spaces, and even perhaps new forms of identity and personality" (Cope & Kalantzis, 2009, p. 167). It therefore becomes pedagogically generative to think about how literacy is becoming socially embedded in larger life practices and discourses (The New London Group, 1996) and to incorporate into formal learning those activities that extend across a range of texts and communicative practices.

Students' reading and writing behaviors generate complex and crucial pedagogical questions on a daily basis. One of the many challenges is to understand how the changing cultural landscape impacts on how on-line reading and writing behaviors are being resituated. Scholarship has drawn attention to the salience of resisting and refuting the paradigm that literacy is only learned within the narrow margins of an established architecture of pedagogic orthodoxy (Snyder, 2008). Roberts (2005) has called for an interrogation of pedagogical approaches that correspond to the social practices of the 21st century learner and, in this chapter, we endeavor to respond to the challenge of making sense of "networked interconnectedness, through globalized and local, virtual and material social fields" (Luke & Carrington, 2002, p. 231). We have sought to understand how "social loafing" online within a global learning network could have a productive pedagogical impact for individual students participating in professional and personalized teacher education dialogue. We endeavor to provide an account of how teacher education students' social loafing, defined as: "the tendency to reduce one's efforts when working collectively" (Karau & Williams, 1993, p. 683) can be thought of as a natural occurring phenomenon of intra-activity and of deep learning in digital domains. Intra-activity as opposed to interactivity signals an ontological shift towards a post human thinking about cultural practices in which "The interest in 'more than human ontologies' lies in understanding the intra-actions or agentic-in-between-ness of humans and non-humans in producing knowledge(s), relationship(s) and reality(ies)" (Kuby, 2017, p. 878). We recognize the problems that accompany any endeavor to untangle the complexity of intra-activity in digital domains. Drawing upon the "social stuff" extracted from out of everyday habits and ways of being between human and nonhumans, we situate social loafing as an affordance within the entangled spaces of contemporary digital communicative practice (Barad, 2007). In this chapter, we have endeavored to think with:

> "More than human ontologies" [as] a perspective that can widen, deepen our understandings of education and provoke new thinking about mainstream accounts of humans interacting with each other and intra-acting with the material world. Posthumanist perspectives in education, specifically literacy, have potential to offer theoretical, methodological, and pedagogical possibilities. (Kuby, 2017, p. 878)

And, in doing so, we pay attention to practices of engagement and relationality as a pedagogical assemblage to provoke new thinking about learning in digital domains. The network spaces that were drawn upon by the participants in the study included online multimedia platforms such as; Facebook group, online blogs, Google docs, Voice thread, and Wikis.

HERE, THERE, AND EVERYWHERE: KNOWLEDGE-BUILDING ACROSS DIGITAL PLATFORMS

In 2012 a global collaboration project was established between teacher education candidates from a University in Victoria, Australia and a University in West Virginia, United States. The Australian university is one of 39 public universities in Australia and is a dual-sector university (students can pathway from vocational education to higher education). There are over 40,000 enrolled higher education, vocational or training students. It is situated in Melbourne's western metropolitan region, a largely urban society, growing fast in size and population and very culturally diverse. In comparison, the U.S. university, also a public university, is regarded as a liberal arts institution, situated in a semirural location with an undergraduate enrolment of approximately 2,000 students.

The goal of the project was to change teacher educational instructional practices from where learners are often passive recipients of information to become more actively involved in the construction of new knowledge. To compare and contrast their current understanding of global education, the project situated learners in shared knowledge-building communities across two very culturally different tertiary educational settings.

The global collaboration was conceived by teacher educators from the two institutions, with participating teacher candidates undertaking similar units of study from their respective degrees. The teacher candidates were required to achieve similar learning intentions from the collaborative examination of the similarities and differences of each nation's education systems. Using a variety of digital resources to exchange, discuss, and cocontribute to shared knowledge-building, the integrated use of specific online applications, as well as those from social media forums, were employed to contextually engage the students in 21st century digital literacies.

The project, in the mutual creation of a shared virtual space was intentionally designed to situate local and international partners in collegial dialogue that foregrounded cultural interpretations of given topics. The participants were asked to explore and compare two diverse school systems and discuss the realities of each other's global context utilizing a range of online digital resources. The information that was exchanged was collectively gathered, shared and coproduced validating knowledge as a social construction and a mutual process of reacculturation (Thompson, 2004). A pedagogic intention for the participants promoted the use of new digital resources in authentic ways to enable the transfer of newfound skills into their own teaching practices.

However, it was quite apparent that some of the participants were at varying stages of competency with digital literacies and the inclusion of digital technologies further challenged them to operate functionally in an online environment. This was especially apparent when participants were required to communicate across cultures with international partners. While some participants reported the online applications as challenging, they also reported it as an opportunity to "have-a-go," For example, the predetermined digital resources (e.g., Skype, VoiceThread, Google Drive) were deliberately selected after ascertaining the prior knowledge of teacher candidates and their identified digital literacies at the beginning of the semester.

Following this determination, the teacher candidates had to utilise and evaluate online resources they may not have previously experienced. Encountering the use of digital resources in an authentic way in an online space, generated opportunities to focus on the learning processes as distinct from the learning of content. As such, teacher candidates initially challenged by the digital platform often reported positive reactions toward the integration of unfamiliar digital resources and were appreciative of the chance to gain in proficiency and confidence.

This chapter presents evidence collected during 2014, a year when four cohorts of students (approximately 40–50 each semester) from the two universities were linked together to participate in the study for a duration of 4–6 weeks. Two cohorts from both universities were selected from the identified units of study from their respective degree programs within each semester. Once initial contact had been made, the teacher candidates were organized by the lecturer's random allocation into teams of four that comprised two local and two international partners (some groups may have had three or five participants depending on available numbers from each university). The participants were provided with learning goals, weekly topics, and specific digital resources, both synchronous and asynchronous to be used as a minimum ongoing contact source. The students were required to exchange and share information, present current local literature and research evidence, and add personal anecdotes to uncover "truths" between the two education systems. They were asked to add to the factual content vignettes taken from their life stories and include subjective opinions, that in discussion with their overseas partners, could be further questioned, analyzed, and evaluated. The following structure was provided to the participants to frame and sequentially structure the online communication:

- In week 1, teacher candidates were required to discover and explain the different school systems, funding arrangements, university requirements, and the perceived value of teachers in society. The information was to be exchanged by creating a shared online space such as a social media platform, for example, Facebook, to co-create with group members.
- In week 2, students linked up using an online forum, for example, Skype, Facetime, to speak with their overseas partners and exchange information about issues confronting education in the respective countries.
- In week 3, students used a multimedia program (e.g., VoiceThread, or a blog or a wiki) to exchange information about the culture and society and the ways teachers adopted strategies to accommodate 21st century learners.
- In week 4, students concentrated on assessment practices and how they impacted teaching and learning. The students used Google Drive to cocreate a shared account of the main facets of assessment happening in schools.
- In the weeks following the initial period after exchanging information, local group members were required to collate and construct an end-product of findings to inform others of their new knowledge and report on the inclusion of digital resources into their online space.

STUDY METHODS AND THE COLLECTION OF DATA

In 2014, 90 students out of a cohort of 183 completed an online survey at the start of their respective semesters and 69 students completed the same online survey at the end of their semester. This data enabled a comparison between pre- and post-responses after having participated in this project as well as other unit of study focused exercises in order to conform to and address their respective unit of study's intended learning outcomes.

All associated unit of study participants were invited to an online interview after the conclusion of semester assessments. Participants were able to asynchronously respond and send their notes directly to the researcher or via online forums, including social network sites (private). The online response was guided by the following evaluation questions:

1. What do you think you have gained from the collaboration for your own learning?
2. What teaching and learning strategies have you gained for your own classroom practice?
3. Were there any issues you encountered that caused you problems in communicating with someone from overseas?
4. What would you like to see changed as a result of your participation in this collaboration?

The use of online data collection methods allowed the participants to respond at their convenience within a given time frame. The survey instruments had been assessed by the research team as being relatively easy to use; they were accessible and safe and encouraged the use of any technology resource, including mobile devices. There continues to be some uncertainties about the efficacy of how technology resources are specifically used to collect data (Beddall-Hill, Jabbar & Al Shehri, 2011). Meho (2006) and Curasi (2001) have reported that the quality of data gained through online research, for example, e-mail, blogs, can be a viable alternative to face-to-face and telephone interviewing.

From the initial evaluation questions, a joint decision was made by the research team to follow up with participants by e-mails and blogs and obtain first-hand accounts of their involvement in the participatory networks. Open-ended invitations were e-mailed to all 90 teacher candidates seeking their feedback on their experiences and, in particular, what would they change in the project. The purpose of the follow up data collection was to try and better understand any perceived relationship between social loafing from their individual practice and the impact within their allocated group. The data did not clearly specify time moments of private study where students may have chosen to "loaf" while working in their own online space. Collated responses from the initial data alerted the researchers to some of the virtual pedagogy challenges (participating in collaborative learning tasks in online web-based platforms) that individuals experienced as they participated in their group's work commitments.

CONTEXTUALIZING THE GLOBAL COLLABORATION

The teacher candidates reported that the selection of local group members was unproblematic. However, the challenge of working in preselected groups was to ensure they self-managed to benefit all online members as an effective way to operate. The group allocation had been determined by the university lecturers prior to the commencement of the project, and the teacher candidates were placed with local randomly preselected partners as well as preselected group members between the two countries to eliminate possible preformed friendship groups. This approach of having two local and two international teacher candidates was considered by the lecturers at the time as the preferred learning model. This sort of online group connection was designed to challenge individuals to be cooperative and collaborative—skills associated with deep learning (Fullan, 2013).

It was reported across groups from both universities that the participants had concerns that the corresponding overseas students allocated to their groups were often perceived as not meeting the demands and expectations of the local group. Team productivity and performance were viewed as inequitable in terms of workload as highlighted by one teacher candidate[1] below:

> Our experience was very frustrating due to the lack of effort on the part of our partners in (country). We made significant contribution from our end—and received the equivalent of about 30 mins work from each of them. This was disappointing as the assignment seemed to have potential to be rewarding. (Jessica e-mail June 2014)

A disconnect between reluctant group members has been noted an ongoing issue in collaborative endeavors (Davies, 2009) and to overcome any perceived disconnect, the University lecturers deliberately organized the teacher candidates to engage with real time, synchronous forms of communication early in the project. The rationale for the early inclusion of week 2's face-to-face contact was in response to the likes of Worchel and colleagues' (1998) identified need to understand and appreciate the social identity of their partners. The intentions to have all partners build a relationship and to encourage comradery among the group were confirmed by the participants as a positive step and helped to lessen the blame game when the task was undertaken:

> Skyping with our group members allowed me to put a face to someone's name, experiences and opinions. By talking to them, I was able to create a better mental image of these people, understanding better their points of view, stopping me from being judgemental or confused. (Amber e-mail Dec. 2014)

However, there was clear evidence to suggest that a portion of the groups encountered some sort of communication problem or resource challenge as part of the overall online connection. There were a large number of individuals who found the online experience frustrating particularly caused by the large time difference between the two countries (14 hours). The time difference often required asynchronous responses which for many young people, is a very different way of operating in their world of instant gratification (Boyd & Onofry, 2013):

> The time differences were difficult as when I had set time aside to get things done they were not available and then their responses would arrive at times when I didn't really have time to spend on that specific component. (Liam e-mail Oct. 2014)

Some individuals thought the delayed online process was a personal imposition as expressed by a teacher candidate in a survey response: *The human aspect of considering time-zones, workloads, other peoples' commitments can be irritating* (Hamish online survey, 2014). And, the experience for the student below highlights personal frustration when there is a reliance on international group members to complete the required tasks and for those participants who did not fully justify their commitment:

> It did feel a little artificial because there was a sense of just getting it done. For example, on the blog, there would be one response from us and one from them, but then nothing. So the opportunity to go deeper into an issue did not happen. (Ken e-mail, Oct. 2104)

In order to assist and overcome connections between group members, the lecturers became the conduit between the two countries: participants would e-mail their respective lecturer who would then email or Skype their overseas colleague in order to address any perceived communication concerns. This was seen as a very effective "push" to have things happen and also enabled the number of contact issues that required their intervention to be quantified. In 2014 there were only 9 interventions required by the teacher educators out of 46 groups overall. This indicated most groups enabled their own group connection and ongoing contact quite readily. It was apparent that many individuals in the different groups were willing to accept the challenges of communicating in a virtual space and were able to reflect on the experience in a positive way:

> There are general issues with virtual collaboration— lack of visibility of participation, lack of accountability etc. but I think these are things that people experience in business every day so they form constructive new learning for students who have not worked in this kind of distributed

> environment before. Challenge is good—as often we find we become more creative in the face of difficulty. (Jade e-mail, Oct. 2014)

For some of the participants, online exchanges were clearly valued and identified as more relevant to them as digital learners and in this context it became important to collect the personal narratives of participants to further examine social loafing as a virtual "socio-cultural practice and process" (Leander & Sheehy, 2004, p. 1). The conceptualization of social loafing from the participants narratives that were considered salient features were: (1) engaging in online virtual spaces which afforded a pedagogic potential, (2) for online participation in collaborative learning to be distributed across geographical and temporal domains, (3) for participants to have agency when operating within their own communities of practice, (4) for participants to deepen knowledge through self directed learning (5) for the emergence of distributed learning to develop in what had been previously been utilized as recreational spaces.

GOING ONLINE AND HOOKING-UP; "SOCIAL LOAFING" A PEDAGOGY IN VIRTUAL PRACTICE

The pedagogic intention underpinning the project was for the participants to learn how to use the digital resources in authentic ways to enable the transfer of newfound skills into their own teaching practices. Neal (2007) has noted, individual teachers who encourage 21st century teaching-learning with digital technologies can scaffold the learning process by encouraging students to apply different thinking strategies to achieve social and academic objectives with an informed criticality that is *less* concerned with "getting the right answer" but is *more* concerned with "getting inside" competing claims, and showing an understanding of how different arguments are constructed. We recognize the *problematic* and *contestable* character of *knowledge claims*, including:

- the presence of underlying values and assumptions (including those embodied in competing paradigms, discourses, rationalities and ethical principles);
- recognition that "meanings" can be conveyed through communicative devices other than formally reasoned argument, for example, via sound and visual images, by use of rhetoric;
- the significance of knowledge communities and cultures, and of claims-makers' interests and allegiances; and
- the associations between knowledge and power.

This prompted our thinking of the ways in which technology has harnessed readerly and writerly behaviors that are connected to "hanging- out" online. The potential of the digital world to throw together people across spaces/ places and texts potentially to form communities of practice, with shared interests and participation has enabled learning to be an online, anytime, anywhere endeavor.

However, within formal education domains an individual's contribution and participation in a group's shared learning process is encountered as a perennial pedagogic problem. Piezon and Ferree, (2007) quantativley surveyed 227 undergraduate and graduate students enrolled in an on line course and employed the concept of "social loafing" to describe the actions of individual students engaging in behavior that lessens the quality of learning for themselves and their group members. Existing research regarding the existence of the social loafing phenomenon in the online learning environments is sparse. One of the few known research investigations that has identified social loafing in technology-supported groups was undertaken by Alnuaimi, Robert, and Maruping (2010) who used an experimental design to test the hypothesis of how individuals worked when placed in groups and reported that team size and dispersion were the two main factors that contributed to a deficit model of social loafing. Piezon and Ferree (2007) also found that distance learning issues such as geographical separation, a lack of visual cues and time zones differences can exacerbate social loafing when students work in online environments. However, both these studies position social loafing as a deficit practice. With the development of global shared knowledge-building communities, where students become active constructors of collective knowledge (Scardamalia & Bereiter, 1999), it is timely to reconsider and re/position social loafing as a productive pedagogy within networked social ethnoscapes of digital learning. The narratives from the students suggests how social loafing was effective in ways that it established consistent task related communication between team members and....

One of the very first social psychologists to investigate social learning in groups prior to the introduction of digital technologies was Latane (1981). His social impact theory stated that individual group members' behaviors change when they join a group and the impact is greater if the group is separated by physical and/or psychological distance. One of the most significant ways to lessen the effect of problems such as this was to build healthy relationships among group members and understand and appreciate the social identity of each other (Worchel, Rothgerber, Day, Hart, & Butemeyer, 1998).

Another challenge clearly evident in digital participatory networks is temporal and spatial separation. Reconsidering how the epistemic landscape around technology has radically altered and how communicative practices are being redefined, Moore-Gilbert (1997) refer to the "imperative to reconsider [pedagogic] positions that once seemed self-evident and normal" (p. 98). Participation in digital networks involves re/negotiating intricate discursive relations with others in which

> fundamental frameworks of knowing, being and acting are challenged ... [As] Our frameworks for understanding the world, ourselves, our actions, our values and our relationships with each other proliferate. Those frameworks cut across each other, overlap with each other, are in tension with each other and may be incommensurable with each other. (Barnett 1998, p. 59)

The narratives from the participants show how the intentions of the project, that aimed to encourage students to experience opportunities to personalize the learning by sharing first-hand accounts and engage in relationship building, were initially challenged by social loafing in online teamwork.

LIFTING THE VEIL

The particular challenge of forming online groups from different countries was in how individual behaviors, attitudes, and cultural influences materialized in the shared virtual spaces.

> There were a number of challenges for me, particularly being partnered with someone I don't know well and was not forthcoming when trying to arrange things. (Carly e-mail, Oct. 2014)

> There was a lack of investment in each other's learning because we didn't really know each other. (Peter e-mail, Oct. 2014)

The glocal (global and local) disconnect of learning in a virtual space for some participants was initially of a technical nature:

> I did not gain any new skills from the process. I stuck to what I was good at (research/answering questions/going off on tangents) and let the other group members pick up the technological requirements (setting up Skype and blog). (Michelle e-mail, Oct. 2014)

This aspect led to a breakdown in participation in some groups particularly when individual students had to contribute to collective responsibility for shared knowledge-building. The challenges of virtual collaboration emerged in a deficit understanding of online synchronous presence: of a perceived lack of visibility, of participation and accountability. However, according to Edwards and Wilson (2004) virtual social presence can assist educators to begin to think differently about social loafing and learning. Engagement with learning and knowledge building was constructed in a "space [that] was increasingly entangled with ongoing situations of breakdown, surprise, bewilderment, or wonder" (Alvesson & Karreman, 2011, p. 722). As one participant noted:

> I found the collaboration to be a "co-operation" rather than a collaboration. We allocated "jobs" and just got through it. At some points, communication dropped off (for various reasons) and certain group members had to chase others. (Trevor e-mail, June 2014)

Despite a decentralization of decision-making some participants took a key role in directing their own learning and in facing the challenges of a virtual collaboration. From the narratives there is support for the view that while social disconnect existed in some of the groups social loafing in a virtual space may in fact be a useful addition to an individual's deep learning. Evidence from the participants indicated how:

> Researching and learning about stuff for my assignment is just one case where I have had a positive experience with ICT in terms of my learning. Although not always easy, the ease of access it enabled me to peer review texts (through Google Scholar), videos where I could see theories or classroom activities in action (via YouTube) and resources collated by other teachers (via Pinterest for example) enabled me to contribute to the group assignment and research in a manner and at times which worked for me. It offered me great flexibility and choice. (Felix online survey, 2014)

> The asynchronous technologies allow for anytime, anywhere contributions and access yet their lack of social presence lead to confusion and rework for the team. Asynchronous technologies are good when working across significant time differences, when you want to give the respondent time to collate information or consider their response or for simple one-to-one threads. But negatives include message threads being lost or people starting new emails or replying to inappropriate ones. (Monica e-mail, June 2014)

Mitigating the deficit understanding of social loafing was made possible when the technology offered sufficient time and space for all individuals in the group to participate and respond dialogically. Murris (2016) suggests how "thoughts … are created in the relational and dynamic process of interaction offering a philosophical justification for interactive, dialogical and democratic pedagogies" (Murris, 2016). An asset understanding of social loafing is how digital domains can maintain engagement and mitigate against the constraints of immediacy and contextual framing as some of the participant's comments have indicated:

> The online access to conversations provided us with an impression of how the students feel about their home towns, the education system they learn in and also their future roles as teachers that you cannot get from static research. In this case, the rich information exchanged, and therefore new knowledge constructed, could not be authentically learned any other way. (Joanne blog, April 2014)

> Sharing personal stories was much more meaningful, it enabled me to relate to the information provided on a deeper level, relating their own experiences to mine. (Kaye e-mail, Oct. 2014)

> I think that accessing real life experiences and having personal exposure to the Australian education system made the information much more relevant to me as I could directly relate or compare to my own experiences of our system. (Gary e-mail, Oct. 2014)

Barad (2007) suggests how increasingly meaning is being produced "in relation to the particular apparatus used" (p. 120) and Murris (2016, p. 6) directs thinking about the being "in" the space "between" the person as embodied organism and the material world [to think through how] space relations between all material organisms act upon each other. If as we suggest social loafing is inseparable from "public displays of connection" (Donath & Boyd, 2004) then what it means to learn with and in digital networks is one in which social loafing is connected to the process of becoming a learner. It draws on as one of the participants noted technology:

> to make social connections at the outset to replace the face-to-face contact we are unable to have. For me the human factors are much more important than the technology in this day and age. What are harder to identify and apply are the extensions [of technology] to our interpersonal skills, to make our intentions visible to the other persons through the technology. (Emily Oct., 2014)

REASSEMBLING UNDERSTANDING

Social loafing, when read against the epistemic space and place of formal learning is in many ways antithetical to dominant educational discourses and practices that are rooted in industrial models of teaching and learning, structured in and through paradigmatic and pedagogic orthodoxies. The tension for educators working with and in digital domains are increasingly connected to what Egan (2002) has suggested are postmodern characteristics of digital literacy in learning. These being how

> fundamental frameworks of knowing, being and acting are challenged. Our frameworks for understanding the world, ourselves, our actions, our values and our relationships with each other proliferate. Those frameworks cut across each other, overlap with each other, are in tension with each other and may be incommensurable with each other. (Barnett, 1998, p. 59)

Social loafing provides a window to understanding what it means to learn with and in digital networks. Vicars (2013, p. 132) suggests how embodied practices in which "students perform individual and collective literacies within complex social worlds should be pedagogical knowledge" and Barad (2007) has urged an understanding of how reading and writing on line has become "horizontal, rhizomatic [in] nature, [in] its virtuality and mutability, its diffraction and reassemblages" (p. 26).

> Social loafing in asynchronous environments as one of the participants commented … allowed me to work independently and conduct the weekly questions and organise the session according to my own schedule. (Marcelle online survey, 2014)

Moving beyond a deficit understanding of social loafing requires acknowledgement of how dominant discourses and practices can become manipulated and in doing so

> afford individuals and collective groups opportunities to experiment with literacy practices that are informal, situated and which operate through horizontal processes and mutual collaboration. (Hickey-Moody & Haworth, 2009 p. 83)

Thinking from the participants' narratives that referenced how the asynchronous technologies allowed for anytime, anywhere contributions (Cogburn & Levinson, 2002), we started to think through spatial, temporal and material interactions of social loafing and the pedagogical implications. Limited synchronous contributions to the group work were initially read as being problematic due to periodic lack of connection. The ways in which information was being accessed, exchanged and new knowledge was being constructed was not immediately visible or recognizable to us, however, the participants' comments indicate they did not share our instructional concerns:

> I have used ICT for learning from watching recorded videos. It was positive as I could learn at my own convenience from my preferred place and time. (Eliza online survey, 2014)

> In the ICT environment I tend to become more self-directed and do a better job at taking learning into my own hands. (Chantal online survey, 2014)

> I would have gained more from completing the collaboration individually and then participating in a group reflection (I quite enjoyed that part). Perhaps I'm not a great team player. I prefer working alone. (Ligia online survey, 2014)

The narratives from the students suggests how social loafing was most effective in ways that it established consistent task related communication between team members. While it might not fit within constructing conventional understandings of deep learning, it does pedagogically point towards how students navigated the thrown togetherness of the project as readers and writers. This increasingly occurred in a digital "space [in which their habits and practices as readers and writers] was [situated out of] an entangled state of 'social' and 'natural', 'material' and 'discursive' negotiations" (Jackson & Mazzei, 2012, p. 269). It is therefore worth considering how as educators we respond to social loafing and interpret it as a practice that is concomitant with 'new' ways of learning within a 24/7 digital literacy landscape.

NOTE

1. Pseudonyms are used for all inserted quotes from the voices of the teacher candidates

REFERENCES

Alnuaimi, O. A., Robert, L. P., & Maruping, L. M. (2010). Team size, dispersion, and social loafing in technology-supported teams: A perspective on the theory of moral disengagement. *Journal of Management Information Systems, 27,* 203–230.

Alvesson, M., & Karreman, D. (2011). *Qualitative research and theory development: mystery as method.* London, England: SAGE.

Barad, K. (2007). *Meeting the universe halfway: Quantam physics and the enlightenment of matter and meaning.* Durham, NC: Duke University Press.

Barnett, R. (1998). Supercomplexity and the University. *Social Epistemology, 12*(1), 43–50.

Beddall-Hill, N. L., Jabbar, A., & Al Shehri, S. (2011). Social mobile devices as tools for qualitative research in education: iPhones and iPads in ethnography, interviewing, and design-based research. *Journal of the Research Center of Educational Technology*, 7(1), 67–89.

Bijker, W. E., & Law, J. (1992). General introduction. In W. E. Bijker & J. Law (Eds.), *Shaping technology/building society*. Cambridge, MA: MIT Press.

Boyd, P. O., & Onofry, R. M. (2013). *Finding lost marbles: Remembering the '50s in River City*. Bloomington, IN: AuthorHouse.

Cogburn, D. L., & Levinson N. S. (2002). Understanding distributed collaborative learning between the United States and South Africa. In *Networked learning in a global environment: Challenges and solutions for virtual education* (pp. 144–159). Berlin, Germany: ICSC Academic Press.

Cope, B., & Kalantzis, M. (2009). "Multiliteracies": New literacies, new learning. *Pedagogies: An International Journal, 4*(3), 164–195. Retrieved from http://newlearningonline.com/~newlearn/wp-content/blogs.dir/35/files/2009/03/M-litsPaper13Apr08.pdf

Curasi, C. (2001). A critical exploration of face-to-face interviewing vs. Computer-mediated interviewing. *Journal of the Market Research Society, 43*(4), 361–376.

Davies, W. M. (2009). Groupwork as a form of assessment: common problems and recommended solutions. *Higher Education, 58,* 563–584

Davies, J. (2012) Facework on Facebook as a new literacy practice. *Computers and Education, 59,* 19–29.

Donath, J., & Boyd, D. (2004). Public displays of connection. *BT Technology Journal, 22*(4), 71–82.

Egan, K. (2002). *Getting it wrong from the beginning: Our progressivist inheritance from Herbert Spencer, John Dewey, and Jean Piaget.* New Haven, CT: Yale University Press.

Edwards, A., & Wilson, J. (2004). *Implementing virtual teams: A guide to organizational and human factors.* Burlington, VT: Gower.

Fullan, M. (2013). Great to excellent: Launching the next stage of Ontario's education agenda. Retrieved from www.edu.gov.onca/eng/document/reports/fullan.html

Gee, J. P. (2008). *Social linguistics and literacies: Ideologies in discourses.* London, England: Falmer Press.

Gee, J., & Gee. P. (1990). *Social linguistics and literacies: Ideology in discourses*. London, England: Falmer Press.

Gibson, J. J (1979). *The ecological approach to perception.* Boston, MA: Houghton Mifflin.

Hickey-Moody, A., & Haworth, R. (2009). Affective literacies. In D. Masny & D. Cole (Eds.), *Multiple literacies theory*. Rotterdam, the Netherlands: Sense.

Hutchby.I (2001). Technology, texts and affordances. *Sociology, 35*(2),441–456.

Karau, S. J., & Williams, K. D. (1993). Social Loafing: A meta-analytic review and theoretical integration. *Journal of Personality and Social Psychology, 65,* 681–706.

Keene, E., & Zimmerman, S. (1997). *Mosaic of thought.* Portsmouth, NH: Heinemann.

Kuby, C. R. (2017). Why a paradigm shift of 'more than human ontologies' is needed: Putting to work poststructural and posthuman theories in writers' studio. *International Journal of Qualitative studies in Education, 30*(9), 877–896.

Lankshear, C., & Knobel, M. (2006). *New literacies: Everyday practices and classroom learning.* New York, NY: Peter Lang.

Latane, B. (1981). The psychology of social impact. *American Psychologist, 36,* 343–356.

Leander, K., & Sheehy, M. (2004). *Spatializing literacy research and practice.* New York, NY: Peter Lang.

Luke, A., & Carrington, V. (2002). Globalisation, literacy, curriculum practice. In R. Fisher, M. Lewis, & G. Brooks (Eds.), *Language and literacy in action.* London, England: Routledge/Falmer

Luke. C. (2003) Pedagogy, connectivity, multimodality, and interdisciplinarity. *Reading Research Quarterly, 38*(3) 397–403.

Moore-Gilbert, B. (1997). *Postcolonial theory: Contexts, practices, politics.* London, England: Verso.

Meho, L. I. (2006). E-mail interviewing in qualitative research: A methodological discussion. *Journal of the American Society for Information Science & Technology, 57,* 1284–1295.

Murris. K. (2016). *The posthuman child.* New York, NY: Routledge.

Neal, G. (2007). Thinking and learning with information and communication technology (ICT): Student voices. *International Journal of Technology, Knowledge and Society, 3*(1), 83–91.

New London Group. (1996). A pedagogy of multiliteracies: Designing social futures. *Harvard Educational Review, 66*(1), 60–93.

Piezon, S. L., & Ferree, W. D. (2007). Perceptions of social loafing in online learning groups. Retrieved from https://www.researchgate.net/publication/267548237_Perceptions_of_Social_Loafing_in_Online_Learning_Groups/download

Roberts, T. (2005). *Computer-supported collaborative learning in higher-education.* Hershey, PA: Ideas Group.

Scardamalia, M., & Bereiter, C. (1999). Schools as knowledge building organisations. In D. Keating & C. Hertzman (Eds.), *Developmental health and the wealth of nations: Social, biological and educational dynamics* (pp. 274–289). New York, NY: The Guildford Press.

Sepie, A. (2017). More than stories, more than myths: Animal/human/nature(s) in traditional ecological worldviews. *Humanities, 6*(78), 2–31.

Synder, I. (2008). *The literacy wars.* Crows Nest, Australia: Allen & Unwin.

St Pierre, E. (2013). The posts continue becoming. *International Journal of Qualitative Studies in Education, 26,* 646–657.

Thompson, J. (2004). *Cooperative learning in computer-supported classes.* Melbourne, Australia: University of Melbourne.

Vicars, M. (2013). Literacy: Books? Who needs books anyway? It is not kewl. In T. Mckenna, M. Cacciatollo, & M. Vicars (Eds.), *Engaging the disengaged.* Cambridge, England: Cambridge University Press.

Worchel, S., Rothgerber, H., & Day, E. A., Hart, D., & Butemeyer, J. C. (1998) Social identity and individual productivity within groups. *British Journal of Social Psychology, 37,* 389–413.

CHAPTER 5

TRANSLANGUAGING AS A (META)COGNITIVE TOOL FOR NAVIGATING AND LEARNING IN THE MULTILINGUAL ONLINE ENVIRONMENT

Kwangok Song
University of Kansas

Byeong-Young Cho
University of Pittsburgh

In this chapter, we challenge the common perception of English centrism in the online world, acknowledging the increasingly diverse situations of digital literacy practices in a today's multilingual environment (Barton & Lee, 2013; Lee, 2017). Our critique of such linguistic status-quo is motivated by the idea of multilingual online users' complex translanguaging practices. Informed by resource approaches to the pedagogy of language and literacy, we view translanguaging as a metacognitive tool that is useful and valuable to learners in a multilingual online setting. To describe the nature of translanguaging situated in online reading, we use bilingual

Negotiating Place and Space Through Digital Literacies: Research and Practice, pp. 77–94

students' think-aloud data from our empirical study of adolescent bilingual learners' use of comprehension strategies and translanguaging strategies in online reading. The verbal excerpts represent how the learners use their two languages as they identify and learn from multilingual texts online. We close the chapter with a discussion of scientific and pedagogical implications for translanguaging as a tool for learning and relevant literacy practices on the multilingual digital media environment.

MULTILINGUAL INTERNET AND HYBRIDIZED DIGITAL LITERACY PRACTICES

Language use on the Internet has become increasingly dynamic and diverse over the last few decades. As of 2017, approximately 75% of Internet participation is carried out in languages other than English, although English as *lingua franca* remains the most common language of the Internet (Internet World Stat, 2018). Examining languages used on the Internet across 12 years, Pimienta, Prado, and Blanco (2009) reported that the Internet usage increased significantly in the countries where English is not the dominant language during the period of their study, suggesting that the Internet activities and online texts have become more linguistically diverse. Thus, the portrait of English-dominating literacy practices in the online environment has been revised to include the assemblage of multiple languages, texts, and codes (Danet & Herring, 2007). Whereas monolingual users may rely on websites written mostly in their native languages, multilingual individuals with experiences in other languages, in one way or another, are likely to traverse linguistic borders in the Internet environment. Not only do they search for information from multilingual sources, but they also engage in online communities using more than one language. The users from different linguistic and cultural backgrounds negotiate differences in their ways of communicating by using their multiple linguistic repertoires and identity representations (Barton & Lee, 2013).

Such dramatic changes in the language usage in communication and textual representations contribute to shifting and problematizing the common perception of English dominance on the Internet. From the perspective of Bakhtin's (1982) heteroglossia, the Internet can be considered to be a hybrid space in which multiple languages, texts, and modalities co-contribute to newly imagined choices and opportunities. On the Internet, language choice matters as one participates in gathering information, building knowledge, and exchanging perspectives. Barton and Lee (2013) noted, "[L]anguage choice is tied in closely with the perceived affordances and action possibilities of the medium. How a site is used is not predetermined but is based on different purposes for different communicative situations" (p. 59). The availability of multilingual information spaces (e.g., personal, commercial, and public websites, communities, and networks) and the language functions of digital tools (e.g., multilanguage information searching, automated translation) on the Internet provide multilingual individuals with a multitude of opportunities to explore information resources in different languages. Flexible uses of such knowledge and skills are crucial as users navigate the multilingual text environment of the Internet to identify, analyze, and make sense of a wide range of information toward achieving their individual and social goals.

Students who have literacy experiences in two or more languages may take advantage of the multilingual Internet by communicating in both languages across physical and virtual borders in the online space (Lam, 2014). Research has documented how bilingual adolescents explore the online spaces by making the most of their repertoires of linguistic and cultural knowledge and strategies. For example, code-switching and transliteration can allow bilingual adolescents to participate actively and confidently in online chatting with other people who use either language or both. These participants share similar linguistic backgrounds, experiences, and resources within the social, epistemic, and emotional space in which they feel free to apply and navigate their knowledge about their two languages (Lam, 2004; Vandekerckhove & Nobels, 2010; Yi, 2009). Bilingual adolescents' language choice is both mediated and constrained by several sociocultural aspects, such as textual languages available on the online space, their interpersonal relationships with other users on the Internet, and genres and medium with which they present themselves (Androutsopoulos, 2015). Language choice in online communication allows bilinguals to enact social roles, negotiate their positions in social structures, and claim their linguistic and ethnic affinity in transnational contexts (Lam, 2014). However, very few studies have examined how bilingual adolescents accessed and utilized multilingual resources on the Internet by activating their knowledge of two languages. To add to the current literature on multilingual learners' use of their two languages to navigate multilingual resources, this chapter reports the findings from a study that examined how Korean emergent bilingual students navigated multilingual online resources by using their skills and strategies in using both of their two languages.

READING AS FOUNDATION FOR LEARNING AND COMMUNICATION IN THE MULTILINGUAL INTERNET

Reading in the Internet context is an integral part of digital literacy practices. Online reading requires specific strategies due to the multiplicity and complexity of the online context. These strategies enable users to search and identify necessary information and synthesize information across different sources while navigating multiple online texts. Furthermore, the Internet users need to make critical decisions to evaluate, explore, select, and read online sources (Leu et al., 2015). Adolescents possessing these skills and strategies can manage their thoughts and actions to search, evaluate, and identify credible information (Coiro, 2011; Coiro & Dobler, 2007).

Culminating research has paid attention to adult English-as-a-second-language (ESL) readers' strategy use in online reading (e.g., Anderson, 2003; Chun, 2001; Huang, Chern, & Lin, 2009; Park & Kim, 2011; Park, Yang, & Hsieh, 2014). These studies indicate that advanced adult ESL readers use not only comprehension strategies similar to those used in reading printed texts but also additional strategies to explore hyperlinked online texts in their second language. However, how biliterate learners can search for and read texts in different languages on the multilingual Internet has rarely been considered in this line of literature. Because online reading is situated in the multilingual text environment of the Internet, bilingual readers are likely to use their knowledge and skills in both languages to access and obtain information in different languages. More research could provide an understanding of bilingual adolescents' use of multilingual sources on the Internet. Building on the previous studies on ESL/EFL students' use of comprehension strategies in an online reading task, the current study aimed to demonstrate how bilingual learners utilize their linguistic resources to comprehend online texts.

TRANSLANGUAGING FOR MEANING MAKING IN READING

Digital literacy practices are multilingual by nature, and translanguaging is central to the multilingual individuals' digital literacies (Lee, 2017). The idea of translanguaging explicates multilingual individuals' transformative and flexible use of their linguistic knowledge and resources for meaning-making in literacy practices across different modalities (e.g., listening, speaking, reading, writing) in their social interactions (García & Li, 2014). Translanguaging encompasses not only shuttling between named languages as in code-switching but also translation and other bilingual abilities (McSwan, 2017). Although translanguaging often explains bilinguals' use of their linguistic repertoire in social interaction, it can also be a metacognitive tool for multilingual individuals to negotiate and create meaning and to evaluate their cognitive processes. In fact, García and Li (2014) indicated that translanguaging is "a meaning-making social and cognitive activity that works in-between conventional meaning-making practices and disciplines and goes beyond them" (p. 40).

With Vygotsky's (1934/1986) idea of language as a mediational tool for cognitive processes, Swain (2006) argues, "[L]anguaging serves as a vehicle through which thinking is articulated and transformed into an artifactual form" (p. 97). Influenced by Swain's notion of languaging, Li (2018) noted that translanguaging helps multilingual learners "gain knowledge, to make sense, to articulate one's thought and to communicate about using language" (p. 1224). Bilingual learners' linguistic repertoires for cognitive processes facilitate their learning in a classroom context in which the socially dominant language is the instructional language. Therefore, the idea of translanguaging reconsiders the role of L1 in bilingual learners' learning and cognitive development in a classroom context (Li, 2018). Multilingual learners can use translanguaging to construct meaning, mediate their use of one language, activate their funds of knowledge, compare meanings across different languages, and monitor their meaning-making processes (Canagarajah, 2013; Martin-Beltrán, 2014).

By using a think-aloud approach, researchers attempted to examine how bilingual readers accessed their two languages during a reading task. Although bilinguals think beyond the boundaries of named languages as Li (2018) indicated, identifying language choice during think-alouds in this line of literature seems to demonstrate how dynamically and flexibly bilinguals use linguistic knowledge and resources in their reading processes. Bilingual readers traverse between their two languages not only to extract, construct, and negotiate meaning but also to evaluate and monitor their comprehension processes when reading in their second language (Kwon & Schallert, 2016; Upton & Thompson, 2001). Translating, using cognates, and using bilingual resources, such as bilingual dictionaries, are identified as reading comprehension strategies that bilingual readers use to clarify, refine, and negotiate meaning across their two languages (García & Godina, 2017; Jiménez, Gacía, & Pearson, 1996). Regardless of their L2 reading proficiency, bilingual readers' use of their two languages during reading represents their strategic decision making on when and how to select a language to facilitate comprehension and monitor their reading processes (Kwon & Schallert, 2016; Seng & Hashim, 2006).

In sum, research has proven that bilingual learners' use of their two languages is integral to their meaning-making from texts. However, most existing studies focused on bilingual learners' use of their two languages only in printed-text reading contexts; very few studies examined the online context that may allow bilingual learners options to read texts of their choice in their both languages. Thus, building on the idea of translanguaging, this study adds to the previous studies by examining adolescent bilingual readers' use of translanguaging for learning from multilingual online texts.

EMERGING BILINGUAL ADOLESCENTS' TRANSLANGUAGING IN ONLINE INQUIRY

Here, we discuss how emerging bilingual adolescents accessed and used their two languages in the online context. Drawing from a more extensive study, we focused on two Korean bilingual adolescents in this chapter: Ho-Youg (All names are pseudonyms), a sixth-grade boy, and Yoonah, an eighth-grade girl. They were invited to participate in our lager study about bilingual learners' use of their two languages in online reading as we looked for emergent bilingual adolescents who had had previous schooling experience in their home country and had spent only up to 3 years in the United States. Both had lived in the United States with their families for approximately two years. They had first learned English as a foreign language when they were in third grade as part of South Korean elementary school curriculum. Ho-Youg had about four years of schooling experience in Korea; whereas, Yoonah had 6 years. Both of them regularly read both in Korean and English. English was the primary language for academic reading; whereas, Korean was for pleasure reading. They had a positive view of themselves as readers in both languages despite their preference for Korean. Their reading ability in Korean was around their grade levels; whereas, their English reading proficiency was slightly lower than their actual grade level. Ho-Youg and Yoonah admitted that they used the Internet almost everyday not only to search for information for school work but also to access social media both in English and Korean and to use online bilingual dictionaries whenever necessary for their understanding of unfamiliar English words.

In examining the metacognitive aspects of Ho-Youg's and Yoonah's translanguaging processes, a think-aloud approach was used in this study. Ho-Youg and Yoonah were asked to select a topic of interest and learn about the topic by using the online resources. To assess their content learning from the online inquiry, the focal participants were also asked to write in English what they had known about the topics before the online inquiry and to write what they learned about their topics after the online inquiry. The language choice for writing tasks was intended to emulate an academic writing task in the United States. The following sections delineate how similarly and/or differently Ho-Youg and Yoonah used translanguaging during the online inquiry. As we explain these two bilingual adolescents' translanguaging as part of their (meta)cognitive processes, differentiating their two named languages is necessary to show how Ho-Youg and Yoonah flexibly used translanguaging for their learning from online sources.

HO-YOUG: TRANSLANGUAGING FOR CONFIRMING AND REFINING INFORMATION

Ho-Youg chose Zika virus as his topic for the inquiry because he learned from the news about the spread of Zika virus. During the online inquiry, Ho-Youg used his skills in both Korean and English and purposefully chose a textual language for his learning on the multilingual Internet. His choice of textual language was somewhat linear. He first examined the information about Zika virus on the Korean version of Wikipedia and then moved to the English edition of Wikipedia to learn further about the topic and to confirm what he had learned from the Korean edition. Thus, he tried to cross-check the information he read in one language by rereading the same information in the other language. In the following excerpt, Ho-Youg acknowledged that he looked up information in both languages when necessary (Please note that the words underlined in translation indicate the ones that the participants code-switched to English while speaking in Korean.).

> 제가 usually 하게는 먼저 영어로 search를 해요. 왜냐하면은, (집에 있는 컴퓨터 키보드에) 한국말 그게 없고, 그래서 영어가 편해서 그렇게 하는데, 그 다음에, 한국 사이트에서도 한 번 봐 봐야 겠다 그러면, command한 다음에 한 글자씩 찾아서 다 쓰고 찾아 보죠.
>
> [I usually search in English first because there are no Korean letters (on the computer keyboard at home), so (searching in) English is convenient. That is why I do so. And then, if I think I need to look up (the information) on a Korean site, I press the command key and look for each (Korean) letter to type (a search term) to look up.]

During the online inquiry for this study, however, the computer offered to him had the bilingual keyboards with letters in both Korean and English. Ho-Youg decided to take advantage of the linguistic affordances of the tool to visit the Korean edition first. Reading the same information both in Korean and in English seemed to enable Ho-Youg to clarify what he learned, enhancing his comprehension. His choice of textual codes during the online inquiry reflected his knowledge about the Wikipedia as a translingual website that provides content in different languages.

Ho-Youg also used both Korean and English to comprehend texts written in either language, and each language has a different role in his think-alouds. His language choice for his think-alouds during the online task suggested that he used Korean to make sense of the content regardless of the language of a text. He intermittently used English words directly from the text without translation to facilitate the flow of his thinking. Some of those words were commonly used in his life; whereas, others were likely to be used only through transliteration when used in Korean. By selecting the Korean language as his primary tool for thinking, Ho-Youg also engaged in translating the information that he read in English into Korean. He was actively paraphrasing and summarizing what has been written in English into Korean. His translation as demonstrated in his think-alouds was not the literal or word-to-word translation. Instead, he selectively chose information from the texts he was reading in English and synthesized multiple pieces of information together. The following excerpt shows how Ho-Youg used his two languages strategically to summarize what he learned from the text.

> 처음에 여기에서 Zika forest of Uganda에서 나왔다니까 우간다에서 먼저 이렇게 발견됐다는 것을 볼 수가 있고, 댕기나 황열 바이러스 아니면 일본 뇌수막염, 그런거 바이러스와 related 되어 있고 댕기열이랑 거의 똑같고, 이렇게 mild symptoms 그런거 있고 ...
>
> [First, here, because it says that it (Zika virus) was originated from the Zika forest of Uganda, I can see it was first discovered in Uganda. And it is related to dengue fever, or yellow fever, or Japanese encephalitis. It is almost similar to dengue fever, and it has mild symptoms like that.]

In the excerpt above, Ho-Youg's translated summary demonstrates several aspects of his translanguaging for cognitive purposes. First, his direct use of English words (e.g., "forest," "related," "mild symptoms") without translation seems to suggest that he might have internalized those words that were frequently used. Thus, such direct use of English words from the text did not hinder the flow of his thinking. Second, although the original text had more detailed information about how Zika virus spread, his summary focused only on where it came from and what other diseases are similar to Zika. By using translanguaging, Ho-Youg selected the information that was important to him and synthesized the information pieces coherently. Third, his translation seemed to benefit from his reviewing of the Korean edition. The names of diseases such as *Dengue* and *yellow fever* might be challenging for Ho-Youg to translate because these words were specialized terms and were not used commonly in his everyday life or at school. Yet, in this excerpt, he successfully recognized these words in English and was able to make connections to the terms in Korean.

Ho-Youg's inference to *Japanese encephalitis* as a relevant disease was interesting because of the lack of the target word in both of the texts that he read. The English entry states, "Zika virus is a mosquito-borne flavivirus closely related to the dengue and yellow fever viruses (Wikipedia, n.d.)" Likewise, The Korean edition of the Wikipedia entry on Zika virus suggests: "보통 가벼운 증상으로 뎅기열과 유사하다 [Usually, the light symptoms are similar to those of Dengue]" (위키백과, n.d.). As shown in these excerpts from the entries from two different language versions, however, there was no mention of Japanese encephalitis [일본뇌염] in either entry. His connection to Japanese encephalitis shows that he might have activated his prior-knowledge to make an inference by using a context clue in the text (e.g., the fact that Zika virus is transmitted via mosquitos) and his cultural knowledge and experiences with Japanese encephalitis vaccination encouraged by Korean Center for Disease Control especially for elementary students. In fact, the Korean word, "뇌수막염" that Ho-Youg chose for *encephalitis* means meningitis, and the correct word in Korean for *encephalitis* is 뇌염. Due to the shared syllables (뇌 and 염) in these two Korean words (뇌수막염 and 뇌염) and his insufficient knowledge about these diseases, his confusion of these specialized terms was understandable. Although his connection was not entirely accurate, it is still notable that Ho-Young was able to activate his cultural and linguistic knowledge to make an inference to try to get a better understanding of the symptoms as he was translanguaging. Overall, translanguaging allowed Ho-Youg to attend to the necessary information selectively, to create a coherent summary of what he read, and to activate his prior knowledge to make an inference.

Additionally, Ho-Youg used translanguaging to regulate and appraise his reading processes during the online inquiry to facilitate his learning. Ho-Youg monitored his understanding during reading, his use of two languages during the inquiry, and his choice of expressions in his think-alouds when reading on a website written in English. The following excerpt is an example of how Ho-Youg used translanguaging for a metacognitive purpose while he was reading about the significant consequence of the infection of Zika virus.

> Zika virus 하면, 이거 소두증? 그런거 같아요. 이렇게 (He points to one photo on the page.) 뇌가 작아진다거나 아니면, 이거 뭐랄까나? bone이 없다는거? Smallness of head, 이게 microcephaly 가 이렇게 작게 된 것 같아요. 소두증.. [Zika virus seems to be related to small, smallness of head? I think it is. Like this. A brain gets smaller or how can I say this? No bone? I think that is. Smallness of head. This, microcephaly, it seems to become small like this. Smallness of Head."

In the excerpt above, Ho-Youg reviewed why Zika virus was particularly dangerous by reviewing the images of microcephaly. His self-questioning about the term ("소두증 [microcephaly]?") and his paraphrasing ("bone 이 없다는거 [no bone]?") demonstrates that he was monitoring his understanding of what microcephaly involved. Furthermore, his use of metalinguistic question (e.g., "이거 뭐랄까나 [How can I say this?]") shows that he might have been considering different ways to express the symptom of microcephaly. Such monitoring of his language use demonstrated that he tried to search the most appropriate expressions or words to refine his understanding of the original texts. Furthermore, re-reading of "smallness of head" in English and re-translating it into Korean ("이렇게 작게 된 것 같아요 [it seems to become small like this]") indicates that he monitored and confirmed his interpretation of what microcephaly is. Throughout this process, as shown in the excerpt, he was traversing two languages across different modes (e.g., reading a text and reviewing images) to reconfirm and refine his understanding of the term microcephaly.

YOONAH: TRANSLANGUAGING FOR MONITORING PLANS AND PROCESSES

Yoonah chose Ebola virus as her topic for the online inquiry because she thought that she might have heard that Ebola virus had spread in South Korea. However, by searching information on the Korean portal site, she soon found out that Ebola virus had not yet been found in South Korea. Like Ho-Youg, Yoonah's textual code-switching was dynamic in that she went back and forth between websites written in English and in Korean several times during her online inquiry. Figure 5.1 shows how Yoonah navigated websites written in Korean and English and how she used two languages to search information about the topic.

To learn about Ebola virus, she first searched how Ebola virus impacted South Korea on Google by using a search term in English. After she found out that no search results were about what she had expected, she accessed the most popular Korean portal site, Naver (www.naver.com). Because this site provides services in Korean, she chose the Korean language to search information about Ebola virus [에볼라 바이러스] by changing the keyboard setting. Her choice of a website seems to reflect her knowledge and experiences that a portal site developed in Korea could provide more comprehensive search results reflecting the relevance of the topic to the Korean context. From the search results, she first chose the link to 네이버 백과사전 [Naver Encyclopedia] to read the entry about Ebola virus. After she skimmed the entry quickly, she went to back to the search results to click the link to another service called 네이버 지식iN [Naver Intellectuals]. This service embedded in the focal portal site allows the Internet users to ask and answer questions. She chose the question about the transmission of Ebola virus. After her initial searches on the Korean portal site, she went to Google again to continue her search in English. Throughout her inquiry process, she revisited the Korean portal site to complement her understanding of what she read in English. Through textual code-switching, Yoonah was able to verify the information across different sites in different languages.

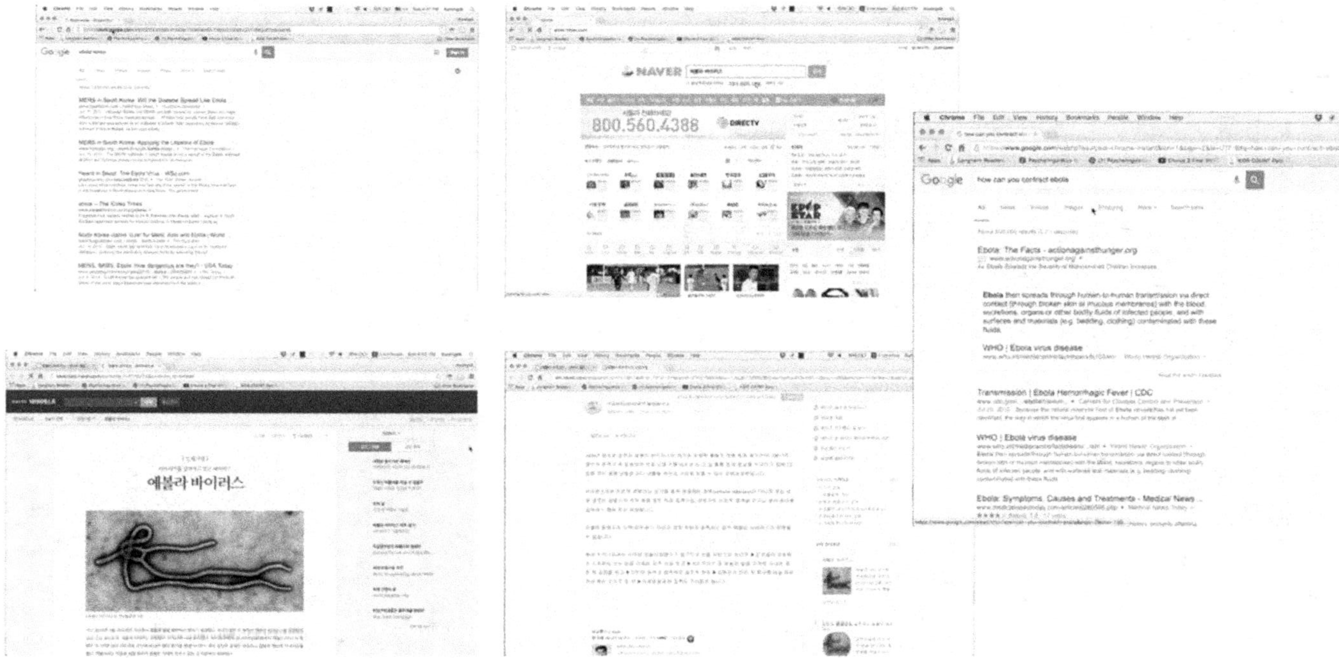

Figure 5.1. Yoonah's textual code-switching during her navigation of different sites.

Yoonah also used both of her languages to understand the content throughout her inquiry process to make sense of what she read. Her ways of translanguaging changed depending on different steps of her processes. During the initial examination of the information about Ebola virus, Yoonah's language choice in her think-alouds generally matched with the language of the text that she read. In other words, she chose Korean in her think-alouds when reading in Korean and English for reading in English. The following two excerpts show how Yoonah switched her primary language for her think-alouds while engaging in reading. The screenshots of the pages that Yoonah was reading are shown on the left side and her verbal reports on the right (see Figures 5.2 and 5.3).

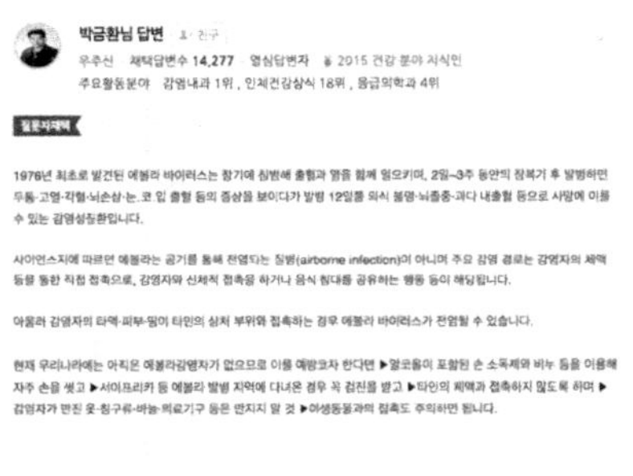

박금환님 답변

우주신 채택답변수 14,277 열심답변자 2015 건강 분야 지식인

주요활동분야 감염내과 1위 , 인체건강상식 18위 , 응급의학과 4위

2014.11.04. 22:21

Figure 5.2. A screenshot of the Korean website (박금환, 2014) that Yoonah was reading.

So they find, they find Ebola virus at first in 1976, and the virus, umm, 2일에서 3주동안 몸에 있다가 병이나면은, 머리가 아프고, 이제 열나고 그 다음에 눈이랑 코랑 입에서 피가 나는 병.. [(the virus) can stay in the body for 2 days to 3 weeks. When symptoms start, there is a headache, fever, and bleeding in the eyes, nose, and mouth.]

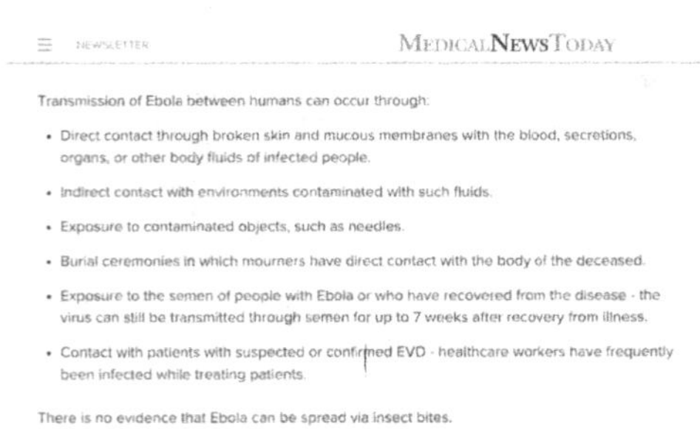

NEWSLETTER MEDICALNEWSTODAY

Transmission of Ebola between humans can occur through:

- Direct contact through broken skin and mucous membranes with the blood, secretions, organs, or other body fluids of infected people.
- Indirect contact with environments contaminated with such fluids.
- Exposure to contaminated objects, such as needles.
- Burial ceremonies in which mourners have direct contact with the body of the deceased.
- Exposure to the semen of people with Ebola or who have recovered from the disease - the virus can still be transmitted through semen for up to 7 weeks after recovery from illness.
- Contact with patients with suspected or confirmed EVD - healthcare workers have frequently been infected while treating patients.

There is no evidence that Ebola can be spread via insect bites.

Figure 5.3. A screenshot of the English website (Nichols, 2017) that Yoonah was reading.

So, you can, you can get … get the virus from the dead body like who has died from Ebola, and, and the blood.

And, the like, umm, needles, and then you can get infected by the animals when they meet. And, it's different like from, umm, normal flus because you cannot get through the air and water, food, and mosquitos, but animals.

As shown in these excerpts, it seems that she relied on the language of the text to frame her thought processes and construct her understanding of the symptoms and transmission of Ebola virus. The content of Yoonah's verbal reports when reading demonstrated that she engaged heavily in summarizing, paraphrasing, and inferring. Although her verbal reports hardly showed how she applied metacognitive strategies to monitor and assess her comprehension processes, her hesitation, pauses, and repeating during think-alouds suggested that Yoonah might continuously monitor and assess her comprehension. Adopting the language of the text as the primary language of bilingual readers' think-alouds was also noted in Kwon and Schallert's (2016) study with advanced bilingual graduate students who strategically chose the textual language to facilitate their analysis of texts.

Interestingly, in the first excerpt, Yoonah initially chose English as her primary language for her verbal reports. Soon, she switched to Korean in her verbal reports. Her code-switching in the middle of her think-alouds seemed to be facilitated by the textual language of the website. On the one hand, it might have been possible that translating from Korean to English was cognitively challenging for Yoonah as shown in her hesitation. On the other hand, it can be viewed as a strategic language choice because Yoonah might have felt that constructing meaning by using the textual language was more effective than using translation because she was able to borrow expressions and specialized terms from the texts. Traversing her two languages across different texts and in her verbal reports seems not to obscure her comprehension of what she read, but it was her intentional and deliberate choice to take advantage of the linguistic resources available in the texts for learning.

Although Yoonah preferred English to answer interview questions and chose English as her major language for her think-alouds for her learning from online texts, it was notable that Yoonah relied primarily on Korean when reviewing the information again for her post-task writing. Her verbal reports revealed that she employed metacognitive strategies to appraise, plan, and regulate her processes as shown in the following excerpts. These excerpts came from different stages of her reviewing processes, and the texts she read during this time were in English.

> 제가 쓰고 싶은 거는 Ebola virus 가 어떻게 음.. 많은 South Africa 에 있는 사람들이 죽었는지에 대해…
>
> [What I want to write about is how <u>Ebola virus</u>, umm, … many people in <u>South Africa</u> came to die] (Then, she opens Google on the screen and types "what is Ebola" in the search box. After the search results appear on the screen, she starts reviewing each of them).

> 잘은 모르겠는데, 그 두 살 아이가 죽었는데, West Africa에서 죽었는데, 그게 Ebola 라는 거는, 그러니까 그 아이가 죽고서, 인제 더 커져서 바이러스가 활동하는게 커져서, 그래서, 어 그래서 이렇게 퍼진 것 같은데
>
> [I'm not sure, not sure, but a two-year-old child died, died in West Africa, that was (due to) Ebola,, which means the child died and then it (the Ebola virus) became more active, the activity of the virus became active, so it seems to come to spread around] (After she took notes of the information about a 2-year-old's death, she went back to the Wikipedia to confirm the information.)

The first excerpt shows how Yoonah planned out what she wanted to write about first, and her planning eventually guided her to carry out an additional search to review the information about how Ebola virus outbreak started in South Africa. The second excerpt demonstrates that Yoonah assessed her understanding about the first outbreak of Ebola virus by expressing uncertainty while reviewing the text written in English: "잘은 모르겠는데 [I'm *not sure*], 퍼진것 같은데 [it *seems to* spread around]." Her uncertainty showed that she monitored her comprehension of what she read, and it further led her to searching for additional information to confirm what she had found was valid. Furthermore, she confirmed and clarified her understanding by repeatedly rephrasing the information about the cause of the Ebola virus diffusion written in English through translation into Korean as shown in: "which means the child died and then it (the Ebola virus) became more active, the activity of the virus became active, so it seems to spread around." In the above examples, translanguaging facilitated her application of metacognitive strategies to monitor her inquiry processes, make and revise a plan, and assess her comprehension.

TRANSLANGUAGING PRACTICES AND ONLINE INQUIRY ON THE MULTILINGUAL INTERNET FOR BILINGUAL LEARNERS

In this chapter, we highlighted two focal Korean-English bilingual adolescents' translanguaging during the online inquiry. The focal bilingual learners were able to traverse between their two languages as they searched for and learned from multiple online texts written in both languages. They also demonstrated their ability to access and utilize multilingual resources as they were given a choice of using their linguistic resources to explore the multilingual Internet. The focal bilingual learners' translanguaging operated both at cognitive and metacognitive levels. Translanguaging, as represented in the focal bilingual learners' think-alouds, suggested that they activated their linguistic repertoire and to make sense of texts (e.g., García & Godina, 2017; Upton & Lee-Thompson, 2001). They drew on their knowledge and experiences with the multilingual Internet while activating their skills in both languages and deliberately pursuing information written in both languages to cross-check different multilingual websites and to make inferences.

Translanguaging is also critical for the participants' application of metacognitive strategies as it facilitates their decision making and planning during reading. Through translanguaging, they monitored their understanding of what they had read and refined their plans to determine what to read in which language. Additionally, the focal adolescent bilingual readers' textual language choice to access multilingual online resources as shown in the findings may have been their purposeful decision to reexamine and reconfirm the information written in two different languages by making the most of their knowledge about the translinguality of information in a particular online space. Such metacognitive use of both languages was to monitor their processes to gain knowledge about the topic and to refine their understanding constructed from reading. Therefore, translanguaging during online inquiry may have the metacognitive nature as it involves explicit and implicit decision making across two different languages to facilitate learning processes (Li, 2018; Swain, 2006; Vygostky, 1986). Decision making with languages during the online inquiry could also suggest that the focal emerging bilingual adolescents had agency in using translanguaging to clarify and refine meaning, to make inferences, and to select and synthesize necessary information.

As shown in this study, bilingual learners may already possess such skills and strategies to take advantage of the affordances of the multilingual Internet to explore, evaluate, and select information written in different languages on the online space (Lee, 2017; Lam, 2014). However, it is imperative that such knowledge and abilities that bilingual learners have developed in an out-of-school context could be further cultivated in a classroom context in which English is the only medium of the instruction. Although the scope of this study was limited, the findings suggest a few pedagogical implications for educators who seek ways to support bilingual learners. It is critical for teachers to acknowledge emergent bilingual learners have agency in using their skills and strategies to explore multilingual resources for their learning. Therefore, translanguaging should be recognized as integral to multilingual learners' cognitive and metacognitive processes when they learn from texts because it facilitates bilingual learners' engagement with texts written in different languages (Li, 2018; McSwan, 2017). Teachers could also encourage bilingual learners to use translanguaging for their content learning in their second language. In supporting bilingual students' learning, therefore, an online inquiry as an instructional approach could be built on the understanding that the Internet as a translingual space in which information could be represented in different languages and that bilingual learners are active participants on the multilingual Internet. Through online inquiry activities that allow bilingual learners to access multilingual resources, bilingual learners with extensive out-of-school experiences with the Internet may be able to leverage knowledge and strategies to navigate resources in different languages to facilitate and strengthen their learning. Therefore, literacy instruction designed to support adolescents' digital literacy skills should provide bilingual learners with authentic opportunities to navigate, compare, contrast, and evaluate resources written in different languages for their learning on the Internet.

CONCLUDING REMARKS

The multilingual Internet offers affordances that bilingual learners can undertake as they search for and learn from online resources, and such affordances can be further activated by users' skills and strategies to use (Barton & Lee, 2013). Furthermore, multilingual users' agentive engagement in digital practices is critical because their intention and willingness to explore multilingual resources on the Internet and to utilize their linguistic knowledge can make the most of what the Internet offers. In some ways, the multilingual Internet can transcend the constraints that monolingual-oriented classroom practices unintentionally impose on bilingual learners. With additional and unrecognized linguistic resources and strategic knowledge excavated from their cross-linguistic experiences in out-of-school contexts, bilingual learners may benefit from exploring and navigating multilingual online resources with a purpose to learn. Ultimately, constructing knowledge and making meaning from texts can take place beyond named languages. Although this study provides an exploratory understanding of adolescent bilingual learners' use of translanguaging during an online inquiry, further research is necessary to investigate sophisticated ways of using translanguaging when searching for information and learning in the online context. Additionally, it is imperative to examine how translanguaging can be implemented in a classroom context to support emergent bilingual students' learning with the multilingual Internet.

REFERENCES

박금환 (2014, Nov. 4). 에볼라바이러스 감염 증상화 전염경로에 대해서. *Naver 지식 iN*. Retrieved from https://kin.naver.com/index.nhn.

위키백과. (n. d.) 지카 바이러스. Retrieved from Korean Wikipedia: https://ko.wikipedia.org/wiki/%EC%A7%80%EC%B9%B4%EB%B0%94%EC%9D%B4%EB%9F%AC%EC%8A%A4

Anderson, N. J. (2003). Scrolling, clicking, and reading English: Online reading strategies in a *second*/foreign language. *The Reading Matrix, 3*, 1–33.

Androutsopoulos, J. (2015). Networked multilingualism: Some language practices on Facebook and their implication. *International Journal of Bilingualism, 19*(2), 185–205.

Bakhtin, M. (1982). *The dialogic imagination: Four essays*. Austin, TX: The University of Texas Press.

Barton, D., & Lee, C. (2013). *Language online: Investigating digital texts and practices.* New York, NY: Routledge.

Canagarajah, A. S. (2013). Negotiating translingual literacy: An enactment. *Research in the Teaching of English, 48*(1), 40–67.

Chun, D. (2001). L2 reading on the web: Strategies for accessing information in hypermedia. *Computer Assisted Language Learning, 14*(5), 367–403.

Coiro, J. (2011). Predicting reading comprehension on the Internet: Contributions of offline skills, online reading skills, and prior knowledge. *Journal of Literacy Research, 43*(4), 352–392.

Coiro, J., & Dobler, E. (2007). Exploring the online reading comprehension strategies used by sixth-grade skilled readers to search for and locate information on the Internet. *Reading Research Quarterly, 42*(2), 214–257.

Danet, B., & Herring, S. C. (2007). Introduction: Welcome to the multilingual Internet. In B. Danet & S. C. Herring (Eds.), *The multilingual Internet: Language, culture, and communication online* (pp. 1–39). New York, NY: Oxford University Press.

García, G. E., & Godina, H. (2017). A window into bilingual reading: The bilingual reading practices of fourth-grade, Mexican American children who are emergent bilinguals. *Journal of Literacy Research, 49*(2), 273–301.

García, O., & Li, W. (2014). *Translanguaging: Language, bilingualism and education.* New York, NY: Palgrave.

Huang, H.-C., Chern, C.-I., & Lin, C.-C. (2009). EFL learners' use of online reading strategies and comprehension of texts: An exploratory study. *Computers & Education, 52*(1), 13–26.

Internet World Stats. (2018). *Internet world users by languages: Top 10 languages.* Retrieved from Internet World Stats: https://www.internetworldstats.com/stats7.htm

Jiménez, R., García, G. E., & Pearson, P. D. (1996). The reading strategies of bilingual Latina/o students who are successful English readers: Opportunities and obstacles. *Reading Research Quarterly, 31*, 90–112.

Kwon, H. J., & Schallert, D. L. (2016). Understanding translanguaging practices through a biliteracy continua framework: Adult biliterates reading academic texts in their two languages. *Bilingual Research Journal, 39*(2), 138–151. doi: 10.1080/15235882.2016.1167139

Lam., W. S. E. (2004). Second language socialization in a bilingual chat room: Global and local considerations. *Language, Learning & Technology, 8*(3), 44–65.

Lam, W. S. E. (2014). Literacy and capital in immigrant youths' online network across countries. *Learning, Media and Technology*. doi:10.1080/17439884.2014.942665

Lee, C. (2017). *Multilingualism online.* New York, NY: Routledge.

Leu, D. J., Forzani, E., Rhoads, C., Maykel, C., Kennedy, C., & Timbrell, N. (2015). The new literacies of online research comprehension: Rethinking the reading achivement gap. *Reading Research Quarterly, 50*(1), 37–59.

Li. W. (2018). Translanguaging as a practical theory of language. *Applied Linguistics, 39*(1), 9–30.

Martin-Beltrán, M. (2014). "What do you want to say?" How adolescents use translanguaging to expand learning opportunities. *International Multilingual Research Journal, 8,* 208–230.

McSwan, J. (2017). Multilingual perspective on translanguaging. *American Educational Research Journal, 54*(1), 167–201.

Nichols, H. (2017, May 23). *Ebola: What you need to know.* Retrieved from https://www.medicalnewstoday.com/

Park, H.-R., & Kim, D. (2011). Reading-strategy use by English as a second language learners in online reading tasks. *Computers & Education, 57*(3), 2156–2166.

Park, J., Yang, J., & Hsieh, Y. C. (2014). University level second language readers' online reading and comprehension strategies. *Language Learning & Technology, 18*(3), 148–172.

Pimienta, D., Prado, D., & Blanco, Á. (2009). *Twelve years of measuring linguistic diversity in the Internet: Balance and perspectives.* The Information Society Division, Communication and Information Sector (Ed.). Paris, France: UNESCO.

Seng, G. H., & Hashim, F. (2006). Use of L1 in L2 reading comprehension among tertiary ESL learners. *Reading in a Foreign Language, 18*(1), 29–54.

Swain, M. (2006). Languaging, agency and collaboration in advanced language proficiency. In H. Byrnes (Ed.), *Advanced language learning: The contribution of Halliday and Vygotsky* (pp. 95–108). London, England and New York, NY: Continuum.

Upton, T. A., & Lee-Thompson, L.-C. (2001). The role of the first language in second language reading. *SSLA, 23,* 469–495.

Vandekerckhove, R., & Nobles, J. (2010) Code eclecticism: Linguistic variation and code alternation in the chat language of Flemish teenagers. *Journal of Sociolinguistics, 14*(5), 657–677.

Vygotsky, L. S. (1986). *Thought and language* (A. Kozulin, Ed.). Boston, MA: The Massachusetts Institute of Technology Press. (Original work published, 1934).

Wikipedia (n.d.). *Zika virus.* Retrieved from Wikipedia: https://en.wikipedia.org/wiki/Zika_virus

Yi, Y. (2009). Adolescent literacy and identity construction among 1.5 Generation students from a transnational perspective. *Journal of Asian Pacific Communication, 19*(1), 100–129.

PART II

DIGITAL LITERACIES FROM WITHIN

CHAPTER 6

FULL OF SOUND AND FURY

Rural Students' Use of Digital Literacies in Exploring Space, Place, and Identity

David L. Bruce
University at Buffalo

Sunshine R. Sullivan
Houghton College

Nichole M. Barrett
University at Buffalo

Charles H. Gonzalez
Alabama A+M University

INTRODUCTION

On a Wednesday evening in mid-June, we gathered with other people from across the region in a school auditorium. Attending were teachers, administrators, and parents, all who chose to take a break from the tyranny of the state exam season to support the crowd of students—all dressed in

Negotiating Place and Space Through Digital Literacies: Research and Practice, pp. 97–116

formal attire—whose video productions had been nominated to represent their individual districts in a first ever, regional student film festival. The foyer had tables of food and drink while ushers passed out programs with voting ballots containing the names of the students and the projects they had created. The 31 student entries had been divided among three viewing flights with a brief intermission between segments. During those breaks, classic movie scenes and montages filled the auditorium screen while attendees ranked their favorites from each division. After all films had been screened, judges tallied the votes. The top winners from each flight were invited to the front of the auditorium and asked to share a few insights about their projects. Finally, an emcee read the names of the audience's choice award and presented them with a trophy.

That evening was the culmination of a year-long effort of a group of teachers from rural contexts who had attended a regional professional development institute called Writing with Video (WWV). In this institute, the teachers formed a community of practice (Wenger, 1998; Wenger, McDermott, & Snyder, 2002) around the use of digital tools. Participation in communities of practice refers to "being active participants in the *practices* of social communities and constructing *identities* in relation to these communities" (Wenger, 1998, p. 4, original emphasis). Wells (1999) adds, "learning is an integral aspect of participation in practices that have some other object in view" (p. 123). In addition to learning how to compose with digital video (DV), they also planned and developed curricular applications of these tools for their shared classroom use.

This chapter situates the ways in which their students used the available resources of their multimodal tools and ruralities as they composed their video projects. We work to illustrate how their students used both spaces and places that were part of their individual and collective ruralities to explicitly complete academic assignments, while tacitly exploring their identities.

REVIEW OF LITERATURE

Our work is informed by issues surrounding space and spatial literacies, rurality, and multimodal literacies, specifically the use of DV as a meaning making tool. In this section, each will be addressed in turn. Theobald (1997) posits that place-conscious pedagogy can occur when we are engaged in educational experiences that lead to *intradependence* between us and our local and broader spaces. Brooks (2003) adds that it is the "[focus] on the necessary relations-cultural, natural, agricultural—that shape a given place and its human communities" (p. 6).

As people move in and out of life experiences, they also move within and across boundaries and spaces that are lived (Lefebvre, 1974/1991). These spaces are inextricably linked to mental and material "biographies and geo-histories" (Soja, 2010, p. 18). Therefore, spatiality can be understood as the result of interactions with historically situated, socially constructed geographies that have impacts—both positive and negative, enchanting or limiting—on the way that individuals conceptualize their surroundings and their role within space. A space becomes a place when we take time to see it, listen in it, or recognize it as a part of our life, our process. Space transforms when a connection is developed (intentionally or tacitly) over time as a result of varied purpose and levels of intentionality and reflection. It is when we take a moment to spend time in spaces, to recognize and embrace them with purpose, that they become an important part of our histories and identities, and influential in the meaning making process. If, as Soja (2010) argues, time and space are both socially constructed through lived experience and shaped by existing circumstance, then understanding how rural students draw on their surroundings as a part of their meaning making processes can be explored by looking at the ways that they negotiate the boundaries between spaces and places.

Both real and imagined places have consequences on learning and affect how individuals reflect upon and negotiate their identities and roles across boundaries. Rural spaces and places are constructed through experience, and although more than half of the students who attend public school in the United States do so in rural spaces, educational research emphasizes the experiences of urban and suburban students (Green, 2013; Schafft, 2016; Tieken & San Antonio, 2016). Current research addressing rural education positions rural students in direct opposition to their urban peers, neglecting to take into consideration realities of rural life (Donehower, Hogg, & Schell, 2007, 2012; Eckert & Alsup, 2004), and the learning and teaching that occurs outside of classroom boundaries (Gruenewald, 2003). Instead, narratives of rurality and rural education construct a deficit view of what it means to occupy spaces and places outside of urban boundaries. These views perpetuate an escape narrative that encourages students to seek out a more urban narrative in favor of their existing impoverished one (Eckert & Alsup, 2014) and strengthen "metro-centric" attitudes towards literacy and learning (Green, 2013). Hodges (2004) also argues that not all rural communities are the same. Each community has its own stories, its own history, and its students will each have their own experiences all connected and defined by their individual rurality. Leveraging a community's resources (e.g., landmarks, museums, local library, landscape), histories, and stories can be a way for students to take ownership over their rural spaces and the affordances they offer.

What is missing from research in rural education is an emphasis on how students draw upon rural spaces and places as they negotiate both their identities and literacy practices. Looking at how students incorporate their rural spaces and experiences as a part of their literacy practices—even implicitly—is one way that we can begin to understand the approaches students use to work to define and redefine themselves in terms of their surroundings, as well as how they negotiate local and global definitions of rurality. Since the research in this chapter occurs within rural spaces, it draws attention to the need for emphasis on the individual stories of rural students and all of their spaces and places.

Drawing on sociocultural views of literacy (e.g., Gee, 1992), educational research exploring the impact of space on student learning and identity has often focused on drawing connections between students' literacy practices in schooled and non-schooled spaces (e.g., Hull & Shultz, 2002; Moje, 2004; Schultz, 2002; Skerrett & Bomer, 2011) as well as the impact that family and community have on students' literacy practices (e.g., Heath, 1983; Moje et al., 2004; Pahl & Kelly, 2005; Street, 1984). There is also a growing body of research that advocates for spatial (e.g., Barton, Hamilton, & Ivanic, 2000; Mills & Comber, 2015) and place-conscious (e.g., Brooke, 2003; Comber, 2015; Mills & Comber, 2013; Somerville, 2013; Theobald, 1997) approaches to literacy and literacy instruction as a way to incorporate the impact that space can have upon student learning and identity development.

Research addressing the positive impact of students' multimodal (e.g., Albers & Sanders, 2010; Cope & Kalantzis, 2000; Miller & McVee, 2013; Ranker, 2008; Siegel, 2006) and digital (e.g., Curwood, Magnifico, & Lammers, 2013; Lankshear & Knobel, 2006; Tavares, 2015; Vasudevan, 2010) literacy practices has gained momentum. However, this research tends to highlight the use of multimodal and digital literacies in relationship to academic gains and/or metrics (e.g., Abrams, 2009; Beach, 2012; Miller, Knips, & Goss, 2013), rather than explore the impact that digital and multimodal literacy practices have upon students' meaning making processes.

As approaches to teaching and learning shift as a result of technological advances, there is need to explore the affordances of DV composition in relationship to space and place. Manovich (2001) notes that digital and new media, as opposed to traditional media and movie making, "is characterized by variability" and "typically gives rise to many different versions" (p. 56). He draws attention to the impact that digital technologies have on an author's interaction with and across modalities. More specifically he notes that, "In the process of interaction the user can choose which elements to display or which paths to follow, thus generating a unique work" (p. 66). While research drawing attention to the value of students' digital compositions as multimodal (e.g., Bruce, 2008; Chandler-Olcott & Lewis, 2010; Doerr-Stevens, 2015; Smith, 2017) and mobile (e.g., Ehret & Hollett, 2014; Wargo, 2015; Warner, 2016) has grown, these studies mostly occur in urban or suburban spaces (e.g., Chisholm & Olinger, 2017; Vasudevan, Shultz, & Bateman, 2010). In the studies where students used DV in rural spaces, researchers found that their compositions were impacted by their settings, with students often highlighting personal connections to the community spaces within their rural settings (Pyles, 2016; Wake, 2012). This study, then, illustrates how students used DV for academic purposes while exploring the spaces, places, and experiences of their rural landscapes.

METHODOLOGY

Context

The data in this chapter are part of a larger study where higher education faculty provided professional development and examined how professional learning communities (PLC) enroot when teachers from across a primarily rural region engaged in digital literacies together.

During the summer of 2016, WWV offered a weeklong summer institute focusing on digital literacies in the classroom. ELA and history teachers from a rural region were invited to participate. Twelve teachers from six school districts participated in developing their own digital literacy competencies and making plans to integrate 21st century literacies in their curriculum. Throughout the following academic year, we met for day-long fall and spring reunions where teachers continued the work they began in the summer as well as shared their teaching and student work within their learning community. In between the reunions, they remained connected with one another through online forums and e-mail threads, sharing ideas and student work samples. Throughout our first year's work together as a community of practice—in our reunions and online forums—the teachers continued collaborating on incorporating the digital literacies in their classrooms. A culminating celebration of both their growth as educators and their students as composers of video occurred in a public venue through a year-end film festival that the teachers collaboratively designed, promoted, and hosted. The videos analyzed for this research were premiered at this film festival.

Participants

Brendan Heaney. Brendan was one of our participating teachers and his school hosted the film festival. He taught an elective film class as well as a World Literature course. In one of his units for the latter, he had students create a video in response to one of the several Shakespeare texts they had read and viewed. Specifically, he gave an open set of directions to the students: interpret your choice of a theme, passage, scene, or play by Shakespeare using DV as your compositional means.

Alicia & Jess. These two students were in Brendan's class and chose to create a video around MacBeth's "Tomorrow and tomorrow and tomorrow" soliloquy (Act V, scene v). Jess was a senior and Alicia was a junior. While they worked collaboratively throughout the project, Alicia originated the concept for their video, and guided much of the content. Jess, having expertise with camerawork and editing, did the majority of the production work. Together, they attended to the content through compositional moves to present a shared vision for the project. Alicia said they wanted to show "the soliloquy though a modern lens and highlight that it's still relevant now and people are still struggling with the same things." We selected their project for analysis because it was textually rich in both production quality and interpretation of the source text.

Data Collection and Analysis

Teacher and student interviews. We conducted two formal interviews with each participating teacher. The first interview occurred near the end of the weeklong summer institute and teachers were asked to share about their learning experiences with digital literacies. The second interview took place during the summer following the academic year. Teachers were asked to share about their curricular use of and student learning through digital literacies. Additionally, the two focal students were interviewed the following academic year. One of the students had graduated high school and gone to college, and the other was now a senior in high school. They were asked about their composition processes and to reflect on what they had discovered through making the DV class project. They also viewed the finished video and were asked retrospective analysis questions about their work.

All teacher and student interviews were listened to in their entirety. While listening, researchers made analytic memos (Strauss & Corbin, 1990). The interviews were transcribed and entered into NVivo qualitative software analysis program. Two researchers looked for thematic connections among the interviews, creating initial coding through open nodes and then coalesced the emergent threads into tree nodes. Where there was congruency in content, these nodes were used to inform the video content analysis.

Teacher artifacts. We collected two types of artifacts from the participating teachers. The first came from their multimodal composition work within the institute, and included conceptual planning, final digital projects, and reflections on their process and product. The second type of artifact was comprised of curricular planning, lessons, and/or projects the teachers planned to enact with their students. Artifacts related to the curricular work that led to student work being entered into the film festival were reviewed for contextual material regarding the student videos.

Online community. We used Schoology as our learning management platform. We posted discussion threads on various topics to which teachers responded. The format was largely dictated by the teachers and became a virtual space for curricular examples, reunion planning and reflections, and a forum for numerous aspects of the film festival.

Video content analysis. There were a total of 31 student videos from five school districts submitted to the film festival. Of these, we completed content analysis of 15 videos, namely, those that used the affordances, spaces, and places of their rural contexts. Specifically we examined the topic/theme, class and assignment, use of indoor spaces and outdoor spaces as well as general production observations. Additionally, we conducted a detailed shot analysis on Jess and Alicia's video, Tomorrow and Tomorrow.

Two researchers concurrently viewed, analyzed, and coded each shot of Tomorrow and Tomorrow. The 3:10 minute video had 73 shots in total, which were analyzed for location, camera angle, visual information, ambient audio, voice-over, music, and special effects.

FINDINGS

In academic assignments, students' assignments and audience are often limited within the four walls of the classroom and the curbs of the school property. While they may use the Internet for virtual explorations, their space within academic boundaries is often within the school confines. Through these video assignments, our teachers' students were given the chance to venture outside of those academic spaces. While some students kept their productions within the school—some by assignment, necessity, time constraints, and so forth—others ventured beyond those borderlines and traversed in and through their community landscapes.

For their literature class assignment of responding to a selection from Shakespeare using DV, Alicia and Jess selected MacBeth's soliloquy, *Tomorrow and tomorrow and tomorrow*. In thinking about making Shakespeare relevant to today, Alicia said,

> I immediately thought about that soliloquy and wanted to capture the idea of somebody struggling with suicidal thoughts and what would be going through their mind rights as they were deciding, when they were on the brink of deciding between life and death.

The audio component of their video had Alicia's voice—halting and pausing throughout the delivery—quoting the text while a haunting instrumental served as background music. The visuals showed her in alternately disheveled and polished appearances, inhabiting spaces around the community, her expressions ranging from contemplative, angry, and weary, to desperate. The penultimate image of the video showed her standing at a waterfall's edge. The final shot was a black screen, the ending left intentionally ambiguous.

In making their video, Alicia and Jess used both spaces and places in their community in two main ways. First, they moved intentionally in and through their landscape, exploring and highlighting a number of community spaces and places. Secondly, through their use of production processes—using camera and editing techniques—they elevated commonplace events in their lives.

Moving in and Through the Community

In making their video, Jess and Alicia operated in and through the landscape of their rural community. Specifically, they used various affordances of their camera as a means of exploration, attending to lighting and time of day, and pushing boundaries of access to capture unique perspectives and vantage points in their production. In their interviews, they indicated that the camera became a source of empowerment—through investigation and exploration—while also using the lens' affordances to compose in purposeful ways. They filmed in nine distinct locations for their production: a waterfall, field, church, gas station, home, grocery store, abandoned house, woods, and trail entrance. However, in each of those settings, their use of space was not limited to one perspective within that location. Instead, they often explored the setting—using the affordances of the camera to see, frame, and record their surroundings. While filming in Alicia's house, for example, they used different places such as her kitchen, living room, and bedroom. In a similar manner, they used their camera to explore each filming location through numerous spaces and places in and around the setting.

One specific way Jess and Alicia moved through and richly explored their selected settings was through their positioning of the camera. This happened in the first scene (shots 1–3) where the central character is introduced in a grocery store. They placed the camera at the floor level so that the audience sees the floor, the feet and legs of the faceless shopper, and the wheels and lower parts of the cart within the shot. This type of exploration is also seen in their footage inside Jess's church. The low level shots (36–39) frame Alicia kneeling along the altar. The camera was situated at the floor level, making the images within the camera's frame—the rail, the altar, and the stained glass window—appear heightened. That sequence—keeping the same scene framing—also showed Alicia sitting with her back against the altar, legs outstretched on the floor. Each of those framing techniques highlighted for the viewer an usual perspective not normally accessible to a shopper or parishioner. Throughout this project, Alicia and Jess were empowered with their teacher's challenge, time, and Jess's camera to tour through their rural community spaces. With their compositional tools, time, and purpose, Jess and Alicia noticed, sought, captured, and edited details of their ruralities that helped them communicate the relevance of Shakespeare's soliloquy to their lives and their peers' lives.

The lighting of the time of day was important to the way in which Jess and Alicia emphasized spaces. In reflecting on the final video, they discussed the importance of the golden hour—first and last light of the day, ideal for photography—in their work as they explored the outdoor landscapes of their community. Tess said, "We had to plan things out because I really wanted to do golden hour so everything looked with the sun, really beautiful." This is most clearly seen and felt in the field setting. A number of shots (15 of the 71) happened within this general setting, in and around an open field. However, they used the golden hour to literally highlight this space, guiding the viewers' ability to see and become aware of this part of their community that reflected different parts of the text's focal soliloquy. Using the golden hour, both the large and the small of the field is accented. The large is felt with the long shot scenes with Alicia walking through the vast space of the open land. The minutia of the surroundings are highlighted through shifting the focus on extreme close ups: the dead blossoms on last year's weed stalks, the emerging buds on twig limbs, and the insects backlit against the light of the setting sun are offerings that were gathered from and for their community. Clearly, their attention to the use of lighting to feature available spaces emphasized elements of their community that might not be seen or felt without the sophisticated use of a camera lens.

The freedom to select and use locations outside of the classroom for their academic project also made room for Alicia and Jess to push their boundaries in ways they may not have otherwise done. Alicia shared that portraying some of the scenes on camera were uncomfortable for her. For example, one of the locales they selected for their video was at an abandoned house. Both had never been there before. In talking about their experience filming there, Alicia said, "I was scared about everything. I was like, I can't believe I'm doing this because I'm the least rebellious person ever." According to Alicia, they are both perceived as "good students" and "rule followers." They would not have considered visiting the abandoned house as part of their normal routines. However, using their camera for this project gave them license to trespass the boundaries of their normal community spaces.

In looking across the larger set of student videos, stretching their identity and community boundaries while moving in and through their lived spaces and places were not unique to Alicia's and Jess's experience. Many of the videos detailed close and expanded perspectives of their rural contexts. In the video "Untitled," the students captured the setting for their story by traversing across fields, through woods and into an abandoned hunting cabin. Another student showed a number of pastoral scenes—including shots of a large pond with ducks— in his rap video, *I Don't Do Poetry.* In the video *Dystopian Asylum,* two students videotaped their entire project by trespassing into a condemned building. Through framing various perspectives and highlighting different angles, the students took exploratory license with their videos as they framed the familiar and unfamiliar spaces in their rural communities, transforming some of their community spaces into places. We contend that these portrayals and representations go beyond students simply 'showing their surroundings.' Rather, the teachers' flexible and responsive mediation supported the students' choices and ability to visually represent the features of their rural experiences, moving away from performative academics to reinforce Theobald's (1997) notion of place-conscious pedagogy.

Elevating the Ordinary

As our teachers' students used the affordances of video composition to move in and through their community landscapes, they heightened the importance of the mundane in their community spaces. Stephen, one of the teachers in our WWV community of practice, developed what he called an *elevation project*. This assignment had students highlight, draw attention to, or elevate an everyday item, event, or routine. While Alicia and Jess were not in Stephen's class or necessarily familiar with the assignment parameters, their project drew attention to and elevated the ordinary elements portrayed in their video. The girls used three specific editing techniques—use of repetition, rapid jump cut edits, and juxtaposing images—to heighten audience attention of the ordinary.

One way they demonstrated elevation was a repetitive series of routine events. Setting their initial footage at a grocery store, a gas station, and a kitchen sink, each of these scenes follow a pattern. At those settings a specific action is repeated in edits 4–16.

Setting	Repeated motion (three times)
Grocery store	opening freezer door, removing item
Gas station	selecting fuel grade, removing nozzle from pump
Kitchen sink	setting dish in sink, lifting dish soap, turning on water

At the different settings, each take was filmed from the same perspective—with Alicia wearing a different outfit for each shot—and then edited together with the voice-over of the opening lines of the text, "tomorrow and tomorrow and tomorrow." The effect of the visual repetition was both to parallel the language and to create a sense of an ordinary event happening the same way repeatedly throughout life. Olivia said, "I was thinking about the idea of life rushing by and the repetitiveness of it that the soliloquy is trying to convey." Even though they are showing the same things happening again and again, the effect elevates the mundane, the routine, by highlighting to the viewer to see, hear, and become aware of something. The girls intentionally used this repetition to make the audience aware how Shakespeare's soliloquy might be relevant to today's tomorrow and tomorrow.

Alicia and Jess used other editing moves that elevated the everyday, specifically their implementation of rapid jump cuts to interrupt the visuals of the scene. For example, in shots 41–44, Alicia is framed within the trailhead exiting a wooded trail system. In this sequence, she looked directly at the camera while standing next to a sign that said DO NOT ENTER. The entire segment lasted approximately 5½ seconds. However, instead of this being a single shot, it was edited into 4 separate scenes, the longer ones interrupted with edits lasting a fraction of a second. Regarding that editing technique, Alicia said, "Obviously the jumpiness of that editing just kind of looked cool ... we liked that part." The effect of having these jump cuts—no transitions to ease switch between images—jars the visual continuity, thus creating a narrative disruptive sense of *pay attention and look closely!* What would be a "normal" shot—albeit beautifully framed—now startles the viewer awake to consider with more care what is being communicated. They used this jump cut editing technique 11 different times throughout their video.

Juxtaposing images was a third editing technique that Alicia and Jess used to elevate the ordinary in their community. By placing dissimilar images next to one another, they drew attention to the similarities and differences among the settings they chose to include and share from their community.

In the most striking instance of juxtaposition, Alicia was framed standing near the edge of a church balcony rail. Jess edited that image, placing it aside a similarly framed shot of Alicia standing on a ledge overlooking a waterfall. They not only framed the images in a parallel fashion, they also kept the continuity of Alicia's movements. For example, at one point, while in the balcony, she looked upward, tilting her face toward the ceiling, as if she were in prayer. As she looked down, the downward movement of her head continued into the next shot of her standing by the waterfall. The parallel images continued with her taking a deep breath, beginning her inhale on the church balcony and then concluding the intake breath at the waterfall's edge. The effect of this not only highlighted the literal setting, it also figuratively emphasized the inner turmoil the character was dealing with. In doing so, the planned sequence leaves the audience with a sense of ambiguity. Alicia said,

> You're not really sure, has she given up hope completely? You're just a little bit unsure. Has she given up on God? Did she find answers? That was supposed to be a little bit ambiguous, but the head placement was intentional.

While this paralleled movement through the two different settings was planned, Alicia and Jess revised their plan through the editing process. In talking about the balcony and waterfall, Jess said,

> We knew we wanted that back and forth because they're kind of like opposites ... they were going to be in different parts of the film. And, at the end we knew we wanted the same shot, we knew we wanted the same shot of her on the church balcony and at the falls, we just didn't know that we were going to put them back to back and like switch them. And, that happened accidentally when I put all the footage into iMovie and it ended up like that and we were like, "Wait, that's really cool. That's what we want."

Originally conceptualized as occurring in different sections of their narrative, they decided to sequence these settings together, creating Alicia's fluid movements across both settings. Their final version called attention to these moments of breathing and choosing that are part of life, elevating the ordinary of their lived spaces and places.

DISCUSSION AND IMPLICATIONS

Before considering some of the implications of this study, we had to return to the issue of identities and ruralities, specifically considering why the rural context mattered. Could researchers find similar findings in urban and suburban settings as well?

In the interview with Jess and Alicia, they never specifically addressed how the rurality of their context affected their identity. However, they did discuss one significant component of their rural community, namely faith and faith-based institutions and the tensions felt in and about these spaces and places. Olivia said,

> We both grew up in church and faith was a big part of our lives and is a big part of our lives. And, I think that we wanted to show that it's not always a comforting thing, even for somebody that grew up in the church, religion isn't always something that you run to when you're sad. Sometimes it's very frustrating and I think that because that part is very personal to us. If we were struggling with something, I think both of us have experienced people from our churches being like, "Pray more" and then maybe we wanted to throw a Bible.

Their video, replete with religious settings and imagery, visualized their verbal affirmation and irritation with church-related issues.

Implicitly expressing their lived ruralities was not limited to Alicia and Jess. Throughout the larger data set of videos, students never explicitly addressed the context of issues surrounding rurality head on. There were no overt signs, statements, or claims to rural identity such as "country life" or "country boy/girl" throughout any of the videos. However, elements of rural life flow through their work, images, and themes.

One such element throughout a number of the videos dealt with an awareness of openness and opportunities for solitude in their surrounding landscape. A number of videos contained images of open fields, farmland and rolling hillsides. Likewise, wooded settings were featured as framing or boundary devices or, conversely, spaces to enter and explore. In highlighting the geographic features of the area, the students implicitly demonstrated the context of their rural experience. Thus, rurality as an expression of identity issues—at least with these students—was never foregrounded but was a constant background in their rural landscapes. While the case could be made that students in urban or suburban spaces would include their surroundings as part of their work, we contend that the rural settings portrayed in these videos were more than mere locations—these spaces and places were deeply embedded into their identities, backgrounds against and within which these students lived, composed, and shared their lives. While students in urban and suburban backgrounds would look and sound necessarily different, bringing these rural backgrounds to the foreground of educational research alongside the urban and suburban spaces and places pushes back against the scant representation in the literature. Additionally, while there was limited explicit talk of rurality, the way that students represented their lived experience demonstrated an implicit awareness.

In the following section, we propose three other implications to this research. First, these student explorations into community spaces would never have occurred without the teachers providing flexible time, resources, and mediation. Secondly, through their work on these projects, students earned a measure of status within the larger community. Finally, these projects were examples of liminal spaces and experiences.

Teachers Mediated Exploration Within and Beyond Classroom Spaces

The students' explorations of their community landscapes were only captured and shared within the school walls because they were given the challenge and freedom to do so for academic purposes. Of the 31 videos that teachers from our WWV cohort submitted for the film festival, all projects had been assigned as academic projects. The assignments varied in nature and included video adaptations of academic assignments, such as personal essays, vocabulary definitions, literary themes, poetry interpretations, short stories, rhetorical analysis, book reviews, and a research thesis.

These varied assignments in which students located opportunities to explore parts of their identity is important to note because a commonplace justification for not using digital literacies in the classroom is that the curriculum does not allow it. These teachers, through the community of practice in our WWV work, identified ways in which curricular objectives and mandates could be met through various DV projects that also invited students to capture, share, and celebrate their lived spaces and places together.

The importance of the teachers' craft in creating these multimodal curricular assignments is paramount: without teachers mediating the content and process of these assignments—originated in classroom settings—the students would not have had the opportunity for academic inquiry to explore their spaces and places within and around the community.

Students Gained Notoriety Through Their Videos

An unexpected outcome of the film festival was how students gained a reputation through their productions. This first happened locally in their classrooms and schools when teachers engaged their classes in viewings and discussion. The regional film festival brought an entirely new level of fame which persisted into the following academic year. One of the many examples of these shifting identities occurred after the viewing of Alec's video, *Dystopian Asylum*. In his school, Alec was perceived as an academic outsider. His teacher recounted the story of showing Alec's video in class and how positively his peers reacted to it, eventually selecting his video as one that would be submitted to the festival. Alec arrived at the film festival without his production partner and chose a seat by himself in the front of the auditorium. During the intermission that followed the session in which Alec's video was shown, he had numerous people talking with him about various aspects of his composition. His video was selected as one of the finalists and he became a defacto celebrity at the festival. Alec and other students found new identities—in his case, a highly visible creator with notable narrative and production chops—through the public viewing and sharing of their projects.

The teachers all agreed to use the festival submissions as content and/or production exemplars in their classes the following year. As videos were shown broadly throughout different districts across the region, the students who produced or starred in the videos earned a reputation for creativity, production skills, and/or artistic credibility. In the WWV discussion boards and reunion gatherings, teachers shared stories of their students mentioning the specific titles and authors of videos produced by students from other districts. As of this writing, another film festival is being planned to culminate the end of the current academic year. The teachers report stories of current students working on their projects, using the content and production quality of last year's submissions as a benchmark for their work. In talking about this phenomenon, the teachers have discussed how no academic assignment they have worked on has been taken up by so many of their students and with so much enthusiasm. This happened, in no small part, because the DV compositions have put students at the front and center of the authorship and audience.

Liminal Spaces and Experiences

A final implication of this research involves the *liminality* by which the students composed the videos. Originally coined in sociology to describe transitional aspects of rites of passage (van Gennep, 1909), liminality refers to what Turner (1967) calls the "betwixt and between" (p. 93). We contend that in making the videos, the places and processes were liminal in terms of space and experience.

In terms of space, "liminality can relate to specific places, thresholds … areas or zones" (Thomassen, 2009, p. 16). The process of students creating these DV projects for academic assignments had these elements to it. DV has often been presented as either an in-school literacy (e.g., Bruce, 2008; Cercone, 2017; Doerr-Stevens, 2016) or as an out of school literacy (e.g., Halverson, 2010; Hull, 2006). However, in making these projects, students often crossed the in/out of school thresholds, not occurring wholly in one or the other. Rather, they could be framed in terms of what Szakolczai (2009) refers to as "the 'in-between' ... a temporary situation betwixt two structured orders" (p. 151). While the projects were technically contained within a curricular unit, the projects had their assignment and assessment origins within the confines of the classroom. However, nearly all of the videos submitted for the festival were completed outside of the physical and temporal confines of the actual class. Namely, it was the *process* of making the video that had transitional elements. Brainstorming may have begun in the clustered desks of the classroom, but the composition process spilled out to continue into hallways, lunchrooms, bus and car rides, homes, chatrooms and phone calls, and extended community spaces. Thus, these projects occurred in the transitional spaces of academic and personal identities.

Liminality also can refer to shared experiences which leave "a common imprint, rendering possible the existence of a group of humans as a community" (Szakolczai, 2009 p. 151). While the latter refers to the binding power of transitional rites and ceremonies, we argue that there was a liminality of experience surrounding these videos. The shared aspect of the videos began in the classrooms where all of the teachers had their students publicly view the finished projects with their classmates. The public audience continued at the film festival where students, teachers, administrators, and parents from all over the region came to view the projects. Aspects of film festival rituals were followed—specifically, formal nominations of submissions, programs and promotional posters, formal attire, refreshments, and award ceremony—in viewing and celebrating these completed projects. Teachers reported that on the returning bus rides to the respective home schools and in subsequent classes following the festival, there were numerous comments and conversations detailing the experience of the festival as well as looking forward to and planning for next year's event. The festival became a sedimented experience, *a common* imprint, for those involved. In the process of spaces and places becoming liminal, the movements created passages for students to share, shape, and evolve in their identities.

CONCLUSION

In many ways, the film festival was both a conclusion and a beginning. It was a culmination of a yearlong effort by a group of committed teachers to highlight and celebrate student work in a communal and public setting. While the film festival lasted only a few hours, the space and experience of that event shaped new curricular preparation, lesson instruction, and student planning for the current academic year. Teachers have been planning for this year's festival, adding more opportunities for student work to be highlighted. There are competitions for the festival posters, programs, and movie trailer style promotional videos. Many students began the year with a goal of having their work submitted to the festival.

The film festival also germinated the research in this chapter. It was only when our research team watched the collective work of the students whose rural geographic boundaries span across an enormous region of our state, that we first saw the students' use of space and place across and within their rural landscapes. We had seen the individual submissions but it was the effect of seeing the totality of the projects—the variety and expanse of their lived spaces—that took us by surprise. Our festival afterglow conversations darted between individual submissions and memorable images within the videos. However, we kept returning to the unique backgrounds of their rural landscapes, imposing facets of its grand visage through the many videos. And we only saw it because the students, in an academic assignment, captured those spaces through their camera lenses, arranged the landscapes with their editing programs, and shared their discoveries and compositions publicly.

REFERENCES

Abrams, S. S. (2009). A gaming frame of mind: Digital contexts and academic implications. *Educational Media International, 46*(4), 335–347.

Albers, P., & Sanders, J. (Eds.). (2010). *Literacies, the arts, and multimodality.* Urbana, IL: National Council of Teachers of English.

Barton, D., Hamilton, M., & Ivanič, R. (Eds.). (2000). *Situated literacies: Reading and writing in context.* New York, NY: Routledge.

Beach, R. (2012). Constructing digital learning commons in the literacy classroom. *Journal of Adolescent & Adult Literacy, 55*(5), 448–451.

Brooke, R. E. (2003). Introduction: Place-conscious education, rural schools, and the Nebraska writing project's rural voices, country schools team. In R. E. Brooke (Ed.) *Rural voices: Place-conscious education and the teaching of writing* (pp. 1–19). New York, NY: Teachers College Press.

Bruce, D. L. (2008a). Visualizing literacy: Building bridges with media. *Reading & Writing Quarterly, 24*(3), 264–282.

Byas, T. & Cercone, A. (2016). HIPs with technology: A peer mentoring journey. *The International Conference on E-Education, E-Business, E-Management, and E-Learning (IC4E) Jakarta, Indonesia–Conference Proceedings.* World Research Library Online.

Cercone, J. (2017). Standing at the crossroads: Content creation in the 21st-Century classroom. *The English Journal, 106*(3), 25–31.

Chandler-Olcott, K., & Lewis, E. (2010). "I think they're being wired differently": Secondary teachers' cultural models of adolescents and their online literacies.

In D. E. Alvermann (Ed.), *Adolescents' online literacies* (pp. 163–182). New York, NY: Peter Lang.

Chisholm, J. S., & Olinger, A. R. (2017). "She's definitely the artist one": How learner identities mediate multimodal composing. *Research in the Teaching of English, 52*(2), 122–155.

Comber, B. (2015). *Literacy, place, and pedagogies of possibility*. New York, NY: Routledge. *Communication, 12*(1), 27–53.

Cope, B., & Kalantzis, M. (Eds.). (2000). *Multiliteracies: Literacy learning and the design of social futures*. New York, NY: Routledge.

Curwood, J. S., Magnifico, A. M., & Lammers, J. C. (2013). Writing in the wild: Writers' motivation in fan-based affinity spaces. *Journal of Adolescent & Adult Literacy, 56*(8), 677–685.

Doerr-Stevens, C. (2015). "That's not something I was, I am, or am ever going to be": Multimodal self-assertion in digital video production. *E-Learning and Digital Media, 12*(2), 164–182.

Donehower, K., Hogg, C., & Schell, E. E. (2007). *Rural literacies*. Carbondale, IL: SIU Press.

Donehower, K., Hogg, C., & Schell, E. E. (2012). Constructing rural literacies: Moving beyond the rhetorics of lack, lag, and the rosy past. In K. Donehower, C. Hogg, & E. E. Schell (Eds.), *Rural literacies* (pp. 1–36). Carbondale, IN: Southern Illinois University Press.

Eckert, L. S., & Alsup, J. (2014). Literacy teaching and learning in rural communities: Problematizing stereotypes, challenging myths. In L. S. Eckert & J. Alsup (Eds.), *Literacy teaching and learning in rural communities: Problematizing stereotypes, challenging myths* (pp. 1–10). New York, NY: Routledge.

Ehret, C., & Hollett, T. (2014). Embodied composition in real virtualities: Adolescents' literacy practices and felt experiences moving with digital, mobile devices in school. *Research in the Teaching of English*, 428–452.

Friesem, E. (2014). A story of conflict and collaboration: Media literacy, video production and disadvantaged youth. *Journal of Media Literacy Education, 6*(1), 44–55.

Gee, J. P. (1992). *The social mind: Language, ideology, and social practice*. New York, NY; JF Bergin & Garvey.

Green, B. (2013). Literacy, rurality, education: A partial mapping. In B. Green & M. Corbett (Eds.), *Rethinking rural literacies: Transnational perspectives* (pp. 17–33). New York, NY: Palgrave Macmillan.

Gruenewald, D. A. (2003). The best of both worlds: A critical pedagogy of place. *Educational Researcher, 32*(4), 3–12.

Halverson, E. R. (2010). Film as identity exploration: A multimodal analysis of youth-produced films. *Teachers College Record, 112*(9), 2352–2378.

Heath, S. B. (1983). *Ways with words: Language, life and work in communities and classrooms*. New York, NY: Cambridge University Press

Hodges, V. P. (2004). Using a sense of place to teach at-risk rural students. *English Journal, 93*(6), 27.

Hull, G. A., & Schultz, K. (Eds.). (2002). *School's out: Bridging out-of-school literacies with classroom practice*. New York, NY; Teachers College Press.

Lankshear, C., & Knobel, M. (2006). Digital literacy and digital literacies: policy, pedagogy and research considerations for education. *Nordic Journal of digital literacy*, *1*, 12–24.

Lefebvre, H. (1991) *The production of space*. (D. Nicholson-Smith, Trans.). Cambridge, MA: Blackwell. (Original published in 1974)

Manovich, L. (2001). *The language of new media*. Cambridge, MA: MIT Press.

Miller, S. M., Knips, M. A., & Goss, S. (2013). Changing the game of literature with authentic assessment: The promise of multimodal composing. *English Journal*, 88–94.

Miller, S. M., & McVee, M. B. (2013). Multimodal composing: The essential 21st century literacy. In S. M. Miller & M. B. McVee (Eds.), *Multimodal composing in classrooms: Learning and teaching for the digital world* (pp. 1–12). New York, NY: Routledge.

Mills, K. A., & Comber, B. (2013). Space, place, and power: The spatial turn in literacy research. In K. Hall, T. Cremin, B. Comber, & L. C. Moll (Eds.), *International handbook of research on children's literacy, learning, and culture* (pp. 412–423). Malden, MA: John Wiley & Sons.

Mills, K. A., & Comber, B. (2015). Rethinking the social constitution and politics of space. In J. Rowsell & K. Pahl (Eds.) *The Routledge handbook of literacy studies* (pp. 91–103). New York, NY: Routledge.

Moje, E. B. (2004). Powerful spaces: Tracing the out-of-school literacy spaces of Latino/a youth. In K. Leander & M. Sheehy (Eds.), *Spatializing literacy research and practice* (pp. 15–38). New York, NY: Peter Lang.

Moje, E. B., Ciechanowski, K. M., Kramer, K., Ellis, L., Carrillo, R., & Collazo, T. (2004). Working toward third space in content area literacy: An examination of everyday funds of knowledge and discourse. *Reading Research Quarterly*, *39*(1), 38–70.

Pahl, K., & Kelly, S. (2005). Family literacy as a third space between home and school: Some case studies of practice. *Literacy*, *39*(2), 91–96.

Pyles, D. G. (2016). Rural media literacy: Youth documentary videomaking as a rural literacy practice. *Journal of Research in Rural Education*, *31*(7), 1–15.

Ranker, J. (2008). Composing across multiple media: A case study of digital video production in a fifth grade classroom. *Written Communication*, *25*(2), 196–234.

Schafft, K. A. (2016). Rural education as rural development: Understanding the rural school–community well-being linkage in a 21st-century policy context. *Peabody Journal of Education*, *91*(2), 137–154.

Schultz, K. (2002). "Looking across space and time:" Reconceptualizing literacy learning in and out of school". *Research in the Teaching of English*, *36*(3), 356–390.

Siegel, M. (2006). Rereading the signs: Multimodal transformations in the field of literacy education. *Language Arts*, *84*(1), 65–77.

Skerrett, A., & Bomer, R. (2011). Borderzones in adolescents' literacy practices: Connecting out-of-school literacies to the reading curriculum. *Urban Education*, *46*(6), 1256–1279.

Smith, B. E. (2017). Composing across modes: A comparative analysis of adolescents' multimodal composing processes. *Learning, Media and Technology*, *42*(3), 259–278.

Somerville, M. (2013). Place, storylines and the social practices of literacy. *Literacy, 47*(1), 10–16.

Soja, E. W. (2010). *Seeking spatial justice.* Minneapolis, MN: University of Minnesota Press.

Strauss, A., & Corbin, J. M. (1990). Basics of qualitative research: Grounded theory procedures and techniques. Thousand Oaks, CA: SAGE

Street, B. V. (1984). *Literacy in theory and practice.* New York, NY: Cambridge University Press.

Szakolczai, A. (2009). Liminality and experience: Structuring transitory situations and transformative events. *International Political Anthropology, 2*(1), 141–172.

Tavares, M. (2015). Digital poetics and remix culture: From the artisanal image to the immaterial image. In E. Navas, O. Gallagher, & x. burrough (Eds.), *The Routledge companion to remix studies* (pp. 192–203). New York, NY: Routledge.

Theobald, P. (1997). *Teaching the commons: Place, pride, and the renewal of community.* Boulder, CO: Westview.

Thomassen, B. (2009). The uses and meanings of liminality. *International Political Anthropology, 2*(1), 5–27.

Tieken, M. C., & San Antonio, D. M. (2016). Rural aspirations, rural futures: From "problem" to possibility. *Peabody Journal of Education, 91*(2), 131–136.

Turner, V. W. (1967). Betwixt and between: The liminal period in rites de passage. In *The forest of symbols.* New York, NY: Cornell University Press.

van Gennep, A. (1960). The rites of passage (Monika B. Vizedom & Gabrielle L. Caffee, Trans.). Chicago, IL: University of Chicago Press.

Vasudevan, L. (2010). Education remix: New media, literacies, and the emerging digital geographies. *Digital Culture & Education, 2*(1), 62–82.

Vasudevan, L., Schultz, K., & Bateman, J. (2010). Rethinking composing in a digital age: Authoring literate identities through multimodal storytelling. *Written Communication, 27*(4), 442–468.

Wake, D. G. (2012). Exploring rural contexts with digital storytelling. *The Rural Educator, 33*(3), 23–36.

Wargo, J. M. (2015). Spatial stories with nomadic narrators: Affect, snapchat, and feeling embodiment in youth mobile composing. *Journal of Language and Literacy Education, 11*(1), 47–64.

Warner, J. (2016). Adolescents' dialogic composing with mobile phones. *Journal of Literacy Research, 48*(2), 164–191.

Wells, G. (1999). The zone of proximal development and its implications for learning and teaching. In *Dialogic inquiry: Towards a sociocultural practice and theory of education* (pp. 313–334). New York, NY: Cambridge University Press.

Wenger, E. (1998). *Communities of practice: learning, meaning, and identity.* New York, NY: Cambridge University Press.

Wenger, E., McDermott, R., & Snyder, W. M. (2002). *Cultivating communities of practice: A guide to managing knowledge.* Boston, MA: Harvard Business School Press.

CHAPTER 7

COMPLICATING PROBLEMATIC NARRATIVES ABOUT SOUTHERN PEOPLE AND PLACES THROUGH COUNTERSTORYTELLING

Sean P. Connors and Erin Daugherty
University of Arkansas

INTRODUCTION

In a popular TED Talk, author Chimamanda Adichie (2009) cautions against the dangers of a single story, a term that she uses to refer to stories that portray a population of people "as one thing, as only one thing, over and over again." As researchers who work at a large university that is located in the South, and more specifically, in the Arkansas Ozark Mountain region, we are aware of a single story that imagines people in this part of the United States as intolerant, backward-looking, and somewhat less well educated than people in other regions of the country. It is possible to understand the iconic figure of the hillbilly, a stereotype that is reproduced in popular culture texts such as the film *Winter's Bone* (Granik, 2010), the

Negotiating Place and Space Through Digital Literacies: Research and Practice, pp. 117–136

book *Hillbilly Elegy: A Memoir of a Family and Culture in Crisis* (Vance, 2016), and the Netflix series *Ozark*, as an embodiment of this single story. While we do not deny that the history of the South, and of the Arkansas Ozark region, includes a troubling legacy of bigotry, fundamentalism, and anti-intellectualism, our experiences as people who live and work in this part of the country allow us to recognize this narrative as grossly incomplete. In our work as educators, we have found that many of the college undergraduates we teach, particularly those who grew up in Southern contexts, are cognizant of (and bothered by) this same single story. As critical educators, we consequently endeavor to create opportunities for students to use digital technologies in the service of producing and disseminating counterstories (Delgado, 1989) about Southern people and places.

One way we seek to accomplish this is through our implementation of the Literacy in Ozark Lives research study, a community inquiry initiative that involves a collaborative partnership between the university where we work and a regional history museum, and which asks preservice English teachers in an introductory literacy studies course to become researchers of literacy in their local contexts. Specifically, the project tasks preservice teachers with collecting oral history interviews from people in the Arkansas Ozark region for the purpose of answering the research question: *What is the relationship between the place where someone lives and the value and purpose of literacy?* Additional research questions include: *What role do literacy sponsors play in the lives of people,* and *how do economic and political systems shape people's literacy?* Having analyzed the data they collect, the preservice teachers produce short digital videos in which they use the oral histories they collected to answer the aforementioned questions. In answering these questions, they are also tasked with using their data to complicate single stories (Adichie, 2009) about people, places, and literacy in the Arkansas Ozark region. To disseminate their findings, the preservice teachers screen their videos for a public audience at the Shiloh Museum of Ozark History, a nonprofit regional museum that is dedicated to documenting and preserving Ozark culture and history. Additionally, to share their work with a larger audience, the preservice teachers embed their videos on an interactive Google Map of the Arkansas Ozark region, which we in turn publish on the course website.

In this chapter, we examine the Literacy in Ozark Lives project for the purpose of demonstrating how it invites preservice teachers to reflect on the relationship between literacy and place, and how, by extension, it challenges them to contest single stories (Adichie, 2009) about people, places, and literacy in the South. To begin, we construct our conceptual framework, drawing on the work of scholars who have discussed the social and political dimensions of place and who theorize it as a site of contested meanings. Next, we introduce the concept of placemaking (McCann, 2002; Sánchez, 2011), a term that is traditionally understood to refer to the work of people who are involved in constructing the built environment of a place. Approaching the concept of placemaking from a critical perspective, however, we argue that it also constitutes a sociopolitical activity wherein people actively "affirm, interrogate, and construct knowledge about place" (Sánchez, 2011, p. 333). As we will argue, telling counterstories (Delgado, 1989) that challenge single stories (Adichie, 2009) about a place and the people who live there is also a form of placemaking. Having established our conceptual framework, we next offer a close reading of a digital video that one preservice teacher, Jordan (first name used with permission), produced for the Literacy in Ozark Lives research study. In doing so, we examine not only how she came to understand the relationship between literacy and place, but also how completing the project challenged her initial perceptions of the working-class community where she conducted her research. Set in the Ozark Mountains, this particular community has a reputation for racial intolerance, an unfortunate legacy that persists to the present day due to the presence of White supremacist groups in the area. Viewed from this perspective, the community appears to reproduce a single story (Adichie, 2009) that equates Southern people and places with racism. As Jordan learned, however, there are also people in the community who are invested in working for change. This understanding led Jordan to argue that "place should not be seen as one stereotyped story, but as an assemblage of thousands of equally important stories," an observation that we suggest approximates Massey's (2005) theorization of place as a product of intersecting stories that come into contact as people attempt to navigate their "throwntogetherness" (p. 141). To conclude our chapter, we address the implications of our work for educators. In doing so, we argue that when teachers tap into the knowledge that is available in their local communities, and when they create opportunities for students to produce and share counterstories (Delgado, 1989) about people and places they come to know, they lay a foundation for rich learning and identity work.

CONCEPTUAL FRAMEWORK

Place as Socially and Politically Constructed

In recent years, literacy researchers have theorized the relationship between power, literacy, and place (see, e.g., Comber, 2015; Green & Corbett, 2013; Leander & Sheehy, 2004). In doing so, they have expressed an interest in understanding place as something more than a built environment or coordinates on a map; instead, they argue that place is characterized by a social, as well as a material, dimension. Massey (2005), for example, theorizes place as the product of human relations, arguing that it is always under construction, and hence always undetermined (p. 7); within this purview, people from different backgrounds and with different life trajectories are understood to contribute to the production of place as they go about their everyday lives and navigate their "throwntogetherness" (p. 141). Important to our argument, Massey explicitly links stories to place when she conceptualizes "space as a simultaneity-of-stories so far" (p. 9). If this is the case, she argues, "then *places* are collections of those stories, articulations within the wider power-geometries of space" (p. 130, emphasis added). Like Massey, McDowell (1997) also establishes a relationship between story and place when he argues "places are both concrete and symbolic. They are literally and metaphorically made up: of buildings, field systems, roads and railways as well as of myths and legends, statues and ceremonies that link people to a place" (p. 2). In the context of these arguments, coming to "know" a place is understood to involve more than developing a sense of familiarity with its built environment. Rather, as Massey argues, it also entails "joining up with, somehow linking into, the collection of interwoven stories of which that place is made" (p. 119). In the context of our argument, we suggest that contributing one's own stories to this larger tapestry is also important.

If place is socially constructed, it also has a political dimension. Mills and Comber (2013), for example, argue that places are organized in ways that "constrain and enable social practices in the interests of maintaining and reproducing established hierarchies" (p. 417). Likewise, Green (2012) observes that because places are realized in social space as much as they are physical space, they are not "positioned equally, or distributed on a level plane, or playing field. Some places are more important socially, and also culturally and economically, than others; they may be bigger, or more prestigious, or powerful, and so on" (p. 379). Green's comments call attention to the fact that places do not exist in isolation; rather, they gain meaning as a result of their position relative to other places. As one example, the South, as a social construct, might be said to take on certain meanings when it is juxtaposed with other regions of the United States. For example, compared to the Northeast, the South may be imagined as both a site of conservatism and evangelicalism, as well as a place of rich tradition. In this way, the region serves as a canvas on which the nation projects both its faults (i.e., racism) and its desires (i.e., national pride) (Duck, 2006). Green's (2012) comments also call attention to the role power plays in constructing place, so that some places—for example, urban centers—are afforded more cultural prestige than others—say, rural areas. Nevertheless, as Mitchell (2000) argues, the possibility for "contestations over meanings, over borders and boundaries, over the ways we make sense of our worlds and the ways we live our lives" (p. 159)—in short, the practicing of cultural politics—enables people who are seemingly without power to contest and resist oppressive narratives about place.

Counterstorytelling as a Form of "Placemaking"

"To say that something is socially constructed," writes Cresswell (2004), "is to say that it is within human power to change it" (p. 30). So too, Mills and Comber (2013) argue that if places are socially produced, they "can [also] be contested, reimagined, and remade" (p. 412). In this chapter, we draw on the concept of placemaking, which is traditionally found in literature that pertains to the work of architects, developers, and others who contribute to the built environment of a place, but which some scholars suggest also encompasses people's interrogating "relationships between power and the production of place" (Sánchez, 2011, p. 333). Reminiscent of Massey's (2005) theorizing place as a product of people's negotiating their "throwntogetherness" (p. 141), Sánchez's (2011) discussion of placemaking is based on his conceptualizing place as "a site of conflict as various constituents struggle over its meaning and identity and wrestle over tensions of transformation and preservation" (p. 333). Moving placemaking outside the realm of professionals, Sánchez (2011) argues that it is "something we *all* do as we affirm, interrogate, and construct knowledge about place" (p. 333). In this chapter, we understand the sharing of stories and counterstories (Delgado, 1989) about place as a form of placemaking.

As educators, we are interested in understanding how teachers can engage students in placemaking by creating opportunities for them to produce and share counterstories, a type of story that, according to Delgado and Stefancic (1995), aspires "to cast doubt on the validity of accepted premises or myths, especially ones held by the majority" (p. 144). Like other kinds of stories, "counterstories can open new windows onto reality, showing us that there are possibilities for life other than the ones we live" (Delgado, 1989, p. 2414). In doing so, "[t]hey invite the reader [or viewer] to suspend judgment, listen for their point or message, and then decide what measure of truth they contain" (p. 2415).

Our understanding of counterstorytelling as a form of placemaking is foundational to our work with the Literacy in Ozark Lives research project, a community inquiry initiative that positions preservice teachers as researchers responsible for collecting, and curating, other people's stories about literacy. The project also invites students to practice counterstorytelling by using the stories they collect to complicate single stories (Adichie, 2009) about people, places, and literacy in the Arkansas Ozark region. To accomplish these tasks, we ask the preservice teachers to demonstrate their learning by producing digital videos, which we later embed in a Google Map and publish online. Our decision to ask students to produce digital videos, and hence to gain experience working with different digital tools, is motivated by several factors. First, in the context of the literacy studies course we teach, our study of literacy is framed by various sociocultural perspectives (Perry, 2012) influenced by Vygotsky's (1978) work, with the result that we acknowledge literacy as a social practice and understand people as practicing multiple literacies. Our understanding of literacy is also informed by scholarship on multimodality and social semiotics (e.g., Kress & Van Leeuwen, 2001; New London Group, 1997; Van Leeuwen, 2005), so that we understand people as communicating through a range of modes, one of which is print. In the context of the course, we consequently aspire to create opportunities for students to gain experience with different forms of composing, and hence with different literacies, one of which is digital literacy.

At the same time, we also understand digital videos as a potentially potent form of storytelling. Delgado (1989) argues that counterstories appeal to an audience's emotions, and as such, have the potential to "quicken and engage conscience" and "stir imagination in ways in which more conventional discourse cannot" (p. 2415). We suggest that this effect is heightened in the case of digital videos, which appeal to multiple senses simultaneously by commingling still images, video footage, and music with spoken narration. In the two iterations of the Literacy in Ozark Lives research project to date, it has not been uncommon for people whose lives have served as the focus of students' videos to express emotion upon viewing them. On a final note, the ability to publish student work online in a digital format permits us to disseminate it more widely, and hence to create a more authentic audience for student writers.

In the next section, we introduce the Literacy in Ozark Lives research project in more detail, and present the methodology preservice teachers employ to conduct their individual research studies. Having done so, we offer a close reading of a digital video that one preservice teacher produced for the purpose of examining how she came to conceptualize the relationship between literacy and place, and how she used her video to respond to a single story about the community in which she conducted her research.

THE LITERACY IN OZARK LIVES RESEARCH PROJECT

Influenced by scholarship on critical pedagogy and place-conscious pedagogy (Comber, 2015), the Literacy in Ozark Lives research project is a whole class, IRB-approved research study that asks preservice teachers taking an introductory literacy studies course to become researchers of literacy in their local communities. The design of the project is influenced by Bruce's (2014) community inquiry cycle (see Figure 7.2). The project begins with preservice teachers *asking* a series of research questions, the central one being: *What is the relationship between the place where someone lives and the value and purpose of literacy?* An additional subset of research questions includes: *What role do literacy sponsors play in the lives of people?* And, *how do economic and political systems shape people's literacy?* As discussed above, throughout the course, the preservice teachers' study of literacy is framed by different sociocultural perspectives (Perry, 2012), specifically the New Literacy Studies, which theorizes literacy as a social practice (e.g., Street, 1984), and scholarship on multimodality and social semiotics (e.g., Kress & Van Leeuwen, 2001; New London Group, 1997; Van Leeuwen, 2005), which argues that the ability to communicate effectively in the 21st century necessitates using multiple modes of representation, one of which is print. As a result, within the context of the Literacy in Ozark Lives research project, literacy is defined broadly, and understood to include new literacies (e.g., blogging; game playing; social media; etc.) as well as old literacy (reading and writing print).

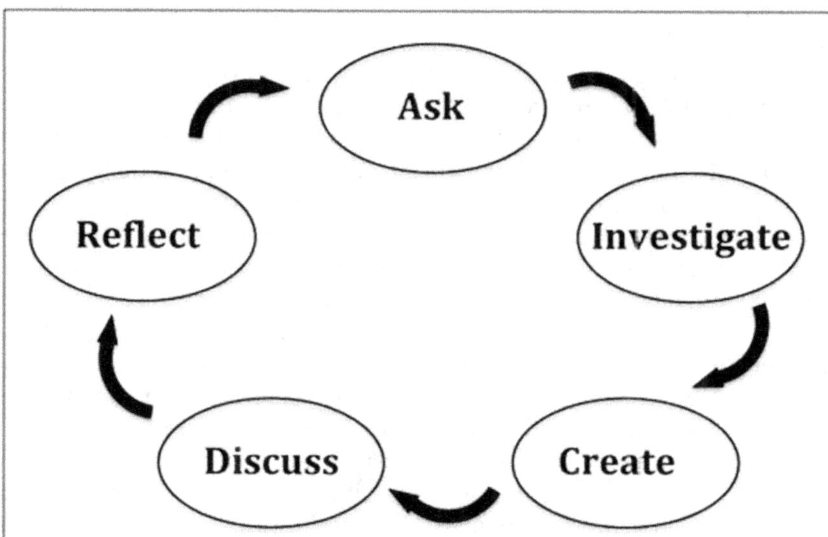

Figure 7.1. The community inquiry cycle.

To *investigate* the aforementioned research questions, the preservice teachers are assigned to collect oral histories about literacy from residents of different counties in the Arkansas Ozark region, an area that spans the northern portion of the state. To recruit participants for the study, we have partnered with the Shiloh Museum of Ozark History, a non-profit regional museum that is dedicated to documenting and preserving the culture and history of the Arkansas Ozarks. Susan Young, the museum's outreach coordinator, has proven to be a valuable asset, as she conducts oral history research in her work at the museum, and is able to tap into its extensive network to identify people who are willing to share their literacy narratives with our students. In spring 2017, the most recent iteration of the project, and the one that serves as the basis for our discussion, we interviewed a total of 20 people. This included college students and senior citizens; college-educated professionals and people from working class backgrounds; and people who traced their roots in the Arkansas Ozarks through several generations and others who had relocated to the area from elsewhere in the United States. The latter group included immigrants whose families had traveled to the region in search of work. The participant pool was also characterized by racial and ethnic diversity, as it included people who identified as European American, African American, and Latino/a. This layering of diversity was intentional: we hoped to help the preservice teachers with whom we worked complicate a single story (Adichie, 2009) that regards people in the Arkansas Ozarks as predominantly White and working class.

Prior to their collecting data for the study, Susan Young visited our class and talked with the preservice teachers about the work involved in conducting oral history research. Specifically, she offered them advice on how to prepare for an interview, how to introduce questions designed to put an interviewee at ease, how to ask follow-up questions to probe points of interest in greater depth, and how to prompt less gregarious informants to share stories and anecdotes. Susan also talked with the students about the ethics of conducting oral history research, and the importance of respecting an interviewee's right not to share information. Having reviewed the interview protocol we created for the study, we set aside time in class for the preservice teachers to pilot it by interviewing each other for practice. Finally, we assigned each of them an interviewee and shared that person's contact information with them. Interviews for the research study took place in a range of settings, including public libraries, coffee shops, an adult English language learning class, and (in a few instances) people's homes. In cases where the ability to conduct interviews entailed traveling long distances, we traveled together in a university van. The interview protocol we used for the research study consisted of 29 questions that examined the following territories: people's memories of literacy in their childhood homes and at school; the ends toward which they put literacy in their work lives; and the ends toward which they put literacy in their personal lives. The interviews were audio-recorded and, on average, lasted approximately one hour. Having collected their data, the preservice teachers transcribed their interviews in their entirety using an agreed upon set of conventions that were established in class. Both the audio-recordings and the transcripts of their interviews were later archived at the Shiloh Museum of Ozark History.

Having transcribed their interviews, the preservice teachers next analyzed their data using structural coding, a process that involved their applying a "conceptual phrase representing a topic of inquiry to a segment of data that relates to a specific question used to frame [an] interview" (Saldaña, 2013, p. 66). Prior to releasing them to code their data independently, we first practiced coding a transcript of an interview that one of us (the lead author) had conducted. To begin, we drew on the research questions that guided the study to establish sensitizing concepts (Charmaz, 2006) we could apply to the data during the initial phase of coding. These included: "literacy," "literacy sponsors," "economic systems," "political systems," "value," "purpose," and "place." As we applied these codes to the data, we developed additional codes that were structured around them. By searching for relationships between codes and placing them into categories, the preservice teachers eventually identified recurring themes, which represented their findings.

To present their findings, the preservice teachers *created* digital videos in which they used the oral histories they collected to answer the research questions that guided the study. In doing so, they identified literacy sponsors (Brandt, 2001), local as well as distant, who appeared to have supported or constrained their interviewees' literacy, and economic or political conditions that impacted their literacy. Additionally, the preservice teachers used their data as the basis for a counterstory (Delgado, 1989) about literacy, people, and places in the Arkansas Ozark region. Prior to producing their videos, the preservice teachers brought their scripts to class and exchanged them with at least three other people during a peer response/editing activity. As they responded to each other's work, they *discussed* their interpretations of their data and the strengths and limitations of their scripts, which promoted *reflection*. They also offered recommendations about how their scripts could be improved. In some cases, this led them to identify additional questions they wanted to ask their interviewees, resulting in their conducting follow-up interviews via e-mail or telephone. Discussion was an integral part of their experience presenting their work at the Shiloh Museum as well. The latter event took the form of a gallery walk, at which time guests moved between computer stations in order to watch the preservice teachers' videos. Throughout the evening, the preservice teachers fielded questions from guests, which prompted still further *reflection*. Finally, to conclude the project, we embedded their videos in an interactive Google Map of the Arkansas Ozark region, which we published on the class website.

To illustrate the learning that occurs when educators position students as researchers of literacy in their local communities, we next offer a close reading of one student's video. While we try to account for the text's multimodal design in our discussion, we encourage readers to view the video online at http://bit.ly/2CTM1Y6.

"LITERACY'S WAY FORWARD"

At the time she completed the Literacy in Ozark Lives research project, Jordan was a junior in college. Bright, self-motivated, and articulate, she aspired to teach secondary English, and she took the introductory literacy studies course we have described to satisfy a prerequisite for admission to the graduate teacher education program at the university she attended. Having grown up in a community that abuts an urban area in the central part of the state, Jordan's familiarity with the Arkansas Ozark region was largely limited to the area where she attended school. Asked in an interview that occurred prior to her completing the project whether she was familiar with stereotypes about people in the Arkansas Ozark region, she, like the majority of her classmates, suggested that people are perceived as "less well educated" and "a little backwards." Significantly, she also shared her belief that people in other parts of the United States were likely to describe people from the state of Arkansas in a similar way.

For the Literacy in Ozark Lives research project, Jordan was assigned to interview John Henderson, a resident of Harrison, Arkansas. A small, predominantly White working-class community with a population of just over 13,000, Harrison is located approximately 76 miles northeast of the university Jordan attended. Beginning with a pair of race riots in 1905 and 1909, and extending through the present day, the city has historically been saddled with a reputation for intolerance. A 2017 article in *Intelligence Report,* a publication of the Southern Poverty Law Center, identified hate groups that are known to operate in the area that surrounds Harrison, and in recent years, the placement of billboards alongside public roadways that have promoted White supremacist ideology has drawn unwanted attention to the community and sparked protests. While she had not previously traveled to this part of the state, Jordan was familiar with Harrison's reputation for racial intolerance. In the same interview referred to above, she volunteered that she had heard the city was "the headquarters of the KKK or something." In this way, the city of Harrison appears to reproduce a single story (Adichie, 2009) about prejudice and intolerance in the South. This is not the entirety of Harrison's story, however.

Chimamanda Adichie (2009) argues, "The problem with stereotypes is not that they are untrue, but that they are incomplete. They make one story become the only story." So too, in the case of Harrison, some local residents are working to change the city's negative image. An article in a 2014 issue of the Southern Poverty Law Center's *Intelligence Report*, for example, described how some city leaders and residents had created a Community Task Force on Race Relations to "counter the city's racist reputation and create a more racially welcoming present and future." In the same article, the Task Force's mission is described as follows: "Reconciling the past. Recognizing the present. Reaching for the future." In 2016, the Task Force received the Dream Keeper Award, which is "presented by the state's Martin Luther King, Jr. Commission for notable efforts to improve race relations, particularly among young people" (Schulte, 2017). Interestingly, although she was unacquainted with either the Task Force or its mission, Jordan's conversation with Henderson, who teaches social studies at a local middle school in Harrison, led her to view him as a person who was also committed to working for the betterment of his community.

Jordan's digital video, which is entitled "Literacy's Way Forward," is approximately seven minutes long and combines still images, video footage, and background music with spoken narration to share Henderson's literacy narrative and consider what it potentially suggests about the nature of the relationship between literacy and place. This relationship is at the center of Jordan's concern, a fact she communicates in the video's opening moments. As footage of a rotating earth as viewed from space gives way to footage of a cityscape, she narrates, "To understand an individual's value of literacy in relation to their place, we must first look at place differently." Suggesting that "place is much more than coordinates on a map," she goes on to argue that it is "socially constructed by sponsors who influence literacy's value, and the economic and political forces that shape its path." As a camera pans an Ozark waterfall, Jordan links her discussion of literacy and place to the concept of the single story (Adichie, 2009). In doing so, she shares a definition of place that strikes us as approximating Massey's (2005) theorization of place as a "simultaneity of stories so far" (p. 9), though we assume that she was unfamiliar with the latter's work. Specifically, Jordan explains, "For the people who call the Ozark region home, they understand all too well how place should not be seen as one stereotyped story, but as an assemblage of thousands of equally important stories."

Having established this point, Jordan introduces the subject of her video, John Henderson, a middle-aged, White male who lives and teaches in Harrison, Arkansas. Born in Phoenix, Arizona in 1957, Henderson grew up in what appears to have been a literacy-rich environment. In his interview with Jordan, he recalled "grandparents who wrote letters and read detective magazines; a grandfather who loved history and read old westerns; his mother, who enjoyed reading; and a sister who wrote letters to pen pals across the world." In addition to modeling different literacy practices, these people also sponsored Henderson's literacy by providing him with access to different resources, such as "books, comics to trade with friends, records, and board games." Henderson recalled a grandmother who gifted him a book about Kennedy's assassination for Christmas one year, sparking his love of nonfiction. Later, when he attended school, he encountered other literacy sponsors, including a friend with whom he competed to see who could read the most biographies. As Brandt (2001) explains, literacy sponsors can constrain as well as support a person's literacy, and this was the case for Henderson, who explained that the library at a school he attended was unable to purchase new books due to limited resources. As a result, once he had finished reading the school's collection of biographies, he was forced to "move on to books he was less interested in," resulting in his reading less often. An encounter with a fifth-grade teacher who belonged to a local chapter of the John Birch Society, a conservative group that gained influence in the 1960s, also appears to have influenced Henderson's attitude toward school. As an image of a child with a teardrop falling from his eye appears on screen, Jordan explains that this particular teacher often shared his political views in class, and once even insisted that a young Henderson attend a Birch Society chapter meeting. This experience tainted Henderson's view of school, and it was not until the following year, when he worked with a teacher who encouraged student confidence, that his interest in school returned.

In her video, Jordan suggests that self-confidence and self-sufficiency were qualities that Henderson's parents valued in the home, and which he later embraced in his life. Henderson recalled his father embarking on a business venture that involved his building a roller skating rink that he owned and operated as a small business. In the absence of any formal training, his father "read books on construction and secured financing in tandem with a few clever tricks." John appears to have acquired his father's business acumen, as he recalled having used his weekly allowance to purchase comic books (a literacy resource he valued) one at a time to avoid meeting the minimum amount required to pay a sales tax. Later, as an adult, Henderson embarked on his own business ventures. As a picture of a video game console gives way to an image of an arcade, Jordan explains that Henderson "dropped out of college to launch a successful video game venture." Later, after arcades grew in popularity, he tried his hand at real estate; still later, he dabbled in trading commodities. Each of these experiences resulted in Henderson acquiring new literacies, thereby expanding his repertoire of literacy practices.

The influence of these collective experiences was felt years later when Henderson followed his parents to Harrison, Arkansas, where they purchased a farm. Having learned that he was unable to work on the farm due to severe allergies, Henderson's interest in history, which he had cultivated reading biographies and nonfiction as a child, led him to develop an interest in teaching. In the absence of a 4-year college that offered a teacher licensure program, and exemplifying the same spirit of self-sufficiency his father had modeled, Henderson completed an online bachelor's degree. Later, he took advantage of a nontraditional teacher licensure program that the state department of education had created to fill teaching positions in high-need schools. Eventually, Henderson was hired to teach social studies at the lone middle school in Harrison, where he spearheaded the development of an EAST (Environmental and Spatial Technology) program. Guided by tenets of progressive education, the EAST initiative is a project-based, service-learning program that aims to provide elementary and secondary students with opportunities to use advanced technologies in the service of addressing authentic problems in their local communities. Henderson's involvement with the EAST program presumably helped him to expand his repertoire of literacies still further. Likewise, as Jordan explains, literacy practices he had cultivated outside of school—for example, reading on an e-reader and consuming digital content on websites such as Audible—began to influence his work in the classroom, as he reported searching for content "that might impact his students, making something he enjoys have a larger purpose." In this way, as Jordan suggests, Henderson has become a sponsor of other people's literacy.

So what did Jordan learn about the relationship between literacy and place as a result of interviewing Henderson? In the final segment of her video, she turns to this question, suggesting that the time and place where a person lives can set the terms and conditions for his or her literacy. As a child growing up in the 1960s, for example, Henderson's literacy practices revolved largely around print, and included his reading nonfiction, biographies, and comic books. Granted, he also recalled playing board games, listening to music, and watching television, but new media were still in their nascent years when he was a child. Years later, after technological advancements made possible the production of video games and other kinds of digital texts, and as Henderson gained experience using technology in the context of the EAST program he had helped develop, his literacy repertoire expanded to include digital literacies, as evidenced by his learning to use devices such as computers, software, and e-readers, and his consuming digital content such as audiobooks and podcasts in his life outside of school.

In Henderson's story, one sees how literacy sponsors (Brandt, 2001) in his local community both supported and constrained his literacy. He credited a book that was given to him by a grandmother with sparking his life-long love of nonfiction, an interest that was further cemented when he participated in friendly reading competitions with a classmate at school.

At home, his father modeled literacy as a form of self-directed learning, reading and writing in order to learn how to build a roller skating rink and run his own small business. Later, Henderson exemplified a similar spirit of self-sufficiency, learning new literacies as he ran his own small business, dabbled in real estate, and traded commodities before finally finding work as a middle school social studies teacher. In this way, as Jordan explains, Henderson's literacy narrative suggests that a person's literacy is "the product of the many interactions that occur over the span of their lifetime." An aspiring educator herself, Jordan's interview with Henderson prompted her to consider how what she had learned from interviewing him might one day inform her own interactions with students. She concluded: "Understanding the effect that place has on a student's literacy, teachers should transform their approach working with students, as each is unique, coming from different places that are actively shaping their literacy."

Jordan was especially impressed with Henderson's contributions to his school's EAST program, which provided students with opportunities to learn different technologies in the service of addressing problems in their local community. Indeed, she came to understand Henderson's work as a form of activism, arguing toward the end of her video: "Every individual can identify improvements to be made in their community and make a difference. John's story proves this by his advocacy despite pushback to implement the EAST program, which focuses on how technology can solve problems in the community." As someone interested in teaching, Jordan's experience interviewing Henderson helped her to appreciate the value of "encouraging students to recognize the impact that their own story has, and how it can shape the place in which they live." Despite preconceptions she had held about the community of Harrison prior to traveling there to interview Henderson, Jordan brought her video to a close by offering a counterstory about this Ozark community. Returning to the same footage of a rotating earth that opened her video, thereby signaling that her argument has come full circle, she revisits her understanding of place as a compilation of stories. "Due to the misplaced stigma that plagues the city, upon hearing Harrison, Arkansas one may not think of education as a priority," Jordan states. "But Harrison, Arkansas is not one story. It is John's story, and thousands of other stories, each bringing rich literacies to form the place they call home."

Asked in an interview that occurred not long after the course had ended why she had chosen not to name the "stigma" she alluded to at the conclusion of her video as racism, Jordan explained that she was hesitant to do so due to her concern that it would reinforce the very stereotype she had sought to complicate in her video. In her opinion, associating Harrison with a single story (Adichie, 2009) of racism in a video she knew would be seen by a larger audience risked perpetuating a deficit view of the community that already plagued it. Moreover, she suggested that to do so would be to overlook the efforts of more progressive-minded people in the community who, like Henderson, were invested in bettering their community. Having paused to collect her thoughts, and without any prompting, Jordan offered the following rationale for her decision to title her video in the way she did:

> That's actually kind of why I named my video *Literacy's Way Forward*, because [Mr. Henderson's] so forward thinking and he is all about the future and teaching students that are learning literacy now to learn to create a better future.... So yeah, I guess just being presented with someone who didn't think that way, who saw the potential, who understands that stigma but who is looking toward the future and finding a way to change it, that's what I wanted to focus on.

We would have preferred that Jordan explicitly name the problem she sought to critique in her video as racism. At the same time, in retrospect, we also appreciate that the nature of the assignment placed her in a difficult position: knowing that she was expected to share her video with a public audience that potentially included residents of the community where she had conducted her oral history research, we suspect that Jordan may have been hesitant to take a strong political stance. We regard this as a limitation on our part as instructors, however, as we could (and should) have done more to support her as she sought to navigate the situation in which she found herself. At a minimum, we could have encouraged Jordan to articulate her vision for her video similar to the way she did in the excerpt above, as this would have allowed her to name the problem of racism while still celebrating the people in the community of Harrison who are committed to addressing it. Nevertheless, we also argue that in electing to understand the city of Harrison as a collection of diverse, sometimes conflicting, stories that come into contact as its residents navigate their "throwntogetherness" (Massey, 2005), Jordan is in the process of developing a more nuanced, more complex understanding of this Ozark community.

IMPLICATIONS FOR EDUCATORS

Having discussed stereotypes of the Australian Outback that are commonly found in popular culture texts, and which they suggest have come to dominate Australian consciousness, Reid et al. (2010) argue that "these are representations. They are not *necessarily* 'truth,' and they are most certainly not the whole truth" (p. 267, emphasis in original). The same can be said of single stories (Adichie, 2009) about people, places, and literacy in the U.S. South. When educators design instruction that invites students to use digital technologies in the service of telling counterstories about their communities, a practice that we have argued constitutes a form of placemaking (Sánchez, 2011), they encourage students to understand themselves as agentive people capable of responding to narratives they recognize as problematic. This work is especially generative for beginning teachers, who may end up teaching in communities that do not resemble the communities where they grew up. In talking with preservice teachers who grew up in urban or suburban contexts, for example, we have noted a tendency for some of them to reproduce a single story (Adichie, 2009) that regards rural communities in deficit terms—that is, as places of lack or want. The opportunity to talk with people from rural communities, and to hear their stories, may help preservice teachers to appreciate the resources and assets that are available to people in those communities. In the same way, talking with people from urban neighborhoods whose schools are deemed "underperforming" may foster preservice teachers' appreciation for the rich literacies that people embrace in their lives.

Encouraging preservice teachers to talk with other people about their literacy practices may also support their moving beyond understanding literacy as a set of autonomous skills. As they develop a sense of appreciation for the many literacies that people employ in their everyday lives, and the different purposes toward which they put them, their understanding of literacy may come to resemble Street's (1984) ideological model, which acknowledges that literacy, far from a mere technical skill-set, is instead embedded in social practices that shape how people use, understand, and value it. From this perspective, literacy "is always contested, both its meanings and its practices, hence particular versions of it are always 'ideological,' they are always rooted in a particular world-view and a desire for that view of literacy to dominate and to marginalise others" (Street, 2006, p. 2). Students intuitively seemed to grasp this point as a result of their having completed the Literacy in Ozark Lives research project. As one student remarked during an interview that occurred at the project's conclusion: "We always say that literacy is the same for everybody, but it's not. It's not just reading and writing; it's how people use reading and writing, their purposes for it and the forms of communication that we use." Other students observed that when schools privilege a narrow range of contexts and purposes for using literacy, and when they limit their definition of literacy to print, they risk marginalizing the diverse practices and purposes that students acquire for using different literacies as they participate in the daily routines of their home and local communities.

Positioning preservice teachers as researchers of literacy in their local communities may also facilitate important identity work. Literacy theorists have argued that learners "try on" new identities as they experiment with new Discourses, a process that involves their "learning how to act and talk so as to take on a particular role that others will recognize" (Gee, 1989,

p. 18). In the case of the Literacy in Ozark Lives research project, preservice teachers experimented with performing the role of researcher as they practiced using an interview protocol, transcribed and coded data, and drafted conceptual memos. Moreover, at the project's conclusion, they presented their work to an audience at the Shiloh Museum of Ozark History, at which time they fielded questions about their research and their videos. Each of these experiences contributed to their gaining insight into what it means to read, write, and talk like a researcher. We also argue that these experiences support Comber's (2015) assertion that students stand to "build a positive sense of their academic identities as they engage with and inquire into the everyday world" (pp. 66–67).

Burke and Greene (2015) argue that young people "learn best when they personally connect to and engage with a given subject like place" (p. 390). Indeed, we have found that positioning students as researchers of their local communities elicits a high level of engagement. As they came to see themselves as curators of other people's stories, a point we emphasized in class, a number of the preservice teachers we worked with expressed feeling a sense of personal responsibility for those stories. In class meetings and post-project interviews, the vast majority of the preservice teachers we spoke with recalled having experienced a desire to honor the stories their interviewees had shared with them. This was due in no small part to their knowledge that the people they interviewed would see their videos, either by accessing the interactive Google Map we created or by attending the public exhibition of their work. In this sense, the opportunity to share their work with an authentic audience, a distinct affordance of digital composing, appeared to change how the preservice teachers approached their schoolwork. As one student explained,

> There's a sense of pride that you get from this project. I'm writing an essay later tonight for this test, and like I'm just getting it done so that I can get to summer break, but that's not what [the Literacy in Ozark Lives] project was, 'cause I know the data I'm analyzing is going to the [Shiloh] museum and I know that my video is going to be seen by the person I interviewed.

Finally, and arguably most importantly, we propose that students benefit when they are given opportunities to share stories and counterstories about people and places they have come to know. According to Ohler (2013), "[Stories] make order out of what would otherwise be the ongoing chaos of life and help each of us create a sense of personal identity in relation to our communities and the world in which we live" (p. 9). In transposing the oral histories they collected into digital stories, the preservice teachers had no alternative but to impose a narrative structure on them. This necessitated their engaging in the kinds of higher-order thinking processes that Robin (2008) suggests digital storytelling encourages, including "synthesizing, analyzing, evaluating, and presenting information" (p. 225). In addition to analyzing the oral histories they collected, the preservice teachers also had to make difficult decisions about which aspects of a person's story were worth sharing in their videos, and which were less relevant in light of their purpose, an undertaking that involves both synthesis and evaluation. While much of this work occurred independently, they were also asked to share drafts of their scripts for their videos with classmates, who critiqued the extent to which they had satisfactorily used the data they collected to persuasively address the specified research questions.

Massey (2005) writes, "There can be no assumption of pre-given coherence, or of community or collective identity. Rather the throwntogetherness of place demands negotiation" (p. 141). At a time when our society is caught in the grips of extreme ideological polarization, and when single stories (Adichie, 2009) about groups of people are carelessly bandied about by politicians and media pundits, our ongoing work with the Literacy in Ozark Lives research project is suggestive of the value involved in creating opportunities for preservice teachers to navigate their "throwntogetherness" (Massey, 2005) in relation to others. In doing so, they may come to appreciate the communities where they teach as constellations of diverse, yet equally important, stories, all of which are worth knowing and sharing.

REFERENCES

Adichie, C. (2009). *The danger of a single story*. Retrieved from http://www.ted.com/talks/chimamanda_adichie_the_danger_of_a_single_story.html

Brandt, D. (2001). *Literacy in American lives*. New York, NY: Cambridge University Press.

Bruce, B. C. (2014). Community inquiry. In B. C. Bruce, A. P. Bishop, & N. R. Budhathoki (Eds.), *Youth community inquiry: New media for community and personal growth* (pp. 1–13). New York, NY: Peter Lang.

Burke, K., & Greene, S. (2015). Participatory action research, youth voices and civic engagement. *Language Arts, 92*(6), 387–400.

Charmaz, K. (2006). *Constructing grounded theory: A practical guide through qualitative analysis*. Thousand Oaks, CA: SAGE.

Comber, B. (2015). *Literacy, place, and pedagogies of possibility*. New York, NY: Routledge.

Cresswell, T. (2004). *Place: A short introduction*. Malden, MA: Blackwell.

Delgado, R. (1989). Storytelling for oppositionists and others: A plea for narrative. *Michigan Law Review, 87*(8), 2411–2441.

Delgado, R., & Stefancic, J. (1995). *Critical race theory: The cutting edge* (2nd ed.). Philadelphia, PA: Temple University Press.

Duck, L. A. (2006). *The nation's region: Southern modernism, segregation, and U.S. nationalism*. Athens, GA: The University of Georgia Press.

Gee, J. P. (1989). What is literacy? *Journal of Education, 171*(1), 18–25.

Granik, D. (Director). (2010). *Winter's bone* [Motion Picture]. USA: Anonymous Content & Winter's Bone Productions.

Green, B. (2012). Literacy, place and the digital world. *Language and Education, 26*(4), 377–382.

Green, B., & Corbett, M. (Eds). (2013). *Rethinking rural literacies: Transnational perspectives.* New York, NY: Palgrave Macmillan.

Kress, G., & Van Leeuwen, T. (2001). *Multimodal discourse: The modes and media of contemporary communication.* London, England: Arnold.

Leander, K. M., & Sheehy, M. (Eds.). (2004). *Spatializing literacy research and practice.* New York, NY: Peter Lang.

Massey, D. (2005). *For space.* London, England: SAGE.

McCann, E. J. (2002). The cultural politics of local economic development: Meaning-making, place-making, and the urban policy process. *Geoforum, 33*, 385–398.

McDowell, L. (1997). Introduction: Rethinking place. In L. McDowell (Ed.), *Undoing place?: A geographical reader* (pp. 2–12). London, England: Arnold.

Mills, K. A. & Comber, B. (2013). Space, place and power: The spatial turn in literacy research. In K. Hall, T. Cremin, B. Comber, & L. Moll (Eds.), *International handbook of research in children's literacy, learning and culture* (pp. 412–423). London, England: Wiley-Blackwell.

Mitchell, D. (2000). *Cultural geography: A critical introduction.* Malden, MA: Blackwell.

New London Group. (1997). A pedagogy of multiliteracies: Designing social futures. *Harvard Educational Review, 66*(1), 60–92.

Ohler, J. B. (2013). *Digital storytelling in the classroom: New media pathways to literacy, learning, and creativity* (2nd ed.). Thousand Oaks, CA: Corwin.

Perry, K. (2012). What is literacy? A critical overview of sociocultural perspectives. *Journal of Language & Literacy Education, 8*(1), 50–71.

Reid, J., Green, B., Cooper, M., Hastings, W., Lock, G., & White, S. (2010). Regenerating rural social space? Teacher education for rural-regional sustainability. *Australian Journal of Education, 54*(3), 262–276.

Robin, B. R. (2008). Digital storytelling: A powerful tool for the 21st century classroom. *Theory Into Practice, 47*, 220–228.

Sánchez, L. (2011). Building on young children's cultural histories through placemaking in the classroom. *Contemporary Issues in Early Childhood, 12*(4), 332–342.

Saldaña, J. (2013). *The coding manual for qualitative researchers* (2nd ed.) Thousand Oaks, CA: SAGE.

Schulte, B. (2017). The alt-right of the Ozarks. *Slate.* Retrieved from http://www.slate.com/articles/news_and_politics/politics/2017/04/what_harrison_arkansas_fight_with_the_kkk_says_about_the_alt_right.html

Southern Poverty Law Center. (2014). Ghosts of Harrison. *Intelligence Report.* Retrieved from https://www.splcenter.org/fighting-hate/intelligence-report/2014/ghosts-harrison

Southern Poverty Law Center. (2017). Active hate groups. *Intelligence Report.* Retrieved from https://www.splcenter.org/fighting-hate/intelligence-report/2017/active-hate-groups-2016

Street, B. V. (1984). *Literacy in theory and practice*. Cambridge, England: Cambridge University Press.

Street, B. V. (2006). Autonomous and ideological models of literacy: Approaches from New Literacy Studies. *Media Anthropology Network*. Retrieved from http://www.philbu.net/media-anthropology/street_newliteracy.pdf

Vance, J. D. (2016). *Hillbilly elegy: A memoir of a family and culture in crisis.* New York, NY: HarperCollins.

Van Leeuwen, T. (2005). *Introducing social semiotics*. London, England: Routledge.

Vygotsky, L. S. (1978). *Mind in society: The development of higher psychological processes*. Cambridge, MA: Harvard University Press.

CHAPTER 8

INDIGENOUS ACTIVISM IN THE DIGITAL SPHERE

A Transrhetorical Analysis of the "Save Longhorn Mountain" Facebook Page

Jordan Paige Woodward
University of Oklahoma

Longhorn Mountain is a sacred site to the Kiowa people. Located near Carnegie, Oklahoma this mountain is visited by Kiowas for spiritual and cultural practices; it is also the only place Kiowas say they can harvest the unique flat leaf cedar that is used ceremonially for protection, healing, and praying. Flat leaf cedar is believed by Kiowas to be a gift from God. In 2013, this geosacred tribal site was threatened after Stewart Stone, a rock crushing company based in Cushing, Oklahoma, stated intentions to mine the western side of the mountain for gravel. As mining the mountain would destroy a site of spiritual and cultural significance to Kiowas, contribute to the destruction of natural landscapes in the area, and potentially lead to negative health ramifications for residents of the area, Kiowas began a movement to save the mountain. This movement has been predominantly carried out through the use of various digital media platforms, one of

Negotiating Place and Space Through Digital Literacies: Research and Practice, pp. 137–153

which is the Save Longhorn Mountain (SLM) facebook. The SLM facebook is a transrhetorical site where Kiowas employ rhetorical strategies, such as appeals to the intersections of geosacrality to cultural identity and cross-cultural alliance building, to protect Longhorn Mountain.

Longhorn is geosacred in that Kiowa, along with Comanche, Kiowa-Apache, and other Plains tribes visit the mountain for vision quests, in times of death and illness, to collect cedar, to fast, and to pray (Ofana 2013). William C. Meadows (2008) describes a geosacred place in *Kiowa Ethnogeography* as a geographical formation or landscape which holds religious or spiritual significance to a people. In geosacred spaces, the land and religious/spiritual connection to it are intertwined. The landscape provides a sanctuary for religious practice while, simultaneously, belief and ritual practices elevate the physical geography into a sacred space. Phil "Joe Fish" Dupoint, a tribal historian at the Kiowa Tribal Museum, stated in an interview with *State Impact OK* (2013), "The old people used to come here [to Longhorn Mountain], and they used to pray. God guided the Kiowas here. This particular mountain here, God gave it to them. And what grows here, God gave it to them." Dupoint's interview describes both the embodied and metaphysical connection Kiowas have to Longhorn. Not only is the cedar seen as a divine gift from God, but Kiowas also physically use their bodies to go to the mountain to collect the cedar, which is then given back as offering in prayer and ceremony. This cyclicality blurs the distinction between the physical and the spiritual. Dupoint's interview was shared on the SLM facebook and illustrates Kiowa rhetorics of geosacrality regarding Longhorn.

Longhorn's geosacrality is the central argument employed on the SLM facebook to protect the mountain from mining, around which other arguments relating to environment, historical preservation, and health circle. As the argument of Longhorn's geosacrality is conveyed via social media, it occurs across physical and digital spaces as well as across time. From this, I argue the SLM facebook is a transrhetorical site in which there is a "movement of meaning across space and time" and "where meaning encounters meaning, concepts change, and rhetorics adapt for multiple audiences" (Jackson, 2016, pp. 9–10). Rachel Jackson (2016) explains that she uses *transrhetorical* in her dissertation, *Red State Reclaimed: The Transrhetorical Recovery of Resistance in Oklahoma*" to characterize the movement of rhetorics themselves, often by individuals acting as rhetorical agents, across multiple location categories—historical, spatial, temporal, cultural, local, regional, national, global, as well as across disciplines" (p. 11). The SLM facebook then, is a site through which Kiowa rhetorical practices from various locations and times travel through and interact with other rhetorics and rhetorical agents.

Jackson (2016) outlines three primary ways transrhetorical sites, and specifically Kiowa transrhetorical sites, function: (1) Kiowa transrhetorical sites and Kiowa rhetorical strategies "work across time. They bridge current Kiowa cultural activist practices with historic practices.... This positions present-day activists as part of a rhetorical continuance of cultural resistance" (p. 177); (2) "they move cultural literacy" from inside a small Kiowa space, "to the Kiowa community more broadly, then beyond to non-Kiowa spaces" (p. 178); and, (3) "Their strategies exemplify cultural and rhetorical adaptations that subvert suppressive rhetorical tactics" (p. 178). It is from within this framework that I ground my rhetorical analysis of SLM facebook, as well as how I understand it to operate as a transrhetorical site by satisfying the above three criteria. Expanding Jackson's framework into the digital realm further complicates the notions of time, space, and subversive rhetorical tactics, as well as understandings of digital literacy as alliance building.

Looked at cohesively, as well as in their disparate parts, the status updates, comment threads, and shared articles on the SLM facebook travel transrhetorically: across time, as movements of cultural literacy from Kiowa to non-Kiowa and non-Native allies, and as subversive rhetorical tactics to (an) oppressive force(s). These interactions occur across time, meaning that communications are not limited to a synchronic moment, but rather move, develop, and evolve diachronically. This distinction between synchronicity and diachronicity only exists in physical spaces. However, in digital spaces, through transrhetoricity (or the movement of rhetorics across time and multiple locations), the distinction between synchronicity and diachronicity blurs. For example, a status update on the SLM facebook can be made in real time, then a week later a person in a different physical location can read and respond to the update (i.e., diachronically). Further, a third person can read the status update and comment as if both happened synchronically, and also comment (diachronically). The convergence of sync/diachronic time in a digital space exemplifies Jackson's point of transrhetorical sites as "movement(s) of meaning" through time (Jackson, 2016, p. 19).

The second indication of a transrhetorical site, and in this case a Kiowa transrhetorical site, is that the site moves cultural literacy from a hyper-localized Kiowa space to a general audience space. The SLM facebook is a repository for various elements of Kiowa cultural literacy, ranging from religious to historical, accessible to both Kiowa and non-Kiowa alike. For example, numerous news articles as well as status updates are shared via the SLM facebook that contain insights and interviews from those within the Kiowa community (such as Dupoint) and information about Kiowa cultural and religious traditions (such as visiting Longhorn to collect flat leaf cedar to be used in prayer and ceremony). The expression of Kiowa cultural literacy directly correlates with the third indication of a transrhetorical site as it "exemplif[ies] cultural and rhetorical adaptations that subvert suppressive rhetorical tactics" (Jackson, 2016, p. 178). The SLM facebook appeals to the emotion and logic of diverse audiences in order to build alliances against the mining of Longhorn. The mining of the mountain can be seen as a suppressive tactic as it would directly impact (and oppress/eliminate) various expression of Kiowa cultural and religious practice. One status update published on July 17, 2013 writes that Longhorn Mountain "has been leased to Stewart Stone ... a rock crushing company that intends to strip mine the Kiowa tribe's sacred mountain, turning it into gravel that would be used to pay our highways. The loss of the mountain would be an act of cultural genocide perpetrated against the Kiowa people." Likening the mining of the mountain to an act of cultural genocide emphasizes the intensity of efforts to protect Longhorn. The SLM facebook thus is a cultural and rhetorical adaption to share efforts of resistance with a broader audience.

The ability to communicate with others in a sync/diachronically convergent way that moves Kiowa cultural literacy to non-Kiowa spaces as an act to subvert suppressive forces (i.e., attempts to mine a Kiowa sacred site) through social media platforms also represents a digital literacy of action and alliance building. Martin (2006) defines digital literacy in "Literacies for the Digital Age" (2006) as,

> the awareness, attitude and ability of individuals to appropriately use digital tools and facilities to identify, access, manage, integrate, evaluate, analyze and synthesize digital resources, construct new knowledge, create media expressions, and communicate with others, in the context of specific life situations, in order to enable constructive social action; and to reflect upon this process. (p. 19)

The SLM page expresses Martin's definition of digital literacy in several ways. For example, the page shares digital resources related to the protection of Longhorn, such as news articles, blog posts, posts from personal or group pages about the topic or other causes related to Indigenous efforts to protect land and culture, numbers and addresses of local and national representatives whom supporters of the SLM should contact regarding Longhorn, and a petition to protect Longhorn (which received 2,122 signatures). The compilation of these shared resources enables the constructive social action of followers of the SLM page, as it provides avenues to become more informed about the issue at hand and to take action (such as contacting representatives and signing petitions).

Within the page, dialogue occurs with native and nonnative participants and makes appeals to concerns of Kiowa cultural preservation and spiritual expression, as well as environmental and historical conservation and public health (i.e., constructive social action). Contributors are physically located in different places and also share information from and to other digital platforms, including other facebook pages, videos, and blogs, which demonstrates a literacy of digital social networks, especially as the page is used to build alliances and ultimately protect Kiowa sacred space. Moreover, the participants' ability to read/write sync/diachronically is evidence of a transrhetorical digital literacy.

Using transrhetorical inquiry, this chapter traces (in brief) the cosmological and historical connections Kiowa have to Longhorn Mountain, the events that lead to the attempts to mine the mountain, and analyzes select posts from the SLM facebook. The analysis explores how the SLM Facebook page not only functions as a transrhetorical site where meaning moves across space, time, and audiences but also how the site is sophisticated in its ability to enable a digital literacy of social engagement through cross-cultural alliance building centered around geosacred space. Participants on the site are simultaneously working towards preservation of the physical, the spiritual, the cultural, and the historical through the digital. Exploring the ways in which multiple locations (digital and physical; Longhorn Mountain and the homes/places of work, and so forth, from which the SLM participants contribute to the page) are entwined and influence one another hints at the simultaneously subtle and complex ways that cultural and digital literacies are utilized for place-based social action.

COSMOLOGICAL AND HISTORICAL CONNECTIONS TO LONGHORN MOUNTAIN

The Kiowa's origin story and migration to Oklahoma beginning in the 1700s illustrate what Elizabeth Maynor (2014) refers to as the Kiowas's "living relationship" to the land in her master's thesis *Native American Cultural Identity and Land Access: The Kiowa Tribe and Longhorn Mountain*. The Kiowas' living relationship to land was impacted by treaties such as the Medicine Lodge Treaty of 1867, the Dawes Act of 1887, and eventually the change in ownership of Longhorn Mountain from Kiowas to non-Native owners (pp. 6–7, 19). These events simultaneously contextualize the current movement to maintain the geosacrality of Longhorn (as the transfer of Longhorn to non-Native landowners made possible the efforts to exploit the mountain for capitalistic enterprises) and highlight the spiritual, historical, and cultural importance of the mountain.

N. Scott Momaday's (1969) telling of the Kiowa origin story illustrates the primordial connection Kiowas have with the land. Momaday writes,

> You know, everything had to begin, and this is how it was: the Kiowas came one by one into the world through a hollow log.... They looked around and

> saw the world. It made them glad to see so many things. They called themselves *Kwuda*, "coming out."

The conception of coming out into the world, through an element of the earth, speaks to the Kiowas' living relationship to the land. The land is intrinsically tied to Kiowa origins of themselves as a people, and that tie is woven into contemporary Kiowas' reverence for and protection of Longhorn Mountain.

This living relationship to land, and specifically to Longhorn, is a longstanding one. Prior to their migration to the southern plains into what is now "present-day western Oklahoma, Kansas, southeastern Colorado, and the Texas panhandle between 1790 and 1830" the Kiowa inhabited the Black Hills area of South Dakota and western Montana (Meadows, 2008, p. 18). A status update on the SLM facebook from September 29, 2013 references the Kiowa's historical relationship Longhorn Mountain, writing, "The Kiowa have been going to Longhorn since the 1700s. Generations of Kiowa medicine men have gone to Longhorn to pray, conduct vision quests, and gather medicine." Meadows contends "that despite migration and changes of residence, the Kiowa maintain a distinct sense of homeland, now centered on dispersed allotted communities in southwestern Oklahoma and the surrounding southern plains" (Meadows, 2008, p. 4). The Kiowa's sense of homeland, their living relationship to land maintained through rituals and stories is dependent upon as well as contributes to the geosacrality of Longhorn Mountain and the sacred cedar that grows there. This sense of homeland and living relationship are the what SLM facebook group was created to protect.

Stewart Stone's stated intentions to mine Longhorn Mountain in 2013 has direct connections to the Medicine Lodge Treaty of 1867 signed by the Kiowa, Comanche, and Apache. The Medicine Lodge Treaty of 1867 placed Longhorn Mountain "within reservation boundaries," and therefore it legally belonged to the Kiowa (Maynor, 2014, p. 6). However, with the Dawes Act of 1887, the land originally included in the Medicine Lodge Treaty "was split into allotments, dividing the landscape among tribal members and selling surplus land to non-Natives.... Due to financial reasons the tribal members who held the Longhorn Mountain allotments, including the Longhorn family, either sold or lost the land" (Meadows, 2008, p. 7). As mentioned previously, currently five non-Native families own Longhorn Mountain and some of the surrounding land. In the early 2000s the non-Native land owners leased their land to Stewart Stone, which lead to plans to mine Longhorn. Thus, Kiowa have had to employ rhetorical strategies to stake their historical, social, cultural, and religious relationships to the land. The Kiowa relationship to the land, and specifically to Longhorn, is nourished and replenished through ritualistic interactions with the mountain, prayers, and activism to protect it. The relationship is corporeal, metaphysical, ongoing—the relationship is living.

The geosacrality of Longhorn Mountain to Kiowa also grows out of various practices and rituals which take place at or because of the mountain. In Meadows's (2008) description of geosacred places to Kiowa, he explains,

> Another geosacred site that has remained particularly important to contemporary Kiowa is Long Horn Mountain, southwest of Mountain View, in Kiowa County, Oklahoma. Because the cedars on this mountain are said to be sweeter than any other in the area, this mountain has become a preferred site for gathering cedar sprigs to dry and use for cedaring ceremonies—prayers and blessings using burning cedar as incense. Cedar incense is commonly used in cleansing and blessing a new home, as a blessing after nightmares, ghost encounters, or funerals, in Peyote and naming ceremonies, prior to a marriage, by dance societies prior to ceremonials, or just for receiving a blessing.... Many Kiowa go to great effort to gather their cedar from this mountain, and a host of offerings, including feathers, tobacco bundles, cloth strips, coins, food, and other items, have been placed on the mountain (p. 93)

The flat leaf cedar has its own unique scent and is believed to hold sacred qualities. Dupoint stated in an interview with KGOU, which was shared on the SLM facebook, in June 2013 that he has smelled cedar across the United States and Canada, "But Longhorn just has its own unique scent, no other place in the world can you get it but here." In the interview Dupoint also explained "they've tried to transplant it but it just doesn't seem to take or grow." Dupoint believes God is the only one who could know why this cedar was given to the Kiowas.

A status update from September 29, 2013 on the SLM facebook elaborates on the importance of the cedar to Kiowa way of life, stating,

> The loss of the mountain would be devastating to Kiowa culture and spirituality as Longhorn Mountain cedar is used in all aspects of Kiowa life.... It also plays a prominent role in Kiowa Native American Church services and all night prayer gathers. Traditional Kiowa households also have it on hand to attend to their daily needs, as they have done for generations.

The September 29th status illustrates the transrhetorical importance of the cedar by describing its connection to various rituals and how the cedar's significance spans generations. This status illustrates transrhetoricity in the ways the past practices with cedar have been carried into the present (meanings from the past encounter meanings from the present). This generational Kiowa cultural literacy regarding the importance of Longhorn cedar to their ways of life is shared on the SLM facebook, with Kiowa and non-Native audiences to resist the mining of the mountain. Thus, the knowledges embedded within the Longhorn cedar are directly threatened by Stewart Stone's plan, as mining the mountain would at the very least endanger, and the worst eradicate, the unique flat-leaf cedar which grows (only) there. The destruction of a historical, cultural, and spiritual component of Kiowa identity and way of life will occur if Longhorn is mined.

ATTEMPTS TO MINE LONGHORN MOUNTAIN

As previously mentioned, Stewart Stone obtained a lease in the early 2000s from the non-Native landowners of the western side of Longhorn Mountain (Maynor, 2008, p. 7). Attempts to protect Longhorn Mountain began in 2013 after Stewart Stone stated plans to mine the western side of the mountain for gravel. As the sacred cedar used ceremonially by Kiowas grows on the eastern side of the mountain, fears arose that the mining would hinder the growth of the cedar, and thus Kiowa tribal traditions. Kiowas, along with other residents of Carnegie, Oklahoma also expressed concerns that the gravel mining would cause impediments to their health "caused by the dust and air pollution from the rock crushing as well as the damage caused to their home due to the dynamite" (Kline, 2013). While health impediments due to mining is a concern both Natives and non-Natives can recognize, bridging an understanding of Kiowa reverence for the geosacrality of Longhorn can prove more challenging for non-Kiowa.

Non-Kiowa and many non-Native communities do not root their ideas of the sacred within the earth. For instance, some evangelical Christian groups understand rooting ideas of the sacred within the earth as blasphemous to God as this would prioritize the creation and not the Creator, which is significant in this particular ideological framework. Meadows (2008) describes the division between Anglo-American and Native conceptions of land by stating, "Outsiders often have difficulty in viewing physical landscapes in the ways the Native Americans do: as physical forms bearing traces of their ancestors, and as form intertwined with the concepts of the past, origins, language, oral history, personal conduct, and spiritual morals and direction" (p. 32). Vine Deloria (1973) also writes in *God is Red* of the contrasting perceptions of land from a Christian worldview compared to an Indigenous one. Deloria writes,

> Tribal religions do not have the massive institutions which Christianity requires to perpetuate itself.... The religious ceremonies of the tribal religions ... [often] take place in sacred locations where the people can be in contact with the spiritual powers who have always guided the tribe. (pp. 220–221)

An August 1, 2013 status on the SLM facebook (described in more detail in the following section) articulates the differences in understandings of sacred spaces for Native and non-Native communities (specifically between Kiowa and Christians). The status appeals to similarities between the faith practices in order to build alliances between these practices. In this way, "meaning encounters meaning" so that concepts are able to change. In other words, *meaning* as Kiowa understandings of sacred space encounters the *meaning* of Christian sacred space, so that concepts of what can be included within a sacred space can change/expand for non-Native audiences. Kiowa cultural literacy is thus shared in such a way as to build alliances. It is important to not romanticize the relationship Native peoples have and continue to have to land, yet understanding the spiritual, cultural, and historical importance of geosacred sites is essential to the protection of the land and to furthering movements such as the SLM.

To mine the mountain for gravel therefore not only hinders generational tribal traditions, but also threatens a core piece of Kiowa identity and way of life for those who currently interact with the mountain as well as for future generations of Kiowa. As Kiowas do not have legal ownership of the western side of the mountain, they had little other recourse against the threat of mining the mountain than to use their voices to bring awareness to and build alliances around the issue, which they did through the SLM facebook.

TRANSRHETORICAL ANALYSIS

The social media platform utilized by SLM functions as an interconnection of rhetorical networks. Jackson (2016) argues that to engage in transrhetorical inquiry is to "look for *networks* of rhetorical locations rather than one, and defines *one location in terms of many*" (emphasis added p. 10). Thus, although the SLM page exists (or can be viewed) as one location, it is embedded within digital social networks of information sharing (personal facebook pages), engaging in asynchronous dialogue (comment threads and status updates), and referencing events which occurred in the past or have the potential to occur in the future (i.e. the historical connections Kiowa have to Longhorn Mountain and the present/future plans to mine it by Steward Stone Rock Crushing Company) or in different places at the same or different time.

The SLM facebook is a digital space connected to the physical place of users through dialogic engagement (in comment threads, status updates, and even silent readers of the page), which integrates and references digital and physical spaces outside of the SLM facebook (most visibly, Longhorn). Additionally, through status updates the SLM facebook shares articles from blogs, news outlets, YouTube, or from other digital or physical networks that either reference Longhorn Mountain directly or are related to other Indigenous movements and issues relating to land. For instance, in 2015, SLM posted about pollution of the Animas River, which runs through Navajo land, protests to protect Sacred Oak Flat from mining, and in 2016, several posts were made about the Dakota Access Pipeline and Standing Rock. Commenters share information from other locations within the digital sphere, discuss their physical (and sometimes spiritual) place, and/or their relationship to the physical space of Longhorn Mountain. From these interactions, the SLM facebook is a nexus where we can see the convergence of "networks of rhetorical locations," which is apparent within the SLM facebook as conversations and statements are both archived and ongoing (i.e., convergent in sync/diachronic time) (Jackson 2016, p. 9). Thus, Kiowa cultural literacies held within a particular post or update can evolve across time or space (i.e., other peoples' facebook pages and/or other digital platforms). Jackson (2016) describes this meeting of temporal and physical/digital as when the "time axis and space axis—intersect" (p. 19). The evolution of meaning across time and space enables participants or readers of the site from various backgrounds, locations, and/or cultural contexts to not only learn about the SLM but also engage in or renew discussions that have happened in the past (i.e., contribute to the site diachronically).

A status update posted September 29, 2013, at the height of the site's activity, particularly illustrates the complex rhetorical engagement within this transrhetorical site, as it moves through the movement of three points outlined by Jackson (2016), while also emphasizing a digital literacy of alliance building through appealing to history, emotion, and health. This status update powerfully describes the connection the Kiowa people of Oklahoma have to Longhorn Mountain through examples ranging from spiritual practice, religious mythology, historical and cultural events associated with Longhorn, and transgenerational interaction. The status update also appeals to the physical health of the community and animals that would be at risk if Stewart Stone were to mine the mountain. The September 29th status is lengthy, detailed, and eloquent in its description of the importance of the mountain to the Kiowa and those living near the area. An excerpt from status emphasizing the historical, cultural, and religious importance of Longhorn (2013) states:

> The Kiowa say God led them to Longhorn Mountain and to use its cedar.... The loss of the mountain would be devastating to Kiowa culture and spirituality as Longhorn Mountain cedar is used in all aspects of Kiowa life.... All Kiowa societies, such as the Black Leggings Warrior Society, Ohoma Lodge, and Gourd Dance Societies utilize the smoke of the cedar in their ceremonies. It also plays a prominent role in Kiowa Native Ameri-

> can Church services and all night prayer gatherings. Traditional Kiowa households also have it on hand to attend to their daily needs as they have for generations.... The Kiowa have been going to Longhorn since the 1700's. Generations of Kiowa medicine men have gone to Longhorn to pray, conduct vision quests, and gather medicine. Some without heirs to their healing powers are said to have also left their spiritual "medicine" to the mountain.

Within this excerpt, the status makes rhetorical appeals to a diverse audience, Native and non-Native alike, who may prioritize different issues. It does so by sharing Kiowa cultural literacy of historical and religious connections of Kiowa to Longhorn, such as that God led Kiowa to Longhorn, that Kiowa have been visiting Longhorn since the 1700s, and that "generations of medicine men have gone to Longhorn to pray, conduct vision quests, and gather medicine," even stating that some of the medicine is left to Longhorn itself. Jackson describes that transrhetorical sites can be seen in "relationships occurring between multiple sites of meaning-making, particularly where they link locations and meaning across difference" (p. 11). These appeals expressed in the status demonstrate the ways the meaning of the geosacrality (the physical intersecting with the sacred) of Longhorn to Kiowa of the past continues to make meaning for present-day Kiowa in similar and different ways, "this positions present-day activists as part of a rhetorical continuance of cultural resistance" (p. 177). Thus the one physical location of Longhorn then comes to symbolize two temporal locations (past and present) where meaning is constructed for Kiowa ways of life. Alongside temporal difference, the September 29th status also links meaning across difference in that this status, and the very existence of the SLM facebook itself, convey that other communities may have different conceptions (or no conceptions at all) regarding the geosacrality, historical, and cultural importance of Longhorn. Linking meaning across difference in this status has the intended effect of both educating diverse audiences and building alliances with them in order to stand against the mining of Longhorn. The September 29th status also references the preservation of historical sites, such as caves bearing pictographs or petroglyphs, as well as the environmental and health implications mining could have on the surrounding area and communities. This excerpt expresses:

> The local farmers around the mountain, many of which have lived there for generations since the early 1900's, do not want the rock crushing to begin either as they fear for their livestock's health as limestone dust adversely affects grass and wears down cattle's teeth. The farmers also fear the negative health effects that breathing the dust will have upon them and their children and grandchildren.... The use of explosives on the mountain would also likely destroy a chambered cave with important historical value.

> The cave is said to have either ancient Kiowa pictographs or petroglyphs on its walls and said to be the place of a unique practice among the Kiowa where men would lure eagles to the cave entrance by placing meat there and then hiding in the cave would grab the eagle by its feet when it landed to get the meat. Thereupon they would pluck a couple tail feathers or so as they needed before releasing them.

This excerpt of the September 29th status frames the issue of mining prismatically through the lenses of agriculture, public health, and cultural and historical preservation. This prismatic framing illuminates components of the issue to mine Longhorn in such a way that appeals to various stakeholders—those who may support maintaining the geosacrality of Longhorn to those whose primary interest is in support of public health. Highlighting the numerous impacts mining could have on different communities demonstrates the intention to build alliances with diverse followers of the page. Jackson, when expressing movements across transrhetorical sites, contends, "Ideas, issues, and events engage multiple groups and locations in the collective construction of meaning. Rhetorics, both as messages and the vehicle for messages, necessarily change as a result of these transactions, yielding generative and cumulative adaptations, co-optations, and applications" (p. 12). The framing of this status excerpt reveals that, by outlining the range of ways mining Longhorn would negatively impact not only Kiowa culture but also non-Natives who live nearby, a variety of ideas and issues were chosen to engage multiple audiences in the cause to stop mining. To a Kiowa-only audience, some of these issues would not be expressed in the same way because of a general consensus of Longhorn's importance. Instead, the construction of a public facebook page, alongside status updates such as this one, convey that multiple audiences are meant to be reached. This underscores a digital literacy employed for efforts of action and alliance building.

The September 29th status itself constitutes a rich site of rhetorical strategies to build alliances cross-culturally. The comment thread also contributes to particular representations of the transrhetorical nature of the site. This particular post was shared 47 times, thus expanding the reach of the information to different digital spaces and communities. Additionally, the comment thread demonstrates the sync/diachronic aspects of the way time functions in this transrhetorical place. For instance, SLM facebook posted the status on September 29th and then commented on the post the same day, asking followers to "Please help us save Longhorn Mountain" (Longhorn Mountain, 2013). A follower of the page commented almost a year later on July 7, 2014 with a link to an environmental forum. In these ways, the comment thread allows for meaning to travel across space and time through connecting multiple networks, such as personal facebook accounts, documentaries, blogs, forums, and other digital spaces in such a way that complicates notions of what it means to participate in dialogue that converges sync/diachronic time.

A later status update from August 1, 2013 also engages in alliance building and displays how "rhetorics adapt for multiple audiences" (Jackson, 2016), specifically with non-Native communities and members of major religious groups. By drawing parallels between other religious traditions' sacred spaces and Longhorn Mountain, the August 1st update encourages non-Native followers or readers of the status to make connections to spaces of cultural and religious importance in their own traditions and/or communities. The status states:

> It may be difficult for non-Native to understand that Native Americans did not build churches, but had sacred places in nature where they went to pray and seek the presence of God.
>
> Christians, Jews, Muslims, Hindus and Buddhists all over the world have sacred places that they have been making pilgrimage to for thousands of years. The Kiowa, Kiowa-Apache, and Comanche have been making pilgrimages to Longhorn Mountain to pray, fast and seek the guidance of the creator for centuries. (August 1, 2013)

The status concludes with a blog post titled "The Importance of Protecting the Kiowa Tribe's Longhorn Mountain and Other Sacred Native American Sites" aims to develop a place of shared understanding through communicating cross-culturally with non-Native religious audiences (Oofana 2013). Oofana (2013) makes the Kiowa veneration of Longhorn Mountain relatable to Christians by drawing similarities between the ways Christians feel about sacred spaces, such as churches, to how Kiowa feel about Longhorn. In other words, the status describes the geosacrality of Longhorn Mountain in such a way that allows various audiences to empathize with the cause. The comment thread on the August 1st status illustrate that the post is effective in its goal to build alliances through cross-cultural engagement.

The first commenter in the comment thread, posting 6 days after the initial post, seemingly positions themself as non-Native by stating, "We as Americans have never did much for the tribes other than try to wipe them off the face of the earth.... We could always build a human chain around this mountain and lay our lives down to help the Indians for a change." The commenter expresses the importance they see in protecting Longhorn, especially in light of the historical colonial forces of oppression and violence against Native people and communities. The commenter also connects their spiritual practice of prayer to efforts to protect the geosacrality of Longhorn by expressing, "I pray good sense and respect win out and this hallowed ground remains untouched." This comment shows a built alliance between a non-Native follower of the page and the SLM movement.

The September 29th and August 1st statuses and comment threads reveal the site as a nexus between multiple networks of relationships and meaning-making, which occurs in a bringing together of past and present times and locations in order to share Kiowa cultural literacy to resist destructive intentions of a geosacred space—in this way they demonstrate the site's transrhetoricity. Transrhetorical sites are ideal locations for alliance building cross-culturally, as well as cross-temporally and cross-spatially, to occur.

Thus the status, shared blog post, and comment thread are dialogic—they begin from multiple origins in terms of physical, temporal, and digital spaces, and therefore depend on and enable social action. In other words, the creation of the SLM facebook depended on social action to create a platform to disperse information regarding the issue facing the Kiowa, and simultaneously the page enables *further* social action through alliance building *because of* the creation of the SLM facebook. Thinking of social media platforms, such as the SLM facebook, as spaces where digital literacies of social action take place independent of a coincidence of place or time opens up new ways of exploring how alliances can be built cross-culturally for a shared goal.

CONCLUSION: A "REVOLUTION OF RELATEDNESS"

The efforts to protect Longhorn's geosacrality are not over. On December 5, 2016 the SLM facebook posted the following status:

> Rock crusher Larry Stewart of Stewart Stone is attempting again to destroy Longhorn Mountain by having it mined for gravel. The Obama Administration has been instrumental in protecting sacred Native American sites, public lands and places of historical significance.. bama remains in office until January 20th. Please call the White House at 202-456-1414 or click on the link below for the White House's contact page and leave a message asking the president to protect Longhorn Mountain by declaring it a Native American sacred site.

The status was shared 19 times. Considering the SLM facebook was most active in 2013, with the most shared post was shared 47 times (September 29, 2013), the amount this call to action was shared is impressive. The amount of times it was shared also highlights that alliances to the SLM are still active and are attempting to build a wider circle of alliances through introducing the information in the status to a personal facebook page. Presently, Longhorn Mountain still remains protected from mining efforts.

In *Back to the Blanket* Wieser (2017) "calls for a revolution of relatedness that we must achieve to save the earth and humanity from environmental destruction" (p. 34). By building alliances transrhetorically, the SLM facebook answers Weiser's call and joins the revolution of relatedness in order to protect a site of cultural, spiritual, and historical significance to the Kiowa. Viewing the SLM facebook as a case study of Indigenous activism in the digital sphere that impacts physical space and reality by enacting a digital literacy of social action contingent upon alliance building reveals the need to further explore the ways in which digital literacies are influenced and created through social action.

The efforts to protect the geosacrality of Longhorn are transrhetorical—they move from the past to the present, from physical space to digital and back to physical again; they share Kiowa cultural literacy, build alliances, and do so in such a way as to subvert oppression forces of mining interests. The digital literacies of action and alliance building enable and are supported by the transrhetoricity of the SLM facebook. It is thus essential to consider how digital platforms contribute to change in the physical realm, and how digital platforms cultivate the digital that take place and grow within them.

In *MixedBlood Messages: Literature, Film, Family, Place* Louis Owens (1998) states,

> The future of that wilderness and, of course, the future of all life depends upon whose stories we listen to: the stories that tell us we are bound in a timeless and inextricable relationship with the earth which gives us life and sustains us, or the stories that tell us the earth is a resource to be exploited until it is used up. (p. 211)

The SLM facebook is a site that share stories of Kiowa culture and ways of life, and also reveals the power in building alliances cross-culturally. Owen's poignant note that "the future of all life depends on whose stories we listen to" is continually relevant—the SLM facebook, and other Indigenous led social media campaigns, provides opportunity for us to listen to those stories that tell us "we are bound in a timeless and inextricable relationship with the earth." The SLM facebook illustrates how meaning-making is woven through, but not limited to, constructs of time and space, and how meaning evolves, who contributes to meaning's making, and who listens.

NOTES

1. For more on cross-cultural alliance building, see Angela Haas's (2008) dissertation, *A Rhetoric of Alliance: What American Indians Can Tell Us About Digital and Visual Rhetoric*.

2. Maynor's (2014) thesis documents interviews with members of the Kiowa community in Oklahoma about their connections to Longhorn Mountain. Her thesis is the only other academic documentation I have found of the attempts to mine Longhorn Mountain and its impact on the Kiowa community in Oklahoma.
3. For more information on the Medicine Lodge Treaty of 1867, see "Medicine Lodge Treaty of 1867" entry in *Oklahoma Encyclopedia of History and Culture* (Rand, n.d.).
4. For more information regarding the Dawes Act of 1887, see "Dawes Commission" entry in *Oklahoma Encyclopedia of History and Culture* (Carter, n.d.).
5. For further reading on the Kiowa's sense of homeland, see Steven M. Schnell's "The Kiowa Homeland in Oklahoma" (2000).
6. For additional information regarding government interference with Kiowa land, look for information regarding the court case Lone *Wolf v. Hitchcock* and the Jerome Commission in *Lone Wolf vs. Hitchcock: Treaty Rights and Indian Law at the End of the Nineteenth Century* (Clark, 1999).

REFERENCES

Carter, K. (n.d.). Dawes Commission. *The Encyclopedia of Oklahoma History and Culture*. Retrieved from www.okhistory.org

Clark, B. (1994). *Lone Wolf v. Hitchcock: Treaty rights and Indian law at the end of the nineteenth century*. Lincoln, NE: University of Nebraska Press.

Haas, A. (2008). *A rhetoric of alliance: What American Indians can tell us about digital and visual rhetoric*. (Doctoral dissertation). Michigan State University, East Lansing, Michigan.

Jackson, R. (2016). *Red State reclaimed: The transrhetorical recovery of resistance in Oklahoma* (Doctoral dissertation). University of Oklahoma, Norman, Oklahoma.

Kline, C. (2013). Longhorn Mountain: Sacred places and cultural genocide. *Intercontinental Cry: A Publication of the Center for World Indigenous Studies*. Retrieved from intercontinentalcry.org/longhorn-mountain-sacred-places-and-cultural-genocide/

Longhorn Mountain. (2013). *Documentary* [Video File]. Retrieved from https://www.youtube.com/watch?v=NzXTGNrkV5g

Martin A. (2006). Literacies for the digital age. In A. Martin & D. Madigan (Eds.), *Digital Literacies for Learning*. London, England: Facet.

Maynor, E. (2014). *Native American cultural identity and land access: The Kiowa Tribe and Longhorn Mountain* (MA Thesis). University of Oklahoma, Norman, Oklahoma.

Meadows, W. C. (2008). *Kiowa ethnogeography*. University of Texas Press, Austin, Texas.

Momaday, N. S., & Momaday, A. (1969). *The way to Rainy Mountain*. University of New Mexico Press, Albuquerque, New Mexico.

Oofana, B. (2013 June 17). The historical and spiritual significance of Longhorn Mountain. *Ben Oofana's Blog*. Retrieved from benoofana.wordpress.

com/2013/06/17/the-historical-and-spiritual-significance-of-longhorn-mountain/

Oofana, B. (2013, August 1). The importance of protecting the Kiowa Tribe's Longhorn Mountain and other sacred Native American Sites. Retrieved from http://benoofana.com/the-importance-of-protecting-the-kiowa-tribes-longhorn-mountain-and-other-sacred-native-american-sites/

Owens, L. (1998). *Mixedblood messages: Literature, film, family, place*. Norman, OK: University of Oklahoma Press.

Rand, J. T. (n.d.). Medicine Lodge Treaty. *The Encyclopedia of Oklahoma History and Culture*. Retrieved from www.okhistory.org

Save Longhorn Mountain | Facebook. (n.d.) *Save Longhorn Mountain | Facebook*, www.facebook.com/SaveLonghornMountain/?fref=ts.

Schnell, S. M. (2000). The Kiowa Homeland in Oklahoma. *Geographical Review, 90*(2), 155–176.

Deloria, V. (1973). *God is red*. New York, NY: Grosset & Dunlap.

Weiser, K. (2017). *Back to the blanket: Recovered rhetorics and lived literacies in American Indian Studies.* Norman, OK: University of Oklahoma Press.

CHAPTER 9

FROM THE SCREENS TO THE STREETS

Translating Digital Engagement Into Performance Practice to Facilitate Multiple Contributions to Placemaking

Wayne Steven Jackson
The Arden School of Theatre, UCEN Manchester

INTRODUCTION

In 2017, Hull became the UK City of Culture, the second city to be awarded the title since it was established in 2009. The focus throughout the year, and throughout the years leading up to it, was on the potential effect that the UK City of Culture status could have upon the people of Hull. However, the decision making, curation, and promotion of the yearlong event was controlled, framed, and only made possible, by the government initiative, which, as an institution in itself, positions the program of cultural regeneration as hegemonically influenced. Furthermore, while a large number of projects aimed to involve inhabitants of Hull, there were limited

Negotiating Place and Space Through Digital Literacies: Research and Practice, pp. 155–176

opportunities for those who, while still identifying the city as home, no longer resided there.

Throughout this chapter I present how a translation of digital engagement into performance practice can be utilized to reach, include, and activate multiple individual contributions to placemaking. To do so, I acknowledge, and exploit, my own connections to the city; I was born and raised in Hull but moved away in 2001. My performance work has always been influenced by my attachment to home and, during 2017, I returned to Hull to present *Now | Then*, a series of performance journeys. My practice investigated how individual experiences of the city, after being uploaded to my website, could be theatrically interpreted. I purposefully located *Now | Then* amidst the cultural celebrations of 2017 but, importantly, outside of the UK City of Culture framework. I did not receive funding from the UK City of Culture program, and while the performance did feature on the event's official website, additional support, such as the production of a promotional video, was only initiated once *Now | Then* had already gained media interest and attention.

Gertner and Kotler (2004, p. 50) suggest that a "place's image is defined […] as the sum of beliefs, ideas and impressions that people have of that place." Throughout this chapter, I position place as a multifaceted projection, constructed from numerous acknowledged, accepted, and amalgamated individual attachments, including those of people who are no longer residents. As such, my research explores how the multiple relationships with Hull that were exposed through *Now | Then* support and evoke individual attachments to the city. Furthermore, I present strategies with which I translated my project's collected individual experiences out of digital engagement and into performance, from the screens to the streets, as examples of how performance can support multiple renegotiations of place.

DEFINING HULL AS A PLACE

I situate my research within the English city of Kingston upon Hull, or Hull as I refer to it throughout this chapter, at a time of its transition into becoming the UK City of Culture 2017. However, while my research is specific to Hull, it is also representative of other urban areas undergoing cultural regeneration; in any process of regeneration, there is an objective for the identity of place to be transformed. Places are ultimately unfixed, experienced, and constructed through practice; "[w]hat begins as undifferentiated space becomes place as we get to know it better and endow it with value" (Tuan, 1977, p. 6). Thus, the transformation of place is heavily reliant on the actions and interactions of its occupants (Cresswell, 2009).

Hull is a working class city, in the north east of England, located at the end of the M62 motorway, atop of the River Humber. Covering an area of 28 square miles, the city has a population of over 260,000 people, and a gross disposable household income that is 6000 pounds less than the national average. Hull is a city undergoing change: cosmetically, economically, and culturally. In 2016, the city reportedly spent 25 million pounds resurfacing its streets, in 2015 it won Siemens's 160 billion pound contract to manufacture wind energy turbines, and, in 2017, it experienced a shift in terms of cultural engagement. The UK City of Culture interim report produced by University of Hull's Culture, Place and Policy Institute (2017) highlights that only 36% of Hull residents engaged in cultural activity during the first three months of 2013. In the same three months of 2017, at the start of the UK City of Culture year, cultural engagement in the city had risen to 90%. However, where the city is situated, its contents, buildings, and its engagement with cultural activities, do not alone make Hull, Hull.

Agnew (1987) suggests that place is constructed and understood through a combination of three elements. Its location, the measurable and literal point in space, and its locale, the place's urban makeup, provide objective definition. However, the third element is much more subjective; it is a definition made from the more nebulous meanings associated with a place, "the feelings and emotions a place evokes" (Cresswell, 2009, p. 1): its sense of place. It is here that the essence of a city is negotiated, both individually and collectively, through how the city is felt and experienced, where "cities' identities are socially produced through the ways we act in them" (Harvie, 2009, p. 47). There is a clear differentiation between a communal understanding of Hull that stands alone from personal relationships to the city and an understanding of Hull that includes emotional connection, where there is an "insistence on the centrality of human consciousness and experience" (Cresswell, 2009, p. 7). Cresswell (2009) further suggests, home is "the location where meanings and attachments are most intense," an extension of the element of place construction Agnew defines as sense of place. The location and locale of Hull are literal and concrete, shared and validated by numerous different people. However, as Etchells (2009, p. xii) explains in relation to performance, a city "is used at the same time by many people, sectors, factions, groups whose interests do not by any mean coincide," and as such, sense of place can be understood as being constructed through an innumerable amount of personal relationships and experiences. Michalski (2009, p. 101) states that a "city becomes fluid, and landmarks and people write themselves upon us. This text, written by the streets has many authors," and thus, the city is a patchwork, created from multiple attachments, memories, and experiences.

As with all constructions of place, Hull, the resulting combination of location, locale, and sense of place, is always in flux. Hull's locale has experienced a number of alterations in recent years, as has its location due to shifting parameters of what is and is not included within its boundaries. As such, and similar to the multiplicity of sense of place, Hull's location and locale can be understood as unfixed entities. Alongside the cosmetic, economic, and cultural changes, Hull has undergone a number of conceptual transformations involving its name, logo, and marketing straplines. There has been a desire to amend, change, and mould Hull as a place contextualized by its history; it "suffered severe deindustrialisation from the 1980s with the loss of its shipbuilding and fishing industries [and as a consequence became] blighted by its drab reputation [and] poor external image" (Julier, 2005, p. 883). For Hull, renegotiations of place focused on the external image of the city, in attempts to unburden itself as England's "Number One Crap Town" (Jordison & Kiernan, 2005).

Methods of reconstructing place, from collective acts of erecting buildings and assigning names, to individual acts of personal experience and memory, parallel the relationship between Agnew's location, locale, and sense of place. Thus, those factors that affect the transformation and definition of a city as place are constant, unrelenting, and subjective. Consequently, as Harvie (2009, p. 6) suggests, cities "are better understood as urban process because they are constantly changing." Goal-Holmes (2012, p. 205) states that the qualities of sense of place give shape to a fixed place that is "only temporarily established, necessitating a continuous state of negotiation and renegotiation," and is thus in constant fluctuation. Furthermore, the multiple individual emotional and experiential connections involved in sense of place leads Parkerson and Saunders (2005, p. 242) to suggest that there is an "elusiveness of any single city image." If in flux, a city, as place, can be renegotiated at any point. By reexperiencing the city through an exposition of subjective connections, individuals contribute to a continual process of placemaking.

Proshansky, Fabian, and Kaminoff (1983) coined the term place attachment in order to articulate the effect that place has upon an individual's sense of self: the emotional, experiential, and subjective connections to place. Furthermore, Morgan (2010, p. 11) highlights humanistic approaches to place theory that "explore the deeper significance of place to human existence and the subjective, emotional quality of people's relationship to places." The similarities between place attachment and Agnew's sense of place create ambiguity and confusion within place theory; place attachment and sense of place are often used synonymously (Jorgensen & Stedman, 2001; Lewicka, 2008). However, Scannell and Gifford (2010, p. 1) offer a distinction between the two, defining place attachment as the meaningful bond an individual has with sense of place. In this reciprocal relationship, I understand place attachment as an individual's abstraction of sense of place, and sense of place as the coalescence of multiple individual place attachments. Sense of place, in this understanding, is formed through majority; it is a representation shared and accepted by a number of individuals. Place attachment, in turn, is an individual's interpretation of, and response to, sense of place, which intrinsically involves a reaction to representation. Place attachment, in this understanding, asks why sense of place has been constructed in that way, and, ultimately, signifies whether an individual accepts or rejects it. As such, the relationship between place attachment and sense of place, through action and response, provides individuals with an opportunity to determine how they understand their city.

PERFORMANCE, CULTURE, AND PLACEMAKING

Millard (2015, p. 4) acknowledges culture as having the "transformational power" to renegotiate, specifically, external impressions of a city. Culture in this way has been utilized successfully in a number of projects for UK cities, such as the European Capital of Culture, which saw Liverpool and Glasgow benefit cosmetically and economically as a result of regeneration. In both of these cases, the renovation of locale played a major part in the cities becoming venues for the practicing of culture and, thus, the renegotiation of place. Similarly, impressions of Hull were undoubtedly affected by a cosmetic restoration that supported the city's cultural regeneration. As well as the repaving of streets, derelict buildings were replaced, water features were introduced in the squares, new street signs were erected, and greenery was planted. However, the cosmetic changes that framed the presentation of cultural events were at times in contrast to existing place attachments, especially those of individuals who did not experience the city's improvements directly. As a consequence, a tension grew between the city's representations from the past and in the present. Humber Street, for example, in contrast to its location as the city's old fruit market with a locale of factories and warehouses, was regenerated for 2017 to house café bars and restaurants, art galleries, and reclamation shops. The renewed facade and atmosphere breathed life into the street's old buildings; live music, street theater, and outdoor socializing became features of its identity.

Hull, as place and home, was confounded by the methods of regeneration that the city employed in order to become a venue for its tenure as UK City of Culture 2017. The winning bid aimed to bring the city "out of the shadows," promising that the UK City of Culture accolade would help shed its external image as a declining and deprived port city. Garcia (2005, p. 844) highlights that the UK government in 2004 was "supportive of the use of culture as a tool for regeneration, with the Department of Culture, Media and Sport (DCMS) framing it as one of its key objectives." In the

Hull 2017 strategic business plan, Green (2015, p. 9) states that the overall objective of the UK City of Culture year was to "position the city as a cultural powerhouse as strong as any other in the north and across the UK." The focus, through utilizing culture as a tool with which to grow capital and boost economy, was "to maximise the benefits and economic impact of Hull's year as U.K. City of Culture and recent private sector investments in the city" (Hull 2017 Strategic Business Plan, 2015, p. 41). In preparation for 2017, a hive of activity took place in Hull that had not been experienced or witnessed before, as though the title bestowed upon the city had given justification and reason to unveil new work and explore new ideas. What began to emerge was a new narrative for the city, established and reinforced through the programming of cultural events, the regeneration of the streets and squares, and the creation of performance.

In their exploration of the effects of social and cultural practices, Dollimore and Sinfield (1988, p. ix) articulate cultural materialism as "inseparable from the conditions of their productions and reception in history." In this way, I suggest, that which constituted Hull as a venue for the yearlong UK City of Culture program also affected individual place attachment. However, the regeneration of the city's locale cannot so easily be isolated as contradictory to understandings of Hull as home; Humber Street has become a popular, reputable, and accepted area of the city. The representations of Hull's past and the present do not necessarily establish a binary opposition; they instead become a continuum of renegotiation. In 2017, the city of Hull became a venue of cultural regeneration that contributed to place attachment in the present *and* a venue of individual experience and history that contributed to place attachment from the past. Undoubtedly, the program of cultural regeneration positively impacted the city in terms of its economy and external image. Support for the regeneration can be seen in the overwhelming response from its inhabitants and local businesses; more than 2,800 events took place across the city that reached an audience of over 5.3 million. Indeed, University of Hull's preliminary outcomes evaluation (University of Hull Culture, Place and Policy Institute, 2018) highlights that three in four residents were proud to live in Hull and that almost half of the population of the United Kingdom and suggests that 2017 had positively changed the perception of the city for almost half of the population of the United Kingdom. However, while there were numerous new and exciting commissions for the yearlong celebrations, the UK City of Culture program not only predominantly engaged those who still inhabited the city, it also promoted a single, albeit new and more positive, narrative of rejuvenation. As such, I question the degree to which this renegotiation of sense of place was conducive to a heterogeneous process of placemaking that aims to include all residents.

Programs of cultural regeneration, such as the UK City of Culture scheme, have the potential to galvanise individual contributions to sense of place. In line with the aims of regeneration that Richards and Wilson (2004, p. 1993) describe, Hull was able to make use of the "particular valuable form of cultural currency, [that of] an image-enhancement tool." The Hull 2017 Strategic Business Plan (2015, p. 14) explicitly outlines this objective, focusing on the transformative nature of culture and clearly states that, for Hull, there would be change. The instillation of pride and community through placemaking is an important cultural practice when renegotiating place attachment. However, sense of place can often be stabilized through hegemonic influence and political power. When a single narrative is promoted through cultural regeneration, that interpretation of the past can become the projected and accepted version of events, regardless of how the city is experientially felt. University of Hull's (2018, p. 214) impact report reflects on the future of the UK City of Culture, stating, "[a]ttention needs to be paid to achieving the right balance of commissioning local and external artistic partners." As such, I highlight a need for performance makers to contribute to cultural regeneration by promoting multiplicity so that processes of placemaking are inclusive of place attachments from a wide range of individuals that identify the city as home.

As Hull underwent a cultural regeneration, I identify a limited number of projects in its yearlong program that challenged the city's renovated narrative. The program instead presented and celebrated Hull's shared history through the frame of, and adherence to, the UK City of Culture's key objectives and thus resulted in a stabilized sense of place. While the UK City of Culture generated a number of positive outcomes, such as a restored sense of pride, a boosted economy, and an increase in cultural engagement, its program supported minimal deviations to, or renegotiations of, the promoted single narrative. In this way, I suggest, culture was utilized as a tool with which to control placemaking as opposed to supporting a renegotiation, and indeed a remembrance, of the city outside of the parameters set, presented, and performed by the hegemonically influenced cultural regeneration.

THE IMPORTANCE OF MULTIPLE NARRATIVES

During the process of placemaking, a stabilized sense of place that concretizes, and constantly reaffirms, a promoted narrative offers little room for the multiplicity of individual place attachments. Instead, reconstructions of place are limited by a frame that is dictated and governed by hegemonic control. Throughout the remainder of this chapter, I present how a translation of digital engagement into performance practice can challenge and destabilize single narratives. In this way, I suggest, multiple place attachments that intrinsically invite varying interpretations of, and connections to, a city should be favored and celebrated.

Robertson (2008) suggests that individual experiences, in contributing to place attachment, can oppose a sense of place manufactured from positions of power. He describes this process as heritage from below. The essence of heritage from below manifests within any proposition that residents take ownership of the contributions to, and interpretations of, sense of place. Here, the power of placemaking is relinquished from any promoted single narrative and relocated within multiple individual narratives. Current research suggests that, unlike in more prominent public spaces where place is constructed through hegemonically controlled social signifiers, ordinary and mundane spaces can elevate individuals to become the producers, curators, and makers of place (Atkinson, 2008). These ordinary and mundane spaces are not typically labelled as sites of cultural significance; they are the derelict buildings, the graffitied walls, and the tenfoots.[1]

Performance opens up potential for change and, as Harvie (2009, p. 7) states, can become more than a reflection of a city by becoming a "*part of* urban process, producing urban experience and thereby producing the city itself" (original emphasis). Thus, I highlight the potential to practically explore performance as heritage from below through utilizing Cresswell's (2014, p. 16) assertion that "[m]ost places have stories [...] that become hidden or silenced only to abruptly re-emerge as new constellations of place appear." I question how, through an engagement with individual experiences of Hull that are not influenced by a promoted single narrative, multiple place attachments can be represented, redefined, and reconstructed.

MY PLACE ATTACHMENT

I pause here to reflect upon my own relationship to Hull, as a researcher, as a performer, and as a nonresident. I acknowledge and appreciate the numerous occasions throughout the course of my life where my home has informed not only my life decisions and my work, but also my identity. A city, as home, harbors the most strongly felt and practiced subjective reconstructions of sense of place, where personal attachments are supported by continued relationships with the city. Hull is maintained as home by its inhabitants through a range of activities that, while including an engagement with the city's location and locale, are ultimately governed by sense of place and the individual experiences of autobiography.

However, I no longer live in Hull. I am not a resident of the city. Jackson (1995, p. 122) articulates home as "a relationship, a tension," whereby an individual's subjective understanding of the place in which they reside is connected to past experiences. This suggests that not only is home underpinned by personal history, but with it there is also "a notion of what is chosen—the open horizons of a person's life" (p. 122). Jackson's depiction of home allows for individual accounts and interpretations of place to be understood as something other than the literal location and locale of habitation. In this way, place attachment becomes more about an individual relationship to, and experience of, a city than a literal choice of residence. While I have un-chosen Hull, deselected my literal connection to its location and locale, I still understand the city as home. My relationship to Hull is now informed by return visits, interactions with family and friends who reside there, and digital engagements with websites and social media. Online, and through digital means, I am able to remotely contribute to the process of placemaking, and thus maintain my own connection and attachment to the city. As a consequence, when developing *Now|Then*, I utilized digital media as a tool with which to engage and include individuals that were outside of the city in Hull's cultural regeneration and in the renegotiation of sense of place.

RESEARCH METHODS AND METHODOLOGY

I identify as Hullian.[2] As a consequence, my research was unequivocally affected by my relationship to Hull as well as my experience of performance making; the theatrical strategies that I engaged with in my research, and my analysis of the ways in which other people viewed my home city, were influenced by my place attachment. Thus, through an ethnographic framework, my first-hand knowledge and experiences of Hull allowed me to not only effectively communicate with the participants, but, as Lahlon, Bellu, and Boesen-Mariani (2015, p. 217) suggest, to "share to some degree their own 'emic' perspective (in the participant's own terms)." The position this created, and the acceptance that the information and data collected is subjectively interpreted, is pertinent to exploring multiple attachments as opposed to a single narrative; my research was conducted from within the heterogeneous social group I was investigating. Therefore, my research benefits from a position of knowledge, whereby my own experiences provide a context for not only the examination and analysis of practice, but also the presentation of the performance outcome as heritage from below.

I began the process of creating *Now|Then* with an online memory collection[3] designed to gather and present individual anecdotes, stories, and personal narratives of Hull. The call for participants had only one criterion for initial self-selection: the participants should identify as being from Hull. This criterion was purposefully ambiguous, allowing for the research project to explore individual relationships to Hull that were not defined through borders or boundaries. Participants were directed to the website via an online social media campaign and a flyer campaign at the city's museums, libraries, and galleries. Furthermore, to avoid the website targeting specific demographics, and to allow for inclusivity, I also hosted a live launch at Hull History Centre on January 16, 2016, where I met with the public and uploaded, live, their experiences of Hull directly onto the website. Between December 2015 and April 2017, 104 experiences of Hull were uploaded to the website from 70 participants. The website included an interactive map of the city (see Figure 9.1) and its surrounding area where participants were able to share their experiences of Hull by locating them at the specific site, street, or building at which they occurred. The digital map provided participants with the opportunity to reflect on their city in isolation to its immediate and literal environment; the city needed to be imagined as opposed to witnessed. The contributions could be viewed, shared, discussed, and extended upon by visitors, strangers, and fellow Hullians. For me, the website became a digital interpretation of the American Political Scientist Benedict Anderson's (1983) imagined community. In his influential exploration of nationalism, Anderson theorized the perception of attachment to place, suggesting that the conception of belonging creates strong connections between people that have not even met.

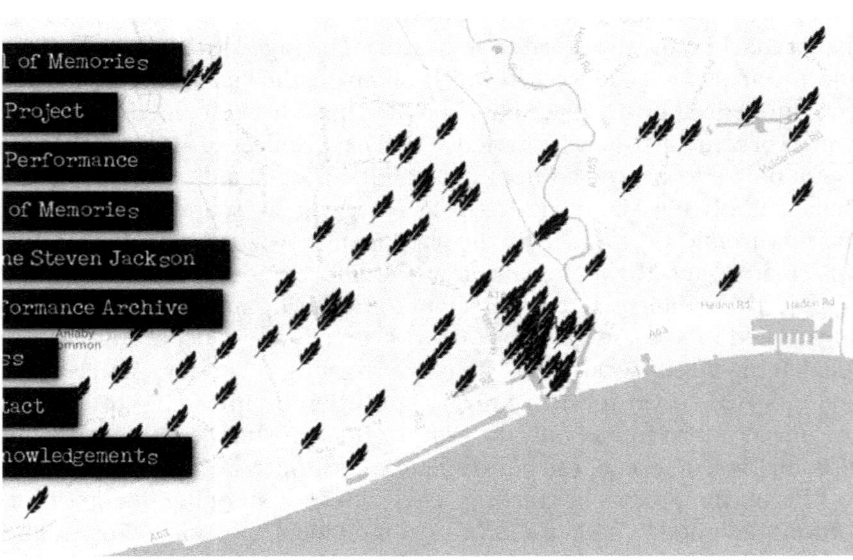

Figure 9.1. The map of memories.

The second stage of my research involved the extraction and analysis of the experiences submitted to the website and their translation into performance. I examined and collated the contributions based on the content, location, themes and issues, and my interpretation of the projected place attachment. Once I had established any commonality between the varying experiences of the city, I categorized the text in order to represent a number of time periods. Ultimately, the experiences I utilized as part of the performance text were selected because of their resonance to my autobiographical memories. This process allowed me, as curator, not only to examine the relationships between the texts, but also to consider the participants' experiences in relation to my place attachment. My adaptation of the text created a disjointed structure that would facilitate multiple contributions to placemaking, without overly editing the participants' contributions and thus distorting their meaning. I delivered the translated text as experiences from one single person, shifting the narratives from first person into second person. My intention was to present the fragmented stories of Hull's past in such a way that invited and instigated the audience to adopt, adapt, or develop, them in relation to their own place attachments.

My translation of digital engagement into performance led to a performance outcome that explored the renegotiation of individual attachments to the city. It focused on the reconstruction, even recreation, of experiences that were widely unknown, as opposed to those already established, accepted, and validated through a stabilized sense of place. My aim was to establish performance as a means of supporting reengagements with Hull, unrestricted by, and unlimited to, any existing or promoted single narrative. Furthermore, the series of performances were also a method of data collection; the audience were invited to answer questions concerning their individual relationship to Hull after they had experienced the performance. I use these responses, as well as my autoethnographic observations and experiences of the project, to inform the subsequent analysis and to draw my conclusions.

STAGE ONE: THE WEBSITE

The contributions to the website ranged in content, length, and style, some were short and succinct bite-sized narratives, others were more descriptive, proffering subjective detail and texture. Each submission to the website offered a unique insight into experiences that the participants felt inclined to digitally share. As such, the online map became a tapestry of fragmented and unconnected stories that, as Calvin Innes (2016) states in his article for Hull Daily Mail, together formed a "deeply personal montage of what Hull looks like to the people who live [there]." There were general stories about street parties, pastimes, and schools, and more specific stories about blades of grass, shop monkeys, and the sound of clogs. The value and relevance of each memory submission was specific to the individual contributor but participants were also able to contribute to other people's experiences by adding comments to the uploaded stories. The website served to map Hull in a digital space through individual experiences, memories, and attachments, and, as a consequence, I understand it not only as an act of placemaking, but also as an act of heritage from below. This digital marking of the city was an opportunity to destabilize sense of place. Importantly, participants who no longer resided in Hull could exercise their own attachments to the city at their leisure, in their absence, by reflecting on the location, locale, and sense of place of their home.

DIGITAL MEDIA IN PERFORMANCE

Before I discuss the ways in which I translated the digital engagement with personal experiences into performance, it is important to expose the effect that developments in digital media have had on theatrical practice. As well as challenging and adapting personal and social engagement through the way in which the fleeting moments of everyday life can be stabilized by photographs, video, and the many varying applications on mobile phones, the possibilities that arise from the inclusion of digital media in performance are constantly increasing. Oddey (2007, p. 43) suggests that these developments have established a "techno-culture, which is about immateriality, the digital and disembodied virtuality, where anyone can make their own computerised Photoshop work of art in an instant." Consequently, subjective interpretations of the world become not only documentation and preservation, but also reconstruction. Digital media frames the content of the experienced past as well as the way in which those past experiences are reengaged with.

The use of digital media within performance, that can be located under the umbrella term intermediality,[4] enhances the unstable nature of performance when the spectator forges a subjective interpretation of the interconnected mediums, actively selecting those moments understood as important. The consequences of this kind of spectatorship support the suggestion by Chapple and Kattenbelt (2014, p. 12) that intermediality becomes "a process of transformation [...] a re-perception of the whole, which is re-constructed through performance." A theatrical use of digital media has the potential to have an impact upon perception by highlighting the disparity that occurs when live and technological materials become symbiotic within the performance's present. The acknowledged and accepted incongruence between the live and the mediatized image becomes the basis upon which Woycicki (2014, p. 39) argues that intermedial techniques and strategies can stimulate "the audience to become more active in the process of meaning-making." Here, performance can embody processes involved in digital literacy in order to support an audience to find and evaluate information that has been interpreted through and from technological practices.

STAGE TWO: THE PRACTICAL OUTCOME

My translation of digital engagement resulted in a series of performances that took place in a taxi (see Figure 9.2) for up to five people at a time, as it journeyed through the streets of Hull. The series of intimate performance journeys, which started and finished at 'oss Wash[5] on Victoria Pier, were open to the general public and so contribution to the website was not a prerequisite. While audiences were driven around the city by my dad, I delivered text, created from the multiple engagements with my website, from the front passenger seat. The performances were accompanied by a soundtrack that blended music, narration, and conversation. Between April and June 2017, the *Now|Then* journey was made 104 times, up to eight times a day, and each time with a new audience, varied routes, and a new backdrop provided by the changing scene of the city. The literal journey through Hull experienced by the audience was echoed in a strand of the narrative, which followed a little boy as he walked through a city that he could not place, among buildings that felt unfamiliar. As the performance progressed, the stories and experiences of others aided his ability to ultimately remember, and reconnect to, home. The story derived from a personal exploration of my own connection to Hull as it underwent its transition to become the UK City of Culture. The little boy was not only the boy of my childhood, lost in an unknown city, he was also the boy of my adulthood, lost within, and yet removed from, a changing city.

Now|Then aimed to directly influence, support, and affect renegotiations of place attachment and it was important to expose and utilize the project's digital roots. Furthermore, the use of intermediality highlighted the duel nature of translation; not only were individual experiences translated through digital engagement with the website, they were also translated through digital engagement with the performance. *Now|Then* was underscored by a soundtrack specifically written for the project that structured the journey and consisted of text, interpreted from the website, and music, written by a composer familiar with the medium of film.[6] A literal conversation was established between the performer past and the performer present; the two mediums of live and prerecorded performance interacted

Figure 9.2. Inside the Taxi.

and, on occasion, shared lines. This dialogue intrinsically created a tension between experience and imagination. Information, stories, and experiences were not simply accepted; previous understandings of the city were juxtaposed or refuted so that any promoted single narrative was questioned in relation to each audience member's individual place attachment.

During the performance, the audience were tasked with completing a card, attached to a feather on a string, with "a word or phrase that describes what the city means to [them], something that makes the city [theirs]." They were invited to tie their contribution to a tree in the city center (see Figure 9.3). Sholette (1997, p. 17) states that "[m]etaphors of urban decay, rebirth and incubation suggest that the process of "constructing nature" has its corollary in the act of naturalizing culture." In this way, Hull's cultural regeneration was not only connected to the concept of natural life cycles, but, through the marking of the city, individual place attachments were being made visible. While the contributions were new, unconnected to the website in terms of content, by utilizing feathers, which were the icons of the original online contributions, digital engagements were being remembered. The task offered a moment for individual reflection in and among the narrative of the little boy and the multiple strands of stories and experiences. HC, a member of the audience, stated that the process of her own contribution "had quite an impact on [her] realising [her] sense of belonging and connection to Hull." These markers, remnants of place attachments that were individually mapped onto the city, together created a visual representation of an alternative sense of place. Collectively, the 361 feathers became signifiers of a heterogeneous process of placemaking. Hull was marked by stories and experiences of the city that included contributions that were not only from those inside of the city, but that were also influenced and informed by the digital contributions of those outside of the city.

Figure 9.3. The feathers and cards left at Queen's Gardens.

APPLICATION AND ANALYSIS

Hull's tenure as UK City of Culture can be understood as a means of making and practicing place. The yearlong cultural event was a framework that supported the renegotiation of sense of place, providing the possibility for Hull to rewrite its external perception, to regenerate itself, and to instil within its residents a sense of pride. However, the framework through which sense of place was renegotiated was hegemonically influenced. The consensus within current research suggests that processes of identity construction, reconstruction, and preservation originate from the authority of political power (Harvey, 2008). Thus, the renegotiation of sense of place is often a tool with which to exercise and influence a city's representation. McLean's (2008) exploration of museums identifies how preservation can be used to promote and amend the reconstruction of place, and thus directly impact upon individual place attachment. An application of this model to a city undergoing cultural regeneration highlights the curatorial role of the political power who, by reconstructing the locale of the city, not only controls *what* is remembered, but also *how* it is performed. In this instance, place is practiced through a frame dictated and enforced by hegemony that projects and promotes a single narrative desired by the political power (Graham & Howard, 2008).

Hull's established and enforced narrative, its external image of economic growth, prosperity, and entrepreneurship promoted as a result of being awarded the title of UK City of Culture 2017, was in contrast to the existing sense of place. As a historically working class city, firmly rooted in the fishing industry, Hull's image is one of poverty and struggle. Agnew's identification of a symbiotic relationship between location, locale, and sense of place in his definition of placemaking suggests that any significant, dramatic, and immediate change to one of the three components could result in the city's identity becoming fractured and manufactured. The possibility, then, is that a hegemonically directed cultural regeneration, commanded to specifically renavigate placemaking, while positive and celebratory, comes in isolation to, and sometimes in spite of, individual place attachments. In these circumstances, those who identify the city as home, particularly those not residing there, become isolated from renegotiations of sense of place and, left outside of the process of placemaking, are in danger of losing their sense of belonging.

My translation of digital engagement into performance during *Now | Then* did not just serve to document individual experiences; it also provided an opportunity to reflect upon place attachment. If place is constructed through an amalgamation of multiple narratives, my digital map, which was collaborative and multidirectional, explicitly offered the opportunity to renegotiate place outside of any promoted single narrative. Furthermore, when I questioned my audience about their experience of *Now | Then*, their responses referenced individual interpretations of not only Hull's changes, but also the ways in which they affected how the city was perceived externally. However, the majority of responses were concerned with how the city was felt on an individual and subjective level. AP discussed how she "reconnected with [her] happy time and sense of belonging [she] had there [and] also felt at peace about where [her] life is at," DK highlighted that "the new confidence [he] felt around Hull [...] was further reinforced by the journey." and EW stated that *Now | Then* "reminded [her] how [the] city is embedded within [her]." Furthermore, those audience members that were not originally from Hull reflected on how the performance exposed their connection to the city. While YO acknowledged that her relationship with the city was still being established, she stated that the performance journey made her "feel more connected, [she was] part of what Hull has always done—made people want to stay once they arrive."

The task of completing the cards on the feathers was inescapably subjective and so any attempt to quantitatively analyze the contributions is redundant; the comments were all incredibly and wonderfully different. However, after coding the responses into Agnew's (1987) categories of location, locale, and sense of place, the responses highlight a clear predilection. After experiencing *Now | Then,* audiences were overwhelming more inclined to reflect on, interpret, and document Hull in relation to sense of place and place attachment (see Figure 9.4). The reflections of place attachment proffered through this task, while varied and unique to each audience member, had reoccurring themes. From the 167 memory cards collected, 24% referenced people, friends, and family, 29% used adjectives to describe the city, of which 44% referenced the notion of home. The contributions were wholly personal, the word "I" was used 13 times, and represented the city through an array of positive interpretations, of hope and new opportunities; of the 20% that referenced emotions, 34% used the term pride. 21% of responses were extremely specific, referencing subjective details such as "hidden secrets," "mushrooms on toast," and "Little Iris and the Iguanas," which out of context do not mean anything except to the individuals who wrote them. These subjective responses are characterised by one individual who stated that Hull was their city of "belonging and knowing who I am."

As a consequence of the structural and intermedial devices I utilized, my translation of digital engagement into performance established a subjective framework through which to explore place attachment. In her book, *theatre & the city*, Jen Harvie (2009, p. 49) discusses the use of performance in urban settings to challenge hegemonic oppression. She highlights Baudelaire's term flaneur, "who confounds dominant uses of the city by casually strolling through it, making his own pathways through it, and so his own *version* of it through his manner of performing it" (original emphasis). Locating *Now | Then* both outside (the screens) and inside (the streets) of Hull was integral to the project's ability to position its audience as flaneurs. As the audience travelled through Hull, both literally and digitally, they were tasked with exploring the city outside of their regular experience and, specifically, reconnecting their own individual relationship to it. As such, no single narrative or interpretation of Hull took precedence. Thus, the contributed experiences I collated as part of *Now | Then* suggest that my audience were not only able to engage with place attachment but were also able to interpret it within a renegotiation of sense of place. Through translating the personal experience of digital engagement from a website into performance, *Now | Then* supported reengagements with Hull, unchained to the promoted single narrative of the program of cultural regeneration, as individual and unique representations of the city.

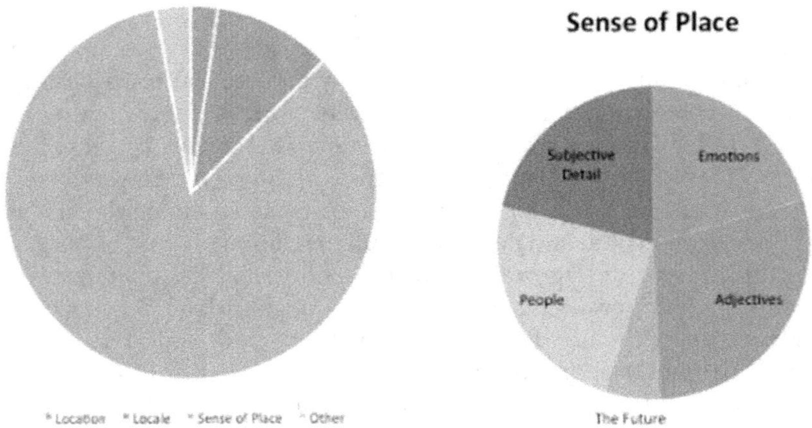

Figure 9.4. The categorized contributions.

CONCLUSION

Now|Then marked the city of Hull through its transition from the screens to the streets. The initial stage of the project asked those who identified as being from Hull to digitally mark the city with their own experiences. The resulting online map documents the ways in which Hull was interpreted and remembered in the build up to 2017 and connects the city to the 104 experiences that were submitted. In the second stage of the project, by utilizing the city as the backdrop to performance, specifically governed by the website's contributions, multiple individual experiences were created that replicated the subjectivity of digital submission. Throughout the project, the 70 participants who submitted memories and the 361 audience members who experienced *Now|Then* were encouraged and supported to resee their city in multiple ways that were unique to individual place attachment. The participants moved through the city, confronted numerous strands of personal narratives, and left traces of place attachments both online and in the streets.

I present the strategies I engaged with in order to translate digital engagement into performance as tools with which to establish heritage from below. This practice, I suggest, transcends the stabilization of sense of place so that individual stories and experiences can become contributing factors in the process of placemaking. Furthermore, *Now|Then* supported the representation, redefinition, and reconstruction of individual place attachment even for those who no longer resided in the city. When place is presented as unfixed, and when the process of reconstruction is embraced, promoted single narratives can lose their dominance to multiple, varying, and subjective experiences. Thus, translating digital engagement into performance supports the multiplicity and idiosyncrasy of individual place attachment. Any definitive position that cements place through location, locale, and sense of place can be challenged through interchangeable and adaptable representations that are open to renegotiation, adaptation, and development.

In its 2018 impact report, University of Hull highlighted that 8 in 10 audience members said that the UK City of Culture provided them with a different experience of the city, and that this "suggests that the programme was successful in exploring and promoting new narratives and ways of seeing the city" (2018, p. 123). However, only 51% of Hull's residents said that they were likely or very likely to continue to attend cultural activities after 2017. The report highlights that this "is perhaps lower than might have been hoped for [which] gives a note of caution on the extent to which audience levels [...] can be sustained in future years" (p. 85). Furthermore, the impact report highlights that less than 35% of the city's inhabitants felt represented by the cultural activities. One resident is referenced as stating "this was a year of events that was used in and done to the people of Hull rather than done with them" (p. 83). This position was mirrored in my audience's reflections of Hull's year as UK City of Culture. When I questioned HC about how the performance journey affected her relationship to the city, she discussed the ways in which the 2017 program of cultural events had left her "feeling at times alienated from the place [...] as it hadn't always reflected [her] experience of coming [...] and choosing Hull as home." In contrast, she stated that her experience of *Now | Then* was "really moving and unusual and intense [...] connecting me to Hull [...] and even if 'I'm not from round here' that I belong here too."

A city is both existing, and continually redeveloping, made up of multiple individual place attachments and, through human interaction, its "space is turned into place. Your place" (Cresswell, 2014, p. 7). When ordinary and mundane sites are promoted through the translation of digital engagement into performance, the power of placemaking is situated outside of hegemonic influence, creating an opportunity "to celebrate and memorialize *from within* the lives and thoughts of those otherwise hidden from history" (original emphasis) (Robertson, 2008, p. 147). It is my conclusion, therefore, that the stabilization of sense of place, through the promotion of single narratives during programs of cultural regeneration, can be rebalanced through a translation of digital engagement into performance. As such, performance making strategies that promote multiple narratives can be utilized in order to create transformative work that facilitates and engages contributions from a wide range of individuals that identify as being from a city in the renegotiation of placemaking, even those that no longer reside there.

NOTES

1. Tenfoots, specific to Hull, refer to the 10-foot wide passageway located behind, typically terraced, houses.
2. Some people prefer to use the term Hullensian to describe those who identify as being from Hull, but I have only ever used Hullian.
3. To view the online map, the participants' contributions, and the visitors' comments, please visit www.waynestevenjackson.co.uk
4. For a detailed exploration of this term and its practices, see Chapple and Kattenbelt's (2014) *Intermediality in Theatre and Performance.*
5. 'oss Wash is Hull slang for "Horse Wash." an area on Victoria Pier, Nelson Street, where workers at the Fruit Market would cool and clean their horses in the River Humber.
6. Christopher Benstead, a fellow Hullian, received an OSCAR and BAFTA for his work on *Gravity* and, when he created the soundtrack for *Now|Then,* had recently finished working on the score for Disney's live action remake of *Beauty and the Beast.*

REFERENCES

Anderson, B. (1983) *Imagined communities.* London, England: Verso

Atkinson, D. (2008). The heritage of mundane places. In B. Graham & P. Howard (Eds.), *The Ashgate Research Companion to Heritage and Identity* (pp. 381–396). Surrey, England: Ashgate,

Agnew, J. A. (1987) *Place and politics: The geographical mediation of state and society.* Boston, MA: Allen and Unwin.

Chapple, F., & Kattenbelt, C. (2014). Key Issues in intermediality in theatre and performance. In F. Chapple & C. Kattenbelt (Eds.), *Intermediality in theatre and performance* (pp. 11–25). Amsterdam, the Netherlands: International Federation for Theatre Research.

Cresswell, T. (2009) *Place.* London, England: Royal Holloway

Cresswell, T. (2014). Place. In R. Lee, N. Castree, R. Kitchin, V. Lawson, A. Paasi, C. Philo, S. Radcliffe, S. M. Roberts, & C. W. J. Withers (Eds.), *The SAGE handbook of human geography* (pp. 4–21). London, England: SAGE.

Dollimore, J., & Sinfield, A. (1988). Foreword: Cultural materialism. In G. Holderness (Ed.), *The Shakepeare myth.* Manchester, England: Manchester University Press

Etchells, T. (2009). Foreword. In J. Harvie (Ed.), *Theatre & the city.* London, England: Palgrave Macmillan.

Garcia, B. (2005). Deconstructing the city of culture: the long-term cultural legacies of Glasgow 1990. *Urban Studies, 42*(5–6), 841–868.

Gertner, D., & Kotler, P. (2004). How can a place create a negative image? *Place Branding, 2,* 43–52.

Goal-Holmes, P. (2012). (Re)calling 'home.' *Crossings: Journal of Migration & Culture, 3*(2), 201–212.

Graham, B., & Howard, P. (2008). Heritage and identity. In B. Graham & P. Howard (Eds.), *The Ashgate research companion to heritage and identity* (pp. 1–18). Surrey, England: Ashgate.

Green, M. (2015). *Hull UK City of Culture 2017 Strategic Business Plan, p. 9.* Hull, UK: University of Hull. Retrieved from https://cmis.hullcc.gov.uk/cmis/Portals/0/HULL2017_STRATEGICBUSINESSPLAN_1518.pdf

Harvey, D., C. (2008). The history of heritage. In B. Graham & P. Howard (Eds.), *The Ashgate Research Companion to Heritage and Identity* (pp. 19–36). Surrey, England: Ashgate.

Harvie, J. (2009). *Theatre & the city*. London, England: Palgrave Macmillan.

Hull UK City of Culture 2017 Strategic Business Plan. (2015). Hull, UK: University of Hull. https://cmis.hullcc.gov.uk/cmis/Portals/0/HULL2017_STRATEGIC-BUSINESSPLAN_1518.pdf

Innes, C. (2016, April 9). Calvin on culture. *The Hull Daily Mail.*

Jackson, M. (1995). *At home in the world.* London, England: Duke University Press.

Jordison, S., & Kiernan, D. (2003). *Crap towns: The 50 Worst Places to Live in the UK.* London, England: Pan Macmillan

Jorgensen, B., S., & Stedman, R. C. (2001). Sense of place as an attitude. *Journal of Environmental Psychology, 21,* 233–248.

Julier, G. (2005). Urban designscapes and the production of aesthetic consent. *Urban Studies, 42*(5), 869–887.

Lahlon, S., Le Bellu, S., & Boesen-Mariani, S. (2015). Subjective evidence based ethnography: Method and applications. *Integrative Psychological & Behavioural Science, 49,* 216–238.

Lewicka, M. (2008). Place attachment, place identity, and place memory. *Journal of Environmental Psychology, 28,* 209–231.

McLean, F. (2008). Museums and the representation of identity. In B. Graham & P. Howard (Eds.), *The Ashgate research companion to heritage and identity* (pp. 283–298). Surrey, England: Ashgate.

Michalski, D. (2009). Cities memory voices collage. In R. Candida Smith (Ed.), *Text & image: Art and the performance of memory.* London, England: Transaction.

Millard, R. (2015). *Hull UK City of Culture 2017 Strategic Business Plan, p. 4.* Hull, UK: University of Hull. https://cmis.hullcc.gov.uk/cmis/Portals/0/HULL2017_STRATEGICBUSINESSPLAN_1518.pdf

Morgan, P. (2010). Towards a developmental theory of place attachment. *Journal of Environmental Psychology, 30,* 11–22.

Oddey, A. (2007). *Re-framing the theatrical: Interdisciplinary landscapes for performance.* Hampshire, England: Palgrave Macmillan

Parkerson, B., & Saunders, J. (2005). City branding. *Place Branding, 1,* 242–264.

Proshansky, H. M., Fabian, A. K., & Kaminoff, R. (1983). Place identity: Physical world socialisation of the self. *Journal of Environmental Psychology, 3,* 57–83.

Richards, G., & Wilson, J. (2004). The impact of cultural events on city image. *Urban Studies, 41*(10), 1931–1951.

Robertson, I. J. M. (2008). Heritage from below: Class, social protest and resistance. In B. Graham & P. Howard (Eds.), *The Ashgate research companion to heritage and identity* (pp. 143–158). Surrey, England: Ashgate,

Scannell, L., & Gifford, R. (2010). Defining place attachment. *Journal of Environmental Psychology, 30,* 1–10.

Sholette, G. (1997). Nature as an icon of urban resistance: Artists, gentrification and New York City's Lower East Side, 1979–1984. *Afterimage.* Retrieved from https://www.questia.com/library/journal/1G1-20236308/nature-as-an-icon-of-urban-resistance-artists-gentrification

Tuan, Y. (1977) *Space and place: The perspective of experience.* Minnesota, MN: University of Minnesota Press.

University of Hull Culture, Place and Policy Institute. (2017). *City of Culture interim impact findings.* Hull, UK: University of Hull. Retrieved from https://www.hull.ac.uk/work-with-us/more/media-centre/news/2017/city-of-culture-impact-findings.aspx

University of Hull Culture, Place and Policy Institute. (2018). *Cultural transformations: The Impacts of Hull UK City of Culture 2017.* Hull, UK: University of Hull. Retrieved from http://impact.hull.ac.uk/

Woycicki, P. (2014) *Post-cinematic theatre and performance.* Basingstoke, England: Palgrave Macmillan.

CHAPTER 10

GEOSPATIAL TECHNOLOGIES IN SUPPORT OF COMMUNITY ENHANCEMENT AND CREATING INCLUSIVE HISTORICAL NARRATIVES

Investigating the Affordances of Collaborative Mapping Software, Location-Based Applications and 3D Reconstructions to Facilitate Place-Based Digital Literacies for the Ecomuseo Della Via Appia in Latiano, Italy

Mark Opmeer, Gert-Jan Burgers, Rosanne Bruinsma, Ron Janssen, Christian Napolitano, and Ilaria Ricci
Vrije Universiteit, Amsterdam

INTRODUCTION

Technology plays an important role in enhancing the discussion on the role of cultural heritage in society. Currently, it is widely recognized that digital

Negotiating Place and Space Through Digital Literacies: Research and Practice, pp. 177–195

applications can be important tools to connect people with shared ideas and interests, to facilitate place-based storytelling, and to foster the debate on the preservation and conservation of heritage resources (Charitonos, Blake, Scanlon, & Jones, 2012; Han, Shih, Rosson, & Carroll, 2014; Sommerville, 2007). Although scholars embrace the potential of digital applications for heritage-oriented organizations, the affordances of these innovative tools for facilitating digital literacies on people's emotional connection with historical objects and events remain comparatively underexplored.

This contribution aims to provide interesting insights on the added value of digital technology for representing a sense of place and belonging within local communities. In particular, we look at how collaborative mapping software, location-based applications, and 3D reconstructions can be successfully employed as workshop instruments to facilitate digital literacies that negotiate place-based narratives and identities in the *Ecomuseum della Via Appia (EVA)* in Latiano, Italy. We argue that these geospatial technologies are powerful facilitators for creating digital literacies that reflect the community's awareness of history and identity and involving local communities in decision-making activities on local heritage management. Our findings are based on activities and stakeholder meetings that were organized by EVA in close collaboration with the *Spatial Information Laboratory* (*SPINlab*) of *VU University Amsterdam* in southern Italy in 2016 and 2017.

This chapter is divided into four sections. Part One aims to explain the ecomuseum philosophy and its current role in developing place-based narratives on local heritage and identity. The second and third part of this chapter describe how the technology-enhanced workshops facilitated digital literacy practices and mediate inclusive place-based associations and fostered feelings of shared heritage ownership and belonging. Finally, the conclusion of this chapter provides an overview of lessons learned to support professionals in different fields of study in successfully employing the discussed technologies for creating digital literacies that represent local voices and identities in an ecomuseum context.

RESEARCH BACKGROUND: ECOMUSEUMS AND THE ECOMUSEO DELLA VIA APPIA

Ecomuseo della Via Appia

The *Ecomuseo della Via Appia (EVA)* is a recent initiative of citizens of the Italian municipalities of Latiano and Mesagne (Brindisi, Italy), implemented in collaboration with *VU University Amsterdam* and the *Soprintendenza archeologia belle arti e paesaggio di Brindisi, Lecce e Taranto*. The installation of the ecomuseum is deeply linked to the gradual reshaping of the cultural landscape between the municipalities of Mesagne and Latiano, and, in particular, to the exploration and valorization of the archaeological site of Muro Tenente. The ruins of this 124 acre site represent more than 3,000 years of local history and include monumental fortifications, cemeteries, and sacred buildings, all buried under extensive vineyards, olive groves, and uncultivated fields. Since the 1970s, they have progressively been unearthed by teams of the regional heritage board, the *Soprintendenza ai Beni Archeologici della Puglia* (now *Soprintendenza archeologic belle arti e paesaggio di Brindisi, Lecce e Taranto)*, and *VU University Amsterdam* (excavations *in concessione* of the Italian Ministry of Culture, *MIBACT*) (Alberda, Burgers, Burgers, Karel, & Yntema, 1999; Burgers, 1998; Burgers & Napolitano, 2010; Burgers & Yntema, 1999). Both institutions have also put much energy into the valorization of the site, in collaboration with the municipalities of Mesagne and Latiano, local interest groups, and the *Università del Salento*. Together, they also proposed the creation of an archaeological landscape park in the area, called the Parco Archeologico di Muro Tenente. Ecomuseum EVA aims to coordinate public activities to foster increased local understanding and awareness of the cultural significance of Latiano's intangible and tangible heritage.

The Role of Place in the Ecomuseum Philosophy

Ecomuseums are not buildings that simply house collections; but rather, they refer to a specific living environment and its inhabitants (e.g., villages, urban neighborhoods, or industrial peripheries). They are important catalysts for promoting continuous discussion on place, heritage, and local identity (Bowers, 2016; Davis, 2011). To this end, a bottom-up approach in the decision-making process was employed in order to create a shared ownership and a sense of awareness of the value of local heritage. Because all involved stakeholder groups had the chance to be heard, a forum for public interaction was created where thoughts, feelings, and interests about the sense of the ecomuseum's place could be expressed more freely. Ecomuseums also commonly aim to strengthen community bonds by engaging communities in the management of their 'own' heritage, thus strengthening links between the present and the past. Indeed, one of the key objectives of the ecomuseum philosophy is to democratize the collective historical memory and to foster a sense of shared heritage ownership and belonging in the local community (Bowers, 2016). Organizing local stakeholder workshops where community members can share previously untold place-based experiences and stories with each other is one of the strategies that ecomuseums employ to ignite intellectual and emotional connections with a region's tangible and intangible heritage (Borrelli & Davis, 2012). These workshops are, for ecomuseum practices, highly rewarding, since it is assumed that the people local to a place offer a better, more in-depth understanding of the locality's heritage features (Davis, 2009). With the local input that were generated during public participatory sessions, multilayered, digital narratives were shared that capture the tone of place and articulate personal feelings on place identity and belonging (Onciul, Stefano, & Hawke, 2017).

The concept of place plays a crucial role in the ecomuseum philosophy. Ecomuseums are considered to be signifiers of a place as they try to connect (local) memories, meanings and events with specific locations. Ecomuseum philosophy promotes the idea that places should be experienced instead of described. The identity of a place can only be understood when one looks beyond its physical appearance and tries to achieve an integral understanding of its social and emotional attributes (Buttimer & Seamon, 1980). As such, place refers not only toward a specific physical reality, but also to a collective sense of belonging as well as personal concepts of identity (Smith, 2015). At EVA, geo-based tools were employed in the summer of 2016 to facilitate these types of digital literacies to negotiate the community's collective image of place.

METHODOLOGY: FOSTERING PLACE-BASED NARRATIVES WITH GEOSPATIAL TECHNOLOGY

Geospatial technology (also known as geo-based or spatial-oriented technology) can be used to support collaborative processes. Typically, geospatial tools combine different methods, such as simulation models, spatial multicriteria analysis, visualization, and optimization. User-friendly interfaces allow multiple users to provide input and to generate real-time output to support negotiated (spatial) decisions (Eikelboom & Janssen, 2015; Geertman & Stillwell, 2009; Janssen & Diaz, 2017). By providing an interactive environment as a common interface, geo-based technology acts as a medium for synthesis to promote exchange among scientists and decision makers, and it can engage stakeholders in developing digital literacies around place-based experiences (Nassauer, 2015; Cunsolo Willox, Harper, & Edge, 2013).

Also for community-led heritage projects, such as ecomuseums, geospatial tools promise to be effective facilitators for developing digital literacies as they are able to amplify the voices of various local stakeholders, including marginalized ones, to help make informed decisions on defining the territory of intangible heritage and historical landmarks (Leanza, Porto, Sapienza, and Cascone, 2016). Moreover, geospatial technology support storytelling about place-based memories and connections. For example, Springett (2015) demonstrated how involving stakeholders in creating maps can contribute to inclusive and democratic representations of time and space, which has the potential to establish multivocal understandings among residents of their community's geographical history.

In this chapter, we postulate that collaborative mapping software, location-based technology ("apps"), and 3D reconstructions are three geo-based tools for facilitating digital tools for reflecting on a community's collective experience. During the last two decades, these resources are leveraged to share cultural and ecological dimensions of one's home, or home-place, with the ecomuseum community and the potential tourist audiences (Kuroczynski, 2017). Accordingly, they provide engaging ways to integrate user-generated content, and to negotiate these materials with visitors and the local community in a dynamic and visually appealing manner.

In the following section we demonstrate how collaborative mapping software, location-based applications, and 3D reconstructions facilitated digital literacies that represent place-based narratives and identities during the EVA ecomuseum workshops with local stakeholders in Latiano.

PROCEDURE: THE WORKSHOPS

Two workshops were conducted at the Palazzo Imperiali in the city center of Latiano on July 18, 2016. About 30 people were involved, representing the various groups in society who had an interest in cultural heritage. This included people from social and agricultural cooperatives, the local tourist board, various associations, city government, the library, several societies, the local music and historic associations, and the local museum.

The objectives of the first workshop with the collaborative mapping software were: (1) to increase the awareness of tangible and intangible heritage of Latiano; (2) to complement and correct the available heritage data; and (3) to design a heritage walking trail and a heritage cycling trail. The first workshop started with an introduction to the various types of heritage. This could be elements, such as churches, but also traditions, such as processions and festas, as well as regional food specialities and local musical traditions. People were asked to comment to the maps presented and make additions were appropriate. The workshop room was decorated with posters with high quality 3D reconstructions of disappeared or transformed historical landmarks in the ecomuseum's territory. These reconstructions were created by professional designers in close collaboration with the local stakeholders. As such, they reflect the community's opinion on which tangible heritage sites collectively tell the historical development of Latiano and its surroundings. For this reason, we argue that 3D reconstructions are digital literacies that negotiate place-based narratives and identities in an innovative, geospatial way.

In the next round of the first workshop, this information was used to design two heritage trails: a walking trail within the city and a cycling trail around the city. Participants interacted with the collaborative mapping application *Phoenix*, a software package designed to support visualization (http://www.geodan.com/products/phoenix/), loaded on a Lenovo Horizon touchscreen device (27"). To draw on the map, a participant first had to select the drawing tool and a color, after which they could use their finger to draw the line.

Figure 10.1. Participants at work with the Lenovo Horizon touchscreen.

The aim of the second workshop was to assess the content quality of the heritage itineraries with a mobile tourist application in the field. The trails are designed to facilitate digital literacies in which place-based narratives and identities were reflected, and during the testing field trip the local stakeholders had the opportunity to see whether the app appropriately told the story of the people of the place.

Two types of a heritage trails were designed in the next round of the workshop: a walking trail within the city and a cycling trail in the region around the city. A content management system for creating mobile tourist apps (IZI.Travel) was used to process the heritage itineraries to mobile devices, such as a smartphones or tablets. IZI.Travel allowed all members of the project team to cocreate and moderate the itineraries simultaneously, without requiring any technical experience in developing software for smart devices. It is also a free service, which enables cultural institutions with tight budgets, such as ecomuseums (us included), to enhance their visitor experience with a location-based, digital heritage storytelling application. Last but not least, the IZI.Travel platform has proven to be highly stable and reliable, which is an aspect that should not be underestimated when employing mobile technology for (ecomuseum) workshop purposes.

During the location-based application workshop, the same people attended who had participated in the previous workshop. Because we were not primarily interested in the cognitive beliefs of tourists (e.g. perceived usefulness) and the itinerary's effect on the appreciation and understanding of the cultural landscape, we focused deliberately on the affordances of mobile technology for facilitating digital literacies that reflected place-based identities and narratives of the local residents.

The participants were divided into a hiking and a cycling group. The hiking group evaluated the urban tour, and the cycling group assessed the rural trail. The duration of both tours was approximately two hours. At the end of the testing session, the participants gathered in the workshop room of the Palazzo Imperiali for an evaluation session on how they had experienced location-based technology as a digital tool to mediate their personal feelings and their connections with the ecomuseum's cultural landscape. In the following, our impressions of using collaborative mapping software, location-based technology, and 3D reconstructions for facilitating digital literacies are discussed.

FINDINGS: GEOSPATIAL TECHNOLOGY IN SUPPORT OF DIGITAL LITERACIES ON CREATING PLACE-BASED IDENTITIES

From the 1970s–2000s, ecomuseums were conceived from an essentialist perspective as relatively closed sociospatial entities. They were established especially in rural communities because of their perceived social stability, traditionalism, and shared, homogeneous history and heritage. However, ecomuseums, as other new museologies, are now increasingly adopting more pluralist and constructivist attitudes towards heritage management. The latter approach is also key to the *Ecomuseo della Via Appia*, with its aim of giving a voice to the multiple stakeholder groups interested in the cultural heritage of the Brindisi district, from civil society institutions to individual citizens and local entrepreneurs. Ultimately, the main aim of the ecomuseum is local dialogue: to open continuous discussions between different views about landscape, history, and heritage, and to foster feelings of shared heritage ownership and belonging among the people of a particular place.

To facilitate such a dialogue, we have experimented with the geospatial tools discussed in this chapter. Inspired by the work of Cunsolo Willox et al. (2013) on digital storytelling with indigenous communities, the outcomes of our investigations have been organized according to Smith's (1999) categorization of indigenous community projects. These communal endeavors are created by indigenous researchers or social scientists and aim to preserve native cultures and languages by fostering the people's self-awareness of their own identity and history. As such, they have similar objectives as EVA, which makes Smith's list with activities suitable to organize our project's findings but from a community building point of view. These categories are: storytelling, creating, sharing, remembering, connecting, representing, networking and intervening. By organizing the workshop outcomes according to Smith's framework, we were able to examine how the geospatial-enhanced workshops evoked specific storytelling actions and responses and facilitated digital literacies that negotiated the community's place-based narratives and identities.

Storytelling and Creating

Storytelling is a highly powerful and creative activity allowing for ecomuseums to explore and develop place-based narratives. It enables the articulation of local landscape experiences, the negotiation of multiple perspectives on the community's history, and the transfer of local wisdom to the following generation (Smith, 1999). Throughout the workshops the participants were very keen to share their stories and to express their sense of connection to their "home place" with other stakeholders. Place-based associations and memories were digitally stored and processed into the collaborative mapping software. This software served as a common frame for discussion and linked the stories of the participants to specific locations. Each contribution triggered additional contributions. This way the stories cascade over the map. As the map was also projected on the wall everybody could see what was happening.

The collaborative mapping software consists of a user-friendly interface. The mapping application is shown in Figure 10.1. The interface shows the list of available map layers on the left, the drawing tool at the top right and the symbol tool on the right. The tool included a library of icons representing different types of heritage. Participants could draw on the map and add icons and text.

A total of 25 map layers were included in the library on the left of the screen. This included festivities, archaeology, historical monuments, music festivals, food festivals, chapels, olive groves, a messaria, traditional industry, local producers, historical monuments, theaters, museums, special restaurants, churches, squares, gardens and parks. The map layers could be opened and closed using the eyes icon in the layer tool. Participants were able to add comments, symbols and drawings to the map. The map layers served as input for the design of the heritage trails in the next step.

Figure 10.2. Interface of the collaborative mapping application *Phoenix*.

Throughout the workshop, a multilayered map with historical, ecological and personal layers was created, which included a multivocal and non-linear spatial representation of the ecomuseums' landscape. This spatial digital literacy can be seen on Figure 10.1: the various drawn shapes and colors highlight the place-based narratives and memories people had when approaching these historical landmarks. For instance, the blue rectangles represented stories that were connected to political or military buildings, such as the Palazzo Imperiali, and the pink and purple shapes reflected the people's associations with monasteries, churches, and other religious buildings. Accordingly, the workshop with the mapping software acted as a rich digital literacy practice that negotiates a local sense of place, identity and belonging.

The cocreated, multilayered map encouraged dialogue between people around different kinds of topics and complex issues. For example, some participants became emotional when discussing the position in Latiano's history and communal identity of newcomers who had arrived in the 1970s. Moreover, the mapping software contributed to the community building process as it stimulated the negotiation about the ecomuseum's strategy and the identification of tangible and intangible heritage that represents the region's collective identity. During the workshop, the community was given the opportunity to discuss and select the elements that better represented the community of Latiano, from the most important landscape and natural elements to tangible heritage to religious celebrations. As one of the participants explained, building collective conservation values and discussing opportunities to revitalize traditional crafts and events "was a real pleasure. It was fun and exciting to meet different people from Latiano and to highlight places on the map that tell the story of the region's past" (personal communication, 2016).

Using the outcomes of this digital mapping sessions, a tangible community map of Latiano was created by an artist that represents the area's local identity and distinctiveness. The artist showed the participants various updates on his drawings, which were then critiqued. The final product is the *Mappa di Comunità del Paesaggio of Latiano* (Figure 10.2) in which the region's collective identity is presented as two pages of a book. We see, for example, references to the local cuisine and to the typical house architecture of the area. The artwork also interweaves examples of folklore, geography, religious artefacts and the natural environment, which makes this multilayered map a multivocal representation of the cultural identity of Latiano and its surroundings. These experiences with collaborative mapping software support Springett's (2015) conclusion that the co-creation of deep maps sparks debate about the documentation and portrayal of people and places (Springett, 2015). As such, we argue—in line with Smith (1999)—that the collaborative mapping software is a strong facilitator of digital literacies; it fosters self-awareness of collective place-based identities in local societies and creates a tangible expression of a community's sense of place.

Sharing, Remembering, and Connecting

The second part of the collaborative mapping workshop was aimed at developing a richly layered narrative that represents the shared and personal histories of Latiano's community. By remembering moments from the collective fabric, incorporating the shared memories and place-based associations within a larger storytelling theme on Latiano's past, and connecting these oral representations to iconic heritage sites within the ecomuseum's territory on the digital map, an inclusive place-based narrative was created that hopefully strengthens local and visitor's awareness of the cultural significance of the tangible and intangible heritage within the ecomuseum's territory. This act of remembering and creating multivocal narratives helps to bring the community's history into the present moment (Cunsolo Willox et al., 2013).

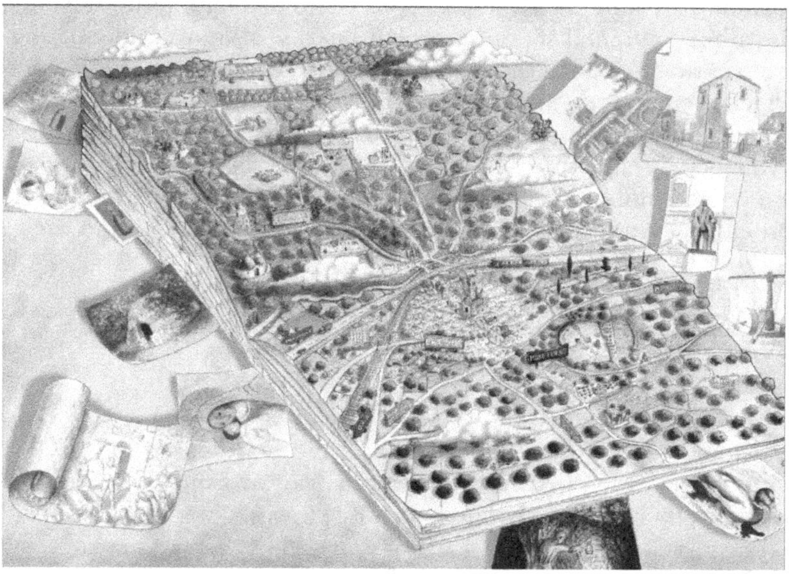

Figure 10.3 Mappa di Comitá del Paesaggio of Latiano (Copyright Vincenzo Camassa).

Smith (1999) explains that remembering is not only meant to focus on positive historical events, but that this activity is also an invitation to talk about specific painful moments in the region's history. In order to prevent the construction of an idealized past narrative that only tells one side of the story, the historical place-based narrative should contain a healthy balance between beloved and painful historical events. For this reason, stories about living conditions during World War II and the impact of mafia violence on the inhabitant's daily life in the second part of the twentieth century—to name a few—were also included in the overall storytelling framework of Latiano's past. Sharing personal memories about these traumatic experiences sparked emotional discussion about the role of the participant's ancestors during these episodes, which resulted in an increased mutual understanding of each other's opinions and perspectives. As one of the workshop participants commented: "storytelling is a great way to gain a better understanding of each other's place-based connections. This activity contributes to the community wellbeing as it brings people together and it strengthens personal relationships in the group" (Surlago, personal communication, July 22, 2016.).

The collaborative mapping software supported the storytelling activities, especially when the group members were invited to assign weights to specific stories and the interrelated tangible heritage sites on the digital map. Accordingly, the Lenovo touch screen with the Phoenix software mediated the community's sense of place and belonging through a digital map with a combined set of iconic landmarks. Moreover, identifying key narratives that represent the city's past contributed to an emotional process in which the participants linked themselves with family and ancestors, the geographical environment, and with the region's inhabitants. To this end, the collaborative mapping workshop acted as a digital literacy practice to enhance a community building activity, and in the words of Smith (1999), to establish good relations between the people of the place and their surroundings.

Representing

The main objective of the third part of the mapping workshop was to create tourist itineraries that negotiated the place-based narratives and identities—as developed in the previous two workshop phases—toward tourists or other community members. By drawing lines between the identified historical landmarks, a walking and cycling tour was created by the workshop participants on the touch-screen device. During the second workshop on the next day, the content of these itineraries were critically evaluated in the field by the workshop participants.

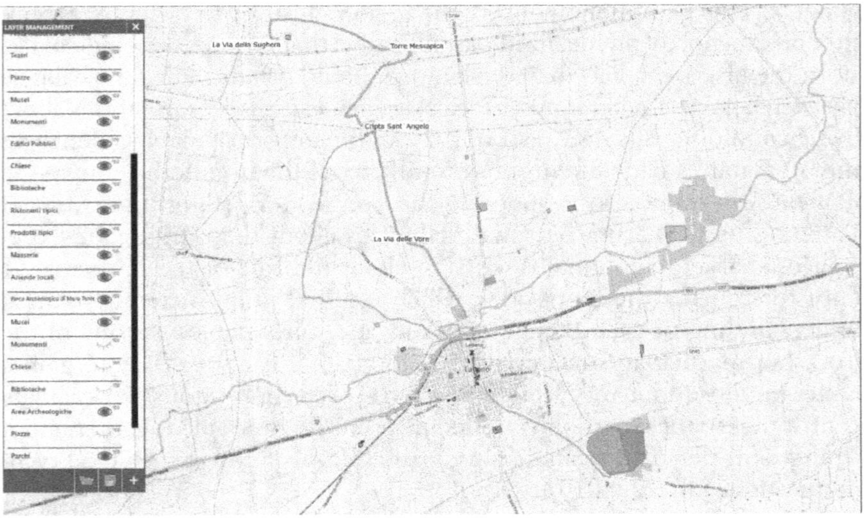

Figure 10.4. Drawing a walking and cycling tour in *Phoenix*.

Developing participant-created tourist itineraries with collaborative mapping software can be fruitfully extended with location-based technology. When integrating the outdoor trails in a mobile application, the local stakeholders have the ability to represent the region's local identity and distinctiveness via a smartphone or tablet device. It allows visitors and other community members to learn about people in other places (Cunsolo Willox et al., 2013). Developing a mobile tourist application becomes then a powerful digital literacy practice through which historical narratives and place-based experiences can be virtually shared with other people—both locals and tourists.

Using location-based technology for creating mobile apps also allows ecomuseum practitioners to mediate the place-based narratives in a multimodal and interactive way. Compared to traditional interpretive materials, such as printed booklets and information sheets, location-based tools for smartphones or tablet devices have the ability to enrich the tour with high quality images, audio and video, and to link these texts and media to the coordinates of a specific point of interests. Because the IZI.Travel platform is a user-friendly service that does not require advanced technical experience, the ecomuseum community can create a mobile tourist application without the need for hiring a professional, often costly, engineer for the technical development of the app.

During the evaluation session, most participants found it highly rewarding to see the outcomes of the first workshop brought together in a professional and intuitive mobile tourist application. Although some mistakes were identified during the testing process (mostly typos), the fact that a small group of volunteers were able to develop a final draft version of a tourist "app" that offers authentic place-based narratives, in a dynamic and multimodal way, was experienced as a rewarding and fruitful activity, capturing local knowledge and sharing this with tourists and other community members. One stakeholder commented that the ability to view context-specific locational information during a landmark visit helped him to critically study the different layers of the cultural landscape and the heritage objects that are located within this environment: "Normally I only looked at one or two specific [landscape] points … but because I know more now about the history, I see more details and I feel personal connections with them" (Personal communication, 2016). Other stakeholders praised the ability to cocreate and adjust the tours to their own insights, and mediate their senses of place and identities through a location-based application.

To this end, the mobile application facilitated the negotiation of digital place-based literacies. The cocreation of a location-based tourist application is a digital literacy practice that encourages people to make new connections with new or existing places and establishes (in)direct connections between places and local identity. We therefore conclude that telling stories with location-based applications allows local communities to represent themselves in an authentic, multimodal, and interactive way, which turns these tools into powerful facilitators of digital literacies that express place-based narratives and identities.

Networking and Intervening

The collaborative mapping and mobile tour-workshops were organized by EVA as social events where local people could foster relationships and share place-based thoughts and feelings. According to Smith (1999), sharing is a form of oral history. Social gatherings are fora that enable communities to disseminate local knowledge and to keep everyone informed about important events and issues (Smith, 1999). But as demonstrated previously in this chapter, sharing memories or stories with geospatial technology is also a fruitful way to negotiate digital place-based literacies and to allow people to rediscover their roots and local identity. Therefore, we argue that ecomuseum workshops are not only storytelling events but are also networking facilitators that provide community members the opportunity to build local movements for protecting and conserving their tangible and intangible heritage.

The ecomuseum movement tries to make local people aware of the intrinsic value of their history and to train them to be agentive ambassadors that help to preserve the landscape's cultural treasures. From this perspective, ecomuseums can be considered as intervention projects that aim to convince policy makers to sustainably develop significant heritage sites and to preserve them for future generations. For EVA this is a major challenge, as most tangible pieces of history from the Classical period are still being excavated. In order to provide a better understanding and appreciation of Latiano's heritage, 3D reconstructions were made to visually inform policymakers, community members, and visitors about the region's historical significance.

Although these reconstructions were designed by professionals, the ecomuseum participants were highly involved in the iterative development process. For example, the initial version of the 3D reconstruction of the imperial palace's internal courtyard was seen from a helicopter perspective and did not include any atmospheric lighting or natural details (Figure 10.5). The same goes for the 3D reconstruction of the Holy Church from the medieval period (Figure 10.6): the first version provided a rather schematic impression of the building. After some discussion with the participants of the ecomuseum, it was agreed upon to add more scenic details to both reconstructions as they remember and experience these sites as highly lively places with their own voice and soul. By choosing a different camera perspective and adding natural atmospheric lighting and environmental details (e.g. trees, grass), these 3D images gave a far more successful impression of the community's sense of place. On the basis of these observations, we concluded that making 3D reconstructions of historical landmarks facilitated a digital literacy through which the community's place-based memories and associations were negotiated.

Figure 10.5. Latiano, Palazzo Imperiali: 3D reconstruction of the internal courtyard.

Figure 10.6. Latiano: 3D reconstruction of the Chiesa Matrice between the 13th and 15th centuries.

During the workshops, the 3D reconstructions were printed on posters with historical representations of Latiano's heritage showcased in the meeting area. We observed that the participants felt encouraged to share their personal stories and memories after viewing the high resolution images. These images functioned as an effective vehicle for engaging the inhabitants of Latiano in bottom-up discussions on the conservation and preservation of their own shared heritage. Because the workshop participants were highly impressed by the historical significance of their region, the 3D reconstructions also sparked fruitful dialogues on their own history and its relationship with a shared cultural identity. They encouraged the participants to actively (re)discover the secrets of Latiano's historical and cultural assets, and fostered a growing understanding and appreciation of the town's history and its heritage features. Second, because the selection of historical landmarks for the 3D reconstructions were chosen by and iteratively developed with local stakeholders, they represented the community's view of the buildings that played a significant role in the historical development of the region. The collection of reconstructed objects explains indirectly which landmarks symbolize Latiano's distinct identity according to the local inhabitants, and as such, can be regarded as artifacts of digital literacies that represent place-based experiences and associations in an innovative way.

CONCLUSION

An important goal of the ecomuseum is to foster the democratization of collective heritage through the involvement and ownership of the community (Davis, 2004, 2008). In this chapter, we aimed to share our findings regarding the use of geospatial technology to co-create inclusive narratives on Latiano's local sense of place and belonging in the context of the *Ecomuseum della Via Appia (EVA)*. In particular, we assessed the affordances of collaborative mapping software, location-based applications, and 3D reconstructions for facilitating digital literacies that negotiated the stakeholder's place-base narratives and identities in an innovative way. The discussions during the workshops provided valuable insights on the added value of employing these tools for mediating local identity and place-based associations.

The geospatial-enhanced workshops were experienced as rewarding digital literacy practices for creating place-based literacies and for representing the community's sense of place and belonging. Participants felt invited to share both positive and traumatic memories and to discuss local particularities with each other. In line with Smith (1999) and Cunsolo Willox et al. (2013), we observed that collaborative mapping software supported storytelling, sharing, creating, remembering, and connecting activities during the first workshop. Secondly, location-based technology allowed the stakeholders to represent their local identity and cocreated place-based literacies towards a broad audience. Last, the public development of the 3D reconstructions of the ecomuseum's heritage sites reflected the community's view of the buildings that played a significant role in the historical development of Latiano and its surroundings. It helped to make local people aware of the intrinsic value of their history and stimulated them to become proactive ambassadors for preserving the landscape's cultural heritage.

On the basis of the findings of this ecomuseum project, we conclude that geo-based technologies are strong facilitators of digital literacies that can negotiate a community's sense of place and belonging. The collaborative mapping software in combination with the 3D reconstructions on display proved to be valuable for facilitating the storytelling process and for connecting personal narratives with historically significant points of interest. Combining fragments of personal stories and knowledge into a richly layered and inclusive narrative on the history of Latiano was broadly considered as fun, challenging, and rewarding. Because all participants had the chance to be heard, a pleasant and democratic atmosphere of interaction was created during the development and evaluation sessions.

Furthermore, the extensive development and testing process of the mobile tourist application gave the participants the opportunity to represent their local identity and distinctiveness on 21st century devices, such as smartphones and tablets, to a wider audience. Because all participants were allowed to share their stories and personal documents during the workshop and because these materials were carefully selected and implemented in an inclusive narrative, the mobile tourist application expressed not only the dominant, but also the personal, histories of Latiano's community. These findings support our assumption that the cocreation and evaluation of a digital community map, mobile tourist application, and 3D reconstructions can be a fruitful digital literacy practices for negotiating place-based narratives and identities for community members and others.

ACKNOWLEDGMENTS

The authors would like to thank the staff members of EVA for helping us to conduct this research, in particular to Fabiana Dirella, Barbara Spigola, Arturo Clavica, Margherita De Matteis. We would also like to thank Heleen Duinker for preparing the touchtable software for the workshop. For the 3D reconstructiosn we would like to thank IMPACT Coop. and Massimiliano Passarelli for *ITLab CNR IBAM-Lecce*. Furthermore, we thank the

Soprintendente Maria Piccarreta at *Soprintendenza archeologia belle arti e paesaggio per le province di Brindisi, Lecce e Taranto*, the architect Francesco Baratti, the *ProLoco Latiano*, the *Biblioteca Civica "G. De Nitto"* of Latiano, the *Università del Salento* and the municipalities of Latiano and Mesagne for assisting in this project. Lastly, we express our gratitude to the reviewers and editors for providing constructive feedback for improvement.

REFERENCES

Alberda, K. van, Burgers, G. J., Burgers, H., Karel, D., & Yntema, D. (1999). *Muro Tenente. Centro messapico nel territorio di Mesagne, a cura di A. Nitti,* Mesagne, Italy: Mandria.

Baratti, F., (2012). *Ecomusei, paesaggi e comunità. Esperienze, progetti e ricerche nel,* Salento, Italy: Sogein.

Bender, B. (1992). Theorising landscapes, and the prehistoric landscapes of Stonehenge. *Man (N.S.), 27*(4), 735–755. doi:10.2307/2804172

Boiano, S., Bowen, J. P., & Gaia, G. (2012). Usability, design and content issues of mobile apps for cultural heritage promotion: The Malta culture guide experience. In S. Dunn, J. Bowen, & K. Ng (Eds.), *E London 2012 Conference Proceedings, Electronic Workshops in Computing (eWiC)* (pp. 66–73). London, England: British Computer Society.

Borrelli, N., & Davis, P. (2012). How culture shapes nature: Reflections on ecomuseum practices. *Nature and Culture*, 7(1). doi:doi.org/10.3167/nc.2012.070103

Bowers, J. (2016). Developing sustainable tourism through ecomuseology: a case study in the Rupununi region of Guyana. *Journal of Sustainable Tourism, 24*(5), 758–782. doi:10.1080/09669582.2015.1085867

Burgers, G.-J. (1998). *Constructing Messapian landscapes: Settlement dynamics, social organization and culture contact in the margins of Graeco-Roman Italy*, Amsterdam, The Netherlands: Gieben.

Burgers, G.-J., & Yntema, D. G. (1999). The settlement of Muro Tenente. Third Interim report. *Bulletin Antieke Beschaving, 74*(2), 111–132.

Burgers, G.-J., & Napolitano, C. (2010). L'insediamento messapico di Muro Tenente. Scavi e ricerche 1998–2009, Mesagne, Italy. In A. Buttimer & D. Seamon (2015). *The human experience of space and place*. Abingdon, England: Routledge.

Buttimer, A., & Seamon, D. (1980). The human experience of space and place. London, England: Routledge. https://doi-org.proxy006.nclive.org/10.4324/9781315684192

Charitonos, K., Blake, C., Scanlon, E., & Jones, A., (2012). Museum learning via social and mobile technologies: (How) can online interactions enhance the visitor experience? *British Journal of Educational Technology, 43*(5), 802–819. doi:10.1111/j.1467-8535.2012.01360.x

Cunsolo Willox, A., Harper, S. L., & Edge, V. L. (2013). Storytelling in a digital age: Digital storytelling as an emerging narrative method for preserving and promoting indigenous oral wisdom. *Qualitative Research, 13*(2), 127–147. doi:10.1177/1468794112446105

Davis, P. (2004). Ecomuseums and the democratization of cultural tourism. *Tourism, Culture & Communication, 5,* 45–58.

Davis, P. (2008). New Museologies and the Ecomuseum. In B. Grahamand & P. Howard (Eds.), *The Ashgate Research Reader in Heritage and Identity* (pp. 397–414) Hampshire, England: Alderhot.

Davis, P. (2009). Ecomuseums and the representation of place, *Rivista Geografica Italiana, 15*(3), 483–503.

Davis, P. (2011). *Ecomuseums: A sense of place* (2nd ed.). London: Continuum International.

Eikelboom T., & Janssen R. (2015). Comparison of geodesign tools to communicate stakeholder values. *Group Decision and Negotiation, 24*(6), 1065–1087. doi:10.1007/s10726-015-9429-7

Geertman, S., J. Stillwell, & Charles, H. (2009). Planning support systems best practice and new methods. *GeoJournal Library, 95,* 490

Han, K., Shih, P. C., Rosson, M. B., & Carroll, J. M. (2014). Enhancing community awareness of and participation in local heritage with a mobile application. *CSCW 2014-Mobile Apps for Enhancing Connectedness* (pp. 1144–1155). New York, NY: ACM Press. doi:10.1145/2531602.2531640

Janssen, R., & Dias, E. (2017). A pictorial approach to geodesign: A case study for the Lower Zambezi valley. *Landscape and urban planning, 164*(3), 144-148. doi:10.1016/j.landurbplan.2017.03.014

Kuroczynski, P. (2017). Virtual research environment for digital 3D reconstructions—Standards, thresholds and prospects. *Studies in Digital Heritage, 1*(2), 456. doi:doi.org/10.14434/sdh.v1i2.23330

Leanza, P., Porto, S., Sapienza, V., & Cascone, S., (2016). A heritage interpretation-based itinerary to enhance tourist use of traditional rural buildings. *Sustainability 8*(2), 47–66. doi:doi.org/10.3390/su8010047

Nassauer, J. I. (2015). Visualization verisimilitude and civic participation. *Landscape and urban planning, 142*(3), 170–272. doi:doi.org/10.1016/j.landurbplan.2015.07.013

Onciul, B., Stefano, M. L., & Hawke, S. (2017). *Engaging heritage, engaging communities.* Woodbridge:, England: Boydell Press.

Sommerville, M. (2007). Place literacies: Significance of space to teaching. *Australian Journal of Language and Literacy, 30*(2), 149–165.

Smith, J. (2015). Anticipating deep mapping: Tracing the spatial practice of Tim Robinson. *Humanities, 4*(3), 283–303. doi:10.3390/h4030283

Smith, P. L. T. (1999). *Decolonizing methodologies: Research and indigenous peoples.* London, England: Zed Books.

Springett, S. (2015). Going deeper or flatter: Connecting deep mapping, flat ontologies and the democratizing of knowledge. *Humanities, 4*(4), 623–636. doi:10.3390/h4040623

PART III

TRACING LITERACIES ACROSS TIME AND SPACE

CHAPTER 11

IMMOBILIZING LITERACIES

Collisions of Difference During the Digital Dialogue Project

Julie E. Rust
Millsaps College

Many in the literacy education research community have been buoyed by the potentials inherent in digital meaning-making opportunities, particularly those that breed collaboration across contexts (e.g., Bruce, 2009; Curwood & Cowell, 2011). However, not all projects that connect participants across divergent political, educational, and religious spheres result in productive dialogue across difference (Mayblin, Valentine, & Andersson, 2016). In this chapter, I explore the resonances of the Digital Dialogue project, a semester-long journey that invited five very different classrooms to share digital compositions virtually in small, heterogeneous groups and then to meet face-to-face for embodied performances of key lines from those compositions. This "throwntogetherness" (Massey, 2005) of students across difference illuminates the wide range of immobilities that can surface when youth from different contexts and age groups are asked to compose multimodally for imagined audiences, watch virtually and comment on

Negotiating Place and Space Through Digital Literacies: Research and Practice, pp. 199–218

each other's digital compositions, and then meet face-to-face to collaboratively construct an embodied skit that mashes up their individual stories.

TRANSLITERACIES AND IMMOBILITY

This chapter pays special attention to the ways the "entangled we" (Ehret, Hollett, & Jocius, 2016, p. 374) brought together during a series of literacy events (from page to screen to bodies) simultaneously creates and breaks down boundaries across difference as human agents experience a myriad of affect-laden (im)mobilities. In this section, I explore the way that transliteracies as a framework foregrounds the degree to which socially-constructed literacy practices across spaces are sometimes inhibited in their mobility.

The framework of transliteracy initially denoted communication across a range of platforms, tools, and media (Liu, 2005; Thomas et al., 2007). In this chapter, I take up Stornaiuolo, Smith, and Phillip's (2017) critical (re) imagining of transliteracies. In their expanded conceptualization, transliteracies perspectives not only aid in tracing the way that meaning-making travels across a range of contexts; but also, they have the capacity to illuminate "how people and things are mobilized and *paralyzed* [emphasis added], facilitated and *restricted* [emphasis added], in different measure and in relation to institutions and systems with long histories" (p. 72). Stornaiuolo et al.'s (2017) transliteracies framework introduces Leonard's (2013) paradox of mobility as one of its central tenants. The paradox of mobility highlights the irony that, while literacy practices are becoming more and more mobile, not all meaning-makers experience the same degree of fluid mobility and uptake from outside audiences. While the paradox of mobility emerged as namely a framework for thinking about traveling multilingual practices, this chapter takes up the concept much more broadly to make sense of how participants affectively experienced meaning-making across a range of platforms, spaces, times, and imagined audiences. Mobility as a construct is utilized in this chapter not merely to focus on "the movement of people, things, modes, and ideas" but instead to more closely pay attention to the circulation of power, emotion, boundaries, and hierarchies that inhibits or invites this movement (Smith & Wargo, 2017, p. 41). In this chapter, I conceptualize *immobilizing literacies* as socially-situated meaning-making that provokes lived experiences that are characterized as constraining, disorienting, lacking, misunderstood, and/or silencing. While those of us who research literacies have been quick to embrace the mobilities inherent in making meaning, we have had a tendency to pay less attention to the sometimes immobilizing nature of meaning-making (Leonard, 2013). The extent to which humans experience immobility in any given moment is a deeply affective experience that is rooted in the agency, power, and connection that is felt in that socially-constructed space. By paying attention to moments when participants describe feeling *less* mobile as they practice space with others during school-sanctioned literacy events, this chapter works to apply the abstract paradox of mobility to applied experiences of youth participating in designed pedagogical interactions. In the sections below, I operationalize immobilizing literacies as sociomaterially constructed, affect-laden, and often inequitable.

Immobility as Sociomaterially Constructed

This chapter takes on immobility as a construct that is sociomaterially produced. Just as space features the "throwntogetherness of human and nonhuman" (Massey, 2005, p. 160), the immobilizing, restricted experience of that space is made up of an entangled constellation of materials, platforms, emotions, and relationships. The introduction of different tools, materials, platforms, and places for meaning-making (e.g., a classroom, a virtual platform, a stage performance) invariably shifts the experience of a moment-in-time to be more or less mobilizing. Adding the digital into spatial assemblages necessarily compels "different socialities," "encounters," "performances," and "enactments" (Thompson, 2016, p. 487).

Massey (2005) similarly reminds us that space is "always under construction … never finished, never closed … a simultaneity of stories-so-far" (p. 9). It naturally follows, then, that space is not a monolithic construct but is one that is continually evolving, experienced differently by socially-contextualized individuals in any given slice of time. For example, at the very same moment that one person feels a sense of *mobilizing* significance and agency after posting their digital story on a virtual platform for an audience, another might experience an *immobilizing* sense of discomfort at the amount of personal details shared as they view the very same story in the same space.

A sociomaterial understanding of immobilizing literacies highlights the seamless flow across channels that makes up constellation of everyday literacy practices. I argue, as many before me (e.g., Buck, 2012; Hollett, Phillips, & Leander, 2017; Leander & McKim, 2003), that the digital doesn't exist in a category distinct from physical realities. The two blur together as youth walk from class to class with their iPhone in hand, laughing with their friends while hitting "like" on an Instagram post. Dovchin and Pennycook (2017) remind us that all spaces "in which …young adults interact are complexly conjoined, with meanings, resources, and identities crossing over from one space to the other" (p. 220).

It is the overarching social purpose, then, that brings the spatial, human, temporal, and material into the realm of meaningfulness. When literacies are experienced as a mobile practice, meaning successfully lands in the proper destination with the intended result. But when literacies are experienced as immobilizing, a much bumpier journey ensues. A sociomaterial view of immobility highlights that this lack of movement is not simply a result of a human agency but arises from an entanglement of humans, emotions, social situations, materials, spaces, and technologies. Broadly conceived in this way, examining "who and what moves, how, why, and under what conditions" (Stornaiuolo et al., 2017, p. 70) aids in making sense of the ways that people make meaning in social contexts with a range of materials, more or less inhibited by micro- and macroconditions.

Immobility as Affect-Laden

Affect, emotion, and the body are indeed central tools for making sense of the entangled assemblage of materials, people, time, space, and technologies that engage in world-making (Ehret & Hollett, 2013; Stornaiuolo et al., 2016). In order to highlight the dance between perceived hierarchies and emotional response, I operationalize mobility as in-the-moment, affective experiences of freedom, agency, joy, confidence, and/or potential to push past previously assumed boundaries. Immobility, in contrast, is operationalized as producing a lived experience that feels more paralyzing or uncomfortable, thus reifying already-existing boundaries or creating new blockades that prevent movement. This emotional mapping of immobility is resonant with Smith, Stornaiuolo, and Phillips's (2018) application of transliteracies when they sought to uncover the ways in which classroom engagement caused students to "feel uncomfortable or comforted, silent or vocal, powerful or powerless" (p. 25). Smith et al. conclude that "students' affective responses were integral to the literacy event, not peripheral or inconsequential" (p. 25). This chapter similarly takes up emotion as central in meaning-making.

Of course, just because an emotion is negative does not mean that students are immobilized by that negative emotion. In fact, oftentimes emotions that are perceived as negative can have mobilizing effects, such as anger or resistance pushing youth to more critically examine a text toward social justice (e.g., Lewis & Tierney, 2013). When anger or sadness result in action or movement, I conceptualize them as mobilizing. When the same emotions result in paralysis and/or deterioration of agency, I conceptualize them as immobilizing. Affect can be characterized, then, not so much by whether it makes an individual feel good or bad, but by what is produced by its presence.

Immobility as Inequity

Perhaps most importantly, I characterize immobility in literacy practice as often highlighting inequities. Whereas mobilizing literacy practices result in boundary-crossing and fluid movement across difference and toward equity, immobilizing literacy experiences are fraught with blockades at every turn. The contemporary understanding of transliteracies crucially adds emphasis on the critical work that is necessary in, not merely celebrating the many literacies that emerge in our diverse landscape, but also noticing the ways in which some groups, media, objects, and individuals experience varying levels of freedom and agency in their production of space (Smith, Stornaiuolo, & Phillips, 2018).

Central to this understanding is the fact that human bodies engaged in this production of meaning and space are not neutral; rather, they carry a diverse set of signifiers (e.g., race, gender, age, dis/ability) that are "consequentially read and produced in everyday human interactions that involve feeling, sensing, touching, and moving" (Hollett, Phillips, & Leander, 2017, p. 149). These heterogeneous agents collide in classrooms to evoke what Pratt (1999) calls a "contact zone," a space marked by difference and inequity rather than sameness and untroubled community. Spaces are not, as Massey puts it, "unproblematically open to all" (p. 153).

Clearly the paradox of mobility has eye-opening implications for issues of equity, access, and justice among youth in traditionally disenfranchised communities. Because it attends to what does and doesn't gain traction for movement, a transliteracies framework "has the potential to orient researchers to everyday, and often systematic, practices of exclusion and marginalization that move with/alongside/against youth and communities" (Stornaiuolo et al., 2017, p. 18). By tracing immobilizing moments that emerged from literacy engagements from page to screen to body among a diverse range of participants, I seek to untangle how one particular collaborative project had the dual capacity to (dis)empower youth. In this particular chapter, I delve into moments that were experienced as confining or restraining rather than agentive. Such a focus is especially valuable because of the need for an honest look at the wide spectrum of ramifications of the pedagogical situations we create.

METHODS

Context and Participants

This study is a small piece of a larger codesigned teacher-researcher partnership, the Digital Dialogue Project, which included 81 participants

(75 students, 5 teachers, and 1 administrator) across a diverse range of schools in a metro area in the Deep South. (See Table 11.1 for a specific description of contexts represented.) Ranging in age (3rd–12th grade), class subject (technology, social studies, English), and school context (rural public, urban public, charter, private), each teacher/class was deliberately invited (via purposive sampling) to help make up a representative slice of the varied communities in the local radius. Teachers interested in joining the project met multiple times throughout the spring semester of 2016 to share information about their schools, discuss their varied goals for their participation, pass along materials and approaches for scaffolding students' digital compositions, create a timeline for the virtual sharing of the compositions, and collaboratively plan the culminating face-to-face field trip.

Table 11.1.
Digital Dialogue Participants

SCHOOL	TYPE/ LOCATION	CLASS	DEMOGRAPHICS
St. Francis Episcopal School	Independent School (2 campuses: Suburban and urban)	3rd Grade Technology 6th Grade Technology	*71.5% White; 13.5% Black; 8.1% Asian; 6.1% Multiracial *Yearly tuition: $17,130
Scholar Prep Charter	Charter School: Urban	5th Grade History	*>95% Black; <5% White, Hispanic *>95% Free/Reduced Lunch
Clark High School	Public School: Rural	8th Grade English	*79% White; 21% Black; .3% Hispanic *52% Free/Reduced Lunch
Smith High School	Public School: Urban	12th Grade AP English	*97% Black; 2%White; 1% Hispanic *100% Free/Reduced Lunch

The Digital Dialogue Project

All participants engaged in three phases of the Digital Dialogue Project, which I logistically directed in partnership with teacher participants:

> *Phase 1: Digital Story Composition*—During this phase, teachers from all five schools designed a prompt and series of scaffolding activities that integrated their own curricular goals (e.g., students

will gain experience comparing/contrasting historical events to current events) with student creation of a multimodal product of some kind (e.g., a podcast or iMovie). For most, this phase took place in the regular classroom during regular class time.

Phase 2: Virtual Sharing, Viewing, and Commenting—Once all digital stories were created, students uploaded them to Voicethread (an online platform that enables multimodal sharing and commenting), and heterogeneous groups of four to five students (typically representing one student from each school and grade) were formed. Students were then instructed to view their group members' compositions and then comment (via text, audio, or video) in a substantive way.

Phase 3: Face-to-Face Collaborative Performative Experience—At the culmination of the viewing/commenting phase, groups met each other face-to-face during a field trip to the college. During the two hours together, students engaged in warm up theater games and were asked to create a skit or poem weaving together key lines from all of the digital stories represented in their group. The event ended with pizza and a vote on "the best" skit in various categories.

Analysis

Analysis initially involved an iterative Critical Discourse Analysis process (Gee, 2014). I first transcribed and emergently coded online comments that took place in each small group's virtual sharing of digital compositions. I then coded reflective interviews accumulated from the 75 student participants after all three phases were over. The initial iterative coding process included marking focal moments in gathered transcripts as "border" or "bridge" to indicate whether students indicated feeling closer to or more distanced from the members of their group from different schools.

At this stage I began to feel limited by the perceived cut-and-dry dichotomy between border and bridge, and I began to do a bit more "thinking with theory" (Jackson & Mazzei, 2012), particularly the ideas outlined above around the paradox of mobility. Thus, I began to be less attuned to borders/bridges and more aware of the various levels of mobility that participants experienced through each of the three phases of the project: from multimodal composition to virtual viewing/commenting to collaborative embodied production. While there were many reported instances of high mobility in youths' literacy practices across the Digital Dialogue Project, this chapter highlights the unanticipated tensions and limitations that participants reported in their interviews. The central question of this chapter thus evolved to become: How did immobility manifest across all three phases of the Digital Dialogue Project?

FINDINGS

In the sections below I trace each of the three phases of the Digital Dialogue Project (described above) with special attention to the ways that participants experienced *immobility* in their meaning-making, which often surfaced as a sense of paralysis or heightened self-consciousness. Findings are organized chronologically in order to juxtapose the different immobilities that emerged for participants as they moved from composing their own digital story in their individual classrooms (Phase 1), to virtually sharing their multimodal production and watching/commenting on their group members' digital stories online (Phase 2), to creating a collaborative dramatic performance with their group members when meeting face-to-face at a culminating field trip (Phase 3). Each subsection begins with a description of the space produced in each phase and then moves to share representative cases of student interview data that point to one foregrounded theme of immobility that surfaced in the data during that phase.

Phase 1 (Multimodal Composing): Imagined Audience as Immobilizing

As they embarked on multimodal design, students were introduced to the fact that they were composing, not just for a grade in the class or for their familiar peers, but for a larger project that would put them in a group of four to five students they had never met who represented five very different schools and age levels in the metro area. While this imagined audience was experienced at times as motivating (which I conceptualize in this chapter as mobilizing), other times participants described moments in which the anticipation of how the unknown others in their small group would react to their posted digital stories stymied their creative process. In this section, I explore the diverse ways that youth in the process of composing their multimodal pieces evoked the notion of *imagined audience* as impeding their design process.

Oftentimes, creating the opportunity for an authentic audience for student writing, outside of just the teacher or their direct classmates, is hailed as a key way for ELA teachers to enhance engagement and relevance for their young writers (Duke, Purcell-Gates, Hall, & Tower, 2006; Kixmiller, 2004). While many interviewed did express a sense of excitement for composing for a diverse youth they had never met, a surprising number described a heightened sense of self-consciousness. For example, a sixth grader who attended St. Francis reported that he'd have preferred to do a paper instead of the podcast because

> writing a paper you can just type down whatever you're thinking and you don't have to talk out loud. But actually making an audio file, you have to talk, which I don't like doing a lot [...] I feel really embarrassed. I've done some stuff with my brother when he has a Youtube account, and when I just watch the video, I sound so dumb. (Personal communication, April 29, 2016)

Note that he transfers his out-of-school experiences making Youtube videos with his brother to inform his affective response to this school-required assignment, thus revealing the interplay between these often dichotomized spaces. His sense of immobility (embarrassment) is closely tied to the multimodality that a digital product affords. He feels safe writing a paper, but sharing an audio file of his voice elicits a sense of heightened vulnerability. This, then, hints at the sociomaterial assemblage (Latour, 2005) contributing to his sense of hesitancy: the audial affordances of the technology are entangled with the social nature of the assignment, thus resulting in an almost paralyzing situation.

While the young man above traced his embarrassment to the sound of his voice, a fifth grader from Scholar Prep described the imagined audience listening to her piece as paralyzing:

> You know how you [feel] standing in front of a crowd doing some type of speech? It felt like I was doing that and [...] it felt like there was a lot of people around me even though there wasn't, it was just y'all. So I decided to- I spoke low. (Personal communication, May 2, 2016)

For this fifth grader, it is less the sound of her voice and more the anticipated crowd of listeners that served as an immobilizing agent, one that caused her to speak so quietly that her words in the video are nearly undecipherable. Newkirk (2017) writes about the original meaning of the word embarrassment as "barrier ... obstacle ... an impediment that might used in a fortification ... barricade" (p. 15). Without a doubt, metaphors, such as barrier, obstacle, and barricade directly elicit immobilizing lived experiences. In both quotes, voice is linked to a sense of embarrassment. Interestingly, the student above likens the experience of making a digital video to the face-to-face experience of giving a speech to a crowd. Immobilization, then, is quite viscerally socially produced through her imagined sense of audience. In addition, note the repetition of the phrase "it felt like." Clearly the affective experience of self-consciousness triggered by the imagined audience of "a lot of people" who were strangers listening to her digital composition inhibited her.

A high school senior in the project felt immobilized, not by embarrassment elicited by imagined audiences, but by a sense of duty to sanitize his message for younger students. Below he describes the way he felt limited in the content he could share with the third through eighth graders in the project:

> So I cut out so much material [...] because like in this class I'm the most behaved [...] and even that's not saying much. In other classes they know how I work [...] Just to put it bluntly, I'm a very vulgar guy, that's how I present myself [...] the way I am really is influenced by the hardness [...] I would wake up where I'm from [...] by hearing somebody, just domestic violence in my neighbors. [Having to make a digital story with] all rainbows and unicorns ... that was weird. (Personal communication, April 29, 2016)

It seems that this young man's sense of disjuncture between his range of experiences and the range of experiences he deemed appropriate for his younger group members (namely "all rainbows and unicorns") triggered self-censorship practices that he felt de-authenticated his story in some ways. Rather than motivating him to go deeper, his imagined audience of younger peers compelled him to water down his truth into something he viewed as more palatable for an audience who did not share his background. This duty to create what he viewed as a more appropriate, but inferior, and less truthful final product reveals the way that this particular multiaged pedagogical situation appear to have immobilized him. This student clearly had internalized the message that his truth, his community, is not deemed acceptable for popular consumption; here immobility as inequity is made manifest.

Phase 2 (Virtual Viewing/Commenting): Unfamiliarity as Immobilizing

In the second phase of the Digital Dialogue Project, participants uploaded their digital compositions to VoiceThread, and they were broken up into small groups of five, generally composed of one student per school. One group, for example, featured five stories: a podcast about school uniforms uploaded by a sixth grader, a "my favorite place" story with voice-over by a third grader, a digital composition connecting civil rights for African Americans with civil rights for Muslims including images and voice-over uploaded by a fifth grader, an artistic rendering of *Lord of the Flies* with a voiced-over artist's statement by an eighth grader, and a personal digital story created with iMovie uploaded by a 12th grader. Each participant was asked to view the other four compositions and then to add a substantive comment. Phase 2, then, consisted of: (1) watching multimodal compositions authored by people from different schools; (2) commenting on the videos watched; (3) reading comments that others posted about one's own composition. During this virtual feedback phase, youth reported feeling immobilized by both unfamiliarity with their diverse small group peers and the experiences/content of the digital stories these peers produced.

Many students reported difficulty with coming up with how to respond to the digital stories uploaded to their group on VoiceThread due to the lack of a previously established face-to-face relationship with the other members of their heterogeneous virtual groups of four to five students. For example, an eighth grade student from Clark High School described hesitancy to post anything critical about the stories produced by younger students he did not know in his group:

> I could give a fair deal if they were my classmates, however they were not. Plus it is impolite to give fair to strict criticism to those I did not even know or first met. Not only is that a formula to make enemies but is also a classless way to make a bad first impression on another individual. (Personal communication, May 16, 2016)

By clearly articulating his culturally-embedded norms of interaction, this young man reveals real discomfort with the charge to engage in honest virtual dialogue with the strangers in his group; critiquing the digital stories of youth he does not know as "impolite" and "a classless way to make a bad first impression." Most fascinating here is his assertion that had he been commenting on his classmates' stories, he could have given them "a fair deal," or more honest and substantive critique and feedback. If immobility is sociomaterially constructed, it naturally follows that a lack of shared social history among group members destabilized the entangled Voicethread-human-digital story-emotion-filled space. In other words, just because a virtual platform affords social interaction through a host of multimodal commenting features does not mean they will be taken up fully. Before delving into these interviews, the classroom teachers and I had assumed that students' often short, surface-level affirmations about their group members' digital compositions were a result of their lack of interest in posting responses on Voicethread. Instead it appears that students were being far from careless—they were deliberately leaving superficial yet positive feedback to avoid hurt feelings and to mirror the lack of depth of relationship and familiarity they had with their group members. More in-depth, specific critique was effectively immobilized because of the social forces acting on the rhetorical situation.

In addition to a hesitancy to go deep in their comments because of their unfamiliarity with their group members, several fifth graders at Scholar

Prep Charter articulated a struggle with responding to very personal details that the seniors integrated into their personal narrative iMovies. For example, a fifth grader from Scholar Prep reported his shocked reaction to his group's twelfth grader's story about her sister having a skin condition: "She was really open with it, and I was like, 'You don't even know who those people are, and you're being really open!' " (Personal communication, May 2, 2016). This particular story featured graphic images of the family member's skin alongside affect-filled narrative about the way this condition impacted everyone's lives, and it is likely that the immobility the fifth grader experienced in commenting after viewing is a direct result of the especially emotionally moving nature of the multimodal composition. While surprise at peers' vulnerability is not by itself immobilizing, it can have the impact of creating a sense of discomfort with the mandate to leave thoughtful comments on such personal stories when shared by a stranger.

Another fifth grader from Scholar Prep explained the strange space created when viewing and commenting on a multimodal story that seemed to confide so much in her, a complete stranger:

> The hardest part about it was finding something to say because this girl she was talking about a really lot of personal stuff, like her mom got divorced. I guess I think she said her dad had died or something. I did not know what to say. I just said, "That's a lot of personal information [...] Maybe you should talk about something a little less personal, but otherwise it's all good." (Personal communication, May 2, 2016)

It appears that the fifth grader above was experiencing some degree of immobility in attempting to interact with this digital story because her own lack of established relationship with the senior composing the video clashes in uncomfortable ways with the vulnerability exposed by the digital piece. The disconnect that the fifth graders described illuminates the dance of affect and social affiliations in literacy enactments. It appears that when social connections are in place, affective responses to vulnerability are experienced as safe and mobilizing. However, without those secure relationships established, these moving digital stories felt risky, as though the seniors producing them were leaving themselves open for attack from outside strangers. The fifth graders were left uncomfortable and, in a sense, unable to virtually respond.

Another reason the student quoted above may have felt uncomfortable was her lack of experience with the personal content shared (e.g., divorce, a parent dying). Given the range of age groups and digital story material, it is perhaps unsurprising that when asked about this phase of the project, the younger students involved in the project experienced a range of immobilizing moments related to how well they did and did not relate to their group members' digital stories as they viewed them virtually. In contrast to the younger students in the project, the high school seniors experienced a much higher degree of mobility as they viewed and commented on the younger peers' digital compositions. One senior from Smith High School listed her connection to each of the digital stories she viewed from her group:

> So for the first girl, she was I believe in Middle School, and she did *Lord of the Flies*. It took me back to when I read the book, and I was like, "OK, I can connect. I can relate. I was there." For the guy, he did a piece on Muslims, and when I watched his I was like, "You're woke." I was like, "You understand." And he was so young; he was like nine! And then I had another girl who did like an interview on school uniforms. Which again, I wore school uniforms, and I could relate. Like, man, I hated it, I could understand [her] pain. And for the last girl, she was really, really, really young and she did it about her best friend's house. And so I liked it because she was so innocent, and I was just like, "Where did the days go?" (Personal communication, April 29, 2016)

Note that, for this (and many) of the seniors, the ability to access group members' digital stories directly correlated with the ability to connect the content of the story to their own past and present experiences. This time-traveling capacity to view text and think "OK, I can connect, I can relate, I was there" is perhaps at the heart of mobility. When youth can activate prior experiences/identities to connect with texts produced by others, they are more equipped to leverage shared affinities to network into new relationships. This, then, enables them to more freely traverse across borders of difference. The senior quoted above is able to remember reading the same novel as the eighth grader, is able to access critical perspectives about oppressed groups that the fifth grader is digging into, and is able to dig deep into her own frustration when she had to wear uniforms for school. In addition, positive emotion colors her recounting of the stories her group members created. She feels sentimental about the novel; she feels amazed and inspired by how "woke" the fifth grader is; she feels deep empathy with the sentiment of the uniform podcast; she feels nostalgia in relation to the third grader's story ("where did the days go?"). In addition, many of her points of connection with the stories revolved around issues of equity (e.g., uniforms are unfair; Muslims are mistreated). Age, affect, and experience, then, served as enhancers of mobility toward equity in this virtual sharing space.

Phase 3 (Face-to-Face Collaboration): Difference as Immobilizing

In the final phase of the Digital Dialogue Project, students moved from screen to face-to-face communication and embodied performance at a culminating meet up at the college. Chairs were set up in small groups of five so that once students arrived they had to break away from their friends and familiar classmates to sit with the members of their virtual groups. After a series of warm-up theater games, the 17 groups of 3–5 participants were assigned their mission for the day: to create a collaborative performance that mashed up a key line from each of the virtual stories represented. The energy of the room was visceral as groups moved around, practiced tableaus, typed scripts for skits, or prepared a snake poem. Each group bravely took the stage to share their quickly-composed creative enactment, and the meet-up concluded with a whole-group reflection on how things went, a vote for the "best of" the performances, a pizza party, and a final announcement of the winners of the day.

For the organizers and helpers in the event, the day felt like a victory. The majority of students interviewed described joyful surprise at the mobility they experienced through the traversing of perceived borderlands at the culminating field trip. Many were amazed how nice they older students were. Others commented that the White children did not make fun of them as they feared. They certainly revealed the fact that, within the 2-hour span of time they spent together physically, students navigated boundaries and difference with a good deal of mobility, much more mobility than they had experienced than when they had viewed each other's videos and commented virtually. But even in the energetic space, there were immobilities being experienced above and beneath the experience related to difference in age, race, and class.

Age, much like in the virtual phase of the project, was experienced as immobilizing by younger students during the face-to-face field trip phase. One third grade girl from St. Francis confessed that during the bus ride conversation on the way to the college they "were starting to go overboard and were talking about all the bad things that could happen" (Personal communication, April 21, 2016) due to their status as the youngest members of each group. Interestingly, the sociomaterial space provoked by the field trip, a large room on a college campus featuring face-to-face collaboration and embodied performance, provoked a particularly unsettling affective impact.

In other words, while age-induced confusion or discomfort merely inhibited the ability of third graders to comment on the virtual platform during Phase 2, age-related immobility during Phase 3 *felt* scarier. One fifth grader from Scholar Prep described a sense of fear when he walked into the room and saw two group members that looked to him like adults: "I thought they would be mean [...] I thought they might be talking about [...] stuff like Facebook, Instagram" (Personal communication, May 2, 2016). It is especially interesting that he links his sense of distance from his older group members to their usage of social media platforms, digital tools that mobilize teenagers to move freely across virtual networks but are experienced as immobilizing by those who cannot yet access them. In both cases, the younger participants experienced immobility in their anticipation of injustice; the third graders were "talking about the bad things that could happen" and the fifth grader feared "they would be mean" simply because of the uneven circulation of power related to age.

In post-interviews, nearly all the young people described being surprised by how kind the older students ended up being, despite the anxiety that preceded the event. But despite the overarching narrative of overcoming age-related boundaries, students occasionally described the process of actually creating the collaborative performance as still impacted by asymmetrical power relations. One third grader from St. Francis recalled her unwillingness to share her dissatisfaction with the skit idea the senior proposed: "We are so young, and they're all so old …I decided it was a good [skit idea] and [to] just go along with it" (Personal communication, April 21, 2016). She effectively felt silenced by the social situation, unable to contribute and collaborate. It is clear that the younger participants almost exclusively faced immobility in relation to their age and expected expertise, while the seniors enjoyed almost unlimited power in shaping the direction of the group skits.

While the sense of self-consciousness and age difference followed across all three phases of the project, differences around categories of race and class came up far more in reflective interviews about this particular face-to-face phase of the project. For example, one fifth grader from Scholar Prep explained: "Not to be racist or anything but they had like there was three white people and only two black people so I only got nervous [...] and I thought the other three white kids would be talking about my color" (Personal communication, May 2, 2016). The nervousness and heightened sense of self-consciousness this young man described worked to immobilize his participation in the initial warm up theater games at the start of the field trip; his typical confident and energetic demeanor was replaced with a much more sober and subdued one. Another fifth grader from the same school articulated his field trip fear that "some people would be like talking to you because you're another race" (Personal communication, May 2, 2016). It was clear by his tone that "talking to you" referred to, not informal banter, but language used to insult, put down, or disempower minority groups. It is heartening that after the event both youth shared that their group members were, in fact, kind. But the fact remains that youth of color reported a greater degree of anxiety as they walked into the physical social space of the final field trip. These affective experiences of nervousness were heightened by the social space produced by the face-to-face collaborative encounter.

While eighth grade students from the predominantly White rural school did not mention race, they did mention class multiple times in their reflection. One eighth grader from Clark High School wrote of her imagination of his group members before meeting them:

> I hadn't really heard of any of the schools that we participated with beforehand, but I did know that they weren't from far out in the country like we are. The only preconceptions that I had about these students were that they probably aren't a lot like us and were raised around different things, for instance nice cars and big houses instead of tractors and cattle farms. (Personal communication, May 16, 2016)

Note the sociomaterial composition of this immobilizing distinction between private school kids ("nice cars and big houses") from the familiar kids at her school ("tractors and cattle farm.") Materials, such as cars and tractors, places, such as big houses and farms, and even animals like cattle lurk large in her social boundary mapping between the self and other. Socioeconomic class is a clear immobilizing agent here, but just as strong is the participant's status as representing the only rural school in the project. It is no coincidence that another eighth grader from Clark reflected that he assumed students from the private school (St. Francis) would "be very clever in a rude way" (Personal communication, May 16, 2016). While this fear did not materialize as true at the field trip, it is accurate that some youth from the rural school walked into the physical space with particular inferior self-positionings in mind. Inequities around class and negative stereotypes about "rural kids," both likely informed by past experiences, are at the center of these immobilizations.

SIGNIFICANCE

Using a transliteracies framework to examine the Digital Dialogue Project highlights traveling literacy practices (from page to screen to body) in socially constructed online and physical spaces. But most poignantly, analyzing with an eye toward the paradox of mobility reveals that not all youth experience the same levels of free-flowing fluidity in all meaning-making situations, even when we design communicative opportunities with the best of intentions. It is essential that we as teacher educators and researchers pay attention to various socially-constructed immobilizing forces if we are committed to preparing young people to dialogue across difference (Burbules & Rice, 1991). As Stornaiuolo et al. (2017) point out, we can no longer afford to pay exclusive attention to triumphs, to "the opportunities and possibilities afforded by people's mobile literacy practices, particularly across digital spaces" (p. 70). We must, instead, turn our eyes to something a bit less sanguine, but equally real: "the contingency, instability, and emergence of mobile literacy practices that simultaneously open some opportunities and foreclose others" (p. 70).

In all phases of the Digital Dialogue Project, participants experienced a range immobilities. The findings in Phase 1 above point to the instability youth face when curating and designing multimodal products for an imagined audience. While creating authentic opportunities for youth to produce multimodal products for audiences beyond their immediate classroom can be an incredibly powerful pedagogical practice, the entanglement of audio-image-words-others can also produce a design space that is experienced as intimidating for some and creatively stifling for others. Both lived realities (the sense of self-consciousness when recording your voice and the impulse to water down your message for a younger audience) can be experienced as immobilizing.

Analysis of Phase 2 (sharing their creations online and commenting on peers' stories they have not yet met) revealed similar immobilizations around accessing and commenting upon the stories made by these unfamiliar others. Students from third grade to eighth grade especially faced immobilizing difficulty in first accessing multimodal content produced by others that was personal and then determining how/if to substantively respond in their virtual comments. For third graders attempting to make sense of an eighth grader's painting of a dead pig from *Lord of the Flies* or an iMovie, this second phase resulted in frustration, miscomprehension, and, for some, refusal to even view or comment on peers' videos. Even when digital stories were accessed and understood, various youth expressed concern with the appropriate level of honesty/vulnerability to share online with strangers they had not yet met. In contrast, most senior participants experienced mobility in both accessing and responding to their group members' produced stories.

Because Phase 3 involved a face-to-face field trip, it elicited a myriad of immobilities around differences in race, age, and class. It is likely that it was the open-ended, spontaneous, face-to-face space of the field trip that made visible these tensions. While the virtual space of Phase 2 enabled teachers to monitor each comment made by students viewing stories in the comfort of their familiar classroom, the sociomaterially produced space in Phase 3 initiated by the entanglement of bodies and collaborative emergent theater activities at the field trip was far less stable, far less predictable. Younger students, students of color, and students from the rural school experienced anxiety on the way to the field trip since, after all, it is much easier to subversively undermine others in an emergent, noisy, collaborative face-to-face space. Before this third phase interviews indicated that many youth involved were still fairly distanced from their group members, informed by a set of assumptions about who they were and were not. However, after the field trip, nearly all youth interviewed described a movement toward increasing mobility across borders. In sum, analysis reveals that pushing young people to virtually view and comment on each other's very divergent digital compositions before they met face to face resulted in a mixed bag of connection, confusion, and surface-level engagement. However, the final face-to-face, collaborative performance phase was vital in (re)shaping students' perceptions of the other members of their groups.

Across all three phases, it became clear that different spaces were produced through the interaction of youth, platforms, materials, time, and emotion. Emotion in particular played a leading role in signifying mapping lived experiences of (im)mobility. Embarrassment, self-consciousness, and nervousness lurked large throughout, and it was clear that particular groups (the younger students, students of color, students from rural areas) were disproportionately impacted by these very real immobilities. Teachers/researchers who design virtual-embodied collaborations across race, class, and other categories of difference must work to design more just interactions that don't unfairly load labor on our students of color, those with dis/ability, or those that come from homes of lower-socio-economic origins (Hollett et al., 2017). Having reflective conversations with youth who have engaged in collaborations across difference after the fact is essential in making visible the ways in which our literacy enactments can work to enhance, rather than inhibit the mobility of others.

Literacies are on the move, and youth engaged in meaning-making are inevitably swimming in a milieu of socio-relationally-produced emotions, identities, and flows that are more or less impeded by inequities, embarrassments, and missed opportunities. We as teachers and educators who appreciate the potential in collaborating across difference and communicating across spaces, times, and platforms must have our eyes wide open to this truth as we seek to make the way clear for youth to curate representations of self and then practice space with a range of others.

ACKNOWLEDGMENTS

I am indebted to Dr. Christy Wessell-Powell, who thought/presented with me during the genesis of this analysis, as well as Dr. Lenny Sanchez, who generously gave his time in reading and providing feedback on an earlier draft.

REFERENCES

Bruce, D. (2009). Writing with visual images: Examining the video composition processes of high school students. *Research in the Teaching of English*, *34*(4), 426–450.

Buck, A. (2012). Examining digital literacy practices on social network sites. *Research in the Teaching of English*, *47*(1), 9–38.

Burbules, N., & Rice, S. (1991). Dialogue across differences: Continuing the conversation. *Harvard Educational Review, 61*(4), 393–417.

Curwood, J., & Cowell, L. H. (2011). iPoetry: Creating space for new literacies in the English curriculum. *Journal of Adolescent & Adult Literacy, 55*(2), 110–120.

Dovchin, S., & Pennycook, A. (2017). Digital metroliteracies. In K. A. Mills, A. Stornaiuolo, A. Smith, & J. Z. Pandya (Eds.), *Handbook of writing, literacies, and education in digital cultures* (pp. 211–222). New York, NY: Routledge.

Duke, N. K., Purcell-Gates, V., Hall, L. A., & Tower, C. (2006). Authentic literacy activities for developing comprehension and writing. *The Reading Teacher, 60*(4), 344–355.

Ehret, C., Hollett, T., & Jocius, R. (2016). The matter of new media making: An intra-action analysis of adolescents making a digital book trailer. *Journal of Literacy Research, 48*(3), 346–377.

Ehret, C., & Hollett, T. (2013). (Re)placing school: Middle school students' countermobilities while composing with iPods. *Journal of Adolescent & Adult Literacy, 57*(2), 110–119.

Gee, J. P. (2014). *An introduction to discourse analysis: Theory and method*. New York, NY: Routledge.

Hollett, T., Phillips, N., & Leander, K. (2017). Digital geographies. In K. A. Mills, A. Stornaiuolo, A. Smith, & J. Z. Pandya (Eds.), *Handbook of writing, literacies, and education in digital cultures* (pp. 148–160). New York, NY: Routledge.

Jackson, A. Y., & Mazzei, L. A. (2012). *Thinking with theory in qualitative research: Viewing data across multiple perspectives*. New York, NY: Routledge.

Kixmiller, L. A. (2004). Standards without sacrifice: The case for authentic writing. *English Journal, 94*(1), 29–33.

Latour, B. (2005). *Reassembling the social: An introduction to actor-network-theory*. New York, NY: Oxford University Press.

Leander, K. M., & McKim, K. K. (2003). Tracing the everyday sitings' of adolescents on the Internet: A strategic adaptation of ethnography across online and offline spaces. *Education, communication & information, 3*(2), 211–240.

Leonard, R. L. (2013). Traveling literacies: Multilingual writing on the move. *Research in the Teaching of English, 48*(1), 13–39.

Lewis, C., & Tierney, J. D. (2013). Mobilizing emotion in an urban classroom: Producing identities and transforming signs in a race-related discussion. *Linguistics and Education, 24*(3), 289–304. doi:10.1016/j.linged.2013.03.003

Massey, D. (2005). *For space*. Thousand Oaks, CA: SAGE.

Mayblin, L., Valentine, G., & Andersson, J. (2016). In the contact zone: engineering meaningful encounters across difference through an interfaith project. *The Geographical Journal, 182*(2), 213–222.

Newkirk, T. (2017). *Embarrassment: And the emotional underlife of learning*. Portsmouth, NH: Heinneman.

Pratt, M. L. (1999). Arts of the contact zone. In D. Bartholmae & A. Petrosky (Eds.), *Ways of reading* (5th ed, pp. 582–596). New York, NY: Bedford/St. Martin's Press.

Smith, A., & Wargo, J. (2017). Experiencing electracy: Digital writing and the emerging communicative landscapes of youth composing selves. In K. A.

Mills, A. Stornaiuolo, Smith, & J. Z. Pandya (Eds.), *Handbook of writing, literacies, and education in digital cultures* (pp. 37–49). New York, NY: Routledge.
Smith, A., Stornaiuolo, A., & Phillips, N. C. (2018). Multiplicities in motion: A turn to transliteracies. *Theory Into Practice*, *57*(1), 20–28.
Stornaiuolo, A., Smith, A., & Phillips, N. C. (2017). Developing a transliteracies framework for a connected world. *Journal of Literacy Research*, *49*(1), 68–91.
Thomas, S., Joseph, C., Laccetti, J., Mason, B., Mills, S., Perril, S., & Pullinger, K. (2007). Transliteracy: crossing divides. *First Monday*, *12*(12).
Thompson, T. L. (2016). Digital doings: curating work–learning practices and ecologies. *Learning, Media and Technology*, *41*(3), 480–500.

CHAPTER 12

ADOLESCENTS IN THE WILD

Critiquing and Arguing Back Through Mediated Social Spaces

Jane M. Saunders
Texas State University

INTRODUCTION

In the current rapid-response networked environment in which we find ourselves, it is difficult to remember a time prior to the onset of social media like Facebook, Twitter, and Instagram, and their primacy over what is left of our free time. The gratification and at times *fixation* with receiving positive responses to postings is evident through even a cursory engagement with social media, one's twitter feed, or viewing the evening's news. In its more negative enactment, we might find a political Twitter spat replete with pithy clapback that goes viral through exponential retweeting. The movie *Ingrid Goes West* (Spicer, 2017) portrays a darker side of social media through its protagonist's cross-country pursuit of an Instagram "influencer" and viral fame. Within the space of social media, literacy educators are called to help students understand and engage with the multiheaded

Negotiating Place and Space Through Digital Literacies: Research and Practice, pp. 219–239

hydra that is the result of a burgeoning cast of social networking sites (SNS) in addition to their other responsibilities.

Recent research suggests that new media show potential for "achieving a more equitable society through increased social participation" (Burnett & Merchant, 2011, p. 41). Scholars call for examples of how students use Web 2.0 tools in and out of schools (Greenhow, Robelia, & Hughes, 2009) and how these tools might leverage greater civic participation in our larger culture (Jenkins, Clinton, Purushotma, Robison, & Weigel, 2006). This call is complicated, however, by school settings that limit students' engagement with the world outside of the classroom either via written restrictions and browser blockers, or the intense focus on standards, scripted curricula, and regimes of testing inside the classroom.

This chapter begins with an innocuous school event—a school presentation by a member of the local community—that burgeons into a public debate about forsaking one's education in pursuit of one's passions and the role that social media play in disseminating competing public messages about schooling, following a dream, and making a difference in the world. I then examine how a group of students draw on social media and public spaces to critique the event, and the ugly and public responses they received in return. Drawing on multiple media sources and conversations to tease out the story behind the story, I provide recommendations for teachers considering entering the "wilds" of mediated online spaces but who may be worrying about the potential fallout from this type of engagement.

A REVIEW OF CRITICAL MEDIA LITERACY

In 2012, the International Reading Association's (now ILA) report on Adolescent Literacy made recommendations for reading and writing instruction that supported adolescents' coming of age in the 21st century. Among these was a request for educators and schools to draw on a variety of print and digital texts; to assist students in connecting with texts and each other orally; and, to help students "use literacy in the pursuit of civic engagement" (International Literacy Association, 2012, p. 10). Likewise, in its 2013 position statement regarding 21st Century Literacies, the National Council of Teachers of English (NCTE) affirmed the importance of helping students to create, critique, analyze, and evaluate multimedia texts (National Council of Teachers of English, 2013). Critical media literacy as it is defined by Alvermann, Moon, and Hagood (1999) includes: the use of print and nonprint materials to construct knowledge of the world; employs the creation of communities of readers who are active and exercise agency; is representative of cultural practice; and can be related to power and popular culture. Enacting a critical media approach, according to Kellner and Share (2005), can be complicated because

> it is not a pedagogy in the traditional sense, with firmly established principles, a canon of texts, and tried-and-true teaching procedures. It requires a democratic pedagogy which involves teachers sharing power with students as they join together in the process of unveiling myths and challenging hegemony. (p. 373)

Indeed, it is often in these power-sharing situations where students begin to understand that information is "never neutral and always mediated by sociocultural, political, and historical contexts of when, where, why, and by whom they were created" (Gainer, 2013, p. 18).

Students today are immersed in a media-rich world that requires a sophisticated set of tools to unpack what is supported by fact, versus infected by misinformation (Burnett & Merchant, 2011; Lewandowsky, Ecker , Seifert, Schwarz, & Cook, 2012). And, it is only by "demystifying media messages through critical inquiry" (Kellner & Share, 2005) that students can develop the tools needed to engage effectively and participate in our larger, socially mediated and connected culture. Jenkins et al. (2006) noted that teachers play an important role "in helping students acquire the skills they need to become full participants in our society" (p. 4). However, there are few roadmaps available for teachers in this new role. Garcia, Seglem, and Share (2013) asked teacher education students to rebrand common everyday products like yogurt or create podcasts that retold a nursery rhyme from a different perspective as a means of modeling what critical media literacy might look like in practice. In doing so, they affirmed critical media literacy as a space to deepen "literacy education to critically analyze relationships between media and audiences, information, and power" (p. 111), while reminding educators of the importance of media production itself, "as it empowers students to create their own messages that can challenge media texts and narratives" (p. 111).

Similarly, Garcia, Mirra, Morrell, Martinez, and Scorza (2015) offered high school students the opportunity to create counterstories to hegemonic norms by asking them to critique the movie *Waiting for Superman* (2010), read and respond to the writings of Antonio Gramsci via social media, and create and curate digital shorts as a means to renegotiate social and power relationships. These examples offer models for teachers interested in helping students hone their tools as critical creators and consumers of text and in developing agency in both in-school and out-of-school literacy practices. And certainly, research related to the role that social media can play in democratizing the spread of information and misinformation is growing in number (e.g., Mihailidis & Viotty, 2017). In spite of these, however, there are few studies that describe students engaging in real-world conversations while navigating the shark-infested waters of public response through social media present in the literature. This chapter offers up just such an example.

METHODS AND DATA

Envisioned as a qualitative case study, the work described here sought understanding about how students draw on in-school learning to engage in both in and out-of-school response and critique through written interactions with teachers, students, and the public at large. It was part of a larger study investigating the critical media literacy practices of high school journalism teacher Isabelle Salazar, her students, and *The Maroon*, the print/online newsmagazine (also publicly available) she oversaw. Those featured in this chapter are not masked by pseudonyms as the bulk of data described are publicly available via the Internet, making it is impossible to mask participants. And, while this research was approved by my university's institutional review board and the participating school district, because of the public nature of the events described in this chapter, I included only the students who were adults at the time of this research (over age 18) and who gave additional written assent (beyond their parent's initial consent for the larger project) to include their work for the purposes of research.

Among the data gathered for this study are in-class observations of Ms. Salazar's class for the documentation of the interaction styles, pedagogical choices, and curricular decisions she employed in helping students critically engage with print, video, and visual media. I kept careful notes of what students were writing and the aesthetic choices they made to strengthen each other's work. Interviews with students and Ms. Salazar, occurring in March 2015 with follow up conversations in April served to clarify students' impressions of their work in the class and reaction to the events described in this chapter. Data were collected from January to May 2015 and subsequently analyzed inductively using guidelines delineated by Huberman and Miles (1983). Triangulation of multiple data sources, such as observations, news articles from *The Maroon*, and so forth, was built into data collection and analysis for the purposes of achieving trustworthiness. Data fall into two categories, providing both an insider/outsider's view to the portrayed events.

In examining data, several of Creswell's (1998) notions of validity and quality were kept in mind. Trustworthiness and triangulation were accomplished through the use of multiple data-collection methods, sources, and perspectives; peer review and debriefing; member checking; and rich, thick descriptions that allow readers to enter the research (pp. 201–203).

Analysis of this data is also informed by Kincheloe's (2005) description of the "interpretive bricolage" (p. 335). This method of interpretation locates the researcher—or bricoleur—inside social spaces "where different perspectives offered by people located in diverse locations" allow for multidimensional interpretations of events "in relation to larger social, cultural, political, economic, psychological, and educational structures" that intersect while conducting research. In addition to multiple perspectives, Kincheloe describes the task of the bricoleur "to move into the domain of complexity … uncovering the invisible artifacts of power and culture" and to use "the tools at hand" (p. 324) in order to explore and explain the complexity and lived experiences of those studied.

Given that the events described here happened quickly, across technological platforms and social spaces, it is difficult to draw on the sanctioned models of written research (research question, review of literature, methodology, and the like) to tell this story. This is also in keeping with employing bricolage as a method, which privileges understanding and the presentation of multiple viewpoints over restrictive research norms. To expedite understanding, I organized the described events sequentially, drawing on students' experiences, their critique and the critique of others, and the way these unfolded publicly. This allowed me to present students as agentive members of social media spaces and to accurately capture the events described in this chapter. The overarching question guiding this work was:

- What critical media literacy practices does Ms. Salazar's employ that support students' identity development and participation in public, civic, and community life?

RESULTS AND DESCRIPTION OF EVENTS

Isabelle Salazar has spent the past decade as a teacher in a large urban school district in the Southwestern United States. Having started her career as a high school English and English language learner teacher, she transitioned to a journalism position when one became available in her district. Upon entering into this position, Ms. Salazar noticed the absence of cultural or linguistic diversity among her advanced journalism students. Because the students responsible for writing and disseminating information through the school newsmagazine, *The Maroon*, hailed largely from the white middle/upper class population of the school, she began informally developing and recruiting students of color enrolled in her entry level journalism I courses. After several years, the demographics of her publications team more closely reflected those of the larger school population, including editors on the leadership team of *The Maroon*. This helped Ms.

Salazar realize the goal of reporting news and human interest stories from a multiplicity of perspectives—both in terms of who covered the news and the stories themselves.

In early conversations with me, Ms. Salazar acknowledged, "I'm always telling students how important their writing is … how important it is to get personal stories out." After a story on depression was pitched at an editor's meeting I attended in January 2015, a student complained, "None of those kids want to talk to me about that." Ms. Salazar responded, "That is such a misconception. Everyone wants to tell their story. But, once it's out, keep in mind you never know where it goes." She reminded students that their news magazine, *The Maroon*, was not just read by the school community; alumni from the school, community members, and professionals regularly commented on student-produced stories. Because the publication comes out both in print and online, the readership has grown exponentially over the past several years. An advocate of teaching skills that prepare students for college and beyond, Ms. Salazar has come to understand that her teaching practice has an impact she did not anticipate when moving into her journalism position. Little could she imagine its reach.

The Assembly

The first week of the spring semester in 2015, students were called to a school-wide assembly. This was not uncommon, as speakers regularly gave pep talks for the following purposes: to rev students up about extra-curricular opportunities, to help prepare students for college applications, and to disseminate information about a particular program or activity. Student and *Maroon* editor Ellie Breed remembered, "Everyone in the building was required to be there. And there wasn't really any information at all. We didn't know what we were walking into. Didn't know what to expect." What the school community encountered was a presentation by local entrepreneur and businessman Kash Shaikh, who spoke of the importance of students identifying and going after their dreams and passions. Kash Shaikh's message drew on a TEDxUWMilwaukee talk he gave (Shaikh, 2014), where he "Called everyone out" (including himself) for being all talk and not following through on their passions. In both speeches—the TEDx talk and at Austin High School—Kash Shaikh wove sensational phrases like "Having no balls," "Calling bullshit," and current business-speak like the "Sharing economy" and "Going all-in" to relay his message.

He told the story of becoming disillusioned with his work and taking an idea he had been harboring—to create a "motivational movement" and platform that allowed people to "do what they love" while "make a living at it." This movement was called #besomebody, and it relied on a blog, app, and the Internet to disseminate its goals for participation in the burgeoning sharing community and to match folks who had similar passions to one another.

Kash Shaikh's (2014) message to the students mirrored Campbell's (1949) "hero's journey" in *The Hero with a Thousand Faces*, a schema useful for mapping plot in stories and novels that many high school students and teachers find familiar. Kash Shaikh placed himself in the role of the hero; in this case, disenchanted with his work as a marketing guru in major companies like Proctor and Gamble and GoPro, he was called to make a change. After finding encouragement from others and developing a plan of action, he created a web blog that evolved into a business, complete with an app that matched "passionaries" (folks with a skill or talent) with those who had an interest in learning about that passion. For example, a person who had expertise in teaching yoga might offer one-on-one classes to a novice hoping to develop a yoga practice. Kash Shaikh's talk used metaphors delineating his journey:

- **the cave**—where the flame of an idea was discovered;
- **the cliff**—where you had to let go of what you were doing to explore what you *really* wanted to do. His suggestion: throw yourself off that metaphorical cliff;
- **the path**—this involved sacrifice, a struggle, and suffering. Then hopefully, success.
- **the bridge**—this was the final path toward realizing your dream—no turning back. Kash Shaikh urged listeners to set fire to the wooden bridge behind them— "No turning back, and No Plan B. If you have a Plan B you will never execute Plan A."

He called students up to the stage to state their passions publicly, to end the event. Although there were those who initially questioned parts of the message, *The Maroon* student reporters Rowan Pruitt and Daniel Wallach acknowledged some attendees who were "positively affected by what he had to say." Upon returning to Ms. Salazar's class, students discussed their impressions of the assembly and considered coverage of it in an upcoming edition of *The Maroon*. This is where the story began to change. What most would view as a typical event in the life of a school—a motivational speaker offered a message of inspiration, students received the message positively or otherwise, and then the community went back to the business of teaching and learning—incited a social media storm extending long past the day of the assembly.

The Critique

In their call for a new view of literacy—one that reflects the growing diversity of learners in schools and the variety of texts with which students engage—the New London Group (1996) envisioned a notably different literacy pedagogy than what students were experiencing in schools. They wrote,

> If it were possible to define generally the mission of education, it could be said that its fundamental purpose is to ensure that all students benefit from learning in ways that allow them to participate fully in public, community, and economic life. (p. 60)

Currently, opportunities for this kind of participation are limited in schools, for reasons as varied as concerns over testing and curricular coverage as an absence of authentic events that necessitate a public response in the first place. Additionally, given the rapid-fire response we are all subjected to after making our voices heard through public spaces (like posting to social media, commenting on web stories, or creating a cogent editorial), teachers may worry over the fallout that could result from such voices rising up. In terms of critiquing Kash Shaikh's presentation, this concern was warranted.

After returning to their classrooms, Ms. Salazar's students discussed writing a story for *The Maroon* about the #besomebody presentation and began conducting background research into the speaker and his organization. After digging into Kash Shaikh and his company, students discovered that the #besomebody app was little more than a matching service that took a 20% cut from all services matched through its interface. They learned the company had received a million dollars in start-up funds to get it online, and to spread its message through the beating heart of the social media system. Students began questioning the central message of the "movement" that the speaker presented at the assembly. They saw the message as somewhat disingenuous given that this was less a movement and more a profit-making endeavor, with Kash Shaikh seeding future customers through his talks at high schools across the country. The conversation evolved into a critique coalescing around three fronts:

- Bro culture—the language Kash Shaikh used at the assembly and the physical nature of his interactions, including fist-bumping, high-fiving, and using "bro" as a familiar;
- Disingenuousness of the message—while the assembly focused on Kash Shaikh's journey from marketing guru to #besomebody startup founder, it omitted the reality that he was selling a service. The students were also critical of the implicit message of his pre-

sentation, suggesting that students—many of whom relied on free and reduced lunches and would need aid to attend college—did not need an education to make a success of their lives;

- Branding over substance—the #besomebody "movement" relied on heavy marketing in person and online, with the potentially dangerous message that followers should let go of fallback plans and focus solely on their passions to realize success.

In addition to conversations in the journalism classroom, visual media arts students from the school—who oversaw its own media channel KHAS (pronounced "chaos")—decided to create a parody of the presentation. Media students regularly uploaded their work to a YouTube channel to make it visible for public consumption; when they finished their lampoon (KHAS, 2015), they tweeted it out to #besomebody, starting a dialogue on Twitter between the journalism and visual media arts students.

Ms. Salazar's students decided that, rather than devoting a full spread to the assembly, they would include an editorial about the presentation instead. *The Maroon* staff writer Sean Saldana penned the piece which appeared in print January 23, 2015 and online February 16, 2015. Unaware that Mr. Gillion, one of the school's teachers, had attempted to post a letter to Kash Shaikh's #besomebody blog (it was not viewable publically on their site until February, 2015), Sean's critique drew on some of the same themes discussed by Gillion. Among these was Kash Shaikh's message of giving everything up for passion and being willing to suffer and struggle in order to realize one's dream seemed unrealistic to students who are not "in the same boat" as he was with a college degree, financial backing, and years of highly competitive corporate experience.

Sean wrote, "For every Kash Shaikh, there are hundreds and hundreds of minimum wage retail workers who couldn't find a sustainable way to practice their passions." Sean acknowledged that while the message of #beseomebody was "moving to anybody who is hesitant to take a non-conventional career path," it was problematic to spread to impressionable high school students who were still forming their identities related to the future, college, and in work. Finally, he critiqued the intent of the presentation, which on the surface appeared as a message of motivation, but in the end was really a pitch for students to explore and spread word of an app, a money-making endeavor. He continued:

> … sure #besomebody has a feel-good message meant to inspire the youth, but at its heart, #besomebody is a company. Companies have a mission to make money, as much money as possible. And there's just something inherently wrong about a company coming to a public school, wasting government resources … to half advertise to people who have no choice

about whether or not they want to hear. The whole thing is just kinda gross. (Saldana, 2015)

Absent the power and reach of social media, Sean's editorial would likely have been read by his immediate community and quickly forgotten as the next big event came to light. But after one of the KHAS media team tweeted from their school media account, "Shout-out to our friends over at *The Maroon*" along with a photograph of the editorial to Kash Shaikh and #besomebody, the story of the speaking event, the critique, and the fallout from the critique spread quickly through both traditional and social media.

The Backlash

Just as we have experienced through current political and news events, Twitter users often strike before thinking through how their message might be received. Kash Shaikh responded quickly through Twitter. He posted his thoughts under the heading "You Have No Idea What PASSION Means," along with links to an extended blog essay that rippled through both the school community and the Twitter-sphere (see Figure 12.1).

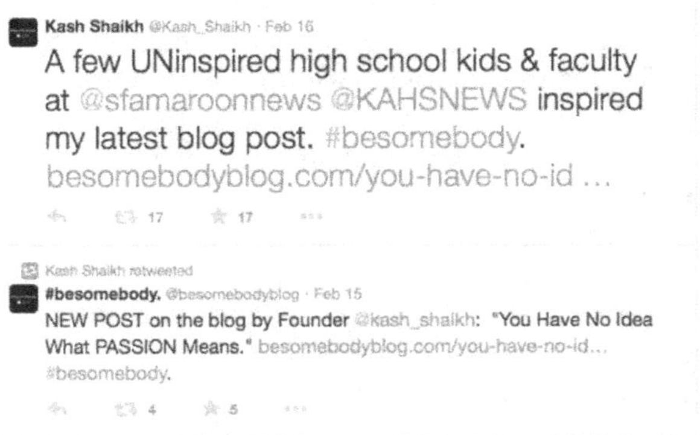

Figure 12.1. Kash Shaikh's tweet, February 16, 2015.

Due to the interconnectedness of social media, Kash Shaikh's lengthy post made its way via a variety of hosts—Twitter, Facebook, the #besomebody app blog—and this served two purposes. One, the blog post allowed Kash Shaikh to speak directly to the editorial and to the parody that critiqued his presentation; two, the post served as an additional tool for branding the #besomebody movement. Kash Shaikh was, after all, a marketing expert. The response began with attacks on his critics as "fear-driven, weak-minded" people who did not understand the role passion played in shaping one's success and included a lengthy explication of the author's understanding of the word passion. Included in this was his belief that passion required: discipline ("the toughest path" requiring "unwavering commitment"); pain ("you have to be willing to take as many punches as you give"); and senselessness ("being blind to criticism ... walking forward without an ounce of doubt"). Employing profanity, business-speak, and an extended discussion of how following one's passions can involve suffering and going against the grain, the post ended with a call to action.

The implication for Sean and *The Maroon* team was they could not possibly be passionate and simultaneously disagree with the messaging presented by the #besomebody author. Through this public posting, Kash Shaikh also reached out to Sean directly, calling Sean's editorial "completely off base" before cataloging all of his accomplishments. He then moved on to what he characterized as "tough love," where he criticized public schools and suggested the need for a new system that did not rely on college degrees to alleviate the growing financial aid debt crisis. This was particularly ill-conceived, given that many of Ms. Salazar's students were relying on their success in public schools to leverage future opportunities. And, unlike Kash Shaikh, who spoke of cashing in a 401K in order to help finance his #besomebody movement, they were not in the position to consider taking on the kind of risks his presentation proposed. In the students' estimation, Kash Shaikh had already earned a college degree and could then discount it; they understood that he was speaking from a position of power that was no doubt available because of that very college degree he then discounted in his direct response to Sean (see Figure 12.2).

The students tuned into various social media channels as this story and its response moved across platforms. What they discovered was a concerted effort by supporters of #besomebody to push back against *The Maroon* editorial through blog posts and tweeted responses, which were then responded to in kind. Teacher Mr. Gillion, seizing this opportunity to repost the letter he had written in January, took issue with Kash Shaikh and his supporters' critique of teachers and the school community, as well as the inappropriate and sexist tone of Kash Shaikh's presentation to the school (see Figure 12.3). Kash Shaikh responded with a defense of his company and reiteration that those who critiqued his presentation were full of "negative energy" reflective of a flawed educational system. He also pitched the notion that Mr. Gillion sign on as a "Passionary" to teach Spanish through the #besomebody app (see Figure 12.4).

In support of Kash Shaikh, commenter Michael Maldonado wrote a lengthy response to Mr. Gillion about his passion for fitness and the lack of support he experienced from his high school teachers in drawing on this as a potential profession. He ended with the rejoinder that schools

Kash

February 16, 2015 at 7:34 pm #

Hey Sean – I am sure you had good intentions in your article. A couple of your teachers questioned my credibility in sharing "my message" of following your passion. I think i'm pretty credible, but you'll have to do your own research and decide on your own. But in the same way, I, of course, can and do question your credibility in your article. Who are you to tell people to not SOLELY and ONLY reach for the stars? And more importantly, how did you get that in your head? I thought your article was completely off base, any I originally referenced it above because a student brought it to my attention.I was shocked to learn that a student wrote that (a few of your classmates told me it was written by a teacher, so that was my bad for being misinformed). When I heard it was a student today, I nearly fell out of my chair.

You're right that I have a good "fall back" plan if needed. I made great grades in school, founded 3 organizations at UT, created the largest single day of community service in the state of Texas, and worked 12 years at two amazing companies. The whole time though, I had the same BS pounded into my head. The same "be reasonable" message that you dangerously wrote to your fellow students. So it took me until I was 30 years old to pursue my passion. I wasted a lot of time… Yes, because of that, I can get a job doing something else if I want Sean, but I don't to! Everyday I'm hit up to do consulting projects for big brands for compensation that ranges from $200-1000/hour. I take ZERO of those opportunities. Instead I use my time to talk to people, speak for free at schools like yours (and, for the first time, in this instance, I witnessed some misguided classmates of yours post racist

Figure 12.2. Response to Sean from #besomebody blog, March 5, 2015.

Kevin Gillion

February 16, 2015 at 4:43 pm #

I am an Austin High School teacher who wrote a letter directly to you via your 'contact us' option, but I never received a response. It is odd that you posted negative statements about my school just when the jokes about you had died down around here. Maybe you are thirsty, as they say. Regardless, I am posting my letter to you here in the spirit of fairness. We are all working very hard here, and you run the risk of appearing the Goliath to our David if you continue to argue with high school students. Please leave us alone. The following was written the evening after I witnessed your 'passion.'

January 5, 2015

Dear Young Motivational Speaker 'Bro' Who Gave My Students Questionable Advice,

All students and faculty at my school were required to attend your presentation this morning, and I am writing to take issue with a couple of the comments you made. Your use of the term 'balls' as a metaphor for courage was inappropriate and sexist, and your depiction of suffering and struggle as traveling in an RV or living in a studio apartment was ridiculous and offensive.

On the matter of balls, did you toss the term around to convey to us that you are somehow edgy, and, as a result, authoritative or trustworthy? If so, I recommend that you revise your strategy by providing data that support your recommendations. You can curse like a Tarantino script, but my students will not benefit from your message if it lacks tangible proof or meaning. Secondly, and more importantly, by invoking 'balls' as a metaphor for courage, you are telling my female students that there is an anatomical requirement for bravery that they lack. It is a worthless cliché both because a truer analogy is that those that possess ovaries have been

Figure 12.3. Kevin Gillion's letter in response to #besomebody presentation, March 5, 2015 (underlined passages enhanced by author).

cause I believe in what we're doing, and I know we're helping people. Our business model for our platform is based on people making money doing what they love. We get 20%, they get 80% of any money they generate on our platform. This is all incremental income for our Passionaries. I know your passion is Spanish, but do some googling of the "sharing economy" or #besomebody and you will learn a lot more. You could be great Passionary for Spanish, for example. And our platform could help provide you with supplemental income that could help those years without a raise. The educational system is flawed, and we are providing a new platform for people to teach and learn.

It's a bummer that you are appear to be one of the people I refer to in the blog post above – negative and insistent on finding the bad in things instead of unearthing and embracing the good. You and some of your colleagues/students spent a lot of time producing and sharing negative energy. Why? Was it helpful to you? I hope so. It did help me, as I wrote above. Tactically, it helped me remember that though I was told to come "share my Ted Talk" at your school (I only spoke 20 mins), that next time I will look to share the broader/original talks from the past that speak more to the universal nature of passion, vs my metaphoric journey. That was a good lesson.

I was blessed to spend two years in some of the poorest neighborhoods in the world, helping people. My career at Procter & Gamble was focused on Cause-related efforts, including providing clothes to families after disasters, or providing food to people living on the streets. These are the people who taught me that there is no correlation between money and happiness. These are the people that reminded me the relative-nature of 'suffering.' My resume may not

Figure 12.4. Kash Shaikh's response to Kevin Gillian, captured from #besomebody blog, March 5, 2015 (underlined passages enhanced by author).

purposefully squelch students' dreams and the #besomebody hashtag, which students came to conclude suggested a relationship. Indeed, students later discovered that almost all of the positive posts about #besomebody were written by "passionaries" who had a financial stake in the success of the business since they were among the instructors. Although silent up to this point, Sean—author of the original editorial—rejoined the conversation, offering a far more balanced perspective of life past high school to Mel, another #besomebody supporter. He offered his bona fides, "Peep my insta if you don't believe me: amnohate" and reminded Mel of the importance of "reaching for the stars" while still having a reasonable plan back here on earth.

While these blog conversations, tweets, and responses were hitting their mark through social media spaces, a local education journalist noticed a parallel conversation taking place on Reddit. Reddit user space_manatee (2015) discussed the assembly at the school, Saldana's *Maroon* editorial, and the blog rebuttal posted to the #besomebody site. In contrast to the comments to Kash Shaikh's "Uninspired" blog which reflected a shared commitment to his message, the Reddit community not only agreed with the students' critique of Kash Shaikh, they also acknowledged the "Bro" demographic targeted by the #besomebody community (see Figure 12.5).

Figure 12.5. Tweet representing the bro culture of #besomebody, captured from Twitter, March 5, 2015.

Honest_arbiter compared #besomebody's message to the "Emperor's New Clothes," reminding the community in that case "the innocence of youth uncovered the scam on the Emperor" much like what was happening here as well. Redditer "spiritofdunkey," a senior at the school at the time, thanked the community for noticing "this little incident that went down" and discussed a blog response (since taken down) from Kash Shaikh noting "how uninspiring our teachers were and how they taught us to not follow our passions," which s/he disagreed with completely (see Figure 12.6).

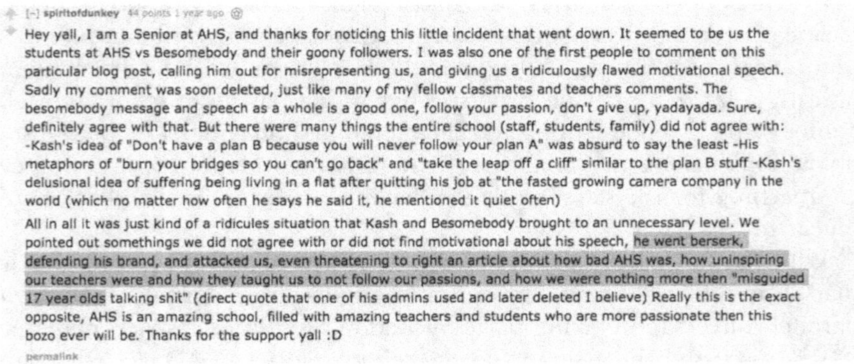
[–] spiritofdunkey 44 points 1 year ago

Hey yall, I am a Senior at AHS, and thanks for noticing this little incident that went down. It seemed to be us the students at AHS vs Besomebody and their goony followers. I was also one of the first people to comment on this particular blog post, calling him out for misrepresenting us, and giving us a ridiculously flawed motivational speech. Sadly my comment was soon deleted, just like many of my fellow classmates and teachers comments. The besomebody message and speech as a whole is a good one, follow your passion, don't give up, yadayada. Sure, definitely agree with that. But there were many things the entire school (staff, students, family) did not agree with: -Kash's idea of "Don't have a plan B because you will never follow your plan A" was absurd to say the least -His metaphors of "burn your bridges so you can't go back" and "take the leap off a cliff" similar to the plan B stuff -Kash's delusional idea of suffering being living in a flat after quitting his job at "the fasted growing camera company in the world (which no matter how often he says he said it, he mentioned it quiet often)

All in all it was just kind of a ridicules situation that Kash and Besomebody brought to an unnecessary level. We pointed out somethings we did not agree with or did not find motivational about his speech, he went berserk, defending his brand, and attacked us, even threatening to right an article about how bad AHS was, how uninspiring our teachers were and how they taught us to not follow our passions, and how we were nothing more then "misguided 17 year olds talking shit" (direct quote that one of his admins used and later deleted I believe) Really this is the exact opposite, AHS is an amazing school, filled with amazing teachers and students who are more passionate then this bozo ever will be. Thanks for the support yall :D

permalink

Figure 12.6. Reddit conversation captured on March 9, 2016.

A highly upvoted comment (author unknown) suggested that the school was fulfilling its job of preparing students to listen and read critically (see Figure 12.7).

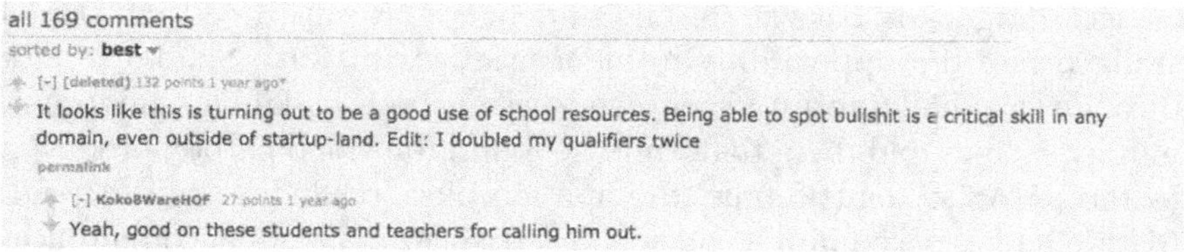
all 169 comments
sorted by: best
[-] [deleted] 132 points 1 year ago*
It looks like this is turning out to be a good use of school resources. Being able to spot bullshit is a critical skill in any domain, even outside of startup-land. Edit: I doubled my qualifiers twice
permalink
[-] KokoBWareHOF 27 points 1 year ago
Yeah, good on these students and teachers for calling him out.

Figure 12.7. Reddit conversation captured on March 9, 2016.

As a result of these conversations Kate McGee, a journalist for the local NPR Station KUT did some detective work, tracking down the #besomebody founder, as well as several students who sat through the presentation. She described the back and forth that transpired through Twitter, Facebook, and the #besomebody blog, offering a balanced account of events. Kash Shaikh conceded to McGee (2015), "I probably got into the debate too quickly and that's some things [sic] I would do differently, probably not get into the back and forth too much. But the one thing we won't do is change our message." Several other publications, like *Texas Monthly* (Solomon, 2015), *BBC News* (Trending, 2015), and the *PBS Newshour* (Segal, 2015) followed suit offering additional perspectives and commentary. Responses to the *PBS* piece posted online supported the students' perspective, with commenter Nimh Frisby acknowledging that while Kash Shaikh's speech "may have been great in starting a discussion amongst the students," it was not "realistically achievable." Frisby noted, "They really did put thought into what he was saying and were paying attention. I give credit for that to their parents and teachers." Miamisid, another commenter on the *PBS* site, concluded

> Feeding students pabulum as if it were a universal truth is an age old tradition. It is good to hear that the students recognized it for what it is. Taking a leap of faith without a backup plan is a luxury most cannot afford. Kudos to the students.

By mid-March, Ms. Salazar asked her students to stop engaging through social media and to turn their attention to other projects. Interestingly enough, several of *The Maroon* editors and Ms. Salazar had secured press passes to attend the multimedia portion of the South by Southwest (SXSW) conference. There, they ran across the #besomebody founder and several of his employees at a marketing booth decorated with graffiti intended to mimic tagging, with loud music pulsating through their space. Folks from the company were high-fiving others walking through the exhibit hall and drawing lottery tickets for an experiential give-away: a motor-cross driving lesson would go to a lucky winner who downloaded the app that day.

According to Ms. Salazar, she and student editors Ellie Breed and Daniel Wallach had the opportunity to meet briefly with Kash Shaikh to talk through what had transpired between #besomebody and their school community. Skaikh told them that while he found the video parody produced by the KHAS students funny, "the opinion piece really hurt him. He felt that we had attacked him ... personally" (I. Salazar, personal communication, March 13, 2005). Ellie Breed suggested,

> I don't think he realized how big his audience was when he tweeted that blog at us. He didn't realize the following we had—the support from the student body that we had. He thought it would be a dialogue between him and our publication and his organization. But then all of the students that were behind us started getting in on it—against him.

This point drove home to students that words have power and they matter—even when the critique is coming from students with less education and experience. Daniel Wallach proposed that the reason Kash Shaikh reacted so negatively to the students' critique was because "he can't really untangle his personal life and what he's doing on the app now." The criticism felt personal. Ellie agreed saying,

> he made [the presentation] a really personal thing. And I think when it's presented to you like that you are less likely to question it if it looks like it's this grassroots 'my story' kind of thing" as opposed to a business trying to sell you an idea. Several students felt that Kash Shaikh had actually enjoyed the opportunity to spar with the school and *The Maroon* publicly as it brought more attention to #besomebody, driving internet traffic and potential users of the app which would filter into the company's bottom line. They speculated he likely "didn't even mind the negative press. Attention was attention and if it brought more clicks to his website, that generated more traffic and advertising dollars.

Student journalist Ana Szachacz viewed the #besomebody assembly as an easy opportunity to build on students' frustration with having "been told to do this stuff so much" [e.g., do well in school, go to college so you can get a job] that they were an easy target for his message of "don't do mainstream stuff. Come and have more fun." That sounded great on the surface, but Ms. Salazar's students saw a college education as necessary for achieving these long-term goals. In the end, the take-away from the experience reflected the hope of most literacy educators: students saw their work as contributing to a larger dialogue as it made its way through a complex and media-saturated world. Their ideas mattered. Ana noted, "we definitely did learn what not to do—we owe it to the person who did the work (as Sean had) to actually read what they say and critically think about it … otherwise, they put it out there for nothing." Reflecting on this Ms. Salazar revealed,

> You know, I don't know how many times in education the things that we are teaching actually get to be applied and authentic. So the things I've been telling my students over the past four years—how important their writing is and how important their voice is. How important to focus on social justice and equity and all those things. I've had students and they haven't had this moment. So I wonder how many teachers really get to have that authentic application. That's what's been the neatest thing.

DISCUSSION

The landscape of public schools is complicated by a host of factors that make researching there difficult when events like those described here surface in public, though social media, web pages, news articles and the like. Kincheloe (2005) explains that "the task of the bricoleur is to attack [the] complexity, uncovering the invisible artifacts of power and culture and documenting the nature of their influence" (p. 324) on scholarly endeavors. Among the data collected for this project were over 200 screen grabs of tweets, blogs with their resulting comments, web pages, photo images, interviews with individual and small groups of students, e-mail correspondence, artifacts of teaching, video, and news articles. In attempting to make sense of these artifacts, I first drew on interviews with the students and with Ms. Salazar; these framed my impressions of Kash Shaikh and what he was promoting at the school. I then investigated #besomebody's web and app presence, confirming students' belief that the company privileged brand over substance, and promoted problematic notions of aspirations versus education through business-speak, persuasive devises, bandwagon presentation skills. This analysis supports the findings that Ms. Salazar's work with students developed them in their ability to read media critically and in terms of acting as agentive participants in the world outside of school.

CONNECTIONS TO THE RESEARCH

In terms of how to support students' "authentic applications," when engaging through Reddit or the twitter-sphere, there is a limited body of research from which to draw. For one thing, social media is continuously morphing into something new and is disseminated widely—with tentacles extending beyond an original posting. And in spite of the Internet and social media's potential for creating spaces for first person accounts, and the inclusion of marginalized voices, it is important to help students gauge the credibility of those who write, blog, post, and tweet. It is impossible to anticipate when something will go viral through the Internet or social media. When this happens to a school community, its draws in a host of complicating issues, like determining how far to let students go in their engagement, reminding them they represent something bigger than themselves when posting, and helping them see the permanence of Internet posts and the consequences that might bring. Jenkins et al. (2006) have explored some of the challenges of a participatory culture in an increasingly connected world, acknowledging that students' "writing is much more open to the public and can have more far-reaching consequences." They go on, "The ethical implications of these emerging practices are fuzzy and ill-defined. Young people are discovering that information they put online to share with their friends can bring unwelcome attention from strangers" (p 17). This was certainly the case with *The Maroon* students, but the experience also provided a valuable learning experience for all involved, particularly as students grappled with the tenets of constructing a sound argument.

In today's world of Facebook and Twitter shaming, anonymous postings to blogs, and a less than civil discourse, it is tricky helping students determine when to put down the mantle and move on to the next thing. That is certainly what Ms. Salazar worried about with her students, eventually asking them to write a reflection on their interactions with Kash Shaikh and the #besomebody community. Student responses varied from questioning his motives, to wondering how Kash Shaikh gained entry into the school in the first place. Calling attention to a "fragile ego," student journalist Lauren Marigold expressed surprise that Kash Shaikh had not received criticism from other school presentations, and worry that he locked down the commenting feature of his blog to limit dissenting voices. Writing a letter as his response, Sonny Stephens discussed #besomebody's favored treatment of "certain passions over others," many of which he saw as hobbies rather than career opportunities. He acknowledged the "amazing school that you attack and denigrate so viciously (has) allowed me to follow my passion" and develop the skills and knowledge to gain entry into a prestigious college. Senior Des Magness conveyed frustration that Shaikh employed "name-calling toward those who critiqued #besomebody," explaining ad hominem arguments diminish the message.

CONCLUSION

In the 3 years since the assembly, the #besomebody brand has changed significantly. After facing a backlash in the Central Texas community, their founder moved the company up to Boston. Media reports (Gallaga, 2016; O'Brien, 2017) indicate that after appearing on the television show Shark

Tank and not receiving the support of any of the investors, #besomebody shuttered its business, morphing into a company that matches employees to jobs and offering life coaching and training. Kash Shaikh deleted the original webpage in early 2017 where the blog, marketing materials, linked tweets, and responses to Ms. Salazar's students lived. Having scrubbed those interactions from the Internet, one has to access the Way Back Time Machine [available at http://archive.org/web/] in order to view earlier iterations of the company, its web presence, and blog. This is a reminder of the ephemeral nature of online spaces and a telling lesson for Ms. Salazar's journalism students who have also moved on to college or work, replete with an entirely new list of responsibilities and learning to undergo.

This chapter suggests that helping students "read the world" and critically examine media is invaluable to navigating their lived experiences—both in person and online. The events explored here happened organically, and students at times adopted pseudonyms (as was the case of the Reddit responders) allowing them to enact their identities more honestly and with greater agency. What is clear from talking with the students in the spring of 2015: they wanted their voices heard, particularly after feeling attacked by Kash Shaikh and his passionary squad. By drawing on their roles as student journalists and enlisting the perspectives of others, students gained efficacy in engaging in literate activities in both familiar and less familiar spaces. These negotiations of public discourse and disagreement taught students about the importance of maintaining their cool in public, given that they were representing not just their school, but their newsmagazine and each other. They were supported by faculty and their local community, which no doubt helped students in balancing multiple identities—that of teenager, writer, editor, critic, and human. In talking with Rowan, who helped edit the newsmagazine and met in person with Kash Shaikh, she acknowledged that the back and forth between students, the public, and #besomebody community was beneficial to Shaikh's company. At South by Southwest he told her, "We have record breaking downloads because of y'all." Rowan told me, "he definitely overplayed things because of the effect it could have" in leveraging more traffic to his app, his webpage, and blog. Because of this, students worried that their critique was more beneficial to #besomebody than a glowing review.

In their discussion about the "spreadable spectacle" of today's media, Mihailidis and Viotty (2017) discuss the notion that teaching students to "question, critique and inquire about the credibility of media" (p. 450) is no guarantee that they will be able to ascertain what is sourced and truthful over what is specious and untrustworthy. The spread of disinformation from human to human, after all, can carry the sheen of reliability once it has passed through large numbers of newsfeeds without critique, particularly as people rely on each other as sources of information more than the mainstream press. We carry an expectation that students today are digitally savvy, yet as Morrell (2012) notes, "for all of their digital expertise, there is still a great deal that [youth] have to learn about how to process the information that they are inundated with via these new portals of information" (p. 301). As we continue to explore the varied literacy practices that our students, schools, and communities engage in, we must help find ways to help students read and respond to their world across platforms and spaces, uncovering truth and calling out fabrication, exaggeration, and other verbal manipulation. It is only through this that students can develop power and agency in their lives as readers, writers, doers, and thinkers.

REFERENCES

Alvermann, D., Moon, J. S., & Hagood, M. C. (1999). *Popular culture in the classroom: Teaching and researching critical media literacy*. Neward, DE, & Chicago, IL: International Reading Association and National Reading Conference.

Burnett, C., & Merchant, G. (2011). Is there a space for critical literacy in the context of social media? *English teaching: Practice and critique, 10*(1), 41–57.

Campbell, J. (1949). *The hero with a thousand faces*. Princeton, NJ: Princeton University Press.

Chilcott, L. (Producer), & Guggenheim, D. (Director). (2010). *Waiting for Superman* [Motion Picture]. United States: Electric Kinney Films.

Creswell, J. (1998). *Qualitative inquiry and research design*. Thousand Oaks, CA: SAGE.

Gainer, J. (2013). 21st-century mentor texts: Developing critical literacies in the information age. *Journal of adolescent and adult literacy, 57*(1), 16–19.

Gallaga, O. (2016). #besomebody, which launched in Austin, brutally turned into chum on 'Shark Tank' Retrieved from http://www.512tech.com/technology/besomebody-which-launched-austin-brutally-turned-into-chum-shark-tank/TC2YxeScUaQTZcK8N7ebsL/

Garcia, A., Seglem, R., & Share, J. (2013). Transforming teaching and learning through critical media literacy pedagogy. *LEARNing Landscapes, 6*(2), 109–124.

Garcia, A., Mirra, N., Morrell, E., Martinez, A., & Scorza, D. A. (2015). The council of youth research: Critical literacy and civic agency in the digital age. *Reading & Writing Quarterly, 31*(2), 151–167.

Greenhow, C., Robelia, B., & Hughes, J. (2009). Learning, teaching, and scholarship in a digital age: Web 2.0 and classroom research: What path should we take now? *Educational Researcher, 38*(4), 246–259.

Huberman, A. M., & Miles, M. B. (1983). Drawing valid meaning from qualitative data: Some techniquest of data reduction and display. *Quality and Quantity, 17*, 281–339.

International Literacy Association. (2012). *Adolescent literacy* (Position statement, Rev. 2012 ed). Newark, DE: Author.

Jenkins, H., Clinton, K., Purushotma, R., Robison, A., & Weigel, M. (2006). *Confronting the challenges of participatory culture: Media education for the 21st century*. Chicago, IL: MacArthur Foundation.

Kellner, D., & Share, J. (2005). Toward critical media literacy: Core concepts, debates, organizations, and policy. *Discourse: studies in the cultural politics of education, 26*(3), 369–386.

KHAS. (2015, January 9). #bekahs. #besomebody [Video]. Retrieved from https://www.youtube.com/watch?v=DUDhJ-KiGLg&t=34

Kincheloe, J. (2005). On to the next level: Continuing the conceptualization of the bricolage. *Qualitative Inquiry, 11*(3), 323–350.

Lewandowsky, S., Ecker, U. K. H., Seifert, C. M., Schwarz, N., & Cook, J. (2012). Misinformation and its correction: Continued influence and successful debiasing. *Psychological Science in the Public Interest, 13*(3), 106–131.

McGee, K. (2015). #besomebody speaker draws controversy at austin high school. *KUT News*. Retrieved from http://www.kut.org/ website: http://kut.org/post/besomebody-speaker-draws-controversy-austin-high-school

Mihailidis, P., & Viotty, S. (2017). Spreadable spectacle in digital culture: Civic expression, fake news, and the role of media literacies in "post-fact" society. *American Behavioral Scientist, 61*(4), 441–454.

Morrell, E. (2012). 21st-century literacies, critical media, pedagogies, and language arts *The Reading Teacher, 66*(4), 300–302.

National Council of Teachers of English (NCTE). (2013). 21st Century Literacies, Curriculum, Instruction, Literacy (Position statement, Rev. 2013 ed.). Urbana, IL: Author.

New London Group. (1996). A pedagogy of multiliteracies: Designing social futures. *Harvard Educational Review, 66*(1), 60–92.

O'Brien, K. (2017). Boston startup Besomebody, once featured on 'Shark Tank,' shuts down app Retrieved from https://www.bizjournals.com/boston/news/2017/01/07/after-sinking-on-shark-tank-boston-startup.html

Saldana, S. (2015, February 16). #Besomebody. [Commentary]. Retrieved from http://sfamaroon.org/593/opinion/besomebody/

Segal, C. (2015). High school kids call out motivational speaker's #besomebody message. *PBS Newshour*. Retrieved from http://www.pbs.org/newshour/rundown/high-school-kids-call-motivational-speakers-besomebody-message/

Shaikh, K. (2014, December 18). Video. Going ALL IN on your passion. Retrieved from https://www.youtube.com/watch?v=hf3_BJ7Lk8Q

Solomon, D. (2015). Austin tech bros from #besomebody are losing the fight they picked against local high school students. *Texas Monthly*. Retrieved from http://www.texasmonthly.com/website: http://www.texasmonthly.com/the-daily-post/austin-tech-bros-from-besomebody-are-losing-the-fight-they-picked-against-local-high-school-students/

space_manatee. (2015). #besomebody founder attacks austin HS students and staff online. [Message board]. Retrieved from https://www.reddit.com/r/Austin/comments/2xd8bt/besomebody_founder_attacks_austin_hs_students_and/

Spicer, M. (Writer). (2017). *Ingrid goes west* [Motion Picture]. In J. Goldman, A. Plaza, T. White, T. White, A. Mirels, & R. Mirels (Producers). United States: Neon.

Trending, B. (2015). Pep talk #besomebody backfires at texas school. *BBC News*. Retrieved from http://www.bbc.com/news/blogs-trending-31754918

CHAPTER 13

IMMATERIALITY REDUX

Tacit Modalities and Meaning Across Timescales

Sandra Schamroth Abrams
St. John's University in New York

Jennifer Rowsell
Brock University

Just now, as I was opening a jar of salsa, I was reminded of my Nana (because just how many jars did we have to open for her, it was a lot) and the feeling that memory brought me was so sweet and happy. For a moment I was standing in the kitchen at the cottage teasing Nana about her wimpy hands and there were two 'toasted cheese' on the stove and an epic game of Rummikub on the table. I will try to hold on to that feeling as long as I can. —Rebecca

I love those fleeting moments when it all comes back so clearly. —Allison

Rebecca's[1] Facebook post and Allison's response call attention to the ways in which human senses play an affective role in meaning making. The simple twisting of a jar's metal cap can spur memory-based feelings associated with images of arthritic "wimpy hands," food on the stove, and intense ("epic") game play under way. All of these images cohere to represent a situated

Negotiating Place and Space Through Digital Literacies: Research and Practice, pp. 241–258

point in time, which, as Allison noted, only surface for "fleeting moments." What happens, however, when a new context, such as an illness, changes the feelings related to the artifact at hand? How can we contextualize and explain how modalities contribute to evolving, affective stances? And how do time and space play a role in understanding such subjective, sensory-based meaning making? How do culture, religion, and social class play a role within this interconnected picture? These and other questions make us wonder how tacit, embodied sensations interact with familiar texts, objects and visuals.

The field of literacy studies has moved beyond representational interpretations with a sole focus on design (Leander & Boldt, 2013; Lewis & Tierney, 2013). To greater explore *meaning making as experiencing*, this chapter introduces the nonrepresentational theory of tacit modalities as a heuristic to better understand how emotions, memories, feelings, sensations, and thoughts play a role in evolving meaning making. This is especially relevant in light of the multimodal production and consumption culture supported by digital spaces and resources.

THEORETICAL PERSPECTIVES

Multimodalities

Inherent in its name, multimodality is the understanding that meaning making occurs through the confluence of modes. The positioning of one's body, the texture and color of a fabric, the way light casts shadows, the musty smell of old books, and so on, all impact one's perception and meaning making. Just as literacy cannot be understood as an "'autonomous' variable, somehow divorced from social and ideological contexts that give it meaning" (Street, 1999, p. 55), so, too, meaning making cannot be reduced to one modality separated from its context. Kress (2010) addressed such complexity when he explained how modes can work harmoniously to convey meaning through "orchestration," which involves "assembling/organizing/designing a plurality of signs in different modes into a particular configuration to form a coherent arrangement," resulting in "ensembles," or the product of such orchestration (p. 162). In other words, multimodality involves the process of modes working in concert to produce an overall effect or meaning; typically, such meaning making is highly nuanced, socially situated and individualized in nature.

When we consider multimodal meaning making, as well as and thoughts and memories of modalities (e.g., smells, sounds, sights, textures), we acknowledge that multimodal literacies also include the connection among "story, memory, images, and experiences" (Vasudevan, 2006, p. 254).

Returning to Rebecca's recollection of her Nana's hands, therefore, we contend that memories are inherently multimodal in nature. The image of the jar, Nana's arthritic hands and the Rummikub tiles, the feeling of resistance from the salsa jar cap, the smell and/or sounds related to the toasted cheese on the stove, all suggest that multimodalities evoke emotions, feelings, and embodiment that are part of the meaning making experienced through such *tacit modalities*. Memories often include sensory-based, multimodal residues (e.g., the scent of a perfume, the sound of a particular song, the image of arthritic hands), and the related sensations are tacit—they are perceived even if they are difficult to identify and/or articulate. Tacit modalities, we argue, are important to meaning making because they bridge experiences across timescales. In what follows, we develop the concept of tacit modalities in relation to affect and timescales.

Tacit Modalities

Tacit modalities include that which is felt and sensed, and by noting emotions and feelings, we are referring to sensations registered within the body and mind, such as, joy, fear, and anxiety (Massumi, 2002). At times, these emotions may be difficult to pinpoint but, nonetheless, are acknowledged and/or believed; often they are articulated through endearing terms, such as "smells like home" or "tastes just like my mother's cooking," or jarring recollections, such as a tone that "sounds just like my ex-boyfriend," or images of recent school shootings that emerge and "make me fearful as I walk down the hall." Tacit modalities also enable readers or listeners to connect with information. Rebecca's account hints at her sentimentality, but we, as readers, cannot sense exactly what she feels. *We interpret it through our own sensed experiences*. Regardless of the subtle or overt nature of tacit modalities, they play a role in the way we construct and reconstruct meaning because tacit modalities facilitate the vivid recollection of moments passed, bringing the past into the present, even if briefly, and sometimes chaining us to a past in ways that can feel traumatic, exhausting, and painful.

What makes tacit modalities so powerful is that they involve embodiment, which represents bodily reactions to instances, spaces, and places and how bodies engage with senses (Enriquez, Johnson, Kontovourki, & Mallozzi, 2015). For instance, entering a room and having felt memories from its smell, design, or visuals on the wall may conjure sensations tied to a past moment. This became clear to Sandra, an author of this chapter, when she struggled to make sense of a traumatic event. In this chapter, Sandra describes the sensation of felt memories when she talks about revisiting her family home when her father was gravely ill. Furthermore, we suggest that these multimodal tacit memories produce an undercurrent of meaning making that may surface in new or extended feelings, interpretations, and actions. As such, an artifact that spurs the memory may have material and immaterial markers, but there are shifts in meaning making that may also complicate and disrupt the way the artifact evokes meaning. The concept of tacit modalities helps to explain why such complication and disruption occur.

Research of artifacts includes an examination of their materiality (something that is tangible, such as a journal) and immateriality (something that is intangible, such as a memory) (Burnett, 2011; Burnett, Merchant, Pahl, & Rowsell, 2014). Pahl and Rowsell (2011) called attention to the ways artifacts, or "objects and their meanings in everyday life" are inherently tied to "the situated nature of texts in places and communities" (p. 130) thereby underscoring the nuanced, culturally embedded meaning that artifacts represent and evoke. Returning to Rebecca's recollection, we can see that her handling of the obstinate lid was a material artifact that also had an immateriality. Had the salsa jar opened easily, it is possible Rebecca might not have recollected her experience with her Nana. However, it was through the struggle with the lid that Rebecca immediately thought of her Nana's hands and the grilled cheese cooking on the stove. Essentially, the immaterial can become materialized through action and intention, which also can occur in and across digital and nondigital spaces (Burnett & Bailey, 2014). We extend this discussion by examining how tacit modalities can take shape in different ways depending on the associated contexts, experiences, and memories. To do so, we first look more closely at mitigating factors—affect, crystallization, and timescales—to offer additional clarity of how tacit modalities transcend temporal-spatial bounds and offer another layer of understanding to multimodal meaning making.

Affect

Though affect has been part of the human experience, it continues to gain attention in education research, especially in relation to literacy. More specifically, Leander and Boldt (2013) addressed how practices are not simply about products and destinations, but are processes imbued with felt experiences and emotion. They perceived

> literacy activity as not projected toward some textual end point, but as living its life in the ongoing present, forming relations and connections across signs, objects, and bodies in often unexpected ways. Such activity is saturated with affect and emotion; it creates and is fed by an ongoing series of affective intensities that are different from the rational control of meanings and forms. (p. 26)

Meaning that stems from tacit modalities can be rational, controlled, and expected or irrational, uncontrolled, and unexpected; affect creates a mind-body connection that is intersensory and can be visceral in nature. The fact is that tacit modalities are related to a "series of affective intensities" that can be ever-evolving even if they are provoked or prompted by the interaction with a particular artifact. For example, Sandra's father encountered near-death experiences, and his hospital stay marked a turning point in his health. When Sandra views pictures of her father from even 5 years ago, she is confronted by the sadness she feels knowing that her father has changed, by the gratefulness she feels knowing that he is still alive, and by the guilt she feels because sadness continues to permeate her thoughts. These tensions are stirred by affective intensities and prompted by interactions with various material and immaterial artifacts. To this day, Sandra cannot listen to David Bowie's *Space Oddity*, a song she listened while negotiating interstate traffic and rushing to see her father before his life-changing surgery; the music triggers a similar psychosomatic response she felt during that drive, underscoring the connection of memory to sensory to body. Even writing about this moment creates affective intensities that Sandra struggles to manage.

Crystallization

Drawing upon this interpretation of literacy as intertextual and intersensory meaning making, we also look to the philosophical discussion of crystallization to emphasize the perception-sensory connection. Perception is hard to grasp; it is slippery, ephemeral and also linked in with synaesthetic responses to artifacts. That is, there are lived memories within artifacts (e.g., the salsa jar for Rebecca, the David Bowie song for Sandra) that resurrect thoughts, feelings, emplaced sensations, and then there are materialities (e.g., colors, textures) that can trigger other sensory responses that could be somatic, sonic, olfactory, or visual. Just as the synaesthetic cross of senses is part and parcel of tacit modalities, so too are the anticipated and unanticipated sensations and memories that the tacit modalities evoke. In other words, felt and remembered experiences create additional tacit modalities that inform the ever-evolving meaning making experiences.

In their narrative about their travels, Laurel Richardson and Ernest Lockridge (2004) explored perception and representations of meaning through sociological and narrative lenses. They discussed memories as "moorings" that guide behavior (p. 123), and the authors recalled Richardson's (2000) qualitative analytical stance of "crystallization," or the understanding *that positioning impacts perception*. More specifically, they contended that "Crystals are prisms, which reflect externalities and refract within themselves, creating different colors, patterns, arrays, casting off in different directions. What we see depends on our angle of vision" (Richardson & Lockridge, 2004, p. 240). The crystal prism and the various refractions of light are metaphors for opportunities to create and recreate, as well as interpret and reinterpret, information, and at the heart of it all is context-based, nuanced meaning making.

In essence, Richardson's image of the crystal helps to underscore the complicated nature of meaning making. What we see is not all that is present. Interpretation is impacted by

> an infinite variety of shapes, substances, transmutations, multidimensionalities, and angles of approach. Crystals grow, change, and are altered, but they are not amorphous ... there is no single truth.... Crystallization provides us with a deepened, complex, and thoroughly partial understanding of the topic. (Richardson & St. Pierre, 2005, p. 963)

In other words, the crystal represents the potential changes and dynamic understandings that stem from tacit modalities and (im)material experiences. Artifacts may be created and consumed at specific points in time, but they are not static entities bereft of emotional connection. For example, photos of Sandra's father once "moored" (Richardson & Lockridge, 2004) her to fond memories, and now the conflation of the material and immaterial trigger mixed emotions. The physical artifact (the photo) has not changed, but it is not static because of the felt experience. Once again, this sense of emotional connection can be a conscious or subconscious response driven by human instincts to colors, textures, and so forth, with tacit modalities concretizing and complicating meaning making.

Furthermore, synaesthesia helps to underscore the dynamic nature and the "constant transition, translation and transduction between modes" (Kress, 1997, p. 37). As stated above, synaesthesia can work off of or in concert with transduction when meaning making moves from one mode to another, such as from speech to writing to image to film (Kress, 2010). Synaesthesia adds texture to memories and is an inherent component of tacit modalities. Engagements with artifacts such as, the Rebecca's jar in the opening, work on similar principles where reactions can lead to meaning making acts that can move from one texture and color to dimensionality. The jar cap is not simply a round metal object; the physical feel of it and the act of twisting (and the activation of related muscles) conjure memories that then bring about other feelings and remembered scents, scenes, and sensories. These, in turn, complicate temporal-spatial boundaries, as a person and an artifact may be physically located in one space, but the feelings can transport one back in time or create new meanings related to the artifact; there are shifts in liminal planes. Lemke's (2000) discussion of timescales helps to situate and clarify the complexity of experiencing and re-experiencing in different spatial-temporal contexts.

Timescales

Lemke's (2000) discussion of timescales helps our thinking by addressing how artifacts may mistakenly be understood as objects indicative of a particular time and place: "*Things*, or *organisms*, or *persons*, or *institutions*, as usually defined, are not dynamical notions: they are ordinarily defined in terms of their stable and persistent, or invariant, properties. They are not about dynamics, not about change and doing, but about being what they are" (p. 275, emphasis in original). However, when taking into account "dynamical theory," attention turns to "what's going on, what's participating and how, and how one going-on is interdependent with another" (p. 275), and Lemke suggests that material objects created or experienced in one timescale can be reexperienced in similar or different ways in another context. For Rebecca, the salsa jar and related tacit modalities figuratively transport her back in time; for Sandra, the *Space Odyssey* song elicits lived memories and psychosomatic responses; for Allison, such memories are but "fleeting moments," that anchor her to a past. The artifacts have a different meaning to different people and connect people to the past in different ways. What is more, artifacts that may have had seemingly static meaning may suddenly change, and this is where tacit modalities offers additional dimensionality to understandings of meaning making as both situated *and* protean. As these examples suggest (and as Lemke contended), moments of experience can be revisited through heterochrony, the phenomenon in which "longer-term processes and shorter-term events [are] linked by a material object that functions in both cases semiotically as well as materially" (Lemke, 2000, p. 281). In other words, meaning making is contextual, embodied, and interactional across timescales, calling attention to various trajectories of learning that inform overall meaning making.

MODE OF INQUIRY

To document and chart tacit modalities, we adopt a method of inquiry that combines the work of Lemke (2000) with Kress (2010) and Richardson (2000) to juxtapose and analyze different multimodal texts that we have collected and to engage in a collective case study of tacit modalities. More specifically, we consider Lemke's point that "every process, action, social practice or activity occurs on some timescale (in complex cases on more than one timescale)" (2000, p. 275). Keeping his discussion of dynamical theory in mind, we aim to describe "what's going on, what's participating and how one going-on is interdependent with another" (Lemke, 2000, p. 275). We ask these questions to examine (a) how material objects are experienced and reexperienced in similar and different ways and on various liminal planes; (b) where one is (e.g., the context and space) when one engages in sensory-based reactions (e.g., memories evoked by smells, sounds, images); and (c) where, how, and in what way the responses figuratively transport one to another dimension. When engaging in such descriptive work, we explore how multimodalities and synaesthetic responses are part of the re-experienced moments and how crystallization and ever-changing understandings help to offer perspectives of positionality, recreations of truth, embodied responses to memory, and spatial-temporal tensions; these perspectives are not mutually exclusive, and, therefore, are not used to categorize our findings. Instead, in this chapter, we feature multimodal texts alongside the producer/meaning maker's stories to extrapolate felt reactions and tacit modalities displayed during meaning making and materialized within the product itself.

Data represented in the paper derive from separate but related research of undergraduate and graduate education students' examinations of artifacts. Our personal experiences offer additional insight into tacit modalities. We mined data from previous research coupled with interviews with various people about objects that they value and objects that tell a story (Pahl & Rowsell, 2010). To analyze the data, we drew on affect theory (Ehret, 2018; Massumi, 2007) to examine how emotions and feelings are registered on the body as participants talked through their object/artifact; we then drew upon Lemke's notion of timescales to connect temporal relations with material engagements and associations that participants had with their objects. Finally, engaging in a collective case study (Yin, 2014), we identified similarities and differences across the cases and developed a greater understanding of how tacit modalities inform situated learning. Inductive data analysis supported the examination of overlapping and contrasting interpretations and the use of expert knowledge to discuss the emerging phenomena in relation to extant research (Yin, 2014).

TACIT MODALITIES

In this section, we present findings from our own research studies to elucidate aspects of tacit modalities. As such, each heading represents a category of tacit modalities and its corresponding concepts.

Entangled Timescales and Tacit Modalities: Ted and His Staged Photo

As a part of Jennifer's methods class, she teaches artifactual and visual methods and asks students to bring in photos and artifacts that they value.

Ted, a 24-year-old Asian Canadian university student, was particularly keen on this activity and promptly brought in a selfie of his family. The photo (see Figure 13.1) is of his Mom, Dad, and Ted at the Toronto airport en route to New York, where his mom would run the New York City Marathon. The photograph evokes many emotions for Ted, but mostly happiness because they had not gone on a family trip for some time and they seldom took photographs of big family events. As well, it is an uncharacteristic photo of both of his Mom and Dad. Ted's Mom typically does not like photos of herself and according to Ted, "my Dad, he has a very goofy personality which does not come out as much in this photo." When he describes the photo, Ted becomes noticeably animated saying,

> This is a very staged photo, but I mean it is a happy photo, and I believe we were all generally happy, but umm it is more of a performance aspect I guess, like that smile I can replicate, like that is my picture smile, because my mom, uhh like I had bad photos for school, like in grade school, and she was like you really need to get like a better, a good smile (both laughing), like you are doing a really cheeky thing, a closed grin thing, you need like an actual smile. Umm so I developed that smile, and then my dad is being very polite.

Within the photo there is the timescale of Ted's school photos when he could not get his "picture smile" right for a long time and then finally got it. Thinking about Lemke's (2000) timescales, the material world has many scales (e.g., space, time, matter), and Ted's reflections harken back to a younger age when he felt awkward during school photos and developed a staged self for more formal shots. He has this same smile in this affect-filled photo. What also arises in this photo is the notion of the performative, Hallmark card family photo wherein people visualize themselves in a particular way to speak to tropes. This kind of visual narrative carries tacit modalities with longer timescales both enacted and experienced.

In addition, speaking to the concept of timescales, Ted reflected on his dad's unusually relaxed smile and his mom's exuberant look, noting, "it was a moment and that is why I keep it." The act of taking the photograph and the resultant image sediments a memory for the family and crystallizes roles within the family. When asked if the photo carries feelings, Ted observed:

> Yeah I think photos are just inherently, like just snapshots, they are visuals, but umm it is more so what the person looking at the photo, umm what emotions they feel when looking at it, due to their past experiences and what visual cues I guess umm bring to mind when they look at a photo.

Looking at and thinking about a photograph ushers in past experiences as longer timescales embedded within photos, as well as visual tropes that exude specific emotions (e.g., joy), but also projected emotions, such as "look at us, we are a happy family."

Figure 13.1. Ted's airport selfie.

Unpacked and Repacked Tacit Modalities: Beyond Chained Elephants

At the end of the interview, Ted referred to a large Richard Avedon photograph (see https://bit.ly/1qV6gme) in Jennifer's office of a woman in a long black gown with two elephants on either side of her. When we discussed photographs, Ted said,

> I also think like if I look at this elephant photo, umm like I can uhhh sympathize with those elephants because they are like chained, so that must not feel good. I mean if I was reading a book about like a bad circus, mistreatment to animals, that feels no good, but I think that is very base level emotion.

Jennifer responded that she admires the woman's elegant black dress and that Jennifer loves the photo because it was in her father's office. In this moment, tacit modalities are entangled within an object, another photo, that signals Jennifer's connections with her father, but also the style of photographs that he loved—carrying her back in time to sitting in his office looking at the very same photo.

During their interview conversation, there is an entanglement emerging again of Ted's selfie with Jennifer's framed Richard Avedon photograph.

Referring to it as a point of contrast, Ted points to the Avedon image as illustrating how it makes him feel sympathetic to the elephant and perhaps angry about the elephants being tethered to chains; nonetheless the photograph is reminiscent of a bygone age with its homage to Audrey Hepburn's classic style in paradoxical juxtaposition with chained elephants. As yet another dimension of the entangled timescale, Jennifer recounts the story behind the Avedon photograph as a treasured artifact from her Dad's office at work and how it makes her feel (calm, usually) when she looks at it and thinks about it. Jennifer thereby refers to the tacit modalities at play as she sits in her office contemplating her Dad's picture and their shared qualities, such as a passion for their work, their love of photography.

Nonetheless, emotions about the Avedon photograph shifted in the interview to sadness—missing her Dad—or even when Ted talks about the cruelty of chaining elephants, Jennifer sees the photo in an entirely different light. In this instance, just as crystals offer various perspectives, materialities coalesce and Ted and Jennifer see the image in a different way after sharing their initial thoughts and telling artifactual stories. This highlights the mercurial, unpredictable character of tacit modalities, which can trigger one emotion in one instance followed by a polar opposite emotion in the next moment. Tacit modalities not only evoke expected meaning (e.g., Jennifer feeling calm), but also are essential for the shifts in meaning making that come rather unexpectedly due to contextual factors, such as new situations, turns in conversations, and interactions with modes. Staged photos, such as selfies, and even images that have been part of daily routines can carry with them loaded meanings that continue to be unpacked and perhaps repacked through each interaction. Sandra describes this motif in the next category when she recalls how her family home registered on her body when she witnessed her father's postsurgery illness and how something that previously was a source of contentment and comfort suddenly fractured and became an object of fright and pain.

Fractured Tacit Modalities: Paradigm Shifts

The introductory vignette of Rebecca's encounter suggests that, through the act of opening a jar of salsa, Rebecca sensed the warmth of family represented in food, play, and time spent together. Memories and artifacts, however, do not remain static, as we see through Jennifer and Ted's interaction. Sometimes changes to liminal planes—shifts of a small or seismic nature—can fracture or even rupture existing directionalities and relationships, resulting in new paradigms that carry with them weighted (or weightless) meanings, affect, and interpretations. Take, for instance, the reflective memos written during a time when Sandra's father experienced a traumatic surgery followed by a series of health issues, and she temporarily returned to her childhood home to help care for him:

> Today is the first day I think I took a breath. Yesterday was hellish; my dad had a fever of 105, and we could not stabilize his vitals. It.Was.Frightening. Today, thank heavens, my father is better. Though they still cannot locate the infection, the cocktail of antibiotics is working, and I'll drink to that (along the cocktail theme). My dad is not ready to leave the CCU [Critical Care Unit], but there's hope in sight.
>
> My dad had a pulmonary embolism and, thus, has had trouble breathing and getting enough oxygen. Things seem to be a bit more under control (knock wood), but there are other repercussions to the treatment and let's just say that I just want to get my dad back … I pray that he will be back to himself—cognitively and with physical improvements—and with as little pain and few issues as possible. I used to like roller coasters, and now I understand the beauty of slow, controlled rides like The Small World.
>
> My dad had to be transported via ambulance (if that gives you an idea of the state he is in), and I helped my mom prepare the house to accommodate my father's needs.... We spent the majority of the time getting things set up here and am now fully versed in the specialist language of medical supplies.... With everything going on, I also have started to rethink affect, the body, data, and energies that simply cannot be named, but rather best described.... My dad is not really the dad I once had—there is a new normal—and yet I still see him/hear him/think of him as he was … until I see him. Then there's a new person, hopefully temporarily. Who is that man? How did [this] transformation take place so quickly? And, if we ever get back to "normal," it will be a different normal, rife with the literal, emotional, and figurative scarring.

During this traumatic family experience, the pain and fear Sandra felt began to influence the way she viewed her home, and the artifacts that once were associated with joy became symbols of emotional torment. Her perception of her father as a "new person"—someone unrecognizable ("Who is that man?")—created sensations that could not "be named, but rather best described." Further complicating the matter were the emotion and sensory-based tensions between how Sandra remembered her father and the way she encountered him in person; the latter included sights, sounds, and smells related to medical supplies, illness, and physicalities unknown (e.g., atrophied muscles; reddened skin; medical tubes emerging from the arm, the nose; eyes with empty gazes).

The convergence of various modalities—the synaesthetic effect of the artifacts in her childhood home and the introduction of new sounds, sights, smells, and felt experiences—created continuous shifts in perceived understandings and sensations, while concretizing a "new normal" that included "literal, emotional, and figurative scarring." Tacit modalities entangled with fractured memories disrupted Sandra's underlying paradigm for home. Her father's deterioration belied representations of strength; the sounds of medical equipment and the stagnant air signaled illness, not growth; and the artifacts of bygone moments emphasized a reversal in roles: Sandra was now the caregiver. Although memories of childhood in that very house still existed, the timescale was fractured and memories soon became tainted by visceral, affective responses. The sounds of childhood joy became muted. Tacit, embodied modalities signaled permutations in meaning and experiential shifts in seemingly non-linear ways. These examples underscore the complex role of tacit modalities in meaning making, especially because these modalities include that which may be difficult to label or define.

Material and Immaterial Dualities Within Tacit Modalities: Genevieve and Her Journal

Genevieve is a 20-year-old undergraduate Hispanic-American Education student who has been journaling "since [she] was a little girl," but has a particular connection to her most recent journal because of its symbolization of freedom and hope. When engaged in a discussion of artifacts and learning, Genevieve explained,

> The first time I wrote in this journal was on my first plane ride to New York on August 5th, 2015. When I look at it I feel a sense of home ... I remember my darkest entry, and that day, and how hopeless and lost I felt moving out of my mom's house when I loved her so much but knew it wasn't a safe place anymore.

Genevieve struggled with the concept of "home," and dualities in meaning supported the material and immaterial entanglements and crystallizing views of what it means to be home and feel safe.

Through the journal, Genevieve's immaterial thoughts and feelings became materialized, and perhaps it is for that reason that she became fearful about "losing it [the journal] I lose things and don't really have anything tangible from childhood, so I feel sort of scared holding it sometimes (like what if I drop it in the subway and the train comes and my life is just rat food now!!)." So perhaps I feel more safe when I just see it laying on my bed or whatever." Because of tacit modalities, the sensory meets the embodied ("what if I drop it in the subway and the train comes and my life is just rat food now!!). To Genevieve, losing the journal would be like losing her identity, and tacit modalities support the material-immaterial duality that enables Genevieve to literally and figuratively hold on to memories.

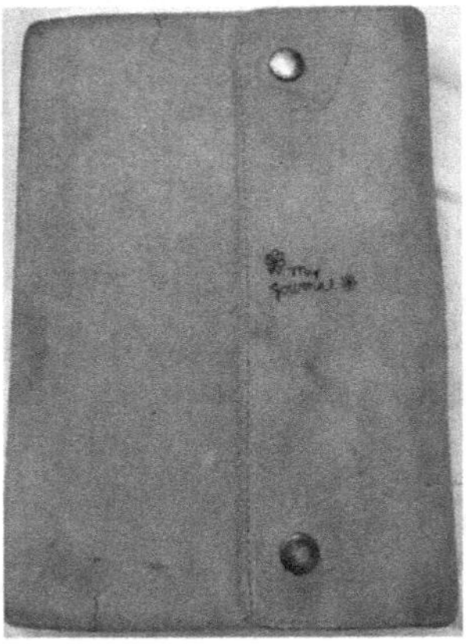

Figure 13.2. Genevieve's journal.

Furthermore, Genevieve seems to feel "moored" to and by her journal, an artifact that she has had for over ten years. She affectionately describes it as she considers how it represents her experiences with it:

> I love the material of the cover of my journal. When you open up the little flap to go inside the journal, you can see it's a lot more vibrant red on the inside. This shows how long I've had it and how it became so faded over the years.

The journal's physical attributes represent longer timescales while its internal links (e.g., the written memories) to other timescales enable Genevieve to move in and out of felt spaces.

Shifting Timescales: Teresa and Her Birds

Above we see how tacit modalities are entwined with identity practices, such as journal writing, as well as complicated timescales that Genevieve traverses when she writes in her journal, when she holds her journal, and when she thinks about her journal. Tacit modalities also highlight identity practices through shifting timescales, something that the story of Teresa helps to exemplify.

Teresa's fascination with birds and photographing birds helps to solidly exemplify visuals that have shifted with time and life changes. Built on her commitment to the work of Richard Shusterman (2008) and somoaesthetics (e.g., the body and its experiences as a sensory and aesthetic entity), Teresa developed a habit of taking photographs as a philosophical and embodied practice. "Somoaesthetics" is an intense look at the body and its function in developing our knowledge and construction of the world. Teresa's doctoral work examines how photography can be an act of consciousness, of actually thinking about the process of making images as a daily, philosophical practice. The lens, therefore, becomes an apt metaphor, capturing the philosophical, the ontological, and the physical, and being behind a camera lens crystallizes how Teresa understands the world in varied ways.

Our interview focused on birds and her lifelong fascination with birds. She talks about birds as messengers and as souls of the earth. She talks about the Janus-faced nature of vultures who are beautiful when they soar, but unattractive when you see them up close. Teresa grew up in Dallas, Texas and talks about growing up with vultures who were in plentiful supply on the "sides of roads, eating." The importance of the triptych in Figure 13.3 is that it reminds Teresa of the importance of her work: "These photographs have literally changed my life in that I can show visually what my work is comprised of ... words fail to convey the concept of 'conscious photographing' as well as the pairing of these three photos." Although Teresa grew up around vultures, it was only a few years ago when she was sitting on the deck at her brother's house in Athens, Texas when she saw the Turkey vultures (Figure 13.3) dancing on the roof. What struck her was the dance that they were engaged in at that very moment. Observing the dance from afar gave Teresa a calmness that stuck, and looking at the photographs even now reminds her of that epiphany.

Since then, Teresa has taken so many photos of birds at different angles and in different postures. Teresa talked far more than other participants about the feeling and affect that she experiences when she takes the photographs as opposed to looking at photographs. Such documentation not only sediments Teresa's identity as a photographer and birdwatcher, but also offers symbolic representations of her academic journey: "the meaning of these photos has increased and become the "solid" proof (to me) that my ideas of photographing, along with the literature have validity. My project is my legacy." In this way, there is a timescale that extends beyond herself; just as photography materializes her philosophies and beliefs, it also creates immaterial, boundless extensions of her values. There are shifts in timescales that enhance Teresa's relationship with photos of birds, especially as these photos are embedded into her everyday and serve as a strong signifier of her identity.

LOOKING FORWARD

A scent. A song. A taste. A texture. An image. These and other modalities individually or in concert with others can trigger an affective response typically associated with memories or physical (dis)comfort, and tacit

Figure 13.3. Teresa's birds.

modalities complicate our notions of place, space and time. Given the communicationally complex texts that students encounter on a minute-by-minute basis, literacy policy and practice need a far more robust and nuanced approach to addressing the orientation and presentation of meaning making.

The concept of tacit modalities supports the exploration of the felt, the sensed, and the imagined, enabling one to experience a mooring to a particular time and space, and yet engage in a reinvention of time, space, and self. Genevieve's journal offered her entree to a space that she could call home during a time she did not have one. Rebecca used Facebook to document her recollection of her Nana's hands, receiving affirmation and creating opportunities for crystallization. Jennifer and Ted found entangled modalities and affective responses prompted by an image that had layers of meaning beyond its physical appearance. We contend that the concept of tacit modalities offers educators and education researchers opportunities to rethink meaning making in light of contextualized, embodied, and interactional aspects that illuminate various trajectories of experience; in essence, the learner can be making meaning on multiple, but distinct planes, something that takes much more time and space to unpack than conventional education spaces and practices support.

Put together with the context of in-school and out-of-school meaning making, the discussion of tacit modalities underscores the ever-evolving nature of meaning. We consider the implications of nondigital and digital artifacts and the tacit modalities that are entangled across timescales. For instance, what does the finger-paint picture mean to the child and the parent today? Tomorrow? In 10 years from now? What happens when a child's work or photo is circulated via social media? How might digital resources and spaces create or mutate tacit modalities, ultimately sedimenting or distorting identities? Relatedly, what and how might digital enhancements and remix, or even the sharing and resharing of material and immaterial artifacts, offer new crystallizations and create alternate timescales rife with permutations and even fractures of meaning?

As we look forward and consider the discussion of tacit modalities and meaning making in and beyond the classroom, we contend that tacit modalities might help to reframe an understanding of progress and formative learning; tacit modalities elicit felt and embodied experiences, which, as the vignettes suggest, can have opposing, fracturing, or reaffirming effects. If progress and formative learning were considered with a holistic view of where, when and how learners make meaning along the way, then perhaps these learning residues will reveal the depth and complexity of each person's ever-changing journey. Furthermore, we suggest that a focus on tacit modalities might help educators, education researchers, and students become more keenly aware of negotiations of place, space, and reimagined meaning, especially as digital and nondigital practices have multiple "truths" and include multiple trajectories moored in one space and crystallizing other dimensions.

NOTE

1. With the exception of author names, all names are pseudonyms.

REFERENCES

Burnett, C. (2011). The (im)materiality of educational space: interactions between material, connected and textual dimensions of networked technology use in schools. *E-Learning and Digital Media, 8*(3), 214–227.

Burnett, C., & Bailey, C. (2014). Conceptualising collaboration in hybrid sites: Playing Minecraft together and apart in a primary classroom. In C. Burnett, J. Davies, G. Merchant, & J. Rowsell (Eds.), *New literacies around the globe: Policy and pedagogy* (pp. 50–72). Abingdon, Oxon: Routledge.

Burnett, C., Merchant, G. H., Pahl, K., & Rowsell, J. (2014). The (im)materiality of literacy: the significance of subjectivity to new literacies research, *Discourse: Studies in the Cultural Politics of Education, 35*(1), 90–103. doi:10.1080/01596306.2012.739469

Bowie, D. (1969). Space Oddity. [Recorded by David Bowie]. On *David Bowie*. [Single]. London, England: Trident Studios.

Ehret, C. (2018). Propositions from affect theory for feeling literacy through the event. In D. Alvermann, N. Unrau, & R. Ruddell (Eds.), *Theoretical models and processes of reading* (7th ed.). Newark, DE: International Literacy Association.

Enriquez, G., Johnson, E., Kontovourki, S., & Mallozzi, C. A. (Eds.). (2015). *Literacies, learning, and the body: Putting theory and research into pedagogical practice*. New York, NY: Routledge.

Jenkins, H. (2006). *Convergence culture: Where old and new media collide*. New York, NY: New York University Press.

Kress, G., & Van Leeuwen, T. (2001). *Multimodal discourse: The modes and media of contemporary communication.* London, England: Arnold.

Kuhn, A. (1995). *Family secrets: Acts of memory and imagination*. London, England: Verso.

Leander, K., & Boldt, G. (2013). Rereading "A pedagogy of multiliteracies": Bodies, texts, and emergence. *Journal of Literacy Research, 45*(1), 22–46.

Lemke, J. L. (2000). Across the scales of time: Artifacts, activities, and meanings in ecosocial systems. *Mind, Culture, and Activity, 7*(4), 273–290.

Lewis, C., & Tierney, J. D. (2013). Mobilizing emotion in an urban classroom: Producing identities and transforming signs in a race-related discussion. *Linguistics and Education, 23*, 289–304.

Massumi, B. (2002). *Parables for the virtual: Movement, affect, sensation*. Durham, NC: Duke University Press.

Pahl, K., & Rowsell, J. (2011). Artifactual critical literacies: A new perspective for literacy education. *Berkeley Review of Education, 2*(2), 129–151.

Richardson, L. (2000). Writing: A method of inquiry. In N. K. Denzin & Y. S. Lincoln (Eds.), *Handbook of qualitative research* (2nd ed., pp. 923–948). Thousand Oaks, CA: SAGE.

Richardson, L., & Lockridge, E. (2004). *Travels with Ernest: Crossing the literary/sociological divide.* Walnut Creek, CA: AltaMira Press.

Richardson, L. & St. Pierre, E.A. (2005). Writing: A method of inquiry. In N. K. Denzin & Y. S. Lincoln (Eds.), *The Sage handbook of qualitative research* (3rd ed., pp. 959–978). Thousand Oaks, CA: SAGE.

Shusterman, R. (2008). *Body consciousness: A philosophy of mindfulness and somaesthetics*. Cambridge, MA: Cambridge University Press.

Street, B. V. (1999). Literacy and social change: The significance of social context in the development of literacy programmes. In D. A. Wagner (Ed.), *Future of literacy in a changing world* (pp. 55–72). Cresskill, NJ: Hampton Press.

Vasudevan, L. (2006). Looking for angles: Knowing adolescents by engaging with their multimodal literacy. *Journal of Adolescent & Adult Literacy, 50*(4), 252–256.

Yin, R. K. (2014). *Case study research: Design and methods 4th edition.* Thousand Oaks, CA: SAGE.

CHAPTER 14

REPATRIATING *DESAPARACIDOS* ACROSS SPACES

Suriati Abas
Indiana University, Bloomington

INTRODUCTION

Earlier studies in the field of linguistic landscape relied on Landry and Bourhis's (1997) definition of linguistic landscape (LL), which is limited to languages in public spaces within a given physical, geographical boundary. The shortcoming of this perspective is that it ignores the reality of space as dynamic, fluid, and mobile. However, an increasing number of studies have expanded the terrain of Laundry-Bourhis's seminal work to examine non-fixed or transient signs (e.g., Abas & Damico, 2018; Hanauer, 2015). Although Troyer (2012) and Chun (2014) had, earlier on, studied physical-digital spaces, both took on an etic perspective in their interpretations of publicly accessible languages. Thus, I aim to fill in the gap by "giving voices" (Silverman, 2014) to these signs. Building on the works of literacy scholars who found that there is a natural transcendence when users treated digital spaces as a continuity to the physical (e.g., Buck, 2012; Leander & Aplin, 2014), my study delved into two areas: the LL created

Negotiating Place and Space Through Digital Literacies: Research and Practice, pp. 259–274

by an American sign-creator named Ben Clark (pseudonym) who resides in Argentina, and the effect of his digital literacy practices leveraging the affordances of technology.

In using LL, I refer to signs that took the form of portraits used in physical spaces, photographed, posted onto digital spaces, and/or resemiotized across spaces. Given that each of these portraits are historically situated, I argue that their circulations across spaces function as teaching and learning tools for raising awareness of the autocracy of the past and present social situations in Argentina. The notion of teaching and learning is viewed from the perspective of Paulo Freire's (1970) critical pedagogy which involves making connections with broader exploitative social, political and structural contexts, to enable social change.

Drawing upon hybrid frameworks of nexus analysis (Scollon & Scollon, 2004), critical pedagogy (Freire, 1970), and Kress and van Leeuwen's (1996) concept of *interactional systems*, the following questions were addressed: (a) How does an American sign-creator attempt to teach people about the Argentine community that he lived with, through the construction of LL? (b) In what ways do particular digital literacy practices that the sign-creator employed challenge monolithic notions of space, his own identities and those of the Argentines?

HYBRID FRAMEWORKS: NEXUS ANALYSIS, CRITICAL PEDAGOGY AND INTERACTIONAL SYSTEMS

I employed hybrid frameworks as the LL data that I collected was shaped by the affordances of technology, moving across physical-digital spaces. Scollon and Scollon (2004) defined nexus analysis as "the mapping of the semiotic cycles of people, objects, and discourses" (p. x). In nexus analysis, the *sites of engagement* occur at the intersections of three elements: *historical body, discourses in place,* and *interaction order*.

Historical body is the background information. For instance, the portraits of *desaparacidos* (the disappeared) that Ben painted were meant to remember victims of Argentina's final military dictatorship (1976–1983), a period where an estimated 30,000 people were forcibly disappeared. The second element, *discourses in place,* which I referred to as *materials in place*, are images and/or texts found at two *sites of engagement*: the physical spaces of Buenos Aires and the digital space that Ben constructed. The last element, *interaction order*, considers social engagements initiated by the sign-creator on sign-viewers and vice versa. In Ben's daily activities, these elements interact with one another to form a *nexus of practice*.

To understand how *nexus of practice* functions as tools for teaching and learning, I refer to Freirean ideas of critical pedagogy. Briefly described as a pedagogical philosophy that challenges the "banking" model of education (a metaphor for a traditional transmission-oriented method of education), critical pedagogy promotes the exploration of real-world problems through reflection, dialogue, and problem-posing. Since the sign-creator's work centered on portraits of *desaparacidos* (the disappeared), Kress and van Leeuwen's (1996) concept of *interactional systems* afforded a means for unpacking how the portraits engaged with viewers. In this system, visual cues such as the direction of the *gaze* (or positioning of a character's eyes) which either conveys a *demand* (when a character is looking directly at viewers) or *offer* (when a character is looking away from viewers), have an impact on the viewer's meaning-making process (Kress & van Leeuwen, 1996).

METHODOLOGY: FOLLOWING THE OBJECTS

I applied the methodological approach of "following the objects" (Lash & Lury, 2007) to track repeated movements of "objects" and their transitions across spaces (see Figure 14.1). The process of data collection comprised two phases which, included the following:

Phase I

While I was in Buenos Aires, I wrote observational fieldnotes, collected photographic data, and conducted interviews with 100 participants on the streets to find out what was going on in the city, which was filled with images and/or texts specific to the 40th commemoration of The Day of Memory, Truth, and Justice. Ben was one of the participants who contributed to the cultivation of LL on that day. The multicolored portraits which he painted and carried down the streets were unique as all other signs of *desaparacidos* (the disappeared) came in somber black and white.

Phase II

Upon returning to the United States, I interviewed Ben several times via Skype. Through his Facebook posts, I discovered multiple online manifestations of the portraits that he had painted. They were produced and reproduced across sites and locales. In following the trajectory of these "objects," I traced their production within and across *nexus of practice*, circulation and mediation. To put this in terms of Scollon and Scollon's (2004) *nexus of practice*, the movements of "objects" can be summarized as in Figure 14.1.

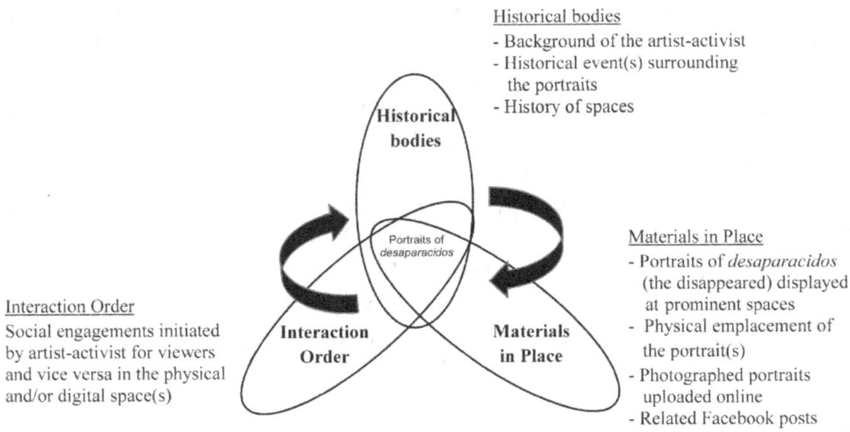

Figure 14.1. Movements of "objects" within and across *nexus of practice* (Adapted from Scollon & Scollon, 2004, p. 3; the arrows were included to indicate physical-digital transitions.)

FRAMING THE "OBJECTS" TO FOLLOW

The "objects" I followed were drawn from two events: the disappearance of Santiago Maldonado in 2017, and the 43 Mexican students in 2014, because they resonated with the historical experiences of the Argentines. First, I examined Ben's Facebook posts on those events. Then, I did online searches with the following keywords: *retratos* (portraits) *y desaparacidos* (the disappeared) and Ben's real name. In the next section, I discussed how Ben navigated across and within *sites of engagement*. I also highlighted the ways in which particular digital literacy practices that he employed challenge monolithic notions of space, his own identities, and those of the Argentines.

FINDINGS AND DISCUSSION

The following section brings together findings across physical and digital spaces.

SITES OF ENGAGEMENT #1 – PHYSICAL → DIGITAL SPACES

For site of engagement #1, Ben navigated linearly, promoting the disappearance of Santiago Maldonado from the physical to digital spaces. To teach people about the Argentine community that he lives with, he posed thought-provoking questions on one space, and re-entextualized the same question in another space. Viewed in the light of critical pedagogy, a question is a call to participate in the pursuit of knowledge. In this case, it is calling viewers to investigate Maldonado's disappearance. Dewhurst (2014) asserts that questioning is "a way of instigating learning with the possibility of transforming how people make sense of the world around them" (p. 69). The questions that Ben posed alongside the portrait that he painted contained particular meanings due to their geosemiotic emplacement, in front of the governmental building of *Casa Rosada*, at *Plaza de Mayo* (see Figure 14.2).

Figure 14.2. Portrait of Santiago Maldonado on the fence of *Casa Rosada* with a slip of note questioning the president at the top left-hand corner.

Posing Thought-Provoking Questions Across Spaces

The *historical bodies* surrounding *Plaza de Mayo* dated back from the years before the military dictatorship of 1976. Recognized as the main square of Buenos Aires, this space has been frequently used for social protests. One of the massive demonstrations that took place on October 17, 1945 involved the release of Juan Domingo Perón, a demagogue, who had been imprisoned. In another instance, during the 2001 economic crisis, people banged pots and pans to protest against devaluation of their savings when the Argentine pesos weakened. When Santiago Maldonado, an indigenous activist disappeared on August 1, 2017, thousands of people demonstrated in front of *Casa Rosada* demanding president Mauricio Macri to "return" him (For details, see https://www.nytimes.com/es/2017/09/06/donde-esta-santiago-maldonado/). For many weeks, this *site of engagement* constituted massive black and white portraits of Santiago Maldonado with the tagline, ¿Dónde está Santiago Maldonado? (Where is Santiago Maldonado?). The appearance of faces of the forcibly disappeared first materialized in 1979 and have since then been incorporated as a central method of protests of disappearances (Longoni, 2010). Daily news reported that Maldonado's disappearance sparked public outrage as it "revived bitter memories of Argentina's 1976-83 military dictatorship" (Goni, 2017).

On the day of Maldonado's disappearance, Ben was one of the sign-creators who contributed to the LL of Buenos Aires:

> I painted his (Santiago Maldonado) portrait the day I heard about his death. I posted it on facebook as a portrait and also presented it as a poster with his name above and the *Presente* (Present), that is characteristic of announcements of victims of state terrorism. The name is said and then *¡Presente!* (Present!). (Interview, 01/01/2017)

Similar to previously held protests, the emplacement of Maldonado's portrait, on the fence of *Casa Rosada,* held a special request from the state who denied culpability for the disappearance. Maldonado's direct *gaze* presented a *demand* for the disappeared to reappear alive (*aparición con vida*). The *demand* could concomitantly be viewed as an invitation to engage with Maldonado and support him in the activist work that led to his disappearance (see Figure 14.1).

***Dónde está?* (Where is he?).** The question, *Dónde está?* (Where is he?), implored through Maldonado's face, provoked further investigations on his whereabouts. His outward *gaze* and the accusatory question of *Dónde está?* by the fence of *Casa Rosada* instigated additional responses, harkening to the dark years during the last dictatorship, to other cases of disappearance after the reestablishment of democracy in 1983 (e.g., Jorge Julio López in 2006, Luciano Arruga in 2009). As Miller (2014) asserts, "meaning is ascribed to a space/place through the dominant historical narratives (in space/places) that are encumbered within specified sociopolitical, educational, cultural and economic policies and laws" (p. 124). Brian's inclusion of another question, *¿Cual es más fácil a descubrir, graffiti o el terrorismo del estado?* (Which is more difficult, to disappear, graffiti or state terrorism?), on the top left-hand corner of the portrait, created possibilities of seeing the everyday issue of graffiti in the capital city through new lenses.

¿Cual es más fácil a descubrir, graffiti o el terrorismo del estado?

(Which is more difficult, to disappear, graffiti, or state terrorism?). This question, as the sign-creator claimed, was added, in response to fleeting graffiti identified as "transgressive signs" (Scollon & Scollon, 2003) or signs that violated the norms, across the city of Buenos Aires.

> at the first march, one month after his disappearance, there was a lot of graffiti, scrawled on government buildings by someone ... purportedly by the unruly demonstrators ... but I never saw anyone doing this. So there was talk about all the destruction (not sure how it occurred in front of many hundreds of police...) but... they had to paint over the graffiti. So I went to the building where they were painting over the graffiti and had a sign that said, "*Es más fácil desaparecer a los seres humanos que desaparecer el graffiti*" (It is easier to disappear human beings than to disappear graffiti). (Interview, 01/01/2017)

Recognizing that the graffiti on this wall was emplaced on an inappropriate space, Ben repositioned his identities as an American, and a sign-creator, to a social activist based in Buenos Aires; he challenged the status quo by transforming the declarative statement, *Es más fácil desaparecer a los seres humanos que desaparecer el graffiti* (It is easier to disappear human beings than to disappear graffiti) on the wall, into a question. This question, which promoted *conscientização* or critical consciousness (Freire, 1970), encouraged viewers to interrogate the commonplace by challenging the unquestioned legitimacy of unequal power relationships between the state, its citizens and those responsible for state terrorism in the previous years. According to Freire (1970), posing and pursuing questions is a means of learning and teaching about social issues. This approach continued and circulated through the digital space that Ben constructed on his Facebook posts as a continuity to the physical space.

Re-entextualization of the Question

A month later, Ben employed re-entextualization where only the question, *Dónde está?* (Where is he?) was "moved" to the digital space (Briggs & Bauman, 1992). He posted his name, current location, and the same question, *Dónde está Santiago Maldonado?* (Where is Santiago Maldonado?) on a solid black background (see Figure 14.3). The simple yet powerful question that formed the *materials in place* had its *historical bodies* circulating across social networks within split seconds; a spontaneous campaign to claim the appearance of Maldonado was initiated using the same form in

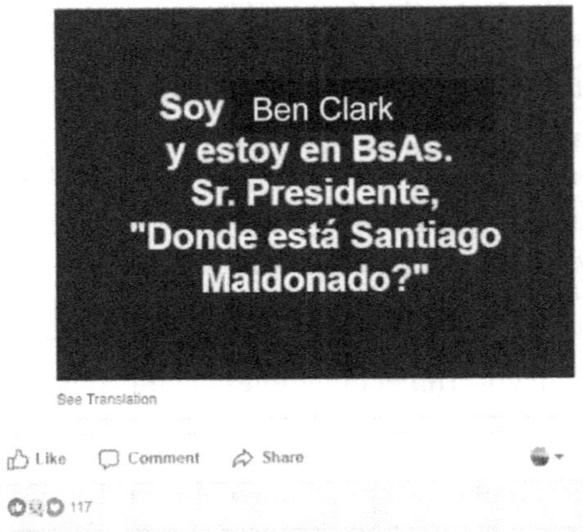

Figure 14.3. A message to all Facebook fans.

all social media (Facebook and twitter) posts. Participants simply mention their names, specify where they are or what they are doing at the time of writing the message, and ask: where is Santiago Maldonado? Argentina's history of political disappearances caused iterations of similar messages to continuously circulate to effect social change. Ben's partcipation could be seen as a form of traversal which Lemke (2001) posited as "catenations of meaningful elements" (p. 86) or extensions of what he did in the physical space, broadening the *sites of engagement* from *Plaza de Mayo* to the digital space on his Facebook. Table 14.1 summarizes the *sites of engagement*, movements of "objects" and the elements that formed the nexus of practice. Further details on sites of engagement #2 will be discussed below.

SITES OF ENGAGEMENT #2 – DIGITAL ↔ PHYSICAL

In *sites of engagement* #2, Ben navigated back and forth, from the digital to physical and vice versa. Drawing parallels with tens of thousands of people who disappeared when Argentina was under the coup (1976–1983), the sign-creator probed into a contemporary problem that happened in another community—the disappearance of 43 Mexican students (For details, see http://www.bbc.com/news/world-latin-america-35539727). Without much knowledge, as he claimed, he turned to the internet, researched the issue, and disseminated the information that he had obtained from the digital space (websites) to his very own Facebook page:

> Unfortunately, I was not aware of what had happened in Mexico until two months after the disappearances. A friend mentioned the Mexican students

Table 14.1.
Summary of Sites of Engagement, Movements and the Elements in Nexus of Practice

Sites of engagement [Event]	**Sites of engagement #1 [The disappearance of Santiago Maldonado]**	**Sites of engagement #2 [The disappearance of 43 Ayotzinapa students]**
Movement between spaces	Physical → Digital	Digital ↔ Physical
Summary of sites of engagement	• Interaction between sign-creator and sign-viewers	• Interaction between sign-creator and online semiotic resources • Interaction between sign-creator and students • Interaction between students, and "place"
Historical bodies	• *Plaza de Mayo,* a historical, physical space of protests • Ben's Facebook posts, a digital space	• *Plaza de Mayo,* a historical, physical space of protests • Ben's Facebook posts, a digital space • *Cinempio Nostos,* a cinema in Colombia
Materials in Place	• Portrait of Santiago Maldonado • Facebook post on Santiago Maldonado	• Portraits of 43 missing Ayotzinapa students

> and asked if I was going to paint them. I began reading all I could about what had happened and also began posting the images on Facebook along with links to articles about them. (Interview, 05/01/2017)

Since he was teaching at the time when the disappearance in Ayotzinapa, Mexico, occurred, Ben took the opportunity to conduct lessons that went beyond painting. Integrating the expertise and interest that he had in portraits of *desaparacidos* (the disappeared), the sign-creator provided spaces for his students to engage in the sociopolitical situations to which he is presently residing (Buenos Aires, Argentina) by getting them to paint portraits of a recent case of disappearance involving students in another community as subjects:

> I was teaching painting at the time, and decided to assign the task of painting the portraits to my class as well, asking them to do research, etc ... quite a challenge for beginning painters. They became very engaged with this as the subject was fellow students and, when their paintings were finished they were displayed at the college. (Interview, 05/01/2017)

Each of the photographs given to the students for painting portraits had its own *historical bodies*—What happened to this person? Why did he/she disappear? Who is responsible for this? How is this related to Argentina? To acquaint students with issues surrounding Argentina's past, Ben created opportunities that connected the *materials in place* (portraits of 43 Aytozinapa students) to real-world context. His pedagogical approach in that sense included teaching how to "read the word and the world" (Freire, 1970).

> I brought a student group from Wisconsin to Argentina as well, for a ten day course in Spanish and political art and, of course, taught these kids, most of whom were not art students, about Ayotzinapa and the disappearances.... I took the students to the *Plaza de Mayo*, with the 45 portraits ... they met one of the founders of the *Madres de la Plaza de Mayo* (Mothers of the Plaza de Mayo), we marched with the *Madres* on their weekly *ronda* or rounds about the central structure there, the *Pirámide de Mayo*. (Interview, 30/12/2016) (see Figure 14.3)

The march down *Pirámide de Mayo*, the oldest national monument in Buenos Aires, offered these students a means for learning "with" places wherein Freire's pedagogy of organizing instruction around students' experiences were adopted. By circling around *Pirámide de Mayo*, students gained understanding of Argentina's past and present. These included recognizing key figures who have been campaigning for state-committed crimes against humanity and enforced disappearances (For details, see https://alborada.net/nora-cortinas-argentina-mothers-of-plaza-de-mayo/), and knowing that the main square of *Plaza de Mayo* is both historical and political *sites of engagement*.

Taken as a *nexus of practice*, these experiences provided a basis for praxis or informed actions aimed at eliminating injustices. From a Freirean perspective, the process of "humanization" or becoming more human by taking responsibility for transformation is only possible through *conscientização* or critical consciousness (Freire, 1970). Although this is already happening locally, at the university spaces that Abas and Damico (2018) investigated, the impact would be greater if it is motivated by those from outside of Argentina. Ben's Facebook pages has the potential for eliciting public participation as it raises societal concerns, reaching out to followers who may not be in the country.

CHALLENGING MONOLITHIC NOTIONS OF IDENTITIES, SPACES, AND COMMUNITIES

Apart from raising awareness on past atrocities that haunted the Argentine community, the circulations of signs within and across the nexus of practice (see Figure 14.1) reflected the dynamic LL. They are not merely portraits that were painted, photographed and disseminated to the world. Rather, the existence of such LL espoused particular ways of thinking about identities, spaces, and communities that were made possible with the affordances of technology, or rather, factors that contributed to the types of interactions using technology (e.g., Facebook).

SOCIAL IMAGINARIES OF "SELF" AND "OTHERS"

The LL that Ben cultivated in a temporal space challenged social imaginaries of "self" and "others". Social imaginaries refers to "the way a given people imagine their collective social life" (Taylor, 2000), are often represented by virtue of how individuals typically position themselves in the world. Given the fact that the sign-creator is American, during his social encounters, many questioned the connections between the portraits that he painted and, his personal self:

> One of the first questions I invariably run into at exhibitions or actions from Latin Americans is, "Why are you, a Yankee, making a memorial to Latin Americans? Did you live here? You have relatives here, etc?" I am not Latin American, of course, and I also have no relatives that are or were, and I am only at a preliminary stage of learning Spanish (unfortunately!). So a side benefit of the work is that people in Latin America must question their notions of what "a Yankee", is or thinks or does. And they end up calling me their Yankee friend, or Yankee brother or whatever…with the irony of course that the real meaning is "the single Yankee who is my friend or is my brother, "a fact that amazes them somewhat more than it does me. (Interview, 30/12/2016)

From the *historical bodies* presented earlier in the chapter, Ben is a rare instance. Many of the memorials, works of human rights and activists in Argentina, were championed by natives who either experienced the brutal dictatorship and/or had families and friends who disappeared. The *interaction order* that this American sign-creator had with Argentines and those residing in Buenos Aires in the physical-digital LL, to a certain extent, transformed his initial perceptions of the "others" or community where he is currently living. As he claimed,

> Likewise, any notions I had or may had about "Latin Americans" have been washed away. My ignorance is corrected by interactions, by living with these people, meeting the diverse group with backgrounds from many indigenous peoples and also from Europe, Russia, Asia, etc. "What is an *Argentino* or an Uruguyan?" The only answer that is somewhat accurate is that they are people who live in these countries and have citizenship there. (Interview, 30/12/2016)

By navigating across multiple *sites of engagement* (see Table 14.1), Ben inherently adopted critical pedagogy. In particular, the real-life experiences enable his students to obtain better understanding of the sociopolitical situations attached to the painting of portraits.

A PORTRAIT WITH MANY "LIVES"

Through the physical-digital LL, Ben bore a portrait with many "lives." One possible reason to account for this was the fluidity of transforming each of them into different dimensions and places:

> I enlarged the painting to a poster a meter by a meter and a half and carried this to the Cabildo, to the Ministry of Justice, to the *Casa Rosada*, to *Congresso*, to all three major *encuentros* about Santiago Maldonado held in the *Plaza de Mayo*, and it has been to universities with me and taken by teachers to schools. Photographs of these actions or uses are online and are widely circulated. So, one small painting has a lot of lives, extensions, effect. It is quite amazing to me. (Interview, 30/12/2016)

While typically paintings of portraits remained dormant in the spaces where the sign-creator chose to place them, those painted by Ben circulated within and across *nexuses of practice*. His openness to sharing them resulted in mutiple series of iterations. As Ben explained:

> Students used them as book covers and for assignments, while teachers in *escuela abierto* (public school) reused them as teaching resources. Some people even reproduced them as Facebook profile. I sent images of the 43 portraits to every Mexican human rights group I could access online, to the Ayotzinapa *escuela*, HIJOS Mexico, etc. I have no idea what any of these people did with them. But one image I attach is from a cinematic school that altered my portraits a bit making posters they set up as an installation in a theater, attaching them to the empty seats. (Interview, 30/12/2016)

The same portraits held at the historic space of *Plaza de Mayo* (see Figure 14.2) "travelled" to a another *site of engagement* in Columbia, at *Cinemplo Nostos* (see Figure 14.3). Through its emplacement in a cinema, the significance of the portraits were artistically represented. Each of the faces communicated a *demand* which suggest some form of participation or invitation to take some actions for their disappearance. Positioned at the back of chairs as if they were in a classroom equipped with a screen, the status of the 43 Ayotzinapa students as *desaparacidos* (the disappeared) was magnified. The movements of these "objects" from Argentina to Columbia suggest global concerns. Since the 1970s and 1980s, the problem of forced disappearances were prevalent in Latin American countries under the governance of right-wing military dictatorships ("Latin America's Disappeared," 2014). In Colombia, reconstructing the immediate and remote past is, to this day, an essential practice due to the exponential rise in human rights violations (Villalón, 2016). With the affordances of technology, the production of itinerant space for memorial installation (see Figure 14.5) was made possible. Through Ben's Facebook posts, portraits were transported digitally in the gallery folder, replicated, printed by the Columbians who were involved in the memorial project and pasted onto a fixed, geographical location.

Figure 14.4. Students from America participated in the weekly rounds at Plaza de Mayo, in Argentina, carrying portraits of the 43 Mexican students who disappeared.

Figure 14.5. Portraits of the 43 disappeared Mexicans used by Cinempleo Nostos, in Columbia, to make a memorial installation for a film about the Mexican students. (https://www.facebook.com/cinempleo)

Another affordance of the digital technology as seen in Figure 14.4 and 14.5 is that its use facilitated a collective process of reconstructing historical realities within (e.g., at *Plaza de Mayo*) and outside the contexts of dictatorship (e.g., in Colombia). These historical realities took the form of *materials in place*, or portraits of *desaparacidos* (the disappeared) painted and digitally disseminated. Together with the *interaction order* which involved circling *Plaza de Mayo*, the portraits and the entire *nexus of practice* promote the social act of reimagining histories to raise critical consciousness.

CONNECTING AND (RE)CONNECTING COMMUNITIES

Although major cities in Argentina are replete with visual reminders of atrocities carried out by the dictatorship, traditional boundaries of engaging in past memories traversed digital spaces. The fluidity of movements in the LL resulted in the production of an "imagined community" (Anderson,

1983) where members who may not know one another face-to-face, were connected and for some, (re)connected online based on a shared sense history:

> My Facebook page … the [online] memorial has connected many people who would not otherwise have met. I have met hundreds of people in person but online, many thousands. At the same time, as we interact, these people are meeting and conversing with each other. many like-minded people, who may have experienced these horrors ... meet one another. It becomes a nexus of hub … for people who care about it, are related. It is an invitation for conversation and exchange. (Interview, 30/12/2016)

Since the movement primarily happened within a shared digital space (in the form of responses to Facebook posts), the *interaction orders* between the sign-creator and his Facebook followers revolved around postings on contemporary issues and informal discussions. Unlike conducting face-to-face discussions, there is no limit to the response time. The unrestricted participation time could only be afforded in digital spaces.

IMPLICATIONS FOR RESEARCH AND PRACTICE

This chapter outlined selected works of an American sign-creator who has been actively involved in the construction of a LL in Argentina. As aforementioned, I used the term LL to refer to signs that took the form of portraits painted for a geographic place, photographed to be posted onto digital spaces, and/or resemiotized within and/or across spaces. In examining the LL, the *nexus of practice* was seen as a blending of the physical, geographical places and digital spaces. The language which comprised images and/texts in the spaces described above is not arbitrary, "rather, there is a goal to understand the system, the messages it delivers or could deliver, about societies, people, the economy, policy, class, identities" (Shohamy & Gorter, 2009, p. 3). Thus, the question of production (LL by whom?) and of reception (LL for whom?) (Backhaus, 2007) is germane in all LL studies.

Although findings from the study showed a clear delineation of how circulations across spaces function as teaching and learning tools (see Table 14.1), the *interaction order* within and across *sites of engagements* were far more complicated in reality than those summarized in Figure 14.1. While there is a nascent body of scholarship that studied physical-digital spaces employing connective ethnographies (e.g., Leander & Lovvorn, 2006; Warner, 2017), the embedded complexity and dynamic nature of movements across spaces foregrounded a methodological challenge, especially with huge data sets. This could be further complicated in a study where the researcher does not occupy the same geographic location as the participants.

In relation to classroom practice, following the pedagogy employed by the sign-creator involves a paradigm shift from commonplace assumptions of the educator as "a sage on the stage" to a "guide on the side." The merits of this approach is that it creates dialogic spaces for interrogating, questioning and learning about how people think and live. While generally viewed as "teaching resistance" (Hardin, 2001), learners should be taught to participate from a detached standpoint. Given the affordances of technology, both educators and learners could coconstruct knowledge together in a safe, shared digital space. Much like the sign-creator described above, learning should be expanded beyond geographical locations and even within and/or across digital spaces.

ACKNOWLEDGMENT

The author wishes to thank Ben Clark (pseudonym) for participating in the study, sharing the photographs and giving consent to use them.

REFERENCES

Abas, S., & Damico, J. (2018). The language of activism. Representations of social justice in a university space in Argentina. In N. Avineri, L. R. Graham, E. Johnson, R. Riner, & J. Rosa (Eds.), *Language and social justice in practice* (pp. 157–165). United States: Routledge.

Anderson, B. (1983). *Imagined communities: Reflections on the origin and spread of nationalism*. London, England: Verso Books.

Backhaus, P. (2007). *Linguistic landscapes: Comparative study of urban multilingualism in Tokyo*. Clevedon, England: Multilingual Matters.

Briggs, C. L., & R. Bauman. (1992). Genre, intertextuality, and social power. *Journal of Linguistic Anthropology, 2*(2). 131–172.

Buck, A. (2012). Examining digital literacy practices on social network sites. *Research in the Teaching of English, 47*(1), 9–38.

Chun, C. W. (2014). Mobilities of a linguistic landscape at Los Angeles City Hall Park. *Journal of Language and Politics, 13*(4), 1569–2159.

Dewhurst, M. (2014). *Social justice art: A framework for activist art pedagogy*. Cambridge, MA: Harvard Education Press.

Freire, P. (1970). *Pedagogy of the oppressed*. New York, NY: Continuum.

Goni, U. (2017, October 21). Argentina—Political storm: The body of missing activist Santiago Maldonado found in icy river. *Dawn News (Argentina)*. Retrieved from https://www.europe-solidaire.org/spip.php?article42291

Hardin, J. M. (2001). *Opening spaces: Critical theory and resistance pedagogy in composition*. Albany, NY: Suny Press.

Hanauer, D. I. (2015). Occupy Baltimore: A linguistic landscape analysis of participatory social contestation in an American city. In R. Rani & S. Ben Selim (Eds.), *Conflict, exclusion and dissent in the linguistic landscape* (pp. 207–222). United States: Palgrave Macmillian.

Kress, G., & van Leeuwen, T. (2006). *Reading images.* London, England: Routledge.

Landry, R., & Bourhis, R. Y. (1997). Linguistic landscape and ethnolinguistic vitality: An empirical study. *Journal of Language and Social Psychology, 1*(16), 23–49.

Lash, S., & Lury, C. (2007). *Global culture industry: The mediation of things.* Cambridge, England: Polity. doi:10.1177/174684770800300603

Latin America's disappeared. (2014, August 29). *Telesur.* Retrieved from https://www.telesurtv.net/english/analysis/Latin-Americas-Disappeared-20140829-0068.html

Leander, K. M., & Aplin, B. (2014). "After apple picking" and fetal pigs: The multiple social spaces and embodied rhythms of digital literacy practices. In C. Compton-Lilly & E. Halverson (Eds.), *Time and space in literacy research*. United States: Routledge.

Leander, K. M., & Lovvorn, J. F. (2006). Literacy networks: following the circulation of texts, bodies, and objects in the schooling and online gaming of one youth. Cognition and Instruction, *24*(3), 291–340.

Lemke, J. L. (2001). Discursive Technologies and social organization of meaning. *Folia Linguistica, 35*(1–2), 79–96.

Longoni, A. (2010). Photographs and silhouettes: Visual politics in Argentina. *Afterall, 25,* 1–10.

Miller, S. (2014). Spatializing social justice research in English education. In C. Compton-Lilly & E. Halverson (Eds.), *Time and space in literacy research*. United States: Routledge.

Scollon, R., & Scollon, S. W. (2004). *Nexus analysis: Discourse and the emerging Internet.* New York, NY: Routledge.

Shohamy, E., & Gorter, D. (Eds.). (2009). *Linguistic landscape: Expanding the scenery.* New York, NY: Routledge

Silverman, D. (2014). *Interpreting qualitative data.* London, England: SAGE.

Taylor, C. (2000). Modernity and difference. In P. Gilroy, L. Grossberg, & A. McRobbie (Eds.), *Without guarantees: In honor of Stuart Hall.* New York, NY: Verso.

Troyer, R. (2012). English in the Thai linguistic netscape. *World Englishes, 31*(1), 93–112.

Villalón, R. (2016). The complexities of memory, truth and justice processes—Art and cultural resistance. *Latin American Perspectives, 210*(43)5, 3–11.

Warner, J. (2017). *Adolescents new literacies with and through mobile phones*. New York, NY: Peter Lang.

Where is Santiago Maldonado? Argentina searches for missing protester. (2017, August). *BBC News.* Retrieved from http://www.bbc.com/news/world-latin-america-41066685

CHAPTER 15

VIRTUAL CARRELS

(Re)Thinking Space(s) for Professional Development

Beth A. Buchholz
Appalachian State University

Sarah Vander Zanden
University of Northern Iowa

Nicholas E. Husbye
University of Wisconsin—Milwaukee

Christy Wessel Powell
Purdue University

Julie E. Rust
Millsaps College

INTRODUCTION

The use of online resources to support professional development for higher education faculty is an established notion (Sherer, Shea, & Kristensen, 2003), though it is argued emphasis needs to shift from static online content

Negotiating Place and Space Through Digital Literacies: Research and Practice, pp. 275–294

to faculty-generated content (Cohn, Stewart, Theisen, & Comins, 2016) and sustained support systems (Anthony, Lawrence, & Reed, 2017). In this chapter, we move from thinking about online resources to consider the kind of space(s) supporting professional, practice-based learning for faculty members. Geographer Doreen Massey (2013) has argued "space" presents a fundamentally social/political question: "How are we going to live[-work-be] together?" (para. 9), and for us this became an invitation to consider how we might *practice space differently* in order to enact more sustainable material ways of being faculty members at geographically dispersed institutions. We explore how we leveraged digital literacy practices to create "virtual carrels," a digital approximation of the boisterous, generative space shared as graduate students that nurtured scholarly body and soul through camaraderie, reciprocity, critical questioning, and practicality.

CONTEXT(S)

While working on our doctorates, we shared a workspace divided into 16 carrels (cubicles) with horizontal filing cabinets delineating our "offices" from the adjacent hallway. Five-foot tall walls cordoned off each desk, marking the space where each of us worked, vented, planned, talked, wrote, conferred, read, laughed, schemed, cried, and consumed many cups of coffee. The physical/material set-up of the space, with its dizzying array of borders and walls, suggested a very different set of social relations and practices than those enacted by users of the carrels (and producers) of the space. In a testament to Massey's (2005) conceptualization of space as "relations of embedded practices" (p. 10), we actively practiced a very different kind of space, one allowing for the forced negotiation of intersecting trajectories. The carrels may have offered a static location, but the space practiced and produced relied on movement, multiplicities, and relationality.

Formal meetings amongst carrel users were rarely planned; rather, a more typical pattern of interaction was rooted in the continual comings and goings of people and artifacts: "the contemporaneous existence of plurality of trajectories: a simultaneity of stories-so-far" (Massey, 2005, p. 12). Each of us, moving along trajectories and traversing along boundaries, at times together and at times alone, inhabited and produced a space responsive to the needs of individuals as well as the collective—in both personal and professional capacities. In the carrels, space and time were intimately connected: space was not the collection of furniture nor the collective square footage but instead cut through the myriad of stories in which we were all living at any one moment. Movement, not stasis, was the norm; the movement of humans, artifacts, ideas, and emotions. This movement continually reshaped the space over our days, months, and years together, providing a sense of "aliveness" invited and evoked by "good community design" (Wenger, McDermott, & Snyder, 2002, p. 54).

Each of us experienced this *aliveness* in slightly different ways, but it was rooted in a sense that anything could happen at the crossroads that were the carrels. If uninhabited by others, it was a space to rest, reflect, read and think, with office chairs pointing deskward toward solitude, head bent. These same carrels could be a semiprivate conference space with students, or, with a passerby or fellow writer's arrival, they morphed into a collective space, office chairs wheeled outward toward conversation, heads up. The carrels were part of our development as scholars: a place for learning, faltering, questioning, complaining, planning, playing with ideas and trying on new identities. Thus, we sought to resurrect and reshape this space in our current practices.

FRAMING SPACE

We begin by situating how we are thinking about/with *space* in this chapter. Massey (2005) moves us from conceptualizing space as a physical or immaterial *container* of people and artifacts (e.g., a classroom, an online forum, a library) to space as the product of our social relations and connections with each other. In the latter understanding, space is the "product of interrelations" (p. 9), where these relations "are understood as embedded practices" (p. 10). Thus, we produce space rather than exist in space, or, as Massey asserts, we *practice* space. Space is not a flat surface we cross in moving from "here" to "there"—nor is space collapsible or reducible with the emergence of digital technologies, but space is alive, political, and open—a "pincushion of a million stories ... in which we are all living at any moment" (Massey, 2013, p. 2). Whereas "time" is the dimension of succession, Massey's "space" is the dimension of multiplicity and movement. These elements of aliveness, heterogeneity, and relationality are central to the "productiveness of spatiality" (Massey, 2005, p. 94).

As literacy education researchers, we are particularly drawn to scholars whose work has taken up generative views of "space," situating it as something more than a passive, predetermined context for learning (e.g., Leander & Sheehy, 2004; Mills & Comber, 2013; Moje, 2004). If we see space as produced anew in each moment people engage in social relations and literacy practices, a learning space is never static but is iteratively (re)produced across minutes, seconds, and hours. Space is produced when people post and comment on social media, just as space is produced when a teacher and child sit together to read a book. A space, then, "is neither a container for always-ready constituted identities, nor a completed closure of holism.... For the future to be open, space must be open too" (Massey, 2005, p. 12). It is this opening up, this enlivening of learning space(s), that offers possibilities for the emergence of new interrelations, actions, and identities for learners of all ages.

CHANGING SPACE(S): LEARNING TO BE-WRITE-TEACH-RESEARCH "HERE"

Over a series of years we each made the move from our shared graduate institution (and those shared carrels) to five different colleges/universities across the country. This move from students to professors involved geographic as well as complex identity shifts, with each of us working to negotiate the new terrains of our departments, institutions, and fields. We each engaged in the highly emotional process of learning how to work, live, write, research, and teach in a new "community of practice" (Lave & Wenger, 1991). Attributed to Lave and Wenger's work studying learning in "natural" settings (e.g., workplace, cultural groups), the term communities of practice (CoP) is rooted in Scribner and Cole's (1981) "practice account" of literacy where a practice "refers to socially developed and patterned ways of using technology and knowledge to accomplish tasks" (p. 236) based on the interactions and interrelations between community members.

Becoming a full participant in any community necessitates more than acquiring discrete knowledge (e.g., reading a handbook, attending an orientation, following rules); it is about learning and taking up the practices, values, identities, and ways of being accepted by the community. Newcomers develop a "changing understanding of practice over time" (Lave, 1991, p. 68) that leads to assuming the identity of a full participant. We find ourselves having to learn how to be recognized as knowledgeable across communities: classrooms, academic programs, departments, colleges/schools, universities, local communities, and academic fields. Each of these communities practice space in very different ways, offering diverse—and sometimes conflicting—practices, values, and ways of being a scholar 'here' in this space/place. The term "landscape of practice" better captures our movement "interact[ing] in a landscape made up of multiple communities," where the landscape necessarily consists of "boundaries, peripheries, overlaps, connections and encounters" (Wenger, 1998, p. 118; see also Wenger-Trayner et al., 2014). Within this frame, our professional development is not directed toward a singular center of expertise or a stable identity; rather, it is multidirectional: knowledges and identities are created in the boundaries traversed within/across the landscape as we learn to serve, teach, and research at/across our institutions.

METHODS

Participants and Context

We are a group of five self-identified early career literacy education faculty members working at a range of institutions (public regional, public research, and small private liberal arts) geographically dispersed across the United States. Collectively we represent a diverse scope of experiences in academia with group members having from 1–7 years of experience in faculty positions. In late May 2017, we arranged a virtual meeting (via Google Meet) to discuss plans for turning a recent AERA symposium into a coauthored manuscript. We never ended up discussing the symposium or a manuscript. Instead, our conversation focused on a seemingly new "turn" in the literacy research field toward posthuman, poststructural theories and postqualitative methodologies. We animatedly discussed our recent experiences attending sessions focused on research informed by/with these theories and expressed a common curiosity (and crankiness) about what these theories meant for the field as well as our own work. What emerged from this virtual meeting was a shared Google Drive folder ("Cranky Pedagogies") with a single subfolder ("Readings"). Our aim was to read a couple of foundational posthuman, poststructual pieces and to virtually meet again in two weeks to discuss. Subsequent biweekly meetings (60–90 minutes) became a part of our scholarly summer routine.

Our time together generally began with an initial "catching up" conversation, which featured an in-the-moment share of emotional states, personal and professional events, and current stressors or successes. We, then, often moved into discussion of an article we had read, which shunted back and forth between questions, critique, and "What might be useful here?" Dialogue about an evolving writing project often followed and featured reporting out progress, questions from the lead authors of the piece, and a dividing up of sections and future assignments. Though there were no formal leadership roles, Nicholas often took the lead in pulling together loose threads during a meeting, thoughtfully synthesizing our production of knowledge, and always propelling us with, 'How should/can we move forward with this work?' By the fall semester, our shared readings turned to shared data analysis and collaborative writing of a conference proposal, and our Google Drive subfolders multiplied (e.g., "Chapter/Article Calls," "Problems of Practice," "Writing," "Meeting Videos").

The meeting subcomponents described above did not exist in discrete categories. A puppy or child jumping into one of our laps during a virtual meeting, for instance, might shift the trajectory of our conversation. As friends, many of us had already been engaged in texting from time to time, which particularly amped up when we attended conferences. However, one day during the summer, we received a group text from Christy sharing her writing goals. She quickly replied, apologizing that the text had been meant for Nicholas. She explained they tried to keep each other accountable by checking in via text with goals. When the rest of us expressed interest in joining in, she and Nicholas included us in their supportive practice, and group texting became another central aspect of our collaboration. This channel of communication evolved to meet a myriad of functions, from scheduling to problem solving to venting about a stressful day.

Data Collection

Across our time of working together, we have utilized four key digital channels to produce space differently: (1) texting (alphabetic text, "stickers," emojis, GIFs), (2) Google Meet (video), (3) Google Docs (writing, commenting), and (4) Google Drive (file sharing). In terms of data collection, Google Docs and Google Drive offer an artifactual, historical record. With hundreds of documents organized across a range of subfolders, our shared Google Drive folder reflects our varied interests across time. More specifically, Google Docs, with saved "histories" (versions) and "comments," offer additional rich data points. Artifacts from Google Meet include video recordings of some meetings as well as notes recorded on paper and in Google Docs. Finally, we have archived our group text messages, which, at the time of writing this chapter, spanned over 180 pages in a PDF file.

Data Analysis

After 6 months engaging in the collaboration, each group member wrote an analytical memo about the experience of participating in this community across time utilizing the various digital channels. In part, we wrote to attend to the "value" of our emerging community of practice. Wenger and colleagues (2002) argue "a key element of designing for value is to encourage community members to be explicit about the value of the community throughout its lifetime" (p. 60). Though many faculty development organizations/structures attempt to predetermine value at the outset, a more organic process is one where communities "create events, activities, and relationships that help their potential value emerge and enable [the community] to discover new ways to harvest it" (p. 60). Our explicit attempt to articulate the value of our shared practices and space(s) allow us to (re) design for even more aliveness moving forward.

We consider writing analytic memos to be a method of discovery, interpretation, and analysis (Richardson & Lockridge, 2004). Writing individual memos and reading across each other's memos offered a formal opportunity for sense-making (Denzin, 2014). Combing through the data collected over time, we considered frequencies, themes, and patterns in relation to two analytical questions: (1) In what ways did we as scholars leverage digital literacy practices to design a professional, practice-based learning community where space could be practiced differently? (2) What kind(s) of space(s) was/were produced? Ultimately, in explicating the value of the community, we found ourselves engaged in an iterative process of moving between—or entangling—data (artifacts collected across time), lived experiences (embodied, affective), memos, and theory.

DATA AND THEORY: AN ENMESHED SPACE

As literacy education scholars sharing a common academic lineage through our preparation, our philosophies and practices in teaching, and the questions we ask about learning and education in our research, we bring particular lenses to understanding our larger collaboration. As we explore the ways in which Massey asserts space is the projection of embedded practices, our understanding of these practices is grounded in social theories of literacy. Literacy practices conceptualized in this chapter, are best understood "as existing in the relations between people, within groups and communities, rather than as a set of properties residing in individuals" (Barton & Hamilton, 2000, p. 8), echoing Massey with the added caveat of considering the use of written language and how it, in the case of our digital collaborations, facilitated the cocreation of space. Based on this theoretical framing, we refer to "[digital] literacy practices" and "space-making practices" interchangeably throughout the chapter. It is critical to note this framing moved the analysis from a focus on digital channels (e.g., tools, software) to digital practices.

By bringing data and theory into conversation, we identified four digital literacy practices that enabled us to produce—and practice—space differently betwixt and between the various channels: (1) maintaining scholarly-ness, (2) assembling knowledge, (3) maintaining community, and (4) bearing witness. Through these practices, we produced space for new possibilities for collective and individual identities with varied intensities. Table 15.1 offers an overview of the four digital practices (rows) and four channels (columns) identified during the analysis process. It is educative at the outset to holistically see the complexity in how these four key practices and channels produced a multiplicity of routes for and levels of participation in our CoP. The table highlights interactions between/across practices and channels, visually demonstrating practices were not isolated to a single channel. Practices (rows) varied in intensity across channels (columns) as represented by varying shades from light gray indicating less activity, to darker gray indicating more activity.

Table 15.1.
Intensity of Literacy Practices That "Produced Space Differently" Across Digital Channels

	Texting	Google Meet/ Video	Google Doc/Writing	Google Drive/File Sharing
Practice 1: Maintaining Scholarly-ness				
Practice 2: Assembling Knowledge				
Practice 3: Maintaining Community				
Practice 4: Bearing Witness				

Our analytical entanglements and insights are organized as follows: First, we *disentangle* the data by identifying, describing, and theorizing four key space-making digital literacy practices emerging across our practice-based, professional learning community. Then, we *(re)engtangle* the data by offering a vignette of one moment/interaction in our shared history to examine how interconnected, intersecting digital literacy practices (i.e., relations of embedded practices) produced (im)material space(s) for learning new ways of being literacy education scholars. The aim in using this structure is to delineate individual practices, providing some rough borders/edges of separation but then to contextualize and complicate this artificial separation by providing a vignette of these intertwined practices in action. If space is the product of interrelations (Massey, 2005), we must move beyond the labeling of individual practices—and individual digital channels/tools—to consider the relations of these practices and channels, as well as the space(s) produced by these interrelations. As part of this process, we recursively turn to Massey's theories to understand how these practices produced space differently and what effect these new spatial relations had on our daily lives and trajectories as faculty members.

Four Space-Making Digital Literacy Practices

Practice 1: Maintaining Scholarly-ness. Our local spaces greatly impact the ways we enact scholarly identities; for those of us at institutions with higher teaching expectations, the time required to stay abreast on developments in the field is scarce. Furthermore, for those of us at institutions with shrinking faculties or who may not have colleagues who actively share our interests, the ability to engage in collaborative exploration of new work is equally scarce. Essential to our coming together was a curation of common readings about poststructural inquiry. Google Drive assisted in our curation, housing a collection of readings, writings, and notes documenting our collaboration. These readings became the bedrock of our collective work, read individually and discussed via video during biweekly meetings. Google Meet allowed opportunities to talk through new ideas and applications to our work. Text messages played an important role in making sense of the new directions our work was taking, as we encountered elements of shared texts or articles, these were often shared with the group via text message (e.g., "This seems relevant, yes?" with a link to an article uploaded to shared Google Drive folder).

Having a face-to-face community actively, publicly engaged in writing agendas was not common, which made safeguarding time for writing difficult. So, early in the collaboration we moved beyond consumption to production as well. While we had often collaborated in graduate school and, to some extent in our careers afterward, Google Docs provided a way to write together and come to understand *how* we enacted our writerly identities, revealing our individual processes as we sought to establish a literature review or tease out nuance in an existing idea. For example, Figure 15.1 illustrates an instance of cowriting in which Sarah, Julie, and Christy were collaborating on a paper. In the process of copy/pasting the entire paper into a new Google Doc, colleagues' "comments"—in essence, markers of their collaborative thinking—were lost. This loss produced a sense of anxiety and disorientation. In response, Christy painstakingly copy/pasted previous comments into the new document to continue to write with Sarah and Julie. Bringing their comments to the new document maintained the line of thinking and collaborative idea expansion their comments held. In Figure 15.1, the dialogic nature of the practice of scholarly maintenance is highlighted. This work more widely constituted the maintenance and stabilization of our identities as scholars; mediated through digital channels, they opened/created space immediately unlike those physical spaces we routinely inhabited. Graduate school trained us each to be scholars, but it did not train us to be scholars, *and* teachers (with heavy course loads), *and* committee members, *and* grant writers, *and* resources for local schools. Collaborative writing projects produced

Figure 15.1. Collaborative writing and theorizing in a shared Google Doc provided opportunities for the practice of *maintaining scholarly-ness* as well as the (re)construction of particular writerly identities.

a commitment and accountability to maintaining scholarly-ness group members desperately needed amidst long "to-do lists" that often crowded out the space and time necessary to write.

Practice 2: Assembling Knowledge. A pressing need in our various roles is fast, reliable information and resources. The practice of assembling knowledge (Gilster, 1997) foregrounds a temporal component, one that carries the expectation of an answer or useful suggestion. Much like Grice's (1975) maxims for conversation, the relevant response is timely, connected, and matches the quantity and quality of the inquiry. Collectively we used language across several channels, text, Google Docs, comments, and so forth, seeking insights to address individual or community responses around particular questions. We worked within a previously curated 'crowd' so the knowledge generated could be trusted. Examples of assembling knowledge included requests for citations, start-up fund usage, reference materials for tenure proceedings, information about how to best navigate a media interview, and so forth. Importantly, when posing a problem or question (implicitly or explicitly), an action, answer, and/or suggestion from the group was largely expected. For example, when Julie explicitly requested "hints" for engaging fellow faculty members in Twitter chats as a form of professional development, group members provided a range of concrete suggestions almost immediately (see Figure 15.2). Wenger and colleagues (2002) argue communities of practice are more suitable for this kind of "collective knowledge stewardship" compared to other organizational structures (e.g., academic departments, professional development workshops), and as a community grows, the development of a "systematic body of knowledge that can be easily accessed" becomes increasingly important (p. 59). As the group needs shifted and stakes for professional success remained high, turning to an external, trusted group of colleagues

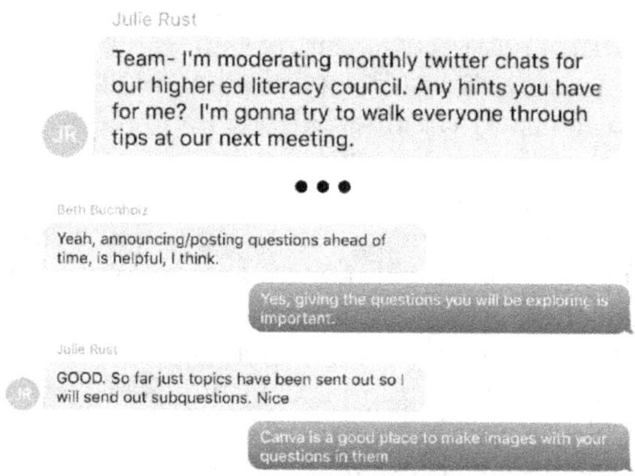

Figure 15.2. The practice of *assembling knowledge* was often initiated through a group member posing a specific question/problem across one or more digital channels with the expectation of an action, answer, and/or suggestion from the group.

offered each of us sounding boards and resource repositories not always found in our respective locations.

Practice 3: Maintaining Community. The glue holding our collaboration together over the busy summer months and the arc of the semester was the practice of community maintenance. Through various channels communication consistently functioned as a way to support one another in meeting individual and collective goals, both scholarly and otherwise. Community maintenance included frequent texts as accountability check-ins (e.g., biweekly Google Meetings structured around shared reading and writing goals; morning texts stating, "What goals are people setting for today?"), opportunities to touch base regularly via friendly pings often laced with humor (e.g. inspirational or funny/relevant GIFs), or as acts of caring (e.g., checking with Beth to be sure she had prioritized lunch in her busy day after skipping the week before, or confirming Julie's commitment to limit advising sessions to 20 minutes). In this way those on the text thread regularly connected, and knew others thought and cared about their well-being. Other examples include weekly shared personal and professional goals on a continuous running Google Doc in which members could bob in and out of when relevant, and the "No Committee" (see vignette below). Over months of meetings and collaborative work, the thrown-togetherness of our place (Massey, 2005) supported engaging with and negotiating how we practiced digital spaces.

Practice 4: Bearing Witness. Over the duration of our collaboration, we have borne witness to one another's experiences and have visibly offered empathy for and acceptance of those experiences through digital channels. From a psychological perspective bearing witness relates to lightening the emotional load an experience or story may hold. Often linked to trauma, bearing witness offers participants, both teller and receiver, validation that something, whatever it may be shared exists-happened-matters. In our almost daily communication, we documented situational administrivia, demands upon our time, teaching strategies, research dilemmas, and deep concern for our profession, usually inextricably interwoven with affect (e.g., annoyance, guilt, humor, worry). One particularly affective example of this was the "#purejoy" text messages exchanged periodically that made 'public' some of the microfrustrations of faculty life (see Figure 15.3).

The practice of bearing witness was most intensely embedded in the text thread (see Table 15.1). Two examples of the ways bearing witness functioned among the group through texting were balancing personal concerns and professional commitments. Given the constraints of our respective institutional locations, untenured, tenured-female, "JR faculty" reaching out prior to decision making facilitated individual and group practice of space in different ways on many occasions. Figure 5.3 shows a sample of "#purejoy" and the opportunities for sharing/validating/hearing/seeing small moments of faculty minutiae that helped to lighten the emotional load. A key component of bearing witness was glimpsing how group members struggled to "negotiate intersecting trajectories" (Massey, 2005, p. 154) in their lives, and, to in some way, participate in the negotiation process itself. This produced a space where the political and the personal were intimately intertwined, and the local context (with localized practices and ways of being) were brought into relief against/within a larger landscape(s) of practice.

DATA AND THEORY: (RE)ENTANGLING PRACTICES, PRODUCING NEW SPACE(S)

Though useful in terms of explicating the value of the community, identifying key literacy practices necessarily imparts artificial dividing lines between "this" practice and "that" practice that do not mirror our lived experiences. We found events/interactions within our community of practice could rarely be labeled by a singular practice. Rather space was constituted by a constellation of interrelated, embedded practices with varying intensities across time and channels, evoking an aliveness critical in good community design. In other words, the space we practiced and produced relied on movement, multiplicities, and relationality; the movement of humans, artifacts, ideas, and emotions via these interconnected and overlapping literacy practices. In this section we offer a vignette highlighting one moment/interaction in our shared history and then explore how this moment/interaction

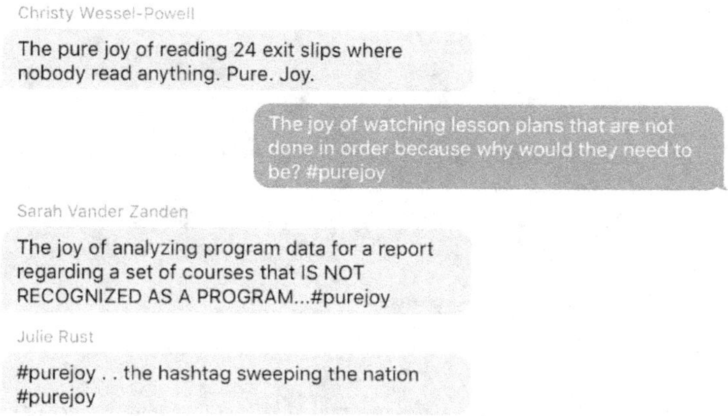

Figure 15.3. The practice of *bearing witness* was intensely embedded across the texting channel.

encompassed the four interconnected, intersecting digital literacy practices (identified above). After fleshing out the practices, we examine how these ways of practicing space produced (im)material space(s) for learning new ways of being literacy education scholars.

A Moment/Interaction: The No-Committee

Fall semester is in full swing. While preparing midtenure review documents one evening, Beth notices the arrival of an e-mail encouraging faculty in the department to attend an important off-campus event later that week regarding the new lab school. In practical terms, attending this event would mean rearranging plans for most of Thursday (a dedicated writing day) and driving 90 miles each way. Glancing at her calendar, Beth has a full week of teaching, meetings, and writing planned, but she worries that many faculty in the department will not attend the event on such short notice. She struggles with the decision, wondering what the 'right' choice is under these circumstances: as a pre-tenure faculty member, she does not want to appear distant or disinterested in a major College of Education initiative, but she also knows that her scholarship is a critical element of her professional life, too.

After wrestling with the decision internally for 24-hours, Beth solicits feedback from the CoP via the texting channel:

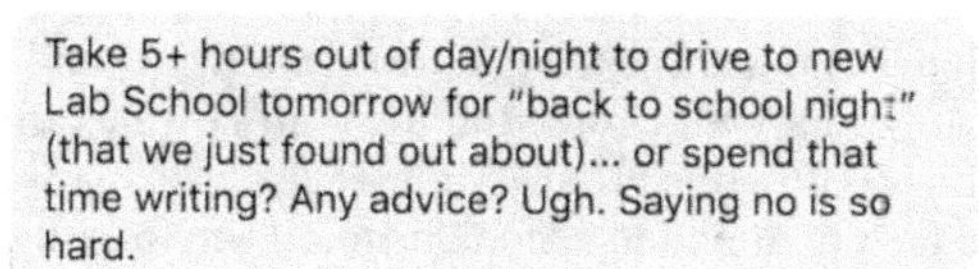

Figure 15.4.

Responses are immediate and decisive:

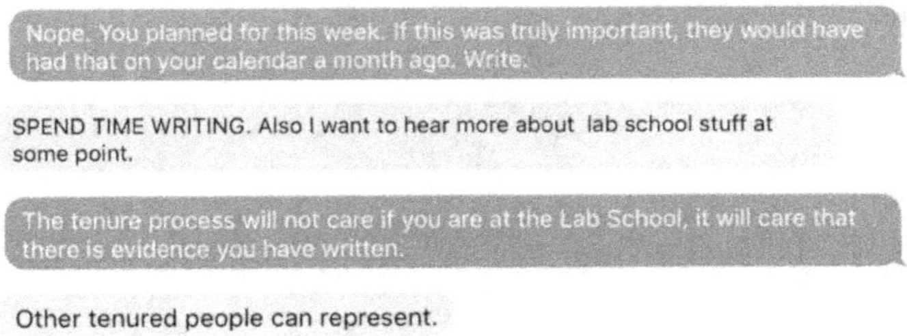

Figure 15.5.

Beth feels relief and a sense of validation. Embedded within these responses is a reminder of the community's commitment to planning for, protecting, and producing scholarly writing: saying "yes" to writing, means sometimes saying "no" to the myriad of requests that vie for our limited time. After this series of texts, Beth sends a quick email to say she will not be able to attend the event and spends Thursday afternoon working on a manuscript.

Analysis of the Intertwined Space-Making Practices

Deceptively simple, this moment/interaction was as typical as it was powerful in producing new ways of doing and being faculty members at our different universities. To understand this particular interaction more clearly, it is important to note two members of the group formally participated in National Center for Faculty Development & Diversity (NCFDD) professional development sessions and often shared insights during our Google Meet sessions. Specifically, the strategy of forming a "No-Committee" (Rockquemore, 2010) was discussed and subsequently taken up heavily within the texting channel. A No-Committee is a trusted group of colleagues who weigh in and filter the "unending stream of requests" (Rockquemore, 2010, para. 3) in faculty life regarding service or administrative tasks.

In relation to the four space-making practices, Beth was seeking to ***maintain scholarly-ness*** by finding time to write, and intentionally reached out to trusted colleagues who supported her inclination to say "no" and clarified writing time as a priority:

> I'm convinced that without this texting conversation, I would have prioritized attending the event over protecting my writing time (and my life outside of work), which is a pattern that I know well across many aspects of my life. As a new-ish faculty member, I am consumed with an ongoing sense of needing to please students and colleagues, and this usually results in me saying "yes" to all things. (Buchholz memo, November, 22, 2017)

Though no formal plan for instituting a No-Committee was created, this group function emerged and gained life in our group message text threads. Group members came to heavily use the texting channel to confirm professional decisions, seek input, and inform others about successful navigation of these kinds of requests (see Table 15.1).

Assembling knowledge in the CoP offered an array of justifications for why sticking to a writing routine was ultimately beneficial and the right choice long-term, and also banished some of the inevitable guilt of saying "no:"

> Beforehand, I dreaded sending the email to my colleague explaining why I wouldn't be at the event, but after our series of text messages, I sent a quick, non-explanatory email and moved on with my writing. That day I worked/wrote until around 6:30 and then cooked dinner at home for one of the first times all week. It was an odd feeling to have said "no" to something and to not feel a lot of guilt about it. (Buchholz memo, November, 22, 2017)

In using digital literacy practices as part of our CoP, a particular kind of space and time was produced in which it became possible for Beth to practice her role(s) as faculty differently, offering opportunities for negotiating the contentious trajectories and boundaries of faculty life collectively and in real time. The practices producing this space and time moved Beth from a fragmented engagement with her own professional development to a more agentic, holistic approach, one where saying "yes" to personal/hidden goals (writing) was as valid as saying "yes" to institutional/visible goals (attending the event). Over time, we have collectively benefited from ***assembling knowledge*** about *how* each of us each makes choices about how to spend our time across the hours, days, weeks, months, and semesters, and how these choices and possibilities are tied to deeper beliefs about our professional "development."

The immediacy and consistency of the group's responses via text actively ***maintained community*** while staring down a professional email request opened up the space for Beth to approach the decision differently: "as a small blip on a never ending timeline of important 'events' " which allowed her to "see/recognize writing as a legitimate event" (Buchholz memo, November 22, 2017). The texting channel is highlighted here, but analyses suggest the embedded and overlapping nature of the digital channels "create[d] points of focus for engaging multiple practices" (Wenger et al., 2014, p. 18). In other words, the spatio-temporal configurations of the digital channels offered a multiplicity of ways to activate, participate in, and maintain the community across time(s). Beth leveraged texting as the most immediate way to energize the community, but biweekly Google Meet gatherings offered extended opportunities to build the deeper structures (e.g., shared goals, empathic listening, collaborative reasoning) necessary for ***maintaining community*** across longer timescales.

In our experiences, universities/colleges largely value face-to-face (and virtual) meetings planned in advance as the main channels for professional development. Our data, alongside spatial and CoP theories, help illuminate that "many of the most valuable community [practices] are the small, everyday interactions" (Wenger et al., 2002, p. 60), such as the text messages exchanged as part of the No-Committee. Daily contact like this allowed our community to maintain its dynamic vitality despite physical distance, settling space among "another set of ideas (heterogeneity; relationality; *coevalness* ... liveliness indeed)" (Massey, 2005, p. 13, emphasis added). Massey's (2005) choice of "coevalness" here, rarely used outside of the field of anthropology, is significant in how its temporal underpinnings frame the production of space as necessitating interactions/practices that are contemporary, simultaneous, and synchronic. It was in texting we experienced the "principle of coexisting heterogeneity" (p. 11), a sense our stories—and development—were necessarily intertwined with others.

Ultimately, ***bearing witness*** undergirded this interaction: the group immediately understood the requirement to spend so much time driving for a last minute back to school night as bordering on absurd. Although we attempt to delineate the four strands of practices, Sarah's response (Figure 15.6) to Beth's query reveals the impossible task of teasing them out as separate:

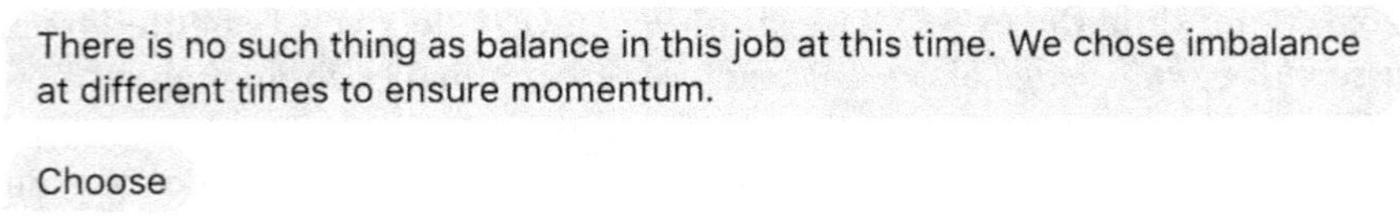

Figure 15.6.

Sarah's reminder bears witness to the impossible task of truly finding balance as early career faculty. Yet her response also served as a kind of deep knowledge now assembled by the community of practice. Taking to heart the notion we must, at times, "choose imbalance ... to ensure momentum" has the potential to aid in the maintenance of scholarly-ness and our community goals for the moments when multiple deadlines call for late nights. Sarah's text produced, then, a sage human encounter. Through coconstruction of deliberative decision making, the group's scholarly-personal relationship shifted away from a writing support or research conversation group. Insight into decisions and feedback from peers became a valued and integral piece of the CoP.

Analysis of Kind(s) of Space(s) Produced. We argue these interconnected digital literacy practices produced a new "here" allowing each of us to move more adeptly across our own multiple and varied 'heres,' across landscapes of practice from the local to the global, extending the face-to-face shared experiences/space(s) of our graduate school carrels. Importantly, these practices made space for the continued exploration of what it means to be a literacy education scholar. In a higher education culture prioritizing efficiency, rationality, self-promotion, and doing more with less (saying "yes"), this constellation of literacy practices across channels produced space for genuine empathy to emerge. Beth later reflected on the impact of her No-Committee interaction:

> The group's text message responses provided the movement/space/opening for something new to happen; for me to be something new; for me to see a new way of being in the world. In a way, the texting channel helped highlight/recognize my humanness over my knowledgeability (and professional responsibility). (Buchholz memo, Nov. 22, 2017)

Virtual carrels, then, ultimately produce a space for humanness, a humanness full and vivid and multi-dimensional. Virtual carrels do not compartmentalize: friends go in this box; colleagues go in that box; work goes in this box; play goes in that box. Rather, they, like the physical carrels that initially served as the epicenter of our successes and challenges and laughter and tears, make a stunning collage of it all. What is it you need today, professor-researcher-mother-person-friend? A push to get productive? Help wordsmithing a sentence? A reminder you are not alone? Confirmation you do not need to always say "yes" to every request? Or perhaps you just need a good idea for a protocol for observing student teachers in the field? It can all be found here, just a text or Google Meet or Google Doc away.

DISCUSSION

The interweaving of humor, levity, truth-telling, resource sharing, academic engagement, goal setting, compassion, and the sharing of lived realities has made our professional-personal trajectories converge in generative ways. Given the origins of this group, it is not surprising scholarly maintenance was a core set of practices cutting across the various technological channels, though the ways these practices were taken up and what they conveyed about our ideas about who we were as scholars was new for us. These practices were both consumptive as well as productive and worked across a variety of digital platforms. Community maintenance practices afforded group members opportunities for maintaining connections and friendship, and to act and be seen as fully human. They represented our mutual investment in one another, taking time out of the day to respond to one another offering support, advice, humor, and group articulations of reasonable boundaries placed around self and career in different situations. Importantly, the practice of maintaining community invited members to participate in varying levels and modes of participation across the days, weeks, and months (Wenger, McDermott, & Snyder, 2002).

The practice of bearing witness was a call to recognize each other's humanness, forcing members to see each other's "and-ness." Our experiences in life—and our decision making therein—do not fit within simplistic labels based on the physical spaces we traverse across the days and weeks. We are teachers, friends, committee members, crafters, confidants, researchers, caretakers, scholars, parents, writers, *and* on and on, and by bearing witness we learned to see each other (and be) at least some of those things simultaneously. In designing a uniquely *human* space "to realize itself, to become 'alive'" (Wenger et al., 2014), we found bearing witness contributed to the "liveliness, the complexity and openness of the configurational itself" (Massey, 2005, p. 13). As Ehlert and Hollett (2016) suggest, affective life is critical in sustaining "placemaking" and "belonging over time"—and here we argue it was affective life, as part of bearing witness, that was critical in sustaining our efforts to practice space differently.

In impromptu and planned encounters across these channels and enacted through a series of digital literacy practices, we produced a sense of "being [here/there] together" that enabled "something new" to happen (Massey, 2005, p. 94). Crucially, it was in our *movement* between "here" and "there"—and the ease in which digital practices unsettled spatial boundaries—that produced possibilities for "bumping into alterity" (Massey, 2005, p. 94). Punctuated by affective intensities, these brushes with "alterity" opened up space(s) for change, disrupting ingrained patterns of living/doing/being a scholar "here," in *this* place.

IMPLICATIONS

New economies have shifted risk and responsibility for professional development from the shoulders of employers to those of the employees; academia has not been immune to these shifts as colleges and universities respond to fiscal challenges and consumer demands. Local professional development opportunities for the professoriate are often minimal, aligned to institutional goals rather than personal, and are rarely longitudinal. In this chapter, we have delineated the ways in which we, as a group of literacy educators and researchers, have occupied this gap through digital literacy practices, creating a space in which we are able to grow as literacy educators and researchers. This digital space was born out of local necessity and, through participation within this space, we have not only addressed our individual, local needs but also have created collaborative agendas and generative space(s) for intellectual work.

This work, however, has not been solely academic; what has been so powerful throughout this experience is the sense of connection, of aliveness permeating our interactions. This, we believe, is a key component to the perceived successes we have felt as we practice in and produce this digital space. We came together as academic siblings, individuals already invested in the well-being of the others within the group, with understandings of how to engage one another to push ideas and individual competencies forward. It is this mutual investment in one another that amplifies and, to a certain extent, gives meaning to the practices outlined in this chapter. Metaphorically, this investment in one another is the waft and the practices the weft of the fabric of this professional development experience.

AUTHOR NOTE

This work is the product of the distributed intellectual efforts of the whole authorial team; all authors have contributed to the analytical methods used, to the research concept, and to the writing of this piece. Buchholz and Vander Zanden have taken on additional pragmatic responsibilities in relation to the preparation of the manuscript for submission and shepherding the manuscript through development, submission, and revision.

REFERENCES

Anthony, L., Lawrence, H., & Reed, A. (2017, December 15). What are you working on today? *Chronicle of Higher Education*. Retrieved from https://chroniclevitae.com/news/1965-what-are-you-working-on-today

Barton, D., & Hamilton, M. (2000). Literacy practices. In D. Barton, M. Hamilton, & R. Ivanič (Eds.), *Situated literacies: Reading and writing in context*. New York, NY: Routledge.

Cohn, J., Stewart, M. K., Theisen, C. H., & Comins, D. (2016). Creating online community: A response to the needs of 21st century faculty development. *The Journal of Faculty Development, 30*(2), 47–57.

Denzin, N. (2014). Writing and/as analysis or performing the world. In U. Flick (Ed.), *The SAGE handbook of qualitative data* analysis (pp. 569–584). London, England: SAGE.

Ehret, C., & Hollett, T. (2016). Affective dimensions of participatory design research in informal learning environments: Placemaking, belonging, and correspondence. *Cognition and Instruction, 34*(3), 250–258.

Gilster, P. (1997). *Digital literacy*. New York, NY: Wiley.

Grice, H. P. (1975). Logic and conversation. In P. Cole & J. L. Morgan (Eds.), *Syntax and semantics: Speech acts* (Vol. 3, pp. 225–242). New York, NY: Seminar Press.

Lave, J. (1991). Situating learning in communities of practice. In L. B. Resnick, J. M. Levine, S. D. Teasley (Eds.), *Perspectives on socially shared cognition* (pp. 63–82). Washington, DC: American Psychological Association.

Lave, J., & Wenger, E. (1991). *Situated learning: Legitimate peripheral participation*. Cambridge, England: Cambridge University Press.

Leander, K. M., & Sheehy, M. (2004). *Spatializing literacy research and practice*. New York, NY: Peter Lang.

Massey, D. (2005). *For space*. Thousand Oaks, CA: SAGE.

Massey, D. (2013, January). Interview: Doreen Massey on space [blog post]. Retrieved from https://www.socialsciencespace.com/2013/02/podcastdoreen-massey-on-space/

Mills, K. A., & Comber, B. (2013). Space, place and power: The spatial turn in literacy research. In K. Hall, T. Cremin, B. Comber, & L. Moll (Eds.), *International handbook of research in children's literacy, learning and culture* (pp. 412–423). London, England: Wiley-Blackwell.

Moje, E. B. (2004). Powerful spaces: Tracing the out-of-school literacy spaces of Latino/a youth. In K. Leander & M. Sheehy (Eds.), *Spatializing literacy research and practice* (pp. 15–38). New York, NY: Peter Lang.

Richardson, L., & Lockridge, E. (2004). *Travels with Ernest: Crossing the literary/sociological divide*. Walnut, CA: Rowman Altamira.

Rockquemore, K. A. (2010, October 4). The n-word. *Inside Higher Ed*. Retrieved from https://www.insidehighered.com/advice/2010/10/04/n-word

Scribner, S., & Cole, M. (1981). *The psychology of literacy*. Cambridge, MA: Harvard University Press.

Sherer, P. D., Shea, T. P., & Kristensen, E. (2003). Online communities of practice: A catalyst for faculty development. *Innovative Higher Education*, *27*(3), 183–194.

Wenger, E. (1998) *Communities of practice: Learning, meaning, and identity*. Cambridge, England: Cambridge University Press.

Wenger, E. C., McDermott, R., & Snyder, W. C. (2002). *Cultivating communities of practice: A guide to managing knowledge*. Cambridge, England: Harvard Business School Press.

Wenger-Trayner E., Fenton-O'Creevy, M., Hutchinson, S., Kuriak, C., & Wenger-Trayner, B. (2014). *Learning in landscapes of practice: Boundaries, identity, and knowledgeability in practice-based learning*. Abingdon, England: Routledge.

ABOUT THE AUTHORS

THE EDITORS

Damiana G. Pyles, PhD, is an Associate Professor at Appalachian State University. Her research interests focus on media production, identity, and media literacy practices in order to understand the intersections of the visual, the spoken, the written, and the performed in digital and print literacies. She created an analytic methodology called *multimodal microanalysis* to understand the media products young people create. She teaches courses for preservice and practicing teachers to learn how to integrate media and technology for teaching and learning. Her current projects include exploring literacy and science learning in kindergarten classrooms, understanding parent and teacher beliefs about preschool literacies, and exploring concepts of space and place around Instagram and local organic farming.

Ryan M. Rish, PhD, is an Assistant Professor at the University at Buffalo (SUNY). His research interests involve the literacy practices of adolescents, especially in regard to how those practices relate to the institutions, social spaces, and geographic places in which they are enacted. This research includes investigations within and across classrooms, online spaces, and communities guided by concerns for learning with participants how to make learning opportunities more equitable for marginalized youth and how to engage students with critical considerations of their social worlds and local communities. Recent projects focus on supporting student inquiry with digital tools that allow for the collection and dissemination of locative data and media.

Julie Warner, EdD, is an Education Research Analyst at the U.S. Department of Education and is also an independent researcher. Her independent research is focused on the digital literacy practices of adolescents, particularly those that happen with and through mobile devices across spaces as explored in her book *Adolescents New Literacies* with and through Mobile Phones (2016) in the series New Literacies and Digital Epistemologies.

THE AUTHORS

Suriati Abas is a PhD candidate in the Department of Literacy, Culture and Language Education at Indiana University. She is currently teaching in the Department of Geography and researching the linguistic landscape of Buenos Aires, Argentina. Her recent coauthored article is on "The Language of Activism: Representations of Social Justice in a University Space in Argentina."

Sandra Schamroth Abrams, PhD, is an associate professor in the Department of Curriculum and Instruction at St. John's University in New York. Her research of digital literacies and videogaming reveals layered meaning making and agentive learning within and across online and offline spaces and practices. She is the author of *Integrating Virtual and Traditional Learning in 6–12 Classrooms: A Layered Literacies Approach to Multimodal Meaning Making* (Routledge), coauthor of *Conducting Qualitative Research of Learning in Online Spaces* (SAGE) and *Managing Educational Technology: School Partnerships and Technology Integration* (Routledge), and coeditor of *Bridging Literacies with Videogames* (Sense). Other publications are featured in *Teachers College Record, Journal of Literacy Research,* and the *Journal of Adolescent & Adult Literacy.*

Nichole M. Barrett, earned her doctorate from the Department of Learning and Instruction from the University at Buffalo in Buffalo, NY. Her dissertation research explored the intersection between digital video composition, identity, and student autonomy in a rural high school film club. Other research interests include finding ways to provide spaces for adolescent students to explore who they are through literacy. More specifically her focuses include digital video composition, rural education, digital literacies, popular culture, and identity. She is currently an adjunct professor at the University at Buffalo specializing in literacy, technology, and foundations of education. She can be reached at nbarrett@buffalo.edu.

David L. Bruce is Associate Professor of English Education in the Department of Learning and Instruction at the University of Buffalo. His research and teaching interests deal with students composing with Digital Video (DV) technology in classroom contexts, incorporating multimodal literacies into teacher education. Together with Sunshine Sullivan, they are Co-PIs with the Writing With Video project. This work centers around the professional learning communities around digital literacies with teachers and students in the rural southern tier of Western New York. He can be reached at dlbruce@buffalo.edu

Rosanne Bruinsma is an archaeologist specializing in heritage theory. She is interested in the relationship between heritage, participation, and social inclusion. In her thesis "Defining Diffusion: A Critical Reappraisal Of Heritage Theory and Practice in the Roman Neighbourhood of Testaccio," she explored the valorization and preservation of Testaccio's diverse heritage in relation to ecomuseological theory, in particular, and critical and recent approaches to heritage conservation, in general. She argued that a re-formulation of the concepts of community and heritage in ecomuseological theory and practice are necessary in order to valorize and preserve heritage in a sustainable and inclusive manner.

Beth A. Buchholz is an Assistant Professor in the Reading Education and Special Education Department at Appalachian State University where she teaches a variety of courses focused on literacy pedagogy and theory as well as qualitative methods. As a researcher, she studies at the intersection of new literacies, play, multimodal composing, and peer culture. She works to extend current sociocultural theories to explore the social, ideological, and critical work of children as they collaboratively compose texts and identities across physical and digital boundaries.

Gert-Jan Burgers has a chair in Mediterranean Archaeology at the Faculty of Humanities of the Vrije Universiteit Amsterdam (VUA). He is also director of CLUE+, the VUA interfaculty research institute for Culture, Cognition, History and Heritage. Over the last few decades, Burgers has developed and directed a series of large scale archaeological field projects in Italy, including others on the famous ancient road of the Via Appia. For the greater part of his academic career to date, Burgers has been concerned with protohistoric and Roman Italy, focusing on urban and rural landscape archaeology and critical heritage studies (conceptual as well as applied).

Sean P. Connors is an associate professor of English education at the University of Arkansas. His scholarship and teaching focuses on multimodality and new literacies, as well as the application of diverse critical perspectives to young adult literature. He has published in a number of scholarly journals and is the editor of *The Politics of Panem: Challenging Genres*, a collection of critical essays about the Hunger Games series.

Erin Daugherty is a doctoral candidate in rhetoric, composition, and literacy studies at the University of Arkansas. Her research focuses on the application of sociospatial and material theories of literacy and how young adults in rural areas can engage in literacy learning by researching and writing about the places they are from.

Mark Diaz is an artist, educator, and arts administrator. As an interdisciplinary artist, he works in various media including video, drawing, and object making to explore issues around migration, memory of place, and natureculture. Related to his arts practice, Mark has taught media literacy, digital arts, and visuals arts courses to inner city youth with several community arts organizations in Chicago. Currently, Mark is the Program Manager at Chicago Arts Partnerships in Education where he manages in-school arts integrated collaborations between teachers and artists.

Charles H. Gonzalez is an assistant professor of Secondary Education in the Department of Educational Leadership and Secondary Education at Alabama A&M University. He has worked with diverse populations of public school students, out-of-school youths, and adult learners and currently teaches literature, pedagogy, and education courses. His research focuses on discovering ways to encourage and support preservice (and in-service) teachers to be culturally relevant and on uncovering ways to develop new culturally sustaining pedagogies. He can be reached at writerchaz@gmail.com.

Nicholas E. Husbye is a teacher educator and literacy education researcher at the University of Wisconsin–Milwaukee, where he is an Associate Professor of Reading Education in the Department of Curriculum and Instruction. A former elementary classroom teacher, his research interests are in literacy teacher preparation, multimodality and learning, and children's literature.

Wayne Steven Jackson is Senior Lecturer in Theatre and Performance at The Arden School of Theatre, UCEN Manchester and a PhD candidate at London South Bank University. He is also a Hull-born performance maker, specializing in contemporary theater and intermedial practices, and a founding member of Escape Theatre. His research focuses on representations of nostalgia and home in the performance of autobiographical memory as a strategy for place making. www.waynestevenjackson.co.uk

Ron Janssen specializes in decision support for environmental and spatial management. His main topics of research are decision analysis, spatial analysis/evaluation, and spatial planning and design. His current topic of interest is the use of geodesign to support interactive land use planning workshops. Examples are the design of a land use plan for the lower Zambezi valley, design of regional adaptation strategies for the Frisian peat meadow areas, locating tidal devices around the Mull of Kintyre and heritage management in Puglia. At present he runs geodesign workshops to support management of road and water infrastructure in the east of the Netherlands.

Chuck Jurich is an Assistant Professor of Language and Literacy in the department of Early Childhood, Elementary, Middle, Literacy, and Special Education at the University of North Carolina Wilmington. His research interests focus on sociocultural and constructivist approaches to both conventional and new literacies practices with particular attention on digital, multimodal, and multi-authored texts. Prior to his work in higher education, Chuck was an elementary classroom teacher for 8 years and program director of a long running after-school video production club for elementary aged children.

Christian Napolitano is a PhD Candidate at VU Vrije Universiteit Amsterdam on Cultural Landscapes of Alto Salento. After obtaining his Master's degree in Archaeology at Università del Salento, he obtained a second level master's, "Geotechnologies for Archaeology," at Università degli Studi di Siena and Scuola di Specializzazione Degree in Classical Archaeology at Scuola di Specializzazione in Archeologia Classica e Medievale "Dinu Adamesteanu." With more than a decade of experience in the archaeological sector, he has worked in several national and international archaeological sites (Turkey, Italy). As a founding member of the Coop. Impact a r. l., he coordinates the management of the Archaeological Park of Muro Tenente, the set-up of museums and archaeological sites and several research projects combining technical, scientific and computer skills with communication and education contribution.

Greg Neal is currently a senior lecturer in the College of Education at Victoria University in Melbourne, Australia. Greg has been involved in a number of research projects over the years with a focus on improving teaching and learning with technology resources. Greg has continued to work with lecturers and teachers in various education settings to explore the ways in which ICT can be in integrated into learning contexts to further engage students and improve learning outcomes. As a course advisor in the Masters of Teaching (Primary) degree at Victoria University, it is Greg's passion to ensure we develop effective teachers prepared for 21st century learners. Greg has a PhD from Melbourne University, an MEd from Ballarat University and a BEd from Deakin University.

Mark Opmeer is a PhD candidate at the Spatial Information Laboratory of the Vrije Universiteit Amsterdam. He received his bachelor's and research master's of philosophy (MPhil) in cultural history where he studied travelers' changing perception of the Dutch cultural landscape in the 19th and 20th century. Currently, he is pursuing his PhD studing the affordances of geospatial technologies (mobile applications and computer games) for teaching ecological thinking in formal and informal learning environments.

Christy Wessel Powell is an Assistant Professor of Literacy and Language Education in the Department of Curriculum & Instruction at Purdue University's College of Education. She is also a former K–2 classroom teacher. Dr. Wessel Powell's research interests include early and elementary literacy (e.g., reading and writing workshops, digital playshops, literacy clinics, and critical literacy); teacher inquiry groups; educational equity and the politics of education; education documentary film; and arts and technology integration.

Erin Preston is an educational researcher and former arts educator who draws upon eight years of teaching visual and digital art. She has worked with the Chicago Humanities Festival, Chicago Arts Partnerships in Education, and Project Zero on program evaluation and research. Her research focuses on tensions of knowing, trust, and values in adult and student collaborative learning in a variety of contexts including professional development settings and arts integrated classrooms. She is particularly interested in the role of tension in learning driven by artistic processes, collaboration, and interdisciplinary inquiry.

Ilaria Ricci is a PhD Candidate in Archeology at Università del Salento and VU Vrije Universiteit Amsterdam focusing on settlement and productive dynamics of the Salento Istmus (Apulia,Italy) from third century BC to first century AD. She received her bachelor and research master in archaeology at Università del Salento (Lecce, Italy). After obtaining her master's degree in 2016, she was involved in Erasmus+ Traineeship for the project "experiencing the diachronic history of Apulia: a Digital Augmented Reality Application" at VU Amsterdam. Since 2016 she has been involved in EVA (Ecomuseo della Via Appia) project coordinated by VU Amsterdam.

Jennifer Rowsell is Professor and a Canada Research Chair in Multiliteracies at Brock University where she directs the Centre for Research in Multiliteracies. Her research interests include: expanding theories of literacy through digital, immersive, and game-based research; conducting longitudinal research in homes; and, applying multimodal, arts-based practices with youth across formal and informal contexts. She is coeditor of *The Routledge Handbook of Literacy Studies* with Dr. Kate Pahl at Manchester Metropolitan University. She is coeditor of the Routledge Expanding Literacies in Education series with Dr. Cynthia Lewis at the University of Minnesota and the Digital Literacy Editor for The Reading Teacher.

Julie E. Rust began her career teaching middle and high school English and then moved on to pursue her PhD in literacy, language, and education at Indiana University Bloomington. She currently works with future teachers as an Assistant Professor of Education at Millsaps College in Jackson, MS. Her research interests include the intersection of new media and ELA classroom spaces, dialogue across difference, and (re)imagining teacher education.

Jane M. Saunders is an Associate Professor of Literacy at Texas State University. She has a keen interest in writing instruction and the ways teachers employ pedagogical and technological innovations to strengthen the literacy learning of students. She is also invested in promoting the professionalism and knowledge of teachers and teacher educators. Dr. Saunders would love to hear from you about this chapter or any interesting new tools you have found that relate to teaching and writing. E-mail her at: janesaunders@txstate.edu

Scott Sikkema is Education Director at CAPE (Chicago Arts Partnerships in Education). At CAPE, he has oversight for programs, partnerships, professional development, and research. He spearheaded the development of research at the organization; in particular, he has focused on research as an aesthetic and pedagogical practice. With the superb CAPE program and research staff, he explores via inquiry site, space, time, process, and other queries, moving away from the immediacy of set answers towards the generative struggle of not knowing.

Louanne Smolin is an urban educator with diverse experiences in technology, arts, teacher education research. Her areas of expertise include curriculum reform through multimedia and arts integration. She currently serves as a researcher on large scale program evaluations for arts organizations serving urban public schools, including working as a principal investigator on studies for U.S. Department of Education funded initiatives Dr. Smolin has experiences with multiple program evaluation approaches. She has published journal articles and book chapters related to program evaluation, multimedia, and teacher professional development. She has presented her work at numerous national and international conferences.

Joseph Spilberg serves as Research Program Manager for Chicago Arts Partnerships in Education (CAPE) managing all after school and family programming. Joseph also manages all research activities across CAPE programs working with external researchers and research organizations to design research, conduct data collection and disseminate locally and nationally

Sunshine R. Sullivan is an associate professor, chair of education, and faculty development coordinator at Houghton College. She teaches literacy and inclusive education courses as well as mentoring student teachers. Together with David Bruce, they are Co-PIs with the Writing With Video project. This work centers around the professional learning communities around digital literacies with teachers and students in the rural southern tier of Western New York. She can be reached at Sunshine.Sullivan@Houghton.edu.

Matthew Thomas-Reid (he/him/his pronouns) is assistant professor of Educational Foundations and affiliate faculty with Gender, Women's and Sexuality Studies. Matthew is faculty advisor for GAPP (Gay and Progressive Pedagogy) and is editor of the South Atlantic Philosophy of Education Society Journal. His areas of research include philosophy of education, social justice education, and queer pedagogy. His current research projects focus on utilizing LGBTQIA histories and narratives with a view toward "queering" pedagogy, praxis, and, most recently, digital literacies.

Mark Vicars is a teaching and research academic in the College of Arts and Education at Victoria University, Melbourne. His main research interests are literacy education, and qualitative research methodologies. An overarching concern of his work is thinking through the connectivities between literacy and identity practices in everyday life. In 2010, he was awarded the Australian Learning and Teaching Council Citation for pedagogical approaches that motivate, inspire and support socially disadvantaged and culturally diverse students to overcome barriers to learning and to experience and attain success. Mark has had his research published in international research journals and edited volumes. He is lead editor of *Qualitative Research Journal.* Mark is a founding member of the International Institute for Critical Pedagogy and Transformative Leadership.

Jordan P. Woodward graduated from the University of Oklahoma in 2017 with her MA in English Composition, Rhetoric, and Literacy, where her research focused on intersections between religious, environmental, and activist rhetorics, community literacy, and digital storytelling. For the 2017–2018 year she was in India as Fulbright-Nehru researcher studying communities' (and especially women's) relationships to water and water bodies through various forms of digital storytelling, ranging from video-making, to soundscaping, and experimental photo essays. She intends to continue research on traditional and alternative forms of storytelling, intersections between religion and environment, activist rhetorics, and local knowledge production.

Sarah Vander Zanden is an Associate Professor at the University of Northern Iowa. She is the Literacy Education Graduate Program Coordinator and Director of the UNI Literacy Clinic. Her areas of interest are critical literacy, multimodal discourse analysis, and literacy teacher education.

www.ingramcontent.com/pod-product-compliance
Lightning Source LLC
LaVergne TN
LVHW052247200926
848481LV00002B/297